To John

with friendship

many thanks

and best

wishes

Gabor Boritt

Spring, 1987

Gettysburg

Lincoln and
The Economics
of The
American Dream

☆ ☆ ☆

I HEAR AMERICA SINGING

I hear America singing, the varied carols I hear,
Those of mechanics, each one singing his as it should be
       blithe and strong,
The carpenter singing his as he measures his plank or beam,
The mason singing his as he makes ready for work, or leaves
       off work,
The boatman singing what belongs to him in his boat, the
       deck-hand singing on the steamboat deck,
The shoemaker singing as he sits on his bench, the hatter
       singing as he stands,
The wood-cutter's song, the ploughboy's on his way in the
       morning, or at noon intermission or at sundown,
The delicious singing of the mother, or of the young wife at
       work, or of the girl sewing or washing,
Each singing what belongs to him or to her and to none else,
The day what belongs to the day — at night the party of young
       fellows, robust, friendly,
Singing with open mouths their strong melodious songs.

Walt Whitman

Lincoln and
The Economics
of The
American Dream

G. S. BORITT

Memphis State University Press

Manufactured in the
United States of America

Library of Congress Cataloging
in Publication Data

Boritt, Gabor S., 1940-
    Lincoln and the economics of the American dream.

    Bibliography: p.
    Includes index.
    1. Lincoln, Abraham, Pres. U.S., 1809-1865—Views on economics.
2. United States—Economic conditions—To 1865.   3.   United States—
Economic policy—To 1933. I. Title.
E457.2.B7   330.1   78-2926
ISBN 0-87880-043-9

Preface

Anno Domini 1865. Oak Ridge Cemetery, Springfield, Illinois. Bishop Matthew Simpson was delivering a funeral sermon. He quoted the deceased in words of deep conviction, words that spoke of a great work to be done. They conjured up the specter of an evil in the land:

Broken by it, I, too, may be; bow to it I never will. The *probability* that we may fall in the struggle *ought not* to deter us from the support of a cause we believe to be just; it *shall not* deter me.

The declaration was that of young Abraham Lincoln on the day after Christmas, 1839. The Bishop interpreted his text in a way and with an authority that seemed wholly natural to the mourning nation. Here was the testament of the beloved martyr dedicating himself in his youth to the great struggle of his life against the Slave Power.

Bishop Simpson quoted Lincoln accurately. He had unearthed a long lost speech that would be soon lost again. But he did make one error. Lincoln's speech had said nothing about slavery. Its subject was banking.

★

This writer made his first acquaintance with American history through a book on the Civil War. In an old bookshop during my childhood in Hungary I came across a copy of Jules Verne's novel *Nord contre Sud*. The picture is vivid in my mind: as I picked up the book I was certain that it was about a war that had raged in the mid-nineteenth century — between North and South America.

The Lincoln image that is the birthright of most American children, as much the creation of mythology as history, was thus not mine. This fact, fortunate for a historian, was enhanced by another auspicious accident. As a sophomore at Yankton College in South Dakota I became intrigued by some early Lincoln utterances and found myself reading the first volume of his collected works before I had read any of his biographies. Having had few preconceived notions about Lincoln, I received my first deep impression of him from his own words.

The remarkable facet of the first volume of Lincoln's writings, which covers half of his public life, is the quantity of material which falls under the heading of economics. The reading of it raised a thirst that took well over a decade to lessen. My exploration of the subject followed the academic pattern, from term paper to thesis to dissertation. I began to know Lincoln. But as I studied him — through his own words — and also the impressive and sometimes brilliant literature about him I intermingled the two with little discrimination. In this lurked the occupational ailment described by Herbert Butterfield: "the tendency to patch the new research into the old story even when the research in detail had altered the bearings of the whole subject." Only after years of further study and thought did a flash of perception illuminate the horizon and reveal the realm of this book: that economics supplied a major key to fathoming Lincoln. In the end the reward waited: the opportunity to present a hypothesis about a substantially new, vigorous image of Lincoln.

To understand the goals of this study requires a glimpse into the history of Lincoln scholarship. The folklore view of Lincoln reigned after his death for about two generations and then its power began to wane. Modern students entered the field late, from the 1920's onward. These sharpened and reinforced an already emerging double portrait. From that time Lincoln had generally been pictured by scholars as a very ordinary politician up to either the repeal of the Missouri Compromise or his election to the presidency — in the words of Albert J. Beveridge, a man "of narrow partisanship and small purposes." In contrast, he had been seen as a statesman of high idealism during the last five or ten years of his life. Repeated attempts to reconcile the two Lincolns have met with less than full success. One of the hopes of this book is to help mend this break, to find a more real, a more believable, Lincoln by illuminating his economic persuasion.

The key to this persuasion was an intense and continually developing commitment to the ideal that all men should receive a full, good, and ever increasing reward for their labors so that they might have the opportunity to rise in life. For the man who in time rose to the White House — son of an almost illiterate father and perhaps illegitimate mother — this commitment was also a personal one. And this, Lincoln's American Dream, became a central theme throughout his entire political life.

In intellectual terms the theme grew from a combination of economic orientation and sympathy for "the many poor," or more accurately "the many," to what might be seen by the 1850's as a full blown ideology. During the first and longer part of his public life it found expression through the support of governmental policies that primarily aimed at economic development — however rudimentarily he, and his age, understood this modern concept. Like thousands of others, Lincoln grasped the fact that such development increased the chances of "the many" to improve their lives.

After the passage of the Kansas-Nebraska Act he came to see his hopes as being mortally threatened by slavery. Thus for the last decade of his life the "peculiar institution" and the Civil War absorbed nearly all his mental powers. His economic views were pushed in the background, but his antislavery and war stance was strongly influenced by them. Most important, his underlying moral assumption, his devotion to the idea that America stood for fair reward for man's labor, for equal, constantly expanding opportunity for all, was strengthened until it became a nation-pervading force. Thus in the end — and in the final analysis — Lincoln accepted the Civil War to save, above all, his Dream — the Union, however precious, being merely its carrying vessel.

Far from being a small opportunist turned statesman, Lincoln must be recognized as a man of consistent, high vision throughout his life — his compromises, blunders, and indiscretions notwithstanding. To say this, and so contradict most academic historians, is not to deny Lincoln's growth over the years. Yet his growth was gradual and continuous from the start rather than concentrated in a few mysterious pre- or post-1854 years. It was also primarily one of degree, not of kind, and involved simultaneous backward motion in some particulars which I will discuss elsewhere.

No attempt is made here to camouflage the fact that Lincoln, the man of principle, was also very much a politician. Practical considerations helped make his economic vision central to his political life. And it hardly need be said that he was also devoted to the Union, liberty, democracy, and the importance of the American example to the world. All these concepts, however, vital as they were, carried a certain aura of abstraction about them by his day, excepting perhaps the last few years of his life. His more down-to-earth, deep commitment to an ordered society in turn was much more contravened than upheld by his decision to "accept war" in 1861. In contrast, the right of each man to the fruit of his labor, the right to rise, was most palpably real — something ordinary people could fully understand and identify with. Thus his American Dream was not only a monument to high ideals but also a design for political victory. He worked for its triumph within the confines of the art of the possible.

Yet, if anything, the young Lincoln was less practical, more constrictingly principle-bound than in later years. The most striking fact about the fledgling politician was his championship of an economic vision — whether represented by internal improvements, banks, taxes, or a fight against repudiation — not only when this was popular but sometimes also when it was dangerously unpopular. Thus it is not surprising to see Lincoln in 1834 demanding, in a minority of six with forty-one opposed, that the Illinois House of Representatives aid the new settlers who had to start at the bottom; or Lincoln in 1837 refusing to condemn the radicalism of the abolitionists unless slavery itself was condemned and casting his "nay" vote with five others against seventy-seven "yeas." The older professional was *much* less often found in such minorities.

Unraveling the intricacies of Lincoln's political workings, however, is incidental to this book. The prime goal is the examination of his economic persuasion, of how it broadly manifested itself in his political life, and how in time it affected American history.

If economic beliefs did play a fundamental role in Lincoln's career, the historian should be able to explain why his colleagues have been unaware of it. A historiographical essay at the end of this volume will attempt both to solve this riddle *and* to review the Lincoln literature. The essay is important because much, though not all, of the material for this study has been long available. The surviving corpus of Lincoln's work brims with economic implications. Just as significantly, in his public life Lincoln probably talked more about economics, to use the term in a broad sense, than any other issue, slavery included. If the bulk of his words preceded the period of his fame and hence went unrecorded, the main lines of his thinking, and frequently details also, are extant. If nothing more, the merely technical enterprise of presenting and analyzing Lincoln's thinking about political economy, "the beautiful science," as his older contemporary Theodore Sedgwick called it, is long overdue.

The book attempts more than this but I hope not too much. The historian must look for meaning but guard against finding more meaning than there is and thus becoming a myth-maker. The danger is very real. The beloved ones of Clio are mere mortals after all with egos common to homo sapiens. The temptation is great to corrupt Descartes' *"cogito ergo sum"* into *"cogito divinum ergo divus sum."** Yet the fear of falling must not be allowed to stop one from advancing.

Whatever significance scholars will hereafter concede to Lincoln's economic persuasion, ignoring it, I would like to think, will no longer be possible. Still it is customary in our day to disclaim having written a definitive study, something close to the last word on a subject. I shall make that disclaimer perhaps with more humility and

---

*"I think, therefore I am," into "I think big, therefore I am big," or literally "I think like a god, therefore I am a god."

more justification than many, because in addition to the usual pitfalls facing the historian, I found parts of my field in the midst of revolution. Some years from now this study might have been written differently. Some years from now, I hope, parts of it will be rewritten by new students. Whether the economic policies Lincoln advocated did in fact substantially further his goals of development and social mobility is not all important. Historians stoutly disagree about the effect of governmental strategies on development, a question they have studied much. They also disagree about mobility, a question they have until recently studied little. That scholars of a later century can still debate indicates that Lincoln's beliefs, though they can be challenged, are not to be casually dismissed even today. For all that, my work is about Lincoln, not about economic much less social history. Any contribution it may make to the latter subjects is quite secondary.

We can not escape here some words about method. In our days, as at times before, many of our finest scholars portray the giants of mankind in the image of Lilliput. One of the desired fruits is the elevation of ordinary folk. But quite the opposite occurs. The historian must be critical. But I believe he also has the *duty* to celebrate — when in his judgment the subject has earned such treatment. This book attempts to reflect this belief, most forcefully in the final chapter. It does so without too many misgivings because of the comforting knowledge that the facts presented will readily permit the able, other-minded student to follow different routes and reach different conclusions. Thus, it should be possible, for example, to depict the Lincolnian struggle for equality of opportunity as leading to inequality, and Lincoln as the politician and ideologist of the nascent industrial capitalist class, still upholding its democratic and humanitarian illusions but readying for the climb to power in America.

Beyond this the methodology needs little explanation. The approach is traditional narrative history, employing both analytical and impressionistic techniques. The order of presentation is largely chronological, with some allowance for exploring topics across time. I found that questions demanding explicit quanto-or psychohistorical tools could be best treated outside of this book. My view that the

Whigs were much more the party of economic development than were the Democrats is true for Illinois and, one suspects, for the entire nation. The problem lends itself to quantitative investigation and its study, as indeed that of the Whig Party as a whole, is sorely needed.

For Lincoln's Illinois years a detailed narrative is necessary because earlier studies have failed to untangle his connections with political economy. Approximately half of the book is devoted to the essential labor of uncovering the foundations. Part of this may appear dreadfully dull to some — but it is indispensable. The detail serves the meticulous student of Lincoln and Illinois; meets scholars such as Beveridge on comparable ground; but above all immerses readers in the kind of work Lincoln immersed himself in throughout much of his public life. Since historians have much more fully investigated the important facts of Lincoln's later career, the second half of this study could become more generously analytical.

During the Civil War period only limited attention is given to the Chief Magistrate's specific views on economics. With the life of the nation at stake, these matters shrank to relatively small significance and Lincoln fully recognized this. His economic beliefs continued to play a vital role in his thinking and actions, often in a less than conscious manner. But their most important manifestations appeared in spheres not strictly economic: in his conduct of war and search for peace. These provide the most convincing evidence of the depth of Lincoln's economic orientation. Thus these are the subjects that had to be more thoroughly examined to maintain a sense of proportion and to serve the overall purpose of the book.

The President's purely economics-related activities do deserve detailed perusal, but in a separate monograph. The new information a summary examination has produced strongly suggests that such an effort would be well rewarded. Yet it must also be recognized that such work would, to paraphrase Butterfield, not alter the bearings of the whole subject. The main themes appeared before the Civil War. They were largely continued thereafter.

The table of contents provides not only chapter titles but also short listings of the topics discussed within each chapter. Students may find it helpful to consult the table before beginning a new chapter. Footnotes are kept as brief as possible for the sake of readability. They generally cite only immediate supporting materials. For the sake of both propriety and scholarship, however, the names of those authors who made a measurable contribution to my understanding of a question under consideration are listed in the footnotes. The titles of their works can be found in the bibliography.

I have endeavored to draw my intellectual bounds widely. I have learned the truth of Emerson's counsel that the "scholar will find Aristophanes and Hafiz and Rabelais full of American history." When a non-English source is cited in the text, it is given in translation, except when the quotation's use has a distinct aesthetic ingredient. Then I have used the original language, bearing in mind the Italian adage, *"traduttore, traditore,"** to which Harold G. Henderson was fond of appealing. An English rendering, however, is always provided in the footnotes, and in this work I was aided by friends.

This book has had its own odyssey. It was conceived in South Dakota, carried to Massachusetts, to Illinois, to Tennessee, to California, and pursued in many parts of the country in between; it traveled to Japan, Taiwan, and Thailand. Work was done on it, yes, in Vietnam, at Phu Cat and Da Nang. Along the way I came to be beholden to many. The note of acknowledgment after the preface touches only the surface of my indebtedness.

When the great poet Bashó traveled to the Kyoto of seventeenth century Japan to partake of greatness past, he could sing only with sadness. He was physically present in the old capital, breathed its air, ate its bread, drank its wine, touched its people, and saw its dwellings and temples, but the old capital eluded him. It was no longer there, could never be there again.

---

*Translator, traitor.

Thus feels this poor student of history at the end of his journey. He tried to find the real Lincoln, like so many better men before him, and in the end found that he could only sing a sad, pale song.

In Kyo I am,
    and still I long for Kyo —
        oh, bird of time!*

Memphis, Tennessee
Bolton, Massachusetts

---

*trs. Harold G. Henderson

cAcknowledgements

At the head of a long list of friendly people I would like to place the names of the two men who first taught me history: one a classicist, the late Fülöp Grünvald of Budapest; the other an economist and art historian, the late Hans Janssen of Cologne, and later of the University of Pennsylvania, and Yankton College. At Yankton, under Professor Janssen, I began the study of Lincoln's economics. Under Cedric C. Cummins of the University of South Dakota my professional training began. At Boston University, under Kenneth A. Bernard, Robert V. Bruce, and Saul Engelbourg, I continued these studies. They supervised my dissertation; later the last two commented on the bulk of the manuscript of this book. Professor Bernard's knowledge of Lincoln is immense and inspiring. Professor Engelbourg was, and I hear is, a hard task master. But I am beholden most profoundly to Professor Bruce — teacher, scholar, friend.

This book represents the third generation of Lincoln scholarship coming out of Boston University and the Chairman of the History Department, Sidney A. Burrell, has earned my respect for his enthusiasm and support.

The generosity of other scholars whom I sought out for help often as a total stranger was moving. Richard N. Current commented on the first half of this study while it was in its early stages. Later he repeated his reassuring performance for the entire work. Bradford Perkins read the study twice — to my considerable advantage. The full manuscript also received the benefit of the learning of Roy P.

Basler, Rodney O. Davis, Sidney Fine, Eric Foner, John P. Frank, and Willard L. King. Earlier my work profited from the encouragement and helpful criticism of the late Paul Angle, Janet Haywood, and George Rogers Taylor.

Various versions of my chapters also received specialist attention: those on internal improvements from John Krenkel and Julius Rubin; those on banking from George D. Green and Erling Erickson; those on the tariff from Paul David; the section on the absence of noneconomic Whig tendencies in Lincoln from Ronald Formisano; those on agriculture from David E. Schob; that on wartime cotton policy from Ludwell H. Johnson (though he strongly disagreed with me); that on wartime policy toward blacks from Leslie Owens; and that on military strategy from John Shy and T. Harry Williams.

The comments of anonymous readers aided me also. So did the encouragement of John F. Robinson of the University of Chicago Press, Lloyd G. Lyman of Louisiana State University Press, and most importantly James D. Simmons of Memphis State University Press. The long delay in publication, caused by budgetary problems, is a sign of the times.

Emily Schossberger, my editor, made valuable and delightful contributions. The cliche that I alone am reponsible for the errors in the book can not be avoided, however. I must also acknowledge — this with pleasure — that the calligraphy at the end of the preface is the work of the brilliant Japanese artist, and friend, Kyoko Kusuda. The drawing of Lincoln after the historiographical essay is by Thomas Nast. It first appeared in *Harper's Weekly,* on April 15, 1865. The organization of the bibliography of cited sources was greatly aided by Daniel Schaffer who was my assistant while I held a visiting appointment at the University of Michigan. I also wish to acknowledge the early encouragement of William E. Baringer. It is with regret that I find myself in sharp scholarly disagreement with him.

I am deeply indebted to many courteous and learned librarians, both inside and outside of the United States. At least one gentle man, Paul M. Spence, Curator of Manuscripts at the Illinois State Historical Library, friend and scholarly helper, must be given the special recognition his competence deserves.

The repeated financial aid and the moral support of the Henry E. Huntington Library and Art Gallery, and of the American

Philosophical Society, through its Penrose Fund, was material to the completion of the book.

A final word of thanks is due to my family. The crewel work of the dedication page was created from my rough sketch by my mother-in-law, Anita Wilson Norseen Hooker. Her encouragement, that of my father, Dr. Paul Szappanos Boritt, and of my father-in-law, Dr. Russell Houghton Hooker were important to me. So were my ever helpful siblings, Drs. Adam and Judith Szappanos Boritt. My brother-in-law, Gregory Hooker, came to my aid at a crucial moment. Finally, to my wife, Elizabeth Lincoln Norseen Boritt, and to my sons, Norse and Jake, who put up with Lincoln, she for all these many years, the boys more recently, I would like to say things of love that my stumbling scholarly tongue can not hope to say.

Contents

Book I

BOOK II

Book One

To [secure] to each labourer the whole product of his labour, or as
nearly as possible, is a most worthy object of any good government.
But then the question arises, how can a government best, effect this?
In our own country, in its present condition. . . .

From Fragments of a Tariff Discussion, c. 1847

I hold the value of life is to improve one's condition. Whatever is
calculated to advance the condition of the honest, struggling laboring man, so far as my judgment will enable me to judge of a correct
thing, I am for that thing.

From Speech to Germans at Cincinnati, Ohio, 1861

1
*c*Adventures in Quest of *c*Advancement

IN THE BEGINNING WERE THE LAND AND THE DREAM. THE LAND, Robert Frost has written, was "vaguely realizing westward, but still unstoried, artless, unenhanced." The dream was as old as mankind, of the "city upon a hill," a light to the world, where men were endowed with the right to rise in life.

The land and the dream drew the Lincoln family from Indiana to Illinois in the spring of 1830. Abraham, twenty-one, guided an ox-cart through flooded creeks and icy rivers, over old Indian trails and roads that were muddy and often under water. The migrants walked, drove, floated, and cut their way into the Prairie State, traveling by way of such places as Purgatory Bottom, toward Palestine and Paradise.

The pioneer journey ended on the Sangamon River in the midst of an election campaign. Here the future president made his first known political speech on, understandably, the need for better transportation — "internal improvements," as Americans called it. This was a small beginning but it led to a big dream. Thirty years later, as Lincoln was about to leave the state for the nation's capital, old settlers remembered that his speech had "pictured out the future" of Illinois.[1]

The young Hoosier immigrant headed in time for Sangamon County and that was a fine place to settle. Centrally located, it was for many years both the largest and most populous county in the state. Its people were both Southerners (mostly from Kentucky,

Tennessee, and Virginia) and "Yankees" (from the Middle States and New England). Although the voters leaned toward Clay's party, nearly a decade and a half passed before, organized as the Seventh Congressional District, the region was recognized as the sole Whig stronghold of a staunchly Democratic state.[2]

This was farm country, potentially rich, with many streams, good timber, the soil "black loam," after a rain "black as a hat . . . from 18 inches to three feet deep." It was not "uncommon," a pioneer declared in the year Lincoln arrived, to find here people "who five years ago were worth little, but a few movables, and had to borrow money to enter their land, who are now in independent circumstances." A "country for poor men," another settler summarized it, for poor men who hoped to rise in life.[3]

The absence of transportation made the people largely creek and river bound, as has always happened to young communities since the days of the Tigris and Euphrates or the Nile. Corn was the important crop, but as late as 1850 little more than half of Sangamon's acreage was cultivated. That in spite of this Governor John Reynolds could correctly judge the area "the great patriarch of agriculture in the State," testifies to both Illinois' underdevelopment and the relative wealth of Sangamon.[4]

The seat of the county government, Springfield, became Lincoln's home and the state capital in the late 1830's, growing from a town of six hundred in 1830 to more than nine thousand, three decades later. Its industries depended largely on the surrounding countryside with pork packing being king. Craftsmen settled in ever larger numbers, as did merchants — most of them selling no specialized wares, all of them plagued by primitive banking conditions and often bartering their goods. It was a bustling land.[5]

Lincoln made his first home twenty miles northwest of Springfield in the pioneer village of New Salem on the Sangamon River. In 1832 he sought his first political post, a seat in the state House of Representatives. Later he learned the necessity of reticence, or at times silence, but at the very start of his political life he already displayed his predisposition toward principled politics. He began his career with a long (and cumbersome) statement about his views, for both custom and "the principles of true republicanism" required this.[6] This first Lincoln platform was largely concerned with internal improvements, and for the next nine years he was to play a rapidly growing role in the state's attempt to join the transportation revolution.

The poor, or more specifically "the poorest and the most thinly populated countries," had the greatest need for improvements, the platform announced. All stood to benefit from railroads and canals, however, and of the two the locomotive was the more desirable. Deciding between these rival modes of transport was a major issue for the advocates of improvements, and perhaps Lincoln's choice was guided by a recognition that in Illinois the iron men were gaining ascendancy. He supported the railroad with sound reasoning, however, emphasizing that it was, as he believed, "a never failing source of communication, between places of business," independent of seasonal variations. He thus displayed early an ability to side in economic matters with what the future would bring.[7]

The subject of improvements was intoxicating, but Lincoln clearly tried to hold to a sober tone. "However high our imaginations may be heated," he warned, railroad building was appallingly expensive. For their new country's "infant resources," therefore, the improvement of the Sangamon River was more practicable. He saw that the crux of the matter was money, and that it would be great folly to undertake works without the capacity to finish them. Nonetheless in the end he ignored his own warning and brashly went on to advocate river improvements, while admitting ignorance of the costs and offering no plan of finance. He did not specify either public or private enterprise, but apparently took it for granted that improvements were a job for the government.

Through his platform and other early declarations Lincoln allied himself with the party of Clay. He did not seem to know that the followers of the Kentuckian were supposed to lean toward aristocracy — as many Democrats and later historians charged. On the contrary, he saw profit in stating the fact that he was "born" and had "ever remained in the most humble walks of life" and had no "wealthy or popular relations." If he also saw political gain in advocating improvements, in 1832 at least he was disappointed by the polls. He remained faithful to his economic message, however, and victories soon followed. Lincoln's law partner, William H. Herndon, a most diligent researcher of Lincoln's early years and not one to discount personal magic as a factor in his success, consistently maintained that the early political triumphs were tied to internal improvements. "This gave him a popularity not otherwise got."[8]

However this may be, only the future would show how deeply committed Lincoln was to developing the country. For now, he demonstrated sincerity (and also bad financial judgment) by backing in a small way the attempt to prove the navigability of the Sangamon. The steamer employed for the purpose proved the reverse, but not before inspiring editorials calling for a general system of internal improvements in Illinois, and beginning what would now be called a boom.[9]

The United States had had a bewildering transportation history. In the early colonial days, individuals and townships took such care as they could of the needs of those who would travel. By the second half of the eighteenth century some government projects were also underway, to be interrupted by the Revolution. After peace came, an improvement convention in Virginia led to the notable assemblage in Philadelphia and to the Constitution of the United States.

We do not know whether the Fathers intended to provide the national government with power to construct canals or to improve rivers and harbors. Alexander Hamilton thought so and recommended accordingly. But Federal assistance was kept at a minimum and state and local authorities preferred to let private enterprise create transportation facilities. In the new century a ten-year plan by Secretary of Treasury Albert Gallatin was interrupted by War. With the return of peace a young John C. Calhoun proposed a new design to bind the union together with a "perfect system of roads and canals," and Henry Clay advanced the American system "to riches, greatness and glory." But presidential vetos, citing the Constitution, delayed the marriage of internal improvement to tariff until the administration of John Quincy Adams.[10]

By the mid-1820's sectionalism grew strong, the Atlantic Seaboard was no longer in so much need of governmental aid, and signs of disenchantment with the frenzied growth of America began to appear. Not unexpectedly, therefore, the constitutional issue was raised again. President Adams had to settle for a fraction of his program and by 1830, under Jackson, hopes for large-scale federal aid to the developing land had evaporated.

Until then the government of Illinois contributed very little to the advancement of transportation. Although under the second Adams, Congress, in an unprecedented move, made a large land grant to the state for the building of a canal to connect the Great Lakes with the Mississippi River system, when Lincoln first entered the legislature, in 1834, nothing of substance had been accomplished.

"Suckers," as Illinoisans were called by themselves and others, were reluctant to embark on improvement projects because they feared high taxation. Lincoln did not like such timidity. Yet as a freshman he could do little but go along with his colleagues' assumption — however disproved by history — that private enterprise would build transportation facilities. In the House he supported the creation of many, though not all, private river, canal, turnpike, and railroad companies. One of his earliest bills was a plan for a bridge. Others came from him in the same vein, and the eager solon even got into what for him were most unusual squabbles over the credit for the introduction of road bills. Thus he indicated the importance he attached to internal improvements.[11]

Promoting the construction of the canal in the Sangamon Valley became Lincoln's special concern, signaling that he took his first platform seriously. He guided an act of incorporation through the House, procured for the company the privilege of not having its stock considered tax-liable personal property, continued to promote the venture to the general public, and put his own assets on the line again.[12]

The young legislator's improvement bills usually contained the somewhat ambiguous admonition that works must cause "as little injury to private property as the public convenience will permit." His developing economic philosophy, however, clearly leaned towards government participation. Even in the case of his favorite company, he secured for both the state and the counties the option of buying out the canal at any time within ten years of its completion. He was also eager to see the state engage in land speculation and voted to request the federal government to sell to Illinois half a million acres at $1.25 an acre, the bill to be paid without interest a decade later. Nor did he shrink from outdoing Clay through an unsuccessful assault upon Illinois' Jacksonian prejudices: he proposed requesting from Congress 20 per cent of the proceeds of the state's public land sales.[13]

These various schemes were aimed at procuring funds to finance improvements. They did not succeed, nor did the sundry private railroad and canal projects. Thus, at last, Illinois' legislators came to see that what Lincoln called the "financial and infantile situation" of the state would prevent them from revolutionizing transportation through private efforts. For the majority the truth had to come, of course, in Democratic garb. When money from the East and London failed to come forth to support the myriad local ventures, the hitherto vague feeling that transportation monopolies should not be placed in private hands suddenly became clear.[14]

Thus although Lincoln and like-minded legislators could not change laissez-faire attitudes, the failure of individual enterprise did. At a special session in the winter of 1835, state backing was finally secured for the Illinois-Michigan Canal. A minor amendment proposed by the New Salem representative, to provide the governor with greater flexibility in financing and operating the waterway, met defeat. But the ground was broken for what would become a vast internal improvement program for the young state.[15]

In the following year Lincoln made improvements the one solid issue of his re-election campaign. As neither borrowing nor taxation was an appealing mode of finance, he again argued for federal aid, through distributing among the states the proceeds from public land sales. The campaign was heated, fights not uncommon, and the Whigs gleefully reported that "a girl might be born and become a mother before the Van Buren men will forget" Lincoln's treatment — verbal, not physical, of course.[16]

By 1837 hopes for internal improvement had grown to a frenzy in Illinois. The former governor now turned Congressman, John Reynolds, removed from the excited atmosphere of his home state, would come to believe his people "perfectly insane on the subject," but the members of the General Assembly, nearly three-fourths of them freshmen and coming straight from an inflamed populace, had little sympathy for such Washington-acquired sophistication. A "veteran" like Lincoln, although trying to remain unimpassioned, wrote his would-be fiancé without batting an eye about a "loan of several milli[ons] of dollars" recommended by an internal improvement convention.[17]

There was much to recommend the glory road. The entire

Western world, a whole civilization, cried out for improvements. England led. Others followed. In one corner of this civilization a poet exhorted:

A hundred railroads, a thousand!
Build them, build them!
Let them be all through the world
As arteries are in man's body.*

From another corner an Illinois pioneer wrote enthusiastically: "i must say to you that this rail road Question is a Question of more importons then enny Question that ever falen in the valys of the massisipy . . . . i should like to see our holl nation paved." And in New York the young Whig lawyer William Seward proclaimed that the history of no land could supply an example of internal improvements leading to impoverishment.[18]

America was young, growing, and optimistic. The iron horse had captured people's imagination and the Erie Canal, completed in 1825, paid off its construction debt eleven years later. Lincoln wanted to be the Dewitt Clinton of Illinois. He was probably not alone in his ambition. In 1839 it was the canal-building Governor of New York (not Washington or Jefferson) who became the only man to have two counties named after him in Illinois. It seemed as though the entire nation was concentrating its energies on building transportation. Illinois' neighbors and rivals, Ohio and Indiana, were launching great projects; Missouri was beginning to move; Michigan entered the Union in 1837 with a constitution that required the state to encourage improvements. Illinoisans would not be left behind.[19]

The state had given years of consideration to possible improvement projects. Lincoln could argue, therefore, that a "general system" of works would not be a leap in the dark. Around him the appetite of farmers was whetted by high agricultural prices. The nation's enormous speculation cycle made land and town lots seem like "the staple" of the state, its "only articles of export," to quote governor-historian Thomas Ford. Its main imports in turn were

---

*Száz vasutat ezret!
Csináljatok, csináljatok!
Hadd fussák be a világot,
Mint a testet az erek.
Freely translated by author from the Hungarian of Sándor Petőfi.

immigrants and foreign capital. Newly chartered banks fed this movement with large issues of money. Local businessmen added their energies. It is not surprising that the spirit of speculation reached the governmental level. Illinois was ready to try what appeared to most as reasonable risks; here, many people thought, was truly the beginning of a new era.[20]

By 1837 Lincoln felt ready to move to the forefront of the state's internal improvement battles. Of course improvements, for him and many others, were ultimately part of broad advancement that was "material, moral, intellectual" — to quote his words from 1859. The material road was merely the means leading toward intellectual and moral elevation. But while we can not say that even as a youth he let the ultimate goals out of sight, he did concentrate the bulk of his energies on the material road. He was after all a politician in a state where economic battles were also the main political battles.[21]

And by 1837 Lincoln's inclinations toward internal improvement were bolstered by a slowly increasing knowledge of political economy. He understood and preached that a better transportation system would quicken the pulse of Illinois economic life, raise living standards for all, enhance property values, and attract immigrants. He was not yet educated in the new science of economics, but he studied law books that contained pertinent lessons. He read newspapers that frequently discussed the subject, often on a high plane. Speeches by the "political economists" of Congress, as Colonel Noah Crocker overgenerously described the lawmakers, also helped his learning. Finally, he listened to his colleagues in the Illinois Assembly and learned. He rose to leadership rapidly, in economic as in other matters.[22]

Illinois' 1837 "internal improvement" assembly passed an omnibus bill allocating $10,000,000 for two trunk railroads, the Illinois Central and the Northern Cross, quartering the state north to south and east to west; six spurs connecting the largest towns; road and river work; and a $200,000 grab bag appropriation to console those areas that did not directly benefit from what became known as the System. These appropriations were in addition to the $8,500,000 thought necessary to complete the Illinois-Michigan Canal. Financing was to be arranged through borrowing. Internal improvement bonds were supposed to sell above par, and the profits from them pay for the interest on the borrowed money. Later the state acquired stocks in local banks, and dividends were also to be applied to the servicing of loans.[23]

Over the long run, tolls charged for the use of the finished facilities were expected to provide for the repayment of the principal of the debt. The separately administered canal was also to be supported by the sale of lands that had been granted to Illinois earlier. The federal government was expected (at least by the Whigs) to provide further aid once work got under way and the party came into power. This manner of financing was not unique. Loans for ultimately self-liquidating projects, encouraged by sometimes grandiose expectations, were part of the American way.

Construction was to begin simultaneously on every project, proceeding from both ends and at times from the middle as well. Private and mixed enterprise was rejected in favor of government entrepreneurship. Since Illinois was the Prairie State, with level topography, preliminary studies were dispensed with as superfluous. Lincoln, former deputy surveyor of Sangamon County, agreed to this — and all the plans.

Historians tend to consider Lincoln the leader of the forces behind this improvement system, but his exact contributions cannot be defined. He appears to have made no major speech on the subject. His party was in the minority. One of the first large development plans was introduced by Stephen A. Douglas. Another Democrat, one of Lincoln's future generals, John A. McClernand, considered himself to be the head of the legislative movement for improvements. Nevertheless, Lincoln, too, was one of its important champions. As a Whig leader of the House he put his full weight behind these plans. Indeed he worked so hard and spent so much time with the committee for internal improvements that years later a colleague remembered him as a member of that bold body.[24]

If we are not certain about the exact role Lincoln played in the creation of the System, we know that after it was adopted he paid attention to even the smallest matters related to it. He recommended a man for the state improvement board and signed a bond for another. He enjoined lawmakers from holding positions with agencies their votes had created, but made an exception for a particularly competent engineer-legislator. Using horse sense, he opposed submitting the improvement act to a referendum, probably fearing delays and parochial politicking. He also found the time and the confidence to introduce additional road bills, to attempt to obtain a bridge on the Sangamon River at New Salem, and to warn his supposed ex-rival for the hand of Ann Rutledge that he had better "get up a remonstrance" if he wished a state road to run in front of his farm.[25]

The work of the 1837 Assembly completed, the people of the state capital, Vandalia, celebrated with bonfires.[26] They should have heard instead the impending death knell of their town. The same session of the legislature that passed the improvement bill also moved the seat of government. The coincidence of the two events spawned the false tale that the Long Nine of Sangamon, as the tall delegation of the county was known, supported all improvement projects in exchange for votes to make Springfield the state capital.[27]

Lincoln himself offered a simple accounting of his fight to relocate the capital. He noted frankly that Springfield was to be his home (and that this was important) and also that he "really believed" that the people would be "accommodated," for the town had a rather central location. Most likely, historians would have accepted his explanation, rather than a hostile one originating with a political rival, but there was a problem. In retrospect Illinois' attempts at improvements appeared foolish. As Lincoln was no fool, folklore, and in time scholarship, decided that he must have supported the System only, or mostly, to obtain the capital for Springfield.[28]

As this shortsighted tale was laid to rest so was its corollary, which vastly exaggerated Lincoln's part in moving the capital and thereby made the event the salient one of his early career. Therefore, we can now focus more plainly on the fact that Lincoln did not champion internal improvements for narrow political reasons. To say this is not to suggest that he did not try to ride political currents or benefit from the popularity of improvements. Indeed, quite probably one cause of his supporting too wide a range of works lay in the politician's desire to have friends in every part of the state.

Lincoln also had, however, an ever deepening commitment to improvements, one that reached beyond expediency and was increasingly tested as the Illinois System lost popularity, and nonpartisan support changed into nonpartisan opposition. As the present study examines the whole spectrum of Lincoln's economic views, it will become clear that his political activity was inspired, beyond the hope of personal or party gain, by a vision of endless material progress, the heritage of Western Civilization. The vision, it is often said, came true swiftly enough only in the New World, where both the individual and society could advance and where it was proclaimed that "all men are created equal." It thus became the American Dream. The Dream as the central commitment of a people was still a hazy idea for Lincoln in the 1830's. For him and the nation, that commitment was taking shape. An adventure was starting.

2

But It Is Pretty to See What Money Will Do

THE MID-1830'S, WHICH SAW ILLINOIS EMBARK ON HER vast internal improvements, also brought to her the mysterious business of banking. If people prided themselves on the former, almost the opposite was true of the latter. Banking was a strange, even shadowy undertaking. Honest men uneducated in the economic science had to have misgivings about it. To the enlightened these feelings were nothing but prejudice, characteristic of an underdeveloped land; to "the many," however, finance seemed full of dark peril. And still, troublesome thoughts and all, Lincoln's countrymen ventured forth with the men of money. Such was their heritage.

Colonial America had few financial institutions that the historian can designate as banks although various paper moneys and loan bills were issued. The situation improved over the years, but inflation was common, bringing delight to debtors and British intervention on the side of the mother country's merchant creditors. Since these parliamentary intrusions to protect fiscal law and order came with what seemed rascally illegality, they gave justification to American rebels who hastened to create banking concerns in their pursuit of happiness.

In the new nation there was staunch opposition to banks. For example, the future Justice of the Supreme Court, Joseph Story, could toast the Newfoundland fisheries thus: "To Banking: May our only Banks be the Grand Banks and may our *Bankers* be rich indeed." Nonetheless, the moneyed institutions flourished — in time Story himself became the president of one.[1]

In Illinois a "state bank" was created even before statehood. It was established by the territorial legislature, chiefly to manufacture paper money. The future state, like her sisters of the Union (but unlike the rest of the world) developed public banks of issue before a private banking system. The venturesome of the New World yearned to develop and exploit America's resources, and banks could help satisfy the yearning.

In 1818 the first Illinois constitution imitated Indiana in excluding the Bank of the United States and chartering a state monopoly. The main business of the institution was, again, the creation of credit through the issue of notes and the lending of money. As a relief agency, the bank succeeded admirably, but the depression that came after 1819 put a quick end to it. The consequent vacuum became more painful as the state's economy grew and memories of earlier misfortunes grew dim. When Lincoln entered the legislature for the first time, the would-be Barings and Rothschilds of Illinois were ready for new ventures.[2]

Hard economic realities in the state buttressed the probank attitude of the mid-1830's. The Bank of the United States faded away under Jackson's policies. The general scarcity of currency was being remedied by the issues of various state banks, whose paper money, often untrustworthy, promised to flood Illinois. The federal funds collected there but placed elsewhere on account of the lack of local depositories fired the imagination of people. Businessmen, as well as speculators, finally demanded banking facilities. Thus early in 1835, after heated debates, the General Assembly chartered the State Bank of Illinois, with headquarters at Springfield.[3]

For Lincoln banking was a special interest. As a freshman, however, he probably helped neither to shape nor to shepherd this legislation. He also, more than most others, faced a difficult problem of political loyalty over the issue — this although party lines were still less than clear at the time, and the bank vote muddied the lines further. The presidential election of 1832 had made the Bank of the United States into a major test of political allegiance. Many Whig-minded Illinoisans took long years to bring themselves to support the local alternative, the state bank. The leading sponsor of the latter was a combination of politicking and entrepreneurial Jacksonians. And yet, Lincoln voted with them.

He did so though he possessed strong convictions about the importance of the Bank of the United States. This was one of the first significant issues, political or economic, studied by him. His one-time law partner, Stephen T. Logan, not one to bestow praise often or lavishly, recalled that in 1832 already Lincoln could make a "very sensible speech" attacking specie currency. In the following years he expressed his opposition to Jackson's bank veto, the removal of national funds from Chestnut Street, the specie circular, the independent treasury, and blamed the Panic on the Jacksonians. Indeed through thirty-three years of public life he would demonstrate a deep commitment to federally controlled banking.[4]

And yet, in the Illinois House of 1835 Lincoln opted for a state bank because he understood that the Bank of the United States could not then be resurrected, and that the state's economy needed banking facilities above all to support internal improvements. By his vote he made his first serious break with his friend and mentor, John T. Stuart, the Whig leader of the House. This was the most important question of the legislative session, and Lincoln took the plunge because, loyal politician though he was, his ultimate loyalty went beyond what he would later deride as "mere party." And his vote was needed: the state bank passed through the House with a one vote majority.

Illinois created a corporation with a capital stock of $1,500,000 of which $100,000 was available to the state and the rest to private citizens. As soon as $250,000 in specie had been subscribed, the institution could begin business. Local residents were favored as stockholders, and the capital was permitted to be increased by $1,000,000 via such individual subscription. The bank could issue notes to the extent of two and a half times its paid-in capital, excluding deposits. Loans were limited to three times the amount of paid-in capital. The charter also provided for forfeiture and punishment should paper bills not be redeemed in gold and silver, and there were to be no notes smaller than five dollars. Such was the rather common fare of banks in America.

Illinois thus joined the national movement of the mid-30's that in five years doubled the number of banks in the country. The establishment of the Springfield corporation was followed by the chartering of two other successful banks. Since state investments in such local concerns were common, by 1837 legislators argued that the interest of all three corporations should be wedded to that of the state government. The immediate goal was to aid the internal improvement system, but the banks also stood to benefit from the connection.

By then Lincoln was a prestigious member of the House Finance Committee, and he could therefore play the role of economic matchmaker. The lawmakers pointed to dividends of 9 per cent declared by two banks in their short existence of a year and a half. It seemed good business for the state to purchase large amounts of bank stock and, with the forthcoming profits, finance improvements. Accordingly, the legislature increased the capital of two of the banks by $3,700,000 and bought nearly all of the stock. The state had to borrow money to complete the transaction, but high bank dividends were expected to pay the interest on this loan as well as on at least some of the internal improvement loans. Since the bonds issued for the purpose did not sell in the open market, the banks accepted them at par in exchange for their stock. About $1,800,000 of this remained with the Springfield bank throughout its existence, drastically reducing its actual operating capital. The state placed its own directors on the governing boards but not in sufficient numbers to control them. The banks were made fiscal agents for the state government.[5]

By 1837 most of the Whigs came around to support the state bank — but so did a substantial segment of the Democrats (despite solidified party lines), for these were optimistic times. A major bloc of Jacksonians, however, remained in opposition. These agrarians put up a strenuous fight when a union of bank and state credit was first proposed. They were backed by some opportunistic politicians, the entrepreneurial rivals of the Springfield corporation, and a few ideological laissez-faire men. Although the contemplated connection between bank and state made a discreet investigation in order, the antibank faction demanded a sweeping inquiry aimed at discrediting the state bank. Lincoln made his debut before the Illinois public as a leader with a fine speech in the bank's defense.[6]

Like so many Whigs, Lincoln regarded a sound currency, meaning an elastic one, as the most important benefit of banking, and he so argued now. Democrats, like the famed publicist William Gouge, tended to revile the wild notion that "the value of Bank medium . . . consists in its elasticity . . . to suit the wants of the community," and Illinois governor Thomas Carlin denounced a "circulating medium which is susceptible of contraction and expansion at pleasure." Lincoln's understanding of the intricacies of elasticity is open to debate. But he saw the need for the credit created by paper money and opposed a specie currency from the beginning of his career. Indeed, what he called "sound currency" remained a constant concern for him, one which he carried to the presidency.[7]

Commending the state bank, Lincoln pointed out that it provided not only sound paper money but also a safe depository for public funds and an end to the abuses of usury. He stood on solid ground in these general propositions. He indicated a considered judgment concerning the virtues of banks — even if in the present case he overenthusiastically claimed that a doubling of farm prices was one of them! He faced a more difficult task, however, in refuting the specific accusations of the antibank forces, which demanded his best political skills.

The General Assembly had intended to create a people's bank owned by small Illinois stockholders. Instead, local businessmen, vying for control, placed large blocks of stock in the hands of Eastern financiers. The ruse of employing names of Illinois citizens as the purchasers accomplished the deed. Thus thousands of farmers who, as Governor Ford wrote, "never dreamed of being banker," became just that — on paper at least.

Spreading ownership over many names to overcome statutory limitations was widely used during this period, most notably by the Second Bank of the United States. In Illinois, however, when one faction won the power struggle, the other (which had employed the same tactics) yelled foul play and helped instigate the attack upon the bank. The commissioners who had distributed the stocks were then charged with chicanery.[8]

In his retort to the accusation, Lincoln gave the first of many clear, lifelong signals that, his real commitment to democracy notwithstanding, when a straightforward assault on public prejudice was hopeless, he would maneuver around it. Accordingly, on the question at hand he upheld his views partly by obscuring them: he belittled the bank controversy as a dispute among the rich. This was a selective use of the facts, yet the underlying point, an acquiescence in out-of-state control of the local institution, was economically sound. Illinois had insufficient capital to support a people's bank, and the provision of the charter requiring citizen ownership was unrealistic. The proper solution, eliminating the offending clause, was impossible in a parochial state that distrusted the moneyed foreigners of the East and England. So Lincoln pragmatically winked at the circumvention of the bank law.[9]

In his speech Lincoln occupied only little firmer legal ground when refuting the complaint that the state bank refused to redeem its paper currency. The institution had nine branches, each of which printed its own notes and redeemed only its own issue. The banks made a practice of bringing their own bills into circulation at a distant branch, making it difficult to have them presented for redemption.[10] The practice was common in America, and Lincoln was technically correct in maintaining that the State Bank produced specie on demand. He neglected, however, to mention the deviousness of the practice.

Once again he had weighed the demands of law against those of economics and found the latter more important. He showed a glimmer of understanding that Illinois was banking on a shoestring, and that trying to work wonders with insufficient capital should be considered meritorious. But it was not. Indeed the practice contained the danger, to cite Bray Hammond, of taking the valid concept that paper currency was as good as gold and silver if it had public confidence, and turning it into "a monetary burlesque of Pauline theology, faith taking the place of works."[11] It is not surprising that the moral sense of much of the community was insulted by such tendencies. With no widespread insight into the needs of an immature economy, that narrow-minded moral sense could only be circumvented over the short run. This was all the more true when the ken of the tall member of the Finance Committee, and that of the bankers themselves, was spotty and groping.

Lincoln's other arguments in defense of the bank were morally and legally less uncertain but politically equally explosive. The attacks on the Second Bank of the United States on constitutional grounds prepared the way for its demise, and the lesson was not lost on the Illinois opponents of lesser monsters. When Lincoln indignantly objected to this weapon being used in his state he cited the approval of the bank by the Illinois Supreme Court.[12] Lincoln also defended the Springfield concern's connections with out-of-state institutions and its right to necessary secrecy in some of its transactions, issues that parochial and paranoid bank opponents made much of. In the end he predicted that an investigation of the corporation would injure its credit and depreciate its currency. Thus the powerful agrarian indictment that banks caused the fluctuations in the value of money was hurled back at the accusers.

Lincoln reached the climax of his speech by pointing out that the charter granted to the state bank did not reserve for the General Assembly the right to investigate the bank. He argued passionately that lawmakers must not act unjustly and meddle with their own acts, "when those acts were made in the nature of contracts, and had been accepted and acted on by other parties." The background for his stance was provided by Jacksonian America's questioning of the sanctity of charter grants, a view voiced in Illinois by Stephen Douglas and others. That for the case in question this Democratic notion had a certain wisdom, Lincoln seemingly refused to consider. Instead, he went so far as to liken his inquisitive colleagues to the mobs that were rife in parts of the state. Magnifying the question out of proportion, he declared:

> I am opposed to encouraging that lawless and mobocratic spirit, whether in relation to the bank or any thing else, which is already abroad in the land; and is spreading with rapid and fearful impetuosity, to the ultimate overthrow of every institution, or even moral principle, in which persons and property have hitherto found security.

Such overblown oratory was out of place in a legislative controversy over banks, even though Illinois was about to become known as the land of Elijah Lovejoy and Joseph Smith. We must also remember that Lincoln himself had pragmatically stretched the bank law. Yet his perceiving a "lawless and mobocratic spirit" in the attack on the bank showed a penetrating, almost eerie ability to judge men; within a month of his House speech, Usher F. Linder, his prime opponent and the spokesman of the antibank forces, became the chief of the Alton mob that murdered Lovejoy.[13]

Defending the bank, Lincoln thus did not mind using either strong rhetoric or the common tricks of his trade. But his politicking carried substantial economic meaning. He seems to have understood his work as serving the upward yearnings of his people. He saw a useless, wide-ranging investigation of a sound bank as irresponsible, likely to result in injury to the state's currency which, he correctly pointed out, would harm not so much the bankers as the "honest and unsuspecting farmer and mechanic." Should the bank, and with it the paper money of Illinois, indeed be annihilated, he said (using words that carried the deepest meaning for him throughout life and which would be at the heart of his fully formed ideology) it would "render valueless in the hands of our people that *reward of their former labors*."[14]

Lincoln showed that he attached substantial importance to public confidence in banks. His view had not only political but economic merit. Studying the problem in the twentieth century, an able scholar cogently argued that a main cause of the intense deflation of the early 1840's, and its grievous harm to the common man, was a decline of public trust in the American banking system.[15]

It was in this bank speech that Lincoln made his subsequently celebrated attack on politicians. He charged that they had placed their own interest above that of the people and tried to create rancor against financial institutions to ride it to power and glory. He explained that his cutting remarks were made "with the greater freedom because, being a politician myself, none can regard it as personal." In the context of the bank debate no doubt many — then and since — dismissed his statement as nothing but rhetoric. Yet a good measure of his perception (and also of the political motivation and the lack of economic sophistication of so many of his Jacksonian opponents) was provided some forty years later. Then the leader of the attack on the Illinois bank, the above mentioned User Linder, recollected cynically that his hopes of becoming a "great man" had set him on his course.[16]

If we ignore certain idiosyncratic alignments, it is possible to conceptualize Jacksonian America's paramount tug of war, in which the bank battles were salient, as not between the haves and the have-nots, as Marx would soon diagnose for Romanticism's *"Alle Menschen."** The conflict then can be visualized as mostly between haves who wanted to have a little more, and other haves who wanted much more and, without fully recognizing the fact, were willing to

*"All mankind."

change the American way of life, indeed the ways of millenia, in order to get it. The former were the diligent and the persevering, a large majority of them husbandmen, the latter the intrepid and the enterprising, the "adventurers in quest of advancement," as James Fenimore Cooper, arraigned them and capitalism in *Home as Found.* One group tended to support the "negative state"; most, but not all, of the other favored the "positive state." Lincoln sided with the second group and led it to victory as President.

His side possessed a much clearer comprehension of economics, an idealistic vision of bettering the lot of all men, and the seemingly natural avarice of humanity. His antagonists, too, possessed a certain idealism (clouded by the rage of the slowly drowning), and also the advantage of larger numbers, which over the short run often frustrated the opposition politically. These somewhat past-directed folk seemed ignorant and rude — the sort that would stand with muddy boots on fine chairs in the White House — but in fact they grasped a basic truth. Though they did not fathom the particulars of the battle — perhaps *because* they did not — they could sense what was ultimately at stake. Lincoln's side understood enough of the new economics to trust and be absorbed in what they could see, and thus they overlooked what could only be sensed beyond the horizon: the revolution they were brewing against their own way of life. All this was perhaps well. Few would be brave enough to embrace the future if its gifts could be faithfully prophesied.

Using strong instincts, the soldiers of Old Hickory pounced on the proper enemy: the banks. Thus they attacked not only the most blatant symbol, but also one of the most effective instruments, of the undesirable new world of growing commercial-industrial capitalism.

The line between the opposing forces was not, of course, as clear as the above paragraphs would suggest. In Illinois many of the agrarians welcomed, off and on, internal improvements although stopped short of their concomitant: banking. If the conservatives were thus not always consistent, their opponents likewise crossed boundaries. Even Lincoln, more steadfast than most, walked a less than straightforward path. And yet, for all the haziness, the contrasting tendencies of Americans were very real. They were certainly so in Illinois. Again and again, the majority of Lincoln's countrymen said nay to banks.

And why did Lincoln say yea, in the Illinois House of

Representatives and ever after? Intricate as the issue is, our most meaningful solution is reached when we reverse the original question: Why should an enterprising young man who expected to get ahead in life reject the Whig view of the American System, which promised to pave his road and that of his countrymen? Lincoln sensed, to borrow the words of Marvin Meyers, that the Whigs tended to speak to the "explicit hopes of Americans" and the Jacksonians to their "diffuse fears and resentments."[17]

As will be shown, economics, and a related vision of America, more than any other factor, made Lincoln a Whig from 1832 to 1854 — and indeed to the end of his life. Suffice it to note here that he entered politics on a platform of internal improvements; indeed, two years before that his first verifiable speech dealt with the same subject. In 1837 his first fully published speech considered banking in Illinois. In 1840 his first political pamphlet focused on banking on the national scene. This effort also obtained for him his first notice in the national press. In 1847 his first address to a national audience, too, took political economy, internal improvements again, for its subject. These "firsts" carried both symbolic and strategic meanings and reveal much about both him and his age. But more important, in between these "firsts," Lincoln made economics the most substantial part of his campaigning, legislative labors, and private studies outside (and not infrequently inside) his legal work.

All this of course went hand in hand with the hope that wide recognition of the benefits of Whig economics would provide its champions with political popularity. Even in the case of banking, such a hope was not as unrealistic in an economically very alive prepanic Illinois as it would become soon after. Lincoln's hopes for America and his Whig attachment thus were firmly intertwined. Yet lest we make too much of his partisan loyalties, of the truth that growing party regularity drew him to espouse the Whig economic platform (sometimes even its contradictions), we should emphasize that for more than a decade and a half the demands of that same regularity failed to induce him to champion *any* of the noneconomic principles of his party. In contrast, he upheld his own brand of the Whig economic vision even in private, whether writing to a political opponent about taxes or to his kinsman about the way to rise in life.

In his 1837 speech, when Lincoln argued that in defending the bank he was also defending the interests of the "farmer and mechanic" he was not merely meeting the requirements of American politics. He was also giving voice to the prime element of his developing economic persuasion. The fact was that for the man who would rise, for the nation that would rise, banks were necessary.

Underneath this larger view of America's future, and beyond party allegiance and the specific economic need for banking facilities in Illinois, Lincoln did have other reasons for succoring the state bank early in 1837.

It was still reasonably well managed, considering the paucity of talent available. Western institutions that consistently followed the better contemporary standards of commercial banking were scarce indeed. Their course was determined by special problems, not the least of which was the need for funds for long-term capital investment. Even the proverbially successful state bank complex of Indiana made a false start. In the interest of economic development, Illinois acted like her neighbors. In Ohio, Indiana, and Michigan, banks made vital contributions to financing railroads and canals. The same was often true in other parts of the nation and the world over.[18]

Defending the state bank, Lincoln also guarded Springfield, as the attackers found it unnecessary to distinguish between the city and its institution. Groaned one legislator: "They are rich enough, God knows, they hold the bag, like Judas; and with as little merit as he." Intercity bank struggles, often senseless, were plentiful in America. Possibly there was such an element of parochialism in Lincoln's early stand, and he did seem less than agreeable towards Springfield's smaller Shawneetown rival. Yet a case could be made for governmental support and control of one strong state banking system and thus there may have been good economics in Lincoln's stance. Certainly there was good politics. In 1835, for example, he undertook to put restrictions on the Shawneetown bank. In 1837, making his speech in defense of banking, he used this attempt (which incidentally failed) as evidence of his severity towards the corporations.[19]

★

The Whig press was greatly impressed by Lincoln's bank defense and printed it in full: the first of his speeches to be so honored. His championship of a Western Whiggish economic vision promised to raise both him and Illinois to new heights; his home newspaper boasted: "Our friend carries a true Kentucky rifle and when he fires seldom fails of sending a shot home."[20] Although the Democratic controlled legislature ordered a limited examination of the Illinois banks, the setback, if it was that, was temporary. The antibank Jacksonians could not, for the moment, rule the state. The bank probe done, the joint House-Senate committee came around to Lincoln's views. It found some irregularities but, on the whole, praiseworthy business operations. The basic question concerning the advisability of forming close ties between bank and state was not raised. Such connections were common in the nation, and Westerners, in any case, were not given to philosophizing. Also, presumably, the satisfactory condition of the corporations was an adequate answer by itself.[21]

The *Sangamo Journal* considered the bank investigation as " 'searching' as could be wished," but put the key word in quotation marks for some reason. Others believed, at least in retrospect, that it mostly consisted of the decimation of the financiers' whiskey supplies.[22] However this may have been, with Lincoln's help Illinois had decided to give a new test to Samuel Pepys's aesthetics of money: to see what banks could do and if it would be pretty.

3

'Hermes' 'Reader

IN THE SPRING OF 1837 THE GENERAL ASSEMBLY COMPLETED ITS
plans for the improvement of Illinois. The new day, when railroads,
canals, and credit would become moving forces of the state, appeared to have almost arrived. Illinois, many thought, was heading
to the forefront of civilization. Then the Panic came.

Lincoln had never seen a depression except as a child, nor had
many of his colleagues. The financial plague, in any case, was slow to
spread to agricultural regions. An emergency session of the legislature during that summer refused the governor's call for the repeal
of the System's legislation. Lincoln, among others, indeed saw fit to
introduce a new road petition and a road bill before adjournment.[1]

Such optimistic innocence seemed to be vindicated when the credit of the state held up through the financial crisis. Work on the railroads and on the Illinois-Michigan Canal, progressed rapidly. By
1838 the nation appeared to be recovering from the Panic. Lincoln
won reelection with ease. In November the appropriately christ-
ened *Experiment,* the pioneer locomotive of the upper Mississippi
Valley, traveled its first eight miles from the Illinois River in the direction of Springfield. For the Whig lawmaker it must have been
satisfying to take his first railroad ride on a line he had helped bring
into existence.[2]

Yet before long Lincoln had to face up to the fact that the depression, after all, refused to go away. For the remainder of his stay in the
Illinois legislature, his main task was to cope with this stupendous
problem. By the time the General Assembly met at the end of 1838 it

25

became clear that the completion of the System would require substantial new funds. Accordingly, Lincoln advanced an eloquent and well-reasoned plan to meet the need.[3]

He had been elected the Whig leader of the House, and we do not minimize his considerable political talent if we also recognize his leadership in the all-important economic matters as material to his rise. His 1838 finance plan ingeniously combined the long-standing Illinois hope of acquiring the public lands within her borders (a very un-Whiglike hope) with the Whiggish desire for federal aid to internal improvements. Lincoln proposed buying all the public lands in the state for twenty-five cents an acre and reselling them for a profit. The five million dollars necessary for the purchase was to be borrowed. He counted on land sales to keep to the pace of "former times," or of sales in Ohio or Indiana, and thus pay comfortably the interest not only on the five million but also on much of the internal improvement debt. Since the scheme was to relieve the government in Washington of the vexation and expense of administering a large parcel of the national domain, there was "some" probability of federal consent. The proposal was also fair, Lincoln urged, for the Treasury had already collected the original price of the Louisiana Purchase from Illinois lands alone. Now it would receive one-third more.

The Western lawmaker chose to ignore the fact that a most controversial issue, the future of the national domain, was involved in the matter. He glossed over another crucial element of his plan, its monetary aspect, which amounted to a request (disguised as a business deal) for an unprecedented act of benevolence by the federal government. There were further obstacles: the state, already indebted, might have met difficulties in securing a new loan of five million dollars, and it was dangerous to assume that Illinois would grow as rapidly as her neighbors had grown in the past.

Yet if Lincoln betrayed some Whiggish naiveté, his work displayed imagination and was buttressed with accurate statistics. Equally impressive is the fact that the next few years bore out his calculations to a remarkable degree. The income from the Illinois public lands sales of 1839 would have amply serviced the state's improvement loans as well as the proposed additional five million loan. Even the diminishing sales of the 1840's would have provided a substantial portion of the payments. It also spoke well for the lawmaker that he was quite ready to dicker with Washington. In the final analysis he relied on Congress's being "in most particular need of money" because of the depression. An unrealistic scheme perhaps, but these were dire times. Lincoln was willing to adventure.[4]

Lincoln pointed out substantial fringe benefits in this plan. Most important, however, was his hope that by controlling its unsettled domains, the state could speed up immigration. Residing in a sparsely settled region, it is understandable that "wealth and population" were practically synonyms for him. Immigrants would bring economic growth and all that it implied. He suggested that large numbers of new settlers could be attracted by favorable land policies, by tax laws, by cultivating timber and experimenting with new methods of fencing, and by shackling speculators. Later, in the White House, his deep belief in the strength that population statistics symbolized was to have fateful results.[5]

Now Lincoln also argued that through his plan the Illinois improvements, made "at great expense," would profit the people of the state instead of Washington. The point was well taken not only because it was attractive to the local citizenry but also in terms of justice — always a salient consideration in his economic arguments. The national government refused to subsidize improvements. This forced the state to take all the risks involved in increasing land values through the building of transportation facilities. It was fair that Illinois receive the benefits of what, among other things, was a business undertaking.

The plan came from one whose education in both the intricacies of finance and national politics needed much strengthening. But equally plainly it came from a man who learned and thought much about the problem of economic development, was strongly committed to it, and dared to dream big. Lincoln had "persevered in opposition to the views of many" of his committee of Finance to present his project before the House. In the end he managed to obtain his colleagues' support on the floor. The state's representatives in Congress were instructed to work in favor of his plan.

Lincoln thought that the federal government should be given two years to accept the Illinois proposal. At least that length of time, he knew, was necessary for Washington to act. He may also have expected the state to be in most acute need of money by 1841. His augury in part proved correct. Some two and a half years after he produced his plan Illinois defaulted on her internal improvement debt. But there was no response from Washington. In 1840, however, he was still urging it on the government, desiring specially Senator Calhoun's attention, because the South Carolinian, for reasons of his own, championed the cession of the public lands to the states.[6]

But by early 1839 growing, popular opposition to the improvement system appeared. Lincoln met the menacing voice with the argument that the deep involvement of the state made retreat a matter of disgrace and huge monetary losses. He expressed confidence that some mode of finance would be found, until the times improved or the Canal and railroads became self-supporting. His judgment was open to question and its sustenance came primarily from an inner vision. The young man of Sangamon never doubted that over the long run economic development would come to Illinois' rescue. Even the *skeletal* records make clear that he painted glorious pictures of the future "wealth and population" of his state, to which the "internal improvement system, now so alarming, in view of its having to be borne by our present numbers, and with our present means, would be a burden of no sort of consequence."[7]

Lincoln's hopes for the future thus were both his strength and weakness. He was so convinced of the economic soundness of Illinois' grand design, and so ignorant of what the business cycle could do, that he felt safe enough to make one of his responses to anti-improvement attacks narrowly political. Since the sources of loudest criticism were the areas of the state that felt neglected by the System, he tried to plug up these sources with new projects. "Economy is to be the order of the day," he declared, and it should have been. But perhaps heartened by a new tax law, his own plan for land speculation, and the optimistic report of the state commissioners of public works, he voted to spend more money in an attempt to recoup the System's popularity. One million dollars were appropriated for general improvements, including five thousand dollars for the little Spoon River that would teach so much to Edgar Lee Masters. An additional four million went to the Illinois-Michigan

Canal. The Springfield lawyer also goaded on his favorite canal company in the Sangamon Valley, threatening it with loss of contract.[8]

Lincoln's proimprovement stance allowed relatively little flexibility. He was willing to see the administration and operation of the System investigated but not the question of its continuation. He opposed ranking projects according to their importance to prepare for the possibility that some of them might have to be abandoned. If this stand was shortsighted, it was not easily escapable. The Democratic organ correctly explained that "classification" was well nigh equal to giving up all improvements, for the regions whose works were rated as low priority would turn on the entire System. In this, too, Illinois acted like most of her sister states.[9]

Thus Lincoln and with him a majority of the legislators would not retreat from their improvement hopes. They failed to fathom the depression in part because the economic signals were confusing. The full downturn of the cycle did not commence until 1839. When that occurred the people watched helplessly as the whole internal improvement scheme, to quote Governor Ford, "tumbled about their ears, and brought down the state." The hard times became extreme, what seemed to be solid financial backing evaporated. Much of the actual work was suspended during the summer, and winter found the Canal the one major unabandoned project.[10]

And yet, in the face of a severe depression, which Douglas C. North thought comparable to the one usually called the "Great," Lincoln remained an obstinate supporter of improvements.[11] That he acted so, even as the popularity of his cause plummeted, tells much about his economic views. Others, equally distributed between the parties, followed both national economic and local political indicators. Nearly all of the leaders who were later to reach more or less prominence, from Democrat Douglas, author of the first improvement bill of 1837, to Lincoln's future Whig rivals, John J. Hardin and Edward D. Baker, stood against the System. Thus if we fail to credit the young Lincoln with deep convictions and, more narrowly, economic convictions, the role he came to play in Illinois' fight for rapid advancement becomes very puzzling.

It is true that more than economic convictions made Lincoln into a stubborn champion of improvements at this hour of despair. The

Democratic press noted with glee his earlier admission that his constituents had received many projects in return for the Long Nine's support of appropriations for other localities. Lincoln said he felt honor-bound to adhere to every part of the System; a hostile reporter added, "through all time to come!"[12]

One is tempted to cherish this moralistic accounting of Lincoln's actions and, indeed, although it was made before the 1839 collapse, it has some merit for this entire period of trouble. The hardihood and ethical compulsion of Nancy Hanks' son were real and earned him the name "Honest Abe." His celebrated pragmatism had strict boundaries. At first only in a single case, that of fraud, did the gentleman from Sangamon back down from his deals unilaterally. Even then he acted through a colleague.[13]

We can go beyond Lincoln's integrity and emphasize his tenacity that bordered on fatalism. Citing his "Old Father," he could reiterate Caesar's "Iacta alea est"* in a frontier version: "If you make a bad bargain, *hug* it the tighter." In another aeon, as it seemed, when doubt rose about the President's steadfastness to his Emancipation Proclamation, he told Charles Sumner "that it was hard to drive him from a position which he had once taken." Indeed it was. Lincoln's mental makeup thus explains to some extent his insistence on the continuation of the improvement system after the depression had worsened.[14]

The psychological ingredient of Lincoln's stance, however, cannot obscure economic convictions which he steadily held throughout his life. Without these convictions his mental traits would have sought other outlets. And, whatever one thinks of psychological determinants, in the final analysis, internal improvements were a matter of political economy. Political profit clearly lay in the direction of turning quickly against improvements. Where economic virtue lay was more open to debate.

By 1839 Lincoln understood that the times had become very hard. In his law practice he had to write: "We regret to say that [there is] the entire certainty that we shall need all the means at our command"; "we shall commence suits"; "they are honest and honorable men, but they are hard pressed." He also saw clearly that the grand improvement plans of the state were lost for a time. To his law partner,

---

*Across the Rubicon for good or for ill, or literally: "The die is cast."

Congressman John T. Stuart, went his terse admission: the "System will be put down in a lump, without benefit of clergy." He thus predicted, and for practical purposes correctly, that for now nothing would survive from Illinois' original design.[15]

Lincoln was sorely beset by the problem before him, his leadership at times faltered, but the direction he took was unmistakable. Realizing that the entire System could not be resuscitated, he hoped against hope that its two most vital projects might be conserved. He could not admit to Illinois being mired in her state of undevelopment, saddled with debt and with nothing to show for it. That would surely set people against the better world he longed to bring them. Thus, although he feared that the outcome of the battle was preordained and that even victory would promise political profit only in the long run, he resolved to fight.

Previous bargains notwithstanding, at the 1839-1840 session of the legislature Lincoln sharply reduced his improvement demands, to the Illinois-Michigan Canal and the Central Railroad. These works not only made the best economic sense but also had the strongest remaining public support. He sought the acquiescence of the "original friends of the system" (with whom he had made his deals) but evidently supported retrenchment without their full backing. His stand in favor of the Central Railroad was very passive, presumably because of his bargains. (The canal, planned separately, was a different matter.) Yet having announced that, apart from the canal, the Illinois Central was his choice as the priority improvement, he was willing to have either the General Assembly or, even better, the Democratic governor carry the burden of that decision. When efforts to sustain the Central failed, Lincoln successfully lowered his sights, in 1840-1841, to the small, half-completed Northern Cross, which required much lighter outlays and promised quick profits.[16]

Lincoln's fight to "save something," as he put it, "from the general wreck" included the tactic of casting some totally unrealistic votes, even opposing the abandonment of the System with ten legislators on his side and seventy-seven on the other. Such stiff-necked (or brave) politics at some moments amounted to protest; at others it may have camouflaged a hope to attain all that was possible by demanding the impossible.[17]

The most significant improvement battle was fought over the

Illinois-Michigan Canal, with Lincoln playing a major part. When late in 1839 a Representative observed that "we have 10 lawyers that take up more time than all the other members," he placed Lincoln at the head of his list. The Whig ex-flatboatman saw the abandonment of the canal as "stopping a skift [sic] in the middle of a river — if it was not going up, it *would* go down." His argument was apt. So was his view, at least in theoretical terms, that "the most economic course" before the state was the completion of the ambitious undertaking. The canal was the strategic project for the development of Illinois, similar to New York's Erie, Georgia's Western and Atlantic Railroad, and the proposed Pennsylvania Main Line. A demand already existed for the services of a waterway connecting the Great Lakes to the system of the Mississippi. The finished work also promised early returns to the state on its investment.[18]

At the 1839-1840 session of the assembly Lincoln used both great economic and political ingenuity to help guide the canal through the House. It is worth noting that when an attempt was made to saddle the canal bill with two other projects he said a firm no. This is revealing because students generally see his votes against the total scrapping of the System as insistence on the completion of all improvement works. Such a stand would have been meaningless, for it was impossible to sustain.[19]

At the 1840-1841 session, with the depression growing ever deeper, Lincoln remained a chief advocate of the project in the House, in committees, presumably in private discussions. He wanted the state to borrow the necessary funds at almost any cost. He even made devastatingly unfair use of his wit, illustrating how personal and heated the fight over improvements was to him. He won in the House but the Senate negated his labors.[20]

The lawmakers of both parties feared the wrath of their constituents: the debt already incurred made them balk at the thought of another large improvement loan. Parochialism also played its paltry part, preaching the fear of "undue" growth in the northern section of the state where the work was located. Many of Lincoln's party friends vacillated because they had nativist leanings and the canal imported Irish laborers. Also the Irish generally voted Democratic. The Illinois-Michigan limped on for a while by temporary expedients, but finally, in the middle of 1842, all work ceased.[21]

Illinois was not alone in its troubles. In the summer of that dismal year canal after canal gave up the ghost — in New York, Pennsylvania, Indiana, Maryland, and Virginia. The systems of the two Carolinas, Georgia, Michigan, and Missouri were also dead. Ohio alone was able to carry its burden through the depression, and she had the advantage of a head start on the Panic of 1837. Enthusiasm for improvements was replaced by disgust.[22]

That in these times Lincoln never questioned the essential rightness of his goals indicates the strength of his developing economic outlook. That he managed to remain the leader of the House Whigs in spite of his often isolated position indicates his political skills and the respect they commanded. It also suggests the extent to which his long-range economic vision was admired by many of his comrades — however unpopular it was for the moment. The tenacity of Lincoln's views is all the more remarkable because mentally he was deeply shaken by the crisis that he had helped guide his people into. Even his private life fell apart, with his engagement to Mary Todd broken. He reached a point of depression where his friends grew anxious about his safety.[23]

In the end, with the people, Lincoln did not escape political punishment for resisting the demand for stopping improvement experiments. Early in 1840 he even feared that he would "not be permitted to be a candidate" for office. Matters stopped short of this because, Lincoln thought, his skills on the stump were deemed indispensable. He tried to explain away his troubles as resulting from the conflict within his party between country and town, a face-off in which he stood for the latter. But these hostilities (not without economic implications) failed to prevent the Whigs from giving the choice spot on the 1840 legislative slate to Edward D. Baker, also of Springfield. Baker was younger, less experienced, and less distinguished — but he opposed the improvement system. On election day, although reelected, Lincoln came in last among his victorious comrades.[24]

Such a state of things presumably helped prompt his retirement from the General Assembly early in 1841. Later when he attempted to obtain his party's nomination for Congress he ran into difficulties. Exactly how much political harm came to Lincoln from his economic stance can not be determined. That the Whigs took the matter into account is clear. As for the Democrats, as late as 1846 (and probably much later than that) they assailed him for his association with what became known as the "misnamed" system of internal improvements.[25]

★

While Lincoln was thus paying the price for nurturing a Dream, Henry David Thoreau lamented that "we do not ride on the railroads; they ride on us." For Illinois this almost became the literal truth. The sage of Walden Pond might have applauded the halting of the iron horse. But a more mundane posterity declared that the state had been led into disaster by politicians ignorant of economics. David Davis summarized this view in 1847: "The Legislature has been the great source of evil in this State. If there had been none in session for 10 years Illinois would have been a very prosperous state."[26]

Such is the judgment of a commonsense hindsight that grew into folklore while Illinoisans paid taxes for forty years to liquidate their $11,000,000 improvement debt. The judgment grew entrenched in scholarship, too, as passing decades brought to America the veneration of laissez-faire and also, in spite of that ideological straightjacket, a deeper knowledge of economics. These factors made the errors of Illinois' governmental enterprise seem elementary.

In the present historical perspective, however, such judgment should not persist. Lincoln's generation of Americans should be seen as more brave than blundering. Illinoisans in particular followed a route similar to that taken by the people of other states, and for similar reasons. Lincoln believed that he saw within his people's grasp wealth and opportunity and preached "that all our energies should be exerted to bring that wealth . . . among us as speedily as possible." At the beginning at least he had the best of company in his opinions. The *Sangamo Journal* proclaimed that the Tenth General Assembly possessed "more talent than any legislative body ever assembled in Illinois." In a year of exaggerations this was an understatement. Among these lawmakers, it is often noted, were future generals and congressmen, three future governors, and seven future United States senators, as well as Stephen Douglas and Abraham Lincoln. Almost unanimously these men supported the improvement system of the state in 1837.[27]

Internal improvements were risky business at best. As developing nations must do, youthful America demanded transportation facilities before conservative private capital was available to provide them. Lincoln and the best of his generation groped toward a concept that modern economists call "social overhead capital." The term, coined by Paul Rosenstein-Rodan, refers to investments in projects that are valuable to society but are not likely to entice businessmen, above all because profits are too far in the future, or can not be captured, or because required capital input is too large. In Lincoln's day even fragments of this fundamental lesson in economic development had to be hard-earned. If the price Illinois thus had to pay was substantial, such often is the history of pioneers, whether the frontier is the prairie, economics, statesmanship, or space.

And there is more. Lincoln and colleagues received financial support to the extent of several million dollars from such reputable bankers as Nicholas Biddle, James Irwine, and John W. Wright & Co. of London. Wealthy, self-made David Henshaw, visiting from Massachusetts, wrote of the Illinois System: "These gigantic works would startle citizens of the east; but any judicious person . . . would say they evince great energy and sagacity." Acting in unison, sophisticated businessmen and hardheaded pioneers apparently confused to some extent the potentials of New York around 1820 and of Illinois in the 1830's. There were warnings that the more developed Atlantic states provided "no fair example or precedent" for young Illinois. But there was also the opinion that she could afford to borrow as much as $100,000,000.[28]

Measured criticism of course is not out of order. The state's improvement attempt was a costly though very temporary setback. Illinois' plans were expensive relative to local resources and far out of proportion to current needs. Economic misjudgments were compounded by the lack of technical knowledge and a shortage of competent engineers. The one completed railroad, the small Northern Cross, was far from successful by American standards of the time. Since votes were often unrecorded on minor issues, it seems impossible to ascertain whether Lincoln joined, for example, in foisting English strap iron on the railroads — in the interest of economy but against sound engineering advice.[29]

The System's cumbersome administration, which the Whig floorleader did not mind seeing investigated, unfortunately included some thieves. Honest ignorance of financial detail also plagued the state, though it acted, to cite Governor Ford, as if it had "a hundred DeWitt Clintons." Costs were consistently underestimated, as they always seem to be, and in the hope of large profits the state made bad investments in local banks.[30]

Lincoln, a prominent member of the House Finance Committee, had a broad knowledge of the fiscal potential of Illinois. But apparently he felt that there was no connection between regular government expenditures and the System. Although it is proper to separate operating and capital budgets, there was a striking contrast in the way he boldly voted millions for improvements while always favoring economy in the normal expenditures of the state, even to the point of squabbling over small amounts of money. He "would grant that 30 or 40 dollars were not worth quarreling about," Lincoln told the House, but leniency here contained the danger that "hereafter, many such sums will be allowed without a quarrel, and without objection." Penny-wise and pound foolish, he acted almost as though possessed by a dream.[31]

This became the most evident during the last years of his legislative service, which coincided with the last years of the improvement attempts. He can be criticized in particular for keeping a too optimistic faith for too long — for allowing his vision of the future to weaken his judgment.

The most devastating part in the internal improvement calamity was reserved not for individuals but for Illinois' collective parochialism, in which Lincoln took part. That the lawmakers made large mistakes in economics, a new science, is understandable and, to a substantial degree, excusable. They thus made Illinois one of the most venturesome states of the Union. Less excusable, however, is their local-mindedness, which, widespread though it was in the nation, was a malaise old enough to have obtained different treatment.

Illinois perhaps could not have been expected to fit its transportation facilities into a national network. Even within the state, however, excessive local rivalries help explain not only the overextension of plans but also the fact that, excepting the Illinois-Michigan Canal, almost nothing was saved from their wreck. All the railroads were constructed simultaneously to assure that no section would profit unduly before another. This extravagance not only produced occasional labor and material shortages but also denied the state revenue from the projects, if there was to be any, until they were all completed.

In the same provincial spirit was the attempt to arrange the System so that it would center at Alton on the Mississippi — in order to make the city a serious rival of St. Louis. Lincoln went along with all this and fought, for example, to locate the authorized Sangamon River bridge near his early home town of New Salem, a town which was destined to fade from the map within a few years. Yet he slowly grew. Some years later he even helped to split the Sangamon delegation in order to defeat a too small and hence wasteful appropriation for their river.[32]

Over the long run Lincoln's years with the improvement system proved profitable for him in many ways and thus proved profitable for the nation. He had been "raised to farm work," his formal schooling no more than a year all told. Many of the advances in this "store of education," as he later recalled, were made "under the pressure of necessity."[33] And Hermes, fickle god of merchants, thieves, and economics, turned out to be a most memorable teacher.

Lincoln's involvement with improvements helped him reach convictions which played a crucial role during his presidency. The disaster that befell Illinois brought Lincoln the realization that public and private enterprise might work hand in hand. He had come to it slowly. In 1837, carried away with enthusiasm, he had approved a House resolution that protested, in language reminiscent of Old Hickory, against trammeling the state with connections to incorporated companies. A large segment of the legislators insisted to the very end on considering individual and public roles incompatible. The young Whig leader himself did not fully learn the error of that view until the continuation of the improvements was at stake. Then he took part in desperate attempts to turn the work over to private business and make the state a stockholder to the extent of its past expenditures. These efforts failed and earned him only the jeer of the ideologue that he had become a "joint-stock-company man." "What an example of good faith!" Yet, for one who was to become a wartime president, learning the importance of intimate cooperation between government and private citizens was essential. So was the even more fundamental lesson about the need to harness man's economic self-interest to the service of the general good.[34]

Herndon, who became Lincoln's law partner toward the mid-1840's, later recalled that his mentor was "purely practicable." The failure of improvements helped Lincoln move in that direction. His experience certainly converted him not only to more prudent economics, but more significantly to more prudent politics. For a more important time the young man was learning to "make haste slowly," to "not go forward fast enough to wreck the country's cause."[35]

Perhaps most fatefully, the improvement episode helped make Lincoln a lifelong opponent of the localism and sectionalism that had proved so destructive in Illinois. Historians before and after Frederick Jackson Turner have pointed to the connection between improvements and nationalism. In Illinois, the failure of the System initiated a nationalizing trend, even among Democrats, the significance of which grew plain in 1861.[36] For Lincoln the lesson of the failure was particularly poignant: he had always leaned toward a broad view of America, but this period marked the lengthiest advance toward his goal "to be no less than National" in all things.[37]

From the unbuilt New Salem bridge the road led to the White House and Civil War. In 1841 Lincoln found himself in a debate over the disposition of state internal improvement property. Nominally the remains of the collapsed System were at stake, but more important here was a clash of two basic American outlooks. And here Lincoln took his stand. One of his House colleagues objected to the use of state possessions by a private company on the grounds that one section thus received an advantage over the others. The Sangamon political economist pointed to the narrowness of such a position. He "shewd in substance that the State property would all be lost and go to ruin, if the principle be adopted that no one shall have any, for fear all shall not have some."

Some years later Congressman Lincoln came up against the same provincialism in Washington which he had learned to battle at home. Still advocating internal improvements, now on the national scale, he resisted the argument that, whereas the whole country had to bear the burden of improvements, only certain sections benefited by them, producing thereby "an obnoxious inequality." To such a view the reply of the representative from Illinois was crystal clear: "No commercial object of government patronage can be so exclusively *general*, as to not be of some peculiar *local* advantage; but, on the other hand, nothing is so *local*, as to not be of some general advantage." In this Lincoln knew there was no difference between the federal and state level. "If this argument of 'inequality' is sufficient any where, — it is sufficient every where; and puts an end to improvements altogether."

More than a decade passed, and on Independence Day, 1861, the President of the United States sent his war message to Congress. Ordinary economic problems were dwarfed by the enormous fact of secession. Searching for an analysis of the Southern stand, the Commander-in-Chief drew on old experiences and used old words:

> This relative matter of National power, and State rights, as a principle, is no other than the principle of *generality*, and *locality*. Whatever concerns the whole, should be confined to the whole — to the general government; while whatever concerns *only* the State, should be left exclusively, to the State.

In reality of course there was no clear-cut line between state and national power. To paraphrase Lincoln, nothing was so local as to not have some general effects; nothing was so general as not to bear some local fruit. Yet American traditions required a line to be drawn somewhere. Individuals had to decide for themselves where that division should be. Opposite stands could be upheld with equal sincerity and logic. For Lincoln internal improvements of old, secession in 1861, came to be matters for the whole nation. In the final analysis his choice was the declaration of a faith that grew over decades — and economics were central to that faith.[38]

4

Egyptian Locust

ILLINOIS' PLAN FOR ECONOMIC DEVELOPMENT FAILED AND LEFT IN its wake a host of problems. Lincoln knew that the setback was temporary but, in the meantime, as a legislator he had to face up to the most pressing issues before the government: the debt created by the improvement attempts. Since he had contributed his strength to creating the crushing problem, and since the signs pointed toward increased taxation as a result, there was poetic justice in the situation.

Mankind seems to have an age-old abhorrence of taxes. The Bible says that divine love was necessary to make the publican Matthew acceptable to the rest of humanity. It would have been even more necessary in America. Although a variety of levies abounded in the thirteen colonies, little was actually collected. Not until the latter half of the eighteenth century and the Revolution did the appetite of armies demand significant revenues. Even then, although patriotism burned high, citizens kept their purse strings tight. Once the battle was won, however, the Constitution granted far-reaching tax powers to the central government. Accordingly, the first rebellion of the new nation was against a levy on such a necessity of frontier life and commerce as whiskey.

The small edifice of taxation that the Federalist Party built was quickly demolished by Jefferson. When in 1812 martial spirit again called for the exercise of this annoying form of governmental power, returns, as before, proved disappointing. Not until the passing of two generations dimmed memories, and war came again, was a similar

41

attempt to be made. Down to the Civil War revenues were extracted largely from import duties and public land sales.[1]

In Illinois fiscal policy reflected, indeed exaggerated, national attitudes. The people were "determined," to quote their historian-governor, "upon the preservation and enjoyment of their liberties." During most of the first two decades of statehood, until the late 1830's, counties were supported mainly by land taxes on residents, and the state government by taxes on nonresidents. Whenever possible the state's constitutional prohibition of discriminatory rates was circumvented and the "foreigners" of the Eastern states, who held a huge acreage for speculative purposes, were treated mercilessly. The rent of state-owned saline lands also put some money into the treasury, as did the borrowing of federal funds which had been provided for a school system that Illinois had not yet created. In harmony with Western traditions, rates were low during this early period, the government was not to do anything that cost money, and if feasible, its functions were to be delegated to private enterprise. When a rare tax increase was placed on the lawbooks by legislators daring to jeopardize their chances for reelection, public clamor was sure to follow.[2]

The advent of the improvement age did not change Illinois folkways. When Lincoln became a leader of the transportation revolution, he accordingly refused to raise the conjunctive specter of taxes. He did not specifically rule out local levies for the support of the System, as mass meetings were prone to do, and this may or may not have been an oversight. But his 1837 report to the House on the financial condition of the state forecast a deficit without recommending the obvious solution of taxation. This was accepted in part because Illinois believed that improvements would not only pay for themselves but produce a profit as well. Thus for some a vote for the System was even a vote against taxation.[3]

Lincoln considered taxation a poor fount of revenue, and justly so. His state was agricultural, and without access to markets investments in land yielded small immediate returns. To add to this small capacity for taxpaying was taxation's disrepute on the frontier. Yet that the Whig lawmaker did not merely take the popular stand but thought long and carefully about taxes is evident. Even in his freshman session in the legislature he showed willingness to use fiscal policy to promote economic development and improve the chances of the poor to rise. Property newly acquired from the public domain was exempt from taxes in Illinois for five years. Both political parties favored the repeal of this arrangement but not Lincoln. He was willing to discuss the issue, yet voted with the few who steadfastly insisted on tax privileges for new settlers starting at the bottom. Since this policy had to be maintained at the expense of more established farmers, his stand resembled his later support of graduated taxation.[4]

If Lincoln was perhaps less reluctant to assess citizens than was the average Illinois politician of the mid-1830's, this says very little in a state with a strong antitax bias.[5] On the one issue wherein taxes figured prominently, that of education, he repeatedly approved the legislature's borrowing school funds to escape taxing. In his first platform Lincoln had declared education to be "the most important subject which we as a people can be engaged in" — words that have been much quoted since. But in the House he sacrificed "the most important subject," year after year, in part, apparently, to avoid levies.[6]

The inherent contradiction between Lincoln's aversion to taxes and his vision of government-supported and -guided development did not come into focus until Illinois' improvement plan began to falter. Then his devotion to improvement was further measured by his willingness to support the assessment of the people. At the 1838-39 meeting of the Assembly a bill was introduced to increase revenues. Its supporters spoke of the need to reform the state's archaic tax structure, and indeed much of the nation was updating its tax laws during this period. In Illinois, however, the taxpayers believed that the financially troubled System was at the heart of the matter. Lincoln advanced his land purchase plan, which if successful, could have minimized taxation. But he also supported the act, which placed a twenty-cent levy on each hundred dollars of real and personal property for the purposes of the state. A fifty-cent ceiling was put on county taxes. At first the fainthearted House intended to adopt a lower rate but the high tax men, with the Whig leader among them, frustrated their wishes.[7]

People thought the law was an important increase in assessment, but comparisons were difficult between old and new levels because the tax base was changed. The fact became clear in time, as revenue receipts increased, but the citizens did not wait that long. A magnificent uproar followed the politicians' betrayal of the American birthright. Opposition reached such a point that some counties refused to list their taxable property. David Davis (who later became Lincoln's close friend, a Supreme Court Justice, and a U.S. Senator from Illinois) was to angrily write to a correspondent in the East. "I am getting heartily tired of this Sucker State. Iowa has no debt . . . no taxes." Lincoln and his colleagues were forced to call a public meeting to explain their stand. Although no account of this confrontation survives, the central argument Lincoln used can be reconstructed from his correspondence.[8]

With considerable skill he showed that the old revenue law badly needed reform to meet the ordinary needs of government.[9] He also emphasized that under the new law justice would be done — an important point that deserves scrutiny here. Until 1839 all taxable land in Illinois was valued at either three or four dollars an acre. No other categories existed, and the levy was set at one-half of one percent. Thus land that was worth less than three dollars an acre carried more than a proportional share of the burden. Much more importantly, because of the large acreage involved, the opposite was true of land worth more than four dollars an acre. The new act abolished this unfair, and for Illinois unconstitutional, system and replaced it with taxation "according to true value."[10]

Lincoln approved the change so heartily that he sounded as if he were defending a progressive tax such as he signed into law during the Civil War. The 1839 measure was just in his eyes because it extended the burden of the wealthy few and not the many poor. The owners of the best lands were to pay more than before and Lincoln spoke about some land being worth fifty or a hundred dollars per acre. Thus some of the well-to-do faced a 24-fold increase of taxes. The owners of the poorer lands on the other hand were to pay no more under the new law than before, and in a few cases less. Such an arrangement, of course, also had political advantages, he thought, and wrote candidly in private:

> if . . . the wealthy should, regardless of the justness of the complaint, as men often are, when interest is involved in the question, complain of the change, it is still to be remembered that *they* are not sufficiently numerous to carry the elections.

Lincoln no doubt recognized that the burden on some land speculators would also be reduced by the elimination of a minimum level of assessments. This, however, was an acceptable price to pay for ending at the same time a maximum limit on levies and having the authority of the state constitution behind the change. Revenue receipts in any case indicated (erroneously as it turned out) that the number of the remaining speculators was exceedingly small.[11]

Lincoln knew that, as always, there might be trouble "before the people" with the tax law. He professed the hope that "the danger is not as great" as some feared, but he was wrong about this. Men who had a murkier vision of the future than he did were less able to dismiss lightly the costs of building that future. His and like efforts notwithstanding, most Illinoisans seemed sure that the new law was a trick to milk them in order to support improvements of dubious value. The rapid decline in the popularity of the System dated from this time. Protest meetings mushroomed, declaring that the tax was "well calculated to arouse the people from the long sleep" of improvement reveries.[12]

Unpopular as taxation was, Lincoln would rather have both improvements and taxes than neither. The depression, however, took the issue out of his hands. With improvement systems collapsing everywhere, not only high taxation but also repudiation began to haunt the nation. During his final General Assembly Lincoln had to serve not only on the Committee of Finance but also on one considering the payment of interest on the state debt. Feeling "his share of the responsibility" in creating Illinois' problem, "revolving in his mind every scheme which seemed to afford the least prospect of relief," to quote his own words, stretching his fiscal ingenuity to the limit, for "he was no financier," Lincoln evolved a clever plan to service the improvement debt with the proceeds of a new loan.[13]

Its main feature was a special tax fund, set irrevocably aside to pay the interest on the new bonds, thus making them marketable and raising the value of previously issued and depreciating state securities. The proposal was economically hazardous but, justifying it, Lincoln produced the best available defense by pointing out that rapid growth would make the payment of debt much easier later. If Illinois wished to remain solvent, there was no clear alternative.

The plan meant still higher taxation and the House scuttled it. Regular securities were issued, and many lawmakers insisted that these be sold at par value. This demand "was tantamount to prohibiting their sale," Lincoln explained, and managed to help defeat at least this much of the majority scheme. By the end of 1841 the bonds sold for fifteen to twenty cents on the dollar. Probably Lincoln's "Illinois Interest Bonds," as he called them, would have done better.[14]

The Lincoln plan had included the lightening of county levies to compensate for the rise of state taxes, but this was not a readily feasible trade-off. Indeed since he expected local governments to continue some of the abandoned improvement projects, we may assume that he proposed such reduction to avoid the responsibility for a heavier tax burden. His job was very difficult: he faced a recalcitrant constituency and even his party colleagues in the House had to be pushed hard to support his high tax stance. One Whig paper labeled Lincoln's finance plan "a mere gull trap," and rebuked him for attempting to "conceal" increased levies. Even the newspaper closest to him, the *Sangamo Journal*, offered more doubts than help.[15]

When his finance plan was defeated, Lincoln concentrated on salvaging the segment of it that increased taxes. Emphasizing that "the faith of the State must be preserved," he would not admit defeat on that question. He was willing to face the anger of both colleagues and constituents. The issue was hardly a partisan one, although under Lincoln's prodding the Whig lawmakers reversed previous history and became somewhat more protax than the Democrats. Still, other Whig leaders such as Hardin seemed to take refuge in the unfairly partisan notion that nothing could be done with "the rascally party in power." Lincoln, however, introduced a second bill and then a third, which finally carried. He not only obtained a ten-cent increase per hundred dollars of property, but also the vital concession that "the said additional revenue . . . shall be set apart exclusively for payment of interest on the state indebtedness." County levies remained unchanged.[16] Lincoln of course knew that for years to come in Illinois even the interest, much less the debt, could not be paid from local assessments. He demanded the raising of property taxes as much to relieve the state until a long-term solution was found via better times and economic growth as to assure Illinois' creditors of her willingness to carry the burden.

Within his high-tax, pro-many stance Lincoln retained his essential pragmatism. By 1840 he evidently came to believe that substantial revenues might be raised from delinquent speculators. Taking aim at their unimproved holdings, he called for a new valuation of land set at a minimum four dollars an acre and then settled for a dollar less. For the sake of desperately needed revenue he thus now gave short shrift to the state constitution which prescribed proportional levies. Furthermore, it is possible that some of the poor, who owned land worth less than three dollars an acre, were hurt by the minimum assessment. Because of the depression land was beginning to be sold at such low prices. However, only a very small quantity of actually settled property on the prairie fell into this category. A year later Democratic Governor Ford singled out the minimum valuation for praise for aiding the state's finances. But with Lincoln no longer a member, the legislature cut the general tax rate in half.[17]

The fifty per cent increase in the existing state tax, together with the floor on land valuation, was a bitter pill for the people in 1841. By then several states, upon whom fell Illinois-like internal improvement disasters, were unable to service their debts. Repudiation was becoming an epidemic. In mid-year Indiana stopped interest payments, although Lincoln justly considered his own state, then still paying, considerably "more embarrassed" by the relative size of its debt. Indeed as Illinois was raising tax rates, her neighbor reduced hers from thirty to fifteen cents per hundred dollars. Many in Lincoln's state wanted to follow suit.[18]

Then in his sixth year of paying an enormous debt of his own from New Salem, and although strongly prodebtor, Lincoln uncompromisingly opposed repudiation — just as he opposed a stay law which benefited his law practice by suspending for all practical purposes the collection of personal debts. (Soon after the U.S. Supreme Court declared the law unconstitutional.)[19] If he was taking some tentative steps toward what another age came to call the redistribution principle of taxation, or more colloquially soaking the rich, he was unwilling to go so far as to encompass the repudiation of debts, personal or state.

In the House he pitted himself against the future Senator, Lyman Trumbull, chief of the forces for partial or complete repudiation of state obligations. These men particularly objected to Illinois' redeeming bonds for which payments had not been received. Among

other things, they chose to ignore the unpleasant fact that the purchasers of the securities often became delinquent because of the
carelessness of state agents in making clear their obligations. In the
end, with Stephen Douglas on his side, Lincoln achieved a victory of
sorts over the repudiators' daring, as he said, the "degradation of the
state." This victory was a far cry from that of Alexander Hamilton
some two generations earlier, but after initial defeat, the House
accepted the proposition that obligations might be disregarded
only if unpaid-for bonds were in the hands of the original purchasers. It is intriguing to note that nearly two decades later, during the Lincoln-Douglas debates, the Little Giant held against his
opponent the "infamous scheme" of repudiation that had been
championed by Trumbull — by 1858 a Lincoln ally.[20]

Lincoln's new high-tax stand did not go so far as to prevent his
proposing privileges for Revolutionary veterans or opposing excessive levies on professionals such as lawyers and doctors. Promoting
the American future, he gave special consideration to cities. He not
only procured benefits for his home town but fought, though in
vain, to give every town half the real estate and personal property
levies collected therein by its county. And declaring against a special
assessment on legislators, he called his colleagues' attention, tongue
in cheek, to the unwritten rule concerning conflict of interests: "it
appeared to him they were interested in this case."[21]

Nevertheless, the fiscal crisis had turned Lincoln into an open
supporter of various austerity and tax measures. His former votes in
favor of higher salaries for public servants now became generally
votes for reductions.[22] By 1839 he also accepted the necessity for
taxing new land improvements and became an open proponent of
Senator Calhoun's cession plans that would have allowed the assessment of newly sold public lands.[23] He even extended his attitude to
the national government and voted to instruct the Illinois delegation
in Congress to resist further appropriations for the military
academy at West Point.[24]

Austerity and increased taxation, however, could not save Illinois
while the depression kept getting worse. Thus in the summer of
1841, after Lincoln completed his final term in the House, the state
defaulted on the interest due on her debt. What followed in his
words, was "a year of almost unparalleled pecuniary pressure . . .

almost insupportable difficulties . . . severest necessity."[25] The Illinois transportation revolution seemed quite dead. But the hair of this Samson grew back in time and the state debt was paid. And the solution to Illinois' plight came along lines the Sangamon dreamer had foreseen.

In the mid-1840's, under Governor Ford, plans were made for the long-term liquidation of the internal improvement debt. A one-mill tax was levied, it was later raised to one and one-half mills, and with its aid loans were secured and the Illinois-Michigan Canal was completed in 1848. The economic impact of the new facility lived up to expectations, the times improved, and the increased wealth of the state returned it to solvency by the end of the decade. Finally, the revenues from the Illinois Central Railroad, built by private enterprise with federal aid in the 1850's, allowed a slow settlement of the old obligations.[26]

But in 1839, 1840, and the years after, the people of the state, indeed much of the Union, came to see internal improvements as just "another name for taxation." An old Illinois settleer recalled half a century later: "The bare mention of the word 'railroad' would have the same effect upon our people that flaunting a red rag would have upon a turkey gobbler."[27] In this unhappy time Lincoln took up the cross of high taxes. In becoming the champion of internal improvements he had reached for the high vision of statesmanship. He followed the same path when the time of consequent troubles arrived. His course deserves respect.

Lincoln learned about taxation during these years, but not how to be fully at ease pleading the unpopular cause. He could still speak strong words against assessments that sounded very much like those of Jefferson's Declaration against George III. Once, while supporting a protective tariff, he had attained almost poetic heights in raising the specter of direct federal taxes: "the land must be literally covered with assessors and collectors, going forth like swarms of Egyptian locusts, devouring every blade of grass and other green thing . . . none can escape." On another occasion (anonymously acting the part of a folksy backwoods lady he called Rebecca) he even bemoaned, in a jocular way, the excessive hardships caused by the very taxes he had worked so hard to put on the lawbooks.[28]

"Rebecca" did not share Lincoln's economic beliefs although she shared the prejudices of his people. Indeed, when Lincoln came to champion taxation for improvements and to stave off repudiation, he began to transcend the limitations of American traditions. From antiquity to modern times the history of taxation had largely been the assessment of the downtrodden and the middling by the aristocrat. Democracies, such as the United States, had much trouble discovering that taxes can be fair, perchance beneficial. In the American West, where there was less sophistication and more liberty, the learning was the more difficult. But by dint of necessity Lincoln had learned. His education reached a plateau from which he could think of tax privileges for those who would plant forests. In a faraway day the Supreme Court of the United States would express the culmination of such learning for a democracy: "The power to tax . . . is not only the power to destroy but also the power to keep alive."[29]

5

"Dead Point"

THE DEPRESSION NOT ONLY FOREDOOMED ILLINOIS' IMPROVE-
ment plans, and brought the dreaded plague of taxes, but also
played havoc with her young banks. Of the struggles waged around
these issues none were more bitter than those that centered on the
banks. This was the Age of Jackson.

Early in 1837, when Lincoln made his important probank speech,
his cause was probably not unpopular among the people. Perhaps a
majority of Illinoisans saw their state on the threshold of prosperity
and greatness and welcomed even the help of these corporations.
Then, a few months later, the Panic struck, and Western banks in
step with the national trend suspended specie payments. Hard times
followed and confirmed the adherents of Old Hickory in their suspi-
cions concerning the wickedness of banks. Never again in Lincoln's
lifetime would banks enjoy the esteem they had in the state early in
1837.[1]

By then Whigs in general had come to support the Illinois banks
— for banks encouraged "industry" and rewarded "virtue" and
helped the industrious man to compete with the wealthy — although
as the crisis deepened the faithful wavered. The majority of the
Democrats, on the other hand, had come to oppose banks because,
as the Whigs thought, they wanted Illinoisans to remain "hewers of
wood and drawers of water all their life," or as Governor Carlin
explained, because banks were "at war with the genius of free
government." In the early depression years, however, as in other
states, enough "tender footed Democrats" (as a stalwart described

51

them) voted with the Whigs to permit the survival of the banks. If thus the corporations managed to carry on, their existence was made ever more difficult as the years wore on. Banks needed staunch champions who could not expect the reward of popularity for their labors. They found one of their best friends in Lincoln.[2]

The Jacksonian onslaught began in the summer of 1837 at the special session of the legislature, called to deal with the Panic. Some Whigs, like young David Davis, complained about the "radicals" and "desporate [sic] men, a great share of whom by some fortuitous circumstances, are members of the legislature . . . ," but the letter of the law was on the side of the radicals: the bank's charter prescribed its forfeiture in case specie payments were suspended.[3]

Lincoln and the Committee of Finance gained a moderate victory by obtaining a temporary legalization of this suspension — at the price of restrictions on the bank. His committee argued that the destruction of the corporation (with resultant loss of expected profits from state-held bank stocks) would lead to taxation to finance improvements. Interestingly, a compromise achieved, Lincoln voted nay on the final roll call.[4]

If Lincoln hoped that an improving economy and resumed specie payments would soon free him of the burden of defending the corporations he was to be disappointed. Illinois Jacksonians felt that the Panic had torn the veil from their eyes, and in the Assembly of 1838-39 raised again the hostile cry of bank investigations. Lincoln frustrated them. Attack being the best defense, his Finance Committee even made a vigorous though unsuccessful move to increase the capital of the State Bank. And he managed to gain a quite substantial victory, both economic and political, when impressive majorities in the House requested the Van Buren government to deposit revenues collected in Illinois in the state's banks rather than in Missouri.[5]

Then in the fall of 1839 many of the Eastern banks suspended specie payments once more, and their Western counterparts inevitably followed. Since the charter of the bank called for forfeiture the legislators met in emergency session. Although members, Whig and Democrat, showed in Lincoln's judgment "verry little disposition" to keep the institution going, he accepted the uphill fight.[6]

But this time a substantial inquiry by the House and the Senate could not be avoided. After some hesitation, Lincoln decided to lead in person his forces on the joint committee which in turn produced three rival evaluations of the bank. Even the majority report that he helped shape was obliged to assume a critical tone. It censured various practices but aimed its roughest barbs at the lending of large sums — however well-entrenched a practice that was (particularly large loans to directors). For Lincoln, banks were to exist only if they served the people, and served them without favoritism. Big loans, at any rate, were unwise even in terms of narrower economic criteria. Big loans risked big losses, and they often supported speculations. The bankers therefore were given some good political advice. To quote what were probably Lincoln's words:

> Nothing is better calculated to engender heartburnings and to enlist enemies of the most hostile character against a bank than for the community to entertain the belief that the institution is used for the benefit of the few to the exclusion of the many.

To make sure that the directors would not make light of this reduction of a business matter to a question of political pragmatism and democracy, they were pointedly reminded of the similar charge made against "the late bank of the United States."[7]

To balance the picture, the Lincoln report stressed the emptiness of much antibank gossip. It provided a friendly history of the corporation and concluded, fairly, that Illinois institutions should not be specially blamed for suspension because "the irresistible law of trade and exchange . . . cannot be controaled [sic] by country banks."[8]

Most important, the majority statement declared the bank solvent and a safe depository for public funds. Accordingly, in the interest of servicing the improvement debt, and after some give and take in the House, suspension was legalized until the end of the next General Assembly. In return, Lincoln supported provisions that reaffirmed the legislature's right to alter the bank charter and also abolished the Chicago branch as a punishment for the cashier's speculations in pork. All the same, his committee took a swipe at the Democratic national administration, which still refused to deposit federal funds in Illinois.[9]

But the great drama of the Illinois bank war was yet to come. Half of the State Bank's capital stock was in increasingly depreciated improvement bonds, which slowly devalued its paper currency. At first the fall was to ninety cents on the dollar, by no means disastrous by post-Panic standards. But Congressman Stuart, presumably in quest of a national bank, estimated that as a result his state lost $160,000 a year in its commerce with the East.[10] Such an inequity, painfully manifest to the public, came in addition to the many loans that had been called in and the many foreclosures that had taken place during these depression years. The promised profits to the state-held stocks had not materialized. The hard times continued, and by the end of 1840 resentment against the state's banks had grown fierce.

When the General Assembly reconvened in December, the Democrats created an unprecedented partisan show. They decided to revoke their concessions of the previous session and oblige the State Bank to return to the specie standard. Since they failed to see that suspension, however hard on the bank's noteholders, would relieve the state's economy, they determined to either make the bank "honest" or destroy it. The phenomenon was nationwide. One historian has quoted the following Mississippi song:

> . . . to the Polls, you noble souls;
> The Banks they cry for quarters;
> And here's their doom, they *shall* resume,
> Or forfeit all their charters.[11]

Since suspension in Illinois had been legalized only until the end of the next meeting of the legislature, the derring-do politicos hit upon adjourning the House on December 5, thus forcing the hand of the bank, and convening it on December 7 to continue business — an unfair scheme but one with the pose of legality. The pressing need to service the state debt had compelled the lawmakers to convene two weeks earlier than usual, allowing the claim of special session that could be adjourned.

The Whigs countered by boycotting the meeting and preventing the quorum required for adjournment. On the appointed day Lincoln remained in the House and watched the sergeant-at-arms fetch delinquent solons by force. What followed was described with such relish in the leading Democratic paper of the state that one might think Lincoln justified in referring to it as "this infernal Extra Register."

Mr. Lincoln . . . who appeared to enjoy the embarrassment of the House, suddenly looked very grave after the Speaker announced that a quorum was present. The conspiracy having failed, Mr. Lincoln, came under great excitement, and having attempted and failed to get out at the door, very unceremoniously raised the window and jumped out, followed by one or two other members. This gymnastic performance of Mr. Lincoln and his flying brethren did not occur until after they had voted and consequently the House did not interfere with their extraordinary feat. We have not learned whether these flying members got hurt in the adventure, and we think it probable that at least one of them came off without damage, as it was noticed that his legs reached nearly from the window to the ground! . . . We learn that a resolution will probably be introduced into the House this week to inquire into the expedience of raising the State House one story higher, in order to set in the third story so as to prevent members from jumping out windows! If such a resolution passes, Mr. Lincoln in future will have to climb down the spout.[12]

This description illustrates nicely how the press then (and historians since) tended to emphasize Lincoln's politicking. Such a treatment has a certain validity but in the end it obscures the ultimate meaning of Lincoln's action. For he acted in such an unorthodox fashion in a desperate attempt to defend the banking system from the forced resumption which was to help pave the way to the destruction of that system.

Elsewhere in the nation the specie standard was maintained only in the banks of New York and New England, and there with much difficulty. These banks could not accommodate the West with coin, and when Illinois resumed payments the exaggerated demand of a whole region was focused upon her. In little over two months almost $500,000 was drained away from the state. David Davis complained bitterly: "The want of money is our great want. Capital there is not enough of to carry on the business of the country . . . yet our wise men are for putting down what banks we had got."[13] Circulation in the state had to be restricted, loans and discounts stopped. The cry of debtors grew shrill. To retaliate in a justified but unseemly show of force somewhat reminiscent of Nicholas Biddle's methods, the bank refused to provide further credit to the state. The legislators thus found that on the free market their salary warrants could be cashed at only half their face value.

Six weeks thus passed, before a banker's agreement that called for a general resumption in the country was to come into effect. Even then, only a few institutions in Pennsylvania, Maryland, and Virginia abided by the plan. The "tender foots" at least saw the absurdity of the Illinois Democratic design, and so the battle could recommence in the House. Lincoln for the last time organized the probank forces. On the other side, his future Civil War general John McClernand marshalled, in the view of one member, "an uncompromising War against all the Banks in the World."[14]

But by the fourth year of the depression the Whig champion began to sound a little like a defeated man. This was generally his winter of discontent, with its sorrowful Mary Todd affair and with the apparently irreversible collapse of improvements. He was tired, he told his House colleagues. He despised the politically inspired, ignorant wrangling over the banks that ignored the public interest. He missed a number of meetings at this session but, in the end, carried on gallantly. He drew up a bill to legalize suspension and to permit for the first time the issue of notes smaller than five dollars. To make the proposal more palatable he added a provision requiring the bank to purchase $200,000 worth of state bonds to help pay the interest on the internal improvement debt. This amendment was unwise, but presumably it measured correctly the limits of the politically possible. He even managed to persuade a "tender foot" to introduce the bill.[15]

The encounters that followed were at times "peculiarly sharp and personal." Lincoln still spoke of the duty to support the interlocked triangle of state, bank, and improvement system obligations. Amendments were added to his bill with his support, among them the limiting of loans made to directors and the prohibition of dividends for private stockholders though not for the state. The bill passed and suspension was once more legalized. Thus after all the Springfield defenestration was not in vain, and the *New York Evening Post* could report that "the Illinois legislature had authorized the sale of indulgences." However, when the moment of truth came, for the second time Lincoln recorded a "nay" on his own work.[16]

There is a remote possibility that in the last moment he had discovered some fatal error in the bill. More likely he simply desired to escape being considered a "special advocate" of banks, to cite his own words. Lincoln saw the great need for money and credit. The majority of his countrymen, however, were no more willing to accept that "bankers are just like anybody else except richer" than Ogden Nash was a century later. Whiggery was vilified "from an excess of hatred," to quote an even-tempered Democratic leader, as the "British bought, Bank, blue-light, federal, whig party." The State Bank was labeled a "whig concern," and with justice, whether we take as the criterion its larger economic goals or the party affiliation of most of its officers.[17]

In the election of 1840 Lincoln made his poorest showing since his first try for office in 1832, in large part it appears because of his economic stands.[18] Although the responsible lawmaker defended the unpopular positions, the politician had to mend fences by votes against banks — when such votes did no harm. Once the support to save the Springfield institution was assured, Lincoln could afford the luxury of a frivolous vote that would be applauded. In this fashion he could lay responsibility for the bank's existence at the doorstep of the Democrats, turning inside out their accusations. How much good this did is open to question, but he continued the practice as long as the bank remained a political issue.[19]

Lincoln's course was very much that of a politician but nonetheless of one who worked for what he saw as the good of his people. His course resembles that of the high-tax Lincoln who on one pressing occasion felt the need to camouflage his demand for increased levies. And it foreshadows the Emancipator who saw slavery as the vilest of evils, yet partly because many if not most of his constituents did not see it so, at any rate because they feared to abolish it, he issued his Proclamation only as a military necessity without appealing to nobler sentiments. Clearly, Lincoln judged that when public prejudice could not be broken down there was glory enough in breaking down its effect.

On the bank issue Lincoln led a more or less united Whig party, but even on this crucial party matter, when warranted, he was ready to carve his own un-Whig-like path. His probank attitude cracked over one substantial question: that of interest rates. This was an important issue, it bred off-and-on local excitement, and loomed sufficiently large even on the national scene to make President Jackson attack creditors in a message to Congress. Lincoln, too, objected to the "baneful and corroding" system of exorbitant interest rates. His first platform had already called for government regulations. He did not change his mind later. With down-to-earth pragmatism he assumed that in extreme necessity laws limiting interest rates could always be circumvented.[20]

Lincoln's financial situation probably had something to do with the beginnings of his attitude. His involvements with a mismanaged store and an incompetent partner had left him with so large an obligation that he and his friends referred to it for years as the "national debt." More significant, however, his antibank stand on this issue indicates that he supported banks not for the sake of banks but for the sake of the better America he envisioned. In the dynamic economy which he was helping to build, the claims of the debtors came before those of the creditors. The debtors were generally not the few destitute, as mythology has it, but the many enterprising — the kind Lincoln attempted to become in New Salem. It was consistent therefore that when he got out of indebtedness he became a money lender himself and continued so until his death. He charged an interest rate of ten to twelve per cent and in the Illinois legislature demanded that these rates, low for that time and place, be made legally binding on all loans.[21]

Lincoln would not have agreed but, given that Illinois was one of the most staunchly Jacksonian states, his leadership on the banking issue was remarkably effective. Of course, on some questions he was generations ahead of his people. He wished, for example, to abolish that practice of the day which made bank stockholders personally liable for a bank's debts. He was not successful and knew that he was forcing the future on the state. Yet probably he would have been surprised to see that the "double liability" of bank stockholders stayed on the lawbooks of Illinois until the middle of the twentieth century.[22]

One of Lincoln's last acts in his House career was to block what would have been a crippling tax on the State Bank's capital stock. His hard labors, however, were for the moment in vain. The improvement system had gone down with a crash, and the bank, weakened by political attacks and some mismanagement, had to attempt to operate with half its capital stock made up of depreciating improvement bonds. The work proved too much for the inexperienced directors, who invested injudiciously in trying to save some of the improvement works. The State Bank went down soon afterwards to the great loss not only of its note holders, but more significantly the economy of Illinois. The end came early in 1842, and the other banks in the state followed, confirming the national trend. Nearly a decade passed before they were allowed a new start. Governor Ford summed up well the thinking embraced even by moderates:

> Whether local banks are necessary and expedient, in highly commercial countries . . . I do not propose to discuss. But if former experience is to be any guide for the future, we must be satisfied, that we in the State of Illinois, are better without them than with them.[23]

Those whose vision of America differed from Lincoln's drew smug satisfaction from the ruin of the 1840's. They delivered innumerable I-told-you-so's. Reported one Illinoisan: "We are getting on slow but sure; the people are pursuing their proper avocation now and will not be allured by your visionary plans of banking. . . ." They had "their noble occupation," as they had had since time immemorial, "in cultivating the land."[24]

The bank privilege of issuing one-, two-, and three-dollar bills, which Lincoln had fought for persistently, aided in the destruction. The state had a real need for small currency, and in that respect its prohibition harmed both bank and public. Such restraints, typical of the age, were claimed to increase specie circulation and protect the poor, who mostly handled small bills of uncertain negotiability. The damage done by the removal of this ban in Illinois after the bank's paper currency had depreciated, however, had a different aspect. The solons, including the Whig floorleader, apparently expected that if the institutions did not have to circulate their silver coins they would be able to accumulate them. Instead, specie currency seemed to disappear from the state altogether.[25]

Thus Lincoln learned Gresham's Law the hard way. He acquired much of his early knowledge of political economy in this manner and frequently at a high cost to his constituents. Yet learning by doing was a virtue where doing was needed and learning unavailable. It was thus that Lincoln became a fine lawyer — but his first murder client was hanged. His over-all stance on economic policies was wise.

His understanding of banking was in some areas surprisingly advanced, in others horrendously deficient. But such was the state of the nation.

Lincoln's gravest error, and Illinois', was in believing that local banks could to a significant extent help finance the state's transportation revolution and so the upward rise of her people. Exceedingly few American banks, certainly none in Illinois could supply such long-term credit. No undeveloped economy possesses in itself the accumulated capital necessary for such an enterprise. The state should not have reached much further than Threadneedle Street would support her in doing. That restraint was too much to expect. Illinois bankers justified large investments in the internal improvement system as Lincoln did, by citing the splendid future of the land. Over the long run their forecast was correct. In the short run, improvements and banks failed together. They fared as badly as the worst of their neighbors.

Not surprisingly, much of posterity bestowed the same contempt on these banking ventures as it had on the internal improvements. The Springfield dreamer however, escaped from the strong censure his support of the System has provoked among scholars.

Lincoln had not merely deferred to the bankers; he had prodded them towards the rainbow on the horizon. And they went. But historians must not be harsh. One of their number found the truth in a happy simile: "Bank credit was to Americans a new source of energy, like steam, and it was not to be known in advance of experience under what conditions it would work well or or ill." It is more than chance that the young Illinois political economist, too, likened finance to Watt's revolutionizing engine. He spoke of its "dead point . . . a point extremely difficult of turning," but once turned "all will again be well."[26]

Too much wisdom can be read into Lincoln's simile: it took the hindsight and scholarship of the twentieth century to speak of the critical point of take off in economic development.[27] Yet Lincoln knew the direction in which he wanted his United States to grow. He knew whom he wished to aid, knew that the task was difficult, and was confident that it would be mastered. Like so many of his countrymen, specially the Whigs, he was ever the optimist in matters economic, often too much so. Often it was not "the many" who benefited by development, particularly not over the short run. Even over the long run, boilers and banks, even national economies, burst many times before they were tamed. But in the distance, truly, the rainbow was waiting.

6
The Log Cabin and The Bank

WHEN LINCOLN RETIRED FROM THE ILLINOIS GENERAL ASSEMBLY his views came to be voiced chiefly on the campaign trail. This at least is what survives to our day. Inevitably, those utterances carried a sharply partisan tone. Through the party feelings, however, we can recognize convictions which generally set him well above his political brethren. Moreover, with seeming indifference to fluctuating national guidelines, he firmly retained economics as his central theme. A fine illustration of his course was provided by the presidential contest of 1840, which he, if not his party, fought on the issue that a later age came to call central banking.

The Constitution of the United States does not mention banks, Bray Hammond thought, because the Fathers feared to raise the divisive issue. Thus banking joined the even more fundamental matters of slavery and the indissolubility of the Union, as great problems that had been bypassed but which would form a fearsome trinity of controversy some two generations hence, in Lincoln's America.

In 1791, constitutional silence notwithstanding, Congress established the first Bank of the United States, legitimizing it by the "general welfare" clause. Modeled after the Bank of England, and inspired by one of the great Hamiltonian sermons in economics, it was intended to provide a safe depository for federal funds, a fiscal agent for the government, a source of paper money, and facilities for commercial operations. The giant was successful in almost every way, including its effort to coexist with state banks and Jeffersonian

63

politicians. This lasted until 1811 when the last-named factions, aided by Western needs and superstitions, managed to put an end to the first Bank.

The chaos that followed this attack of the rustic knights, and the War of 1812, led to reconsideration of the matter and to a new bank, to be known in contemporary jargon as the BUS, or the "national bank." After a jolting start it followed the well-trodden road to become even more of a public-oriented organization than its predecessor. This very accomplishment marked it as a "monster" in certain quarters.

The assault on Philadelphia's Chestnut Street temple that commenced in 1832 was armed with condemnation of the rich, financiers, Easterners, the English, and federal power. The fundamental and perhaps somewhat abstract question concerning the propriety of a semi-private corporation with substantial public power was relegated to the background. Lincoln entered the political arena as the debate between the opponents and proponents of central banking reached its peak. He immersed himself in the debates deeply enough to acquire convictions that stayed with him for life.[1]

If Lincoln acquired firm opinions about national banking early in his career, he also strove, from the first, to be master of the art of the possible. Not until the thirties were about to end did he think the time ripe for renewed battle. The Panic had demonstrated the limitations of state institutions in handling federal money. Since the government could not function without a fiscal agent, the economic-oriented segment of the Whigs revived the design of the national bank. Van Buren had proposed an alternative: the government handling its funds solely through its own officers in an independent treasury. But the plan died thrice in Congress, even though an important clause of the original blueprint, limiting transactions to specie, was abandoned.[2]

In spite of this, and sound as the call for a new central bank was, when the election of 1840 approached politics alone came to rule the majority of the Whig party that nominated William Henry Harrison — "General Mum" as the Democrats called him. Issues were ignored almost entirely. Lincoln, notwithstanding his strong political loyalties, refused to go along and travel the unmarked road. He supported the party's nominee fully but also decided to stake a full years' campaigning on the question of national banking.

His first clashes came in the late fall of 1839, in debates with Stephen Douglas and others. Lincoln emphasized the failure of Jacksonian financial policy over the previous decade and sustained himself with "an array of documentary evidence." Although Douglas was said to have earned some years earlier his sobriquet of the "Little Giant," with his expertise on the BUS, his opponent's opinion of their debates was blunt: "The Democratic giant is here; but he is not worth talking about." And this opinion is underscored by one of Lincoln's speeches which survived in its entirety. It gives impressive evidence of Lincoln's strong convictions, of the progress of his learning in economics, and also of his ability to use that learning for political combat.[3]

The burden of this well-researched, sometimes lecture-like address was a comparison of the national bank and the independent treasury, to the enormous disadvantage of the latter. Lincoln's approach was analytical and relied primarily on "the experience of the past" rather than on economic theory. His first and most important argument, however, was based on the quantity theory of money.

The subtreasury, he charged, would drastically reduce the circulating medium of the country even though "money is only valuable while in circulation." Government funds that formerly had been part of the money supply would be allowed to rust in iron boxes. Since the intention was to collect revenues in specie, the effect of the system would be doubly disastrous. Both the nation's gold and silver supply and the paper issues based on it would be curtailed. The United States had $60 to $80 million in precious metals, at most, Lincoln judged, and the federal expenditures of $40 million during the previous fiscal year suggested to him a 50% reduction of the currency.

While arguing thus he used an extremely conservative ratio of specie to paper in circulation, four to ten, and so underestimated the issue of banks.[4] He more than balanced the picture, however, by assuming in his calculations that all revenues would be collected at once, producing a sudden disappearance of much precious metal, and assuming also that the large federal deficits of recent years would be a permanent feature of Democratic governance. He thereby exaggerated the foreseeable effect of the subtreasury on circulation and found himself unable to "contemplate without terror, the distress, ruin, bankruptcy and beggary, that must follow." Still, his central point was very much worth listening to, for it was well to use federal funds to stimulate the economy.

The deflationary effect of the independent treasury was overestimated by many Democrats and Whigs alike. A former president turned opponent of the BUS, Langdon Cheves, expected a $20 million drop in the nation's specie supply. Whig pamphleteer Calvin Colton spoke of a two-thirds loss, and in Congress conservative Democrat William Cost Johnson predicted a 92% reduction of the total amount of American currency, from $1 billion to $80 million. They, like Lincoln, used an extreme quantity theory of money that was defended by such of the learned as George Tucker, the University of Virginia's professor of moral philosophy and political economy.[5]

Lincoln turned his mathematics into homespun, as was his wont, basing his calculations on the above theory which assumed that prices would vary directly with the amount of money in circulation. He could thus explain that if a farmer bought a $100 horse on credit, with the subtreasury in effect the animal would be worth only $50 on pay day. The ordinary purchase price, of course, would still have to be met. The traditional view of deflation, that "the debtor loses, the creditor gains," he found applicable only to a "very limited extent." He argued perceptively that when the price level change is drastic, "it is more generally true that *all* lose by it."

Lincoln admitted that the economy could adjust to a vast contraction of the currency. The pain would be great but only temporary. Thus conceding more than reason required, a tactic he developed in his law practice, he moved in for the kill. In the West, where the public lands were, the adjustment could not be full. Land was "the great gulf by which all, or nearly all, the money in them is swallowed up." Government land prices, however, were fixed by slow-changing law and could not fluctuate with the general price level. As always, there was the homely illustration: "the *produce* or *labor*" that now bought 80 acres of land would buy only 40 if the undemocratic "plot" succeeded. It is a little frightening to note that Lincoln evidently took the existence of the "plot" seriously.

The alternative to such an economic muddle was in the Bank of the United States. Deranging "contractions and expansions" of the currency were not permitted during its past tenures. With good reason Lincoln did not think that the shaky first and last years of the second Bank forced a meaningful diminution of his claim. He explained that these difficulties came before the institution had gotten on its feet or after politics had crippled it:

> We do not pretend, that the National Bank can establish and maintain a sound and uniform state of currency in the country, in *spite* of the National Government; but we do say, that it has established and maintained such a currency, and can do so again, by the *aid* of that Government; and we further say, that no duty is more imperative on that Government, than the duty it owes the people, of furnishing them a sound and uniform currency.

Lincoln spoke sufficiently to the point to be repeatedly cited by an outstanding historian of banking more than a century later. For as Bray Hammond explained: "The Bank was never more justly and understandingly defended" than in the above words.[6]

Lincoln's appreciation of the regulatory function of the Bank implies the recognition of a need to which twentieth century America pays homage with the Federal Reserve System. The *depth* of his understanding is problematic. Albert Gallatin, Biddle, and some others set high standards of comprehension for the age and made some modest efforts to diffuse their views. John Quincy Adams, Webster, and particularly Clay were at times perhaps more vehement than knowledgeable, and when Gallatin asked Jackson what he meant by uniform currency he received no intelligible reply.[7]

From keen insight the range of American thought extended to utter ignorance vis-á-vis the BUS. In between Lincoln failed to elaborate his discussion. Or perhaps he did elaborate. Only two dozen of his speeches can be identified for the 1840 campaign, although he may have made twice that number. The text of only one speech is extant. Had others been recorded for posterity, the historian could better gauge Lincoln's sophistication in the matter of central banking. At any rate, one can be reasonably certain that the lessons of history were more important to him than theory. In the final analysis he supported the national bank because, as he said, it had been "tested by the experience of forty years."[8]

One of the most heated points of the Bank debate concerned the institution's constitutionality. We have noted earlier that though a lawyer, Lincoln was much more concerned with the economic than the legal ramifications of economics policy. The Bank was no exception. He had little patience for questions of its constitutionality. Since they could not be avoided, however, he marshalled the Fathers, the Supreme Court, and what he thought was an original observation, that the founding document of the nation provided no more explicitly for an independent treasury than for a bank. Both can be "necessary and proper" under the general welfare clause, he argued, and the choice between the two should be made purely on their economic merits.

In citing the general welfare clause, Lincoln expressed a preference for Webster and Clay over Calhoun, who based his support for the Bank on its monetary function and on the constitutional right of Congress to regulate the currency. Lincoln, too, stated, much more emphatically than Calhoun, that the provision of sound uniform currency was an imperative duty of the government and that through the Bank of the United States this had been attained. That the Illinoisan did not point to the more narrowly proper authorizing clause of the Constitution illuminates not as much a weakness of his understanding of central banking, or lack of an innovative legal mind, as his economically significant Whig enthusiasm for the general welfare clause.[9]

The refusal of Jackson's party to accept judicial supremacy in the case of the Bank irked Lincoln. Yet he learned some lessons that helped him grow into what, many would argue, was a wiser interpreter of the Constitution. In his 1858 debates with Douglas he recalled "the long and fierce war" over the BUS. Since by then he himself was fighting a decision of the Supreme Court then headed by Old Hickory's Bank-killing Secretary of the Treasury, Roger Taney, the senatorial challenger crowed: "Will you not graciously allow us to do with the Dred Scott decision precisely as you did with the Bank decision?" Indeed, the Republicans would do just about that. Although Lincoln thus changed his view of the Constitution, as we shall see in economic terms his two causes flowed into the same ultimate channel.[10]

In the 1839 speech Lincoln also made a substantial effort on behalf of the commonplace Whig arguments that the Independent Treasury would be unsafe and expensive. Although these forebodings turned out to be exaggerated, he carefully rounded downward all of his ample and accurate supporting statistics. And it was true that with the government handling its own funds, losses caused by embezzlement were to be borne by the nation. The 1830's seemed to have brought an epidemic of such crimes, and the point was a popular one. Yet that Lincoln considered the problem serious was demonstrated twenty-four years later. Reviewing Treasury regulations in the White House, he would then suggest to Secretary Salmon P. Chase that the bonds of agents working with large sums of money be increased.[11]

Lincoln's calculation of the subtreasury's costs yielded a large enough figure to purchase a forty-acre tract for each of eight thousand "poor families." With such statistics about "poor families," "poor people," meaning of course ordinary people, he arrived at the heart of his message. The national bank served all the people of America. The independent treasury — "was such a system for benefiting the few at the expense of the many, ever before devised?" He even saw fit to repeat the charge that subtreasury officers would have a monopoly on good money and the rest of the country the "rags and shin-plasters." And in the printed form of the speech he buttressed this with a scholar's footnote that cited a Senate-ordered study of Hamburg's ill-favored specie currency.

In the heat of debate he reached a climax where to the opponents of central banking he refused the excuse of ignorance; he attributed to them corruption and an evil partisan spirit. Through their labors, he warned, the nation may lose its liberty. Lincoln had seen the light and climbed a height of partisanship that his later words would never again match. Yet in this context he also put forward for the first time an implied definition of free government as one that aids the "many" in their economic endeavors, a definition he later made explicit.

One of the most enlightening parts of Lincoln's speech is a long digression, in reply to Douglas and other opponents, which displayed his meticulous craftsmanship. He had made the unusually large federal spendings of 1838 an essential part of his antisubtreasury argument. The Little Giant tried to check him by listing the extraordinary demands the government had to meet during that year. Lincoln replied, however, with a multitude of statistics showing that such Douglas-claimed expenditures as those for the removal of

certain Indians, purchase of lands, indemnities for the French, post
offices, and war preparations, were either nonexistent or else had
taken place before or after 1838. Lincoln must have taken great
satisfaction in this exercise, showing, for example, that the patriotic
$10 million appropriated for the Maine "war" against England was
not in the fiscal year his opponent claimed and at any rate was not
"expended at all." He concluded bluntly that "Mr. Douglas . . . was
stupid enough to hope, that I would permit such groundless and
audacious assertions to go unexposed."

This was the Prairie State, the Christmas season of 1839, stump-
speaking country. With his speech Lincoln was launched on a campaign that lifted him once again above his environs. In format to be
sure he continued to observe the code of the West. He used as plain
language as the science of political economy would allow. He devised
homely examples and was true to the humor that was his trademark.
He exaggerated, and in conclusion delivered what appears to
another age as a touch of demagoguery about liberty. His carefully
researched economic discussion, however, was most extraordinarily
outside the custom of stump politicking.

Lincoln's speech showed little original thinking about the dismal
science, but he had mastered his subject sufficiently to select most of
the best arguments of the decade. Nor did he merely mouth the
thoughts of others, as politicians often did with questions of
economics. The ideas he used were well digested by his thorough,
grinding mind. Not surprisingly, many in Illinois were impressed.
The economic problems he had helped guide the state into had not
weakened his convictions and many seemed still willing to listen to
him. Indeed, the Whigs published his speech as a campaign pamphlet and advertised it widely. Lincoln himself was sufficiently
pleased with his effort to send it to his law partner in Washington.
Congressman Stuart probably sent the pamphlet on to the *National
Intelligencer*, the most important Whig newspaper of the country,
which then gave Lincoln his first, brief moment in the national
limelight.[12]

In Illinois the Democrats were forced to concentrate their attention on Lincoln, their leading organ devoting several editorials to
refuting his views. In an age when newspapers, particularly at the
local level, rarely conceded virtues to an opponent, the *Illinois State*

Register could not but express hope that the extraordinary Whig adversary would no longer "lend his brilliant powers to give currency to mischievous errors." Both friends and foes long remembered his expertise on the subject. The Little Giant himself never forgot these first Lincoln-Douglas debates. At the commencement of a more momentous encounter in 1858, his description of his opponent fitted eminently the Lincoln of 1840: "He is the strong man of his party — full of wit, facts, dates, and the best stump-speaker . . . in the West . . . if I beat him, my victory will be hardly won."[13]

The implications of Lincoln's rather scholarly discourse were very political. They indicted the Democratic destruction of the BUS as a major source of America's current economic distress. Yet this indictment, political aims aside, was fully consistent with his overall outlook. For Lincoln was possessed by the optimism of Western Civilization, reborn in the Renaissance, grown to maturity in the Enlightenment, and triumphant in nineteenth century America, which saw man as the master of his own destiny. Perhaps nowhere was this world view stronger than in American conceptions about economics, particularly among Whigs. Lincoln never doubted that the business cycle was directed by man. Faced with the problem of an economic downturn after his election to the presidency, he demanded in private, that "the *'respectable scoundrels,'* " meaning Eastern capitalists, who got up the hard times, "go to work and repair the mischief of their own making." His faith in man's vast economic prowess was lifelong. This faith helps explain why he attached so great, and to some extent unrealistic importance to governmental economic policies. This faith also helps explain why in the late 1830's and early 1840's he could hold Jacksonian policies so largely responsible for the hard times and why he dared to base a full year's campaigning on the call for national banking.[14]

Even Lincoln's peroration, which tied liberty to the Whig cause, in effect to the Bank, becomes less questionable if put in contemporary perspective. It should be remembered how seriously Americans of the time took their politics, and how strong were the feelings President Jackson and his followers exhibited on the subject of the Bank of the United States. And if we see Lincoln's intense words, his "I swear eternal fidelity to the just cause, as I deem it," in the light of his growing dream, the passion may still not become acceptable, but at least it becomes understandable.[15]

It is poor history to dismiss the Whig Lincoln's message as largely empty political rhetoric, while placing a high valuation on the Republican Lincoln's message. Not only does a basic harmonious current flow in both his works and his words, from the time of his first platform in 1832 to the second inaugural of 1865, but in addition no evidence indicates that the early Illinois politician was less sincere than the Republican politician and President.

That Lincoln found in Whiggish economics a vehicle for a high vision of America does not imply that most others of his party did so, too. Many became Whigs because of largely accidental, or opportunistic attractions; many had divergent understandings of what the party stood for. The log cabin campaign of 1840 demonstrated this all too fully. Lincoln, too, long thought that Whiggery would lead to political advancement. Yet he, and others like him, were also shaping the American Dream. This in turn suggests that the ideological heart of Republicanism came from Lincoln's kind of moral-economic Whiggery.

In 1840 as an elector Lincoln canvassed a good part of the state. In rough and tumble debates he often met Douglas. The scanty surviving evidence indicates that if he did not repeat the substance of his one extant speech, he never strayed far from its theme. He introduced speeches with a discussion of "the design and object of all Governments," no doubt elaborating on his view that "the many" had to be aided on the road to economic elevation. He "drew a vivid picture of our prosperous and happy condition previous to the time of the war which was waged against the U.S. Bank." He "fearlessly and eloquently" exposed the "iniquities" of the subtreasury scheme; demonstrated "the constitutionality, as well as great utility" of the BUS "in a most triumphant manner"; or as the Democrats thought, gave an "elaborate defence of Federal principles under the name of Whiggery." He labored the economic truth "that errors may have occurred under all administrations; but we insist that there is *no parallel* between them and those of the two last," under Jackson and

Van Buren. His foreign method of debating, "highly argumentative and logical," using economic learning and statistics, was both educating and exasperating. At one point he was even brought to the verge of a duel as the result of a speech and had to use great circumspection to avoid it.[16]

While Lincoln was fighting for the Bank and Whig triumph, the Harrison campaign turned into a collossal camp meeting across the nation, in one sense into an orgy of nostalgia. The log cabin and hard cider candidate seemed certain of victory as the spirit of things past possessed the land. The Whigs took "to the woods," as John William Ward has felicitously said of them, and the good politician Lincoln went along. He did not even complain, as his future friend David Davis could not help but do, about "the hurrah boys." Indeed twenty years later, the same logs split into rails, with Davis giving a hand, helped bring him and his economic philosophy into the White House.[17]

> Without a why or a wherefore
> we'll go for Harrison therefore

the Whigs sang and so did Lincoln, but *he* also insisted on the "wherefore," which he expressed in terms of the national bank. He placed himself among the select few of his party who demanded issues in addition to the hullabaloo and thus injected substance into the Harrison effort in Illinois. Elsewhere in the country Whigs charged that Van Buren was an aristocrat and consorter with bankers, and "Old Tip" declared in a clear but untruthful language, "I am not a Bank man." Clay had already been told that he could not be the Whig nominee, in good part because of his past identification with the BUS, and it was not until late in the year that Webster at last spoke out on the subject. Even such a firmly economic-oriented young Whig as Horace Greeley, who argued issues in his campaign newspaper the *Log Cabin* in un-Whig-like fashion for 1840, tended to use the euphemism "sound currency" for the Bank of the United States.[18]

In contrast Lincoln's uncamouflaged arguments made the "rounds of the federal papers" in his state, as the opposition bemoaned, and became the Whig "text book" of Illinois. He set the keynote for the entire campaign. To the extent substantial issues were discussed they centered on the independent treasury and the national bank. Lincoln's achievement depended not only on his already superior abilities but also on the unabated depression and the fact that it and the Bank could be used as symbols of mass politics. By midsummer it seemed to some that the election in Illinois would turn on this question alone. Others reported that the issue was "well calculated to make converts to the Whig cause," and that some Democrats would not admit to ever having opposed the BUS.[19]

Lincoln's leadership even shamed politicos into recognizing the importance of the issue at hand. His crony Joseph Gillespie, for example, upheld the Bank although he apologized that he knew "it was not a topic suited to the present enthusiasm." If Illinois Democrats jeered with justice at the opposition party which dared champion no policies in this election, they had to qualify their taunts for their own state where the Whigs stood, as the Democrats said, "for nothing except a national bank." In 1840 that was quite a lot.[20]

Condescending broadly to low levels, as some Whig leaders understood the 1840 campaign, insulted Lincoln's political preconceptions. Bringing a sense of plain realty, of solid content, into an emotion-charged atmosphere fitted his mental makeup. He had little use for the nostalgia that was a mainstay of the Log Cabin syndrome. He had barely moved from the real cabins of Salem to Springfield. It bears repeating that *his* Whig party stood not for the past but the future of America. Thus Lincoln, the poor man, rising in life, nurturing a Dream for the nation, was again making a declaration of faith in 1840. Few things proved his sincerity better than the fact that while elsewhere in the country most of his party brethren spoke only of log cabins, he spoke mostly of banks.

Indeed railroads, or William Strickland's Philadelphia Parthenon, that housed the Bank, were truer symbols of the party than backwoods cabins. They squarely identified the tools through which the hopes of "the many" might be attained. If Benton and other Democrats were sincere in believing that the Bank tended "to make the rich richer, and the poor poorer," Lincoln with equal earnestness believed that it would help people to rise and make the whole country richer.[21] As he apparently felt that stark prejudice had killed the "late Bank of the United States," his willingness to battle anew is an eloquent testimony to his faith in the common sense of democracy. The increasingly unhappy state of Illinois' own banks, and his own involvement in attempting to direct economic policy, made the need for a central institution all the more clear and urgent to him. Not that he forgot Jackson's war, but he saw the economic facts as being so much on the side of the national bank that he felt confident in staking the election on them, particularly during a depression, under a President nicknamed Martin Van Ruin.

If Lincoln's national party rather disagreed, in one respect it was beginning to come into step with him: it, too, argued that theirs was the "poor" man's party. Calvin Colton's succinct verbalization of the Whig faith was still a presidential campaign away:

> Ours is a country, where men start from a humble origin, and from small beginnings rise gradually in the world, as the reward of merit and industry. . . . This is a country of *self-made* men, than which nothing better could be said of any state of society.

In the 1840 contest the party was finding its way toward this definition. If politics had much to do with the Whig search there nonetheless remained an essential truth in Thurlow Weed's explanation that the Log Cabin stood for "the hopes of the humble."[22]

In this hectic contest Lincoln found the energy to be one of the editors of the *Old Soldier*, the campaign newspaper of the Illinois Whigs. Typical of its genre, it was a low-caliber affair. But when not repelling Democratic attacks or whipping up pandemonium, it too emphasized economic questions, particularly the subtreasury. It even dared to report a new movement for a national bank which it labeled "absolutely necessary." Its more meaningful economic arguments very probably were the fruit of Lincoln's pen.[23]

Still, not all could comprehend economic ideas and the accusations of the nescient against Lincoln were bitter; he "seemed like a man travelling over unknown ground." That he felt compelled to identify the expense and the insecurity of the subtreasury as his most telling argument provides a fair indication of the level of economic sophistication he expected to find among his audiences.[24]

What Lincoln left out of his discussion is also revealing. He ignored the services the national bank could provide for commercial operations because of their hue of special interest advocacy. He also neglected rebuttals to antibank utterances that rested on a dim view of the federal government, Easterners, foreigners, and "moneyed power." All of this he probably regarded as mere claptrap, and with much justice in 1840, particularly in economic terms. The need of antebellum America was for more government not less. The Jacksonian complaint against outside capital is often echoed by the developing nations of the twentieth century, but they have found no real alternatives. Since in the days of yore the Bank had functioned properly, its potential for misusing power did not bother the pragmatic Lincoln. His eyes were fastened on his hopes for America, and what the Bank could do in its building.

In the economic spectrum of the United States, at one end were the inflationists who condemned the BUS for exerting too much control and at the other the agrarians demanding the hard metallic currency of the Middle Ages. Lincoln as a practitioner of a fledgling science in the Illinois House may have been too permissive toward the state banks, as some may conclude their failure has proved. His policies on internal improvements put him among the more unbridled developers of America who at times also played havoc with business and set back the economy. But in his theory Lincoln stood for what he understood as the middle way of the national bank and solid economic growth. It is instructive to note that the great Biddle himself turned out to be a better preacher than practitioner of state banking. In time Lincoln learned to implement his ideals more successfully. That acquiring the proper theory of banking itself was significant, became manifest when he rose to be the President of the United States.

By 1840 Lincoln's principled electioneering became so much a matter of course that if he seemed to descend even briefly to the common denominator of the campaign, reproach was immediate. He was expected to occupy unswervingly the "high and lofty ground."[25] If one disregards personal indiscretions, Lincoln indeed appears to have departed from his "lofty" and single issue politics only on what in 1840 was a relatively minor question, that of race, and he did this only in defense against the Negro-baiting of Douglas and others.[26] Otherwise he clung to his economic theme. One can not help wondering how different, perchance more successful, not to mention how much more honest, the course of Whig history might have been over the long run if elsewhere, too, the Bank had been tied to the Log Cabin in the Harrison campaign. If the Whigs were to succeed this was the time. They had an attractive candidate to carry their economic program at a juncture when America was desperately looking for a cure for a depression. That the Whigs did not travel Lincoln's road indicated that they were shortsightedly both more pragmatic and less principled than he was. And to some it indicated that they had no meaningful road to travel at all.

In economic terms, too, the historian is tempted to support Lincoln's judgment. Although the country learned to live with the subtreasury after 1846, few can doubt, with another century's appreciation of the import of monetary and credit policies, that national banking as it promised to develop would have done better.

In the autumn of the year, when the votes were cast and counted the Whigs stood overwhelmingly triumphant. But Harrison lost Illinois in a close contest. Lincoln, and nearly all of his party friends, expected victory and the loss of what he called "this loco — I mean democratic state" was a bitter blow. Illinois, after all, was confirmed as one of the most unrelentingly Jacksonian states in the Union. To make matters worse for Lincoln, he ran last on the losing electoral ticket — as he had earlier run poorly for a seat in the General Assembly.[27]

It could not but seem to him that the people had judged the whole of his political economy. The election seemed to question his faith in their intellect, to prove the high level of his campaign an error. This, however, was not the lesson he drew from the defeat. Lincoln might go on grumbling to the end of his days, as the Civil War diary of his friend, Orville H. Browning testifies: "Why will men believe a lie, an absurd lie, that could not [be] impose[d] upon a child, and cling to it and repeat it in defiance of all evidence to the contrary." Yet he never abandoned his "patient confidence in the ultimate justice of the people." His 1840 campaign and the whole history of the Bank of the United States perhaps helped him toward a better understanding of the ways of prejudice and the extreme difficulty of combating it. Later he would concede: "universal feeling, whether well — or ill — founded, can not be safely disregarded."[28]

Nor did Lincoln change his mind about the value of meaningful politics. In after years, when he remembered his 1840 efforts it was with both pride and nostalgia. Politics to him was a serious matter of serious principles, "dear" principles, as he said. Men were mere vehicles — in the case of the hero of Tippecanoe a popular vehicle to be sure, and so much the better for the Whigs. But looking back in 1843 on the contest, Lincoln declared flatly that "It was not the election of Gen. Harrison that was expected to produce happy effects, but the measures to be adopted by his administration." Herndon later recalled somewhat unfairly: "I think he cared for principles, and not much for men."[29]

The campaign of 1840 signaled a turning point for the "lion of Sangamon," as the Democrats described him (while suggesting that his ancestry was African). Lincoln stood up against the national party managers. He seems to have judged that his political apprenticeship was over, that he was ready to lead on national issues. Thirty years after, Herndon thought that in the year of hard cider his partner had come to believe that a larger destiny awaited him: "I think it grew and bloomed and developed into beauty, etc., in the year *1840 exactly*. Mr. Lincoln told me that his ideas of something burst in him in 1840." This we do know: soon the bank champion was to write to comrades, "Now if you should hear any one say that Lincoln don't want to go to Congress, I wish you as a personal friend of mine, would tell him you have reason to believe he is mistaken."[30]

7

'Et In ᴄArcadia 'Ego *

THE HERO OF AMERICA IN LINCOLN'S TIME WAS THE FARMER. He was the hero in part because of the complex psychological needs of the nation and in part because he was the Common Man, the representative of the largest population segment in the land. Befitting a people whose religion was democracy, those who were the most numerous determined that the nation's idol should be in their own image — in the manner of the ancients with their gods. Americans were a people who liked themselves.

Thus the nostalgia of the aristocracy in the Old World had become the norm of democracy in the New. But European romance was only one of the cultural roots of the "agrarian myth" of America. The Bible exalts the life on the land, despite the few hostile nomadic memories of such as farmer Cain. The beauty of the pastoral poetry of Rome was given the sanction of economists in the eighteenth century by Francois Quesnay and the followers of *physiocratie* (the rule of nature). Rousseau labored in the same cause with the tools of the *philosophe*. In America, Crevecoeur, Jefferson, and an ever-growing host naturalized the worship of husbandmen, the Virginian making them "the chosen people of God, if ever He had a chosen people." This may have insulted the orthodox sectarian sensibilities of many of his countrymen but not their developing social values. Professors such as Doctor Thomas Cooper or the Reverend John McVickar also affirmed the superiority of life close to the soil. By the time the "farmer of the Hermitage" willed his name to the age, and the Whigs fought the Log Cabin campaign of 1840, Pan, god of Arcady, ruled the native Pantheon.[1]

---

*"I, Too Have Lived in Arcady." From the painting of Guercino.

That in this atmosphere Lincoln became an advocate of change, that he wanted Illinois' "Arcadian repose disturbed by the puffing of the locomotive," as a New York clergyman lamented, was not unique. Nor, probably, was his motivation although, as nearly always in such cases, the historian must be satisfied with a largely impressionistic understanding. If the locomotive, and the bank, and the way of life Lincoln believed they promised, were a strong attraction to him, the "Arcadian repose" was itself a strong repellent. The most popular teacher of Whig economics to the West, Horace Greeley, was said to have left the farm because in his boyhood it offered work only for an ox. So it had been with Lincoln, too, "with trees and logs and grubs he fought until he reached his twentieth year," as he recounted three decades later. He, too, left the land behind as permanently as had the Vermont-born master of newsprint.[2]

Significantly, Lincoln had not only left the farm, but he never learned to romanticize the plowman and the railsplitter. Thus he showed more down-to-earth realism, perhaps even more honesty, than did most of his countrymen. His regard for the laboring man was deep. But America's longing for rustic simplicity, like her hero-building, her guilt over her chasing after riches, her indulgence in a sometimes unprogressive outlook, and her Democratic politics, could claim him not. The introductory words of his 1859 speech at the Wisconsin State Fair could have been given by him at any juncture of his adult life:

> I presume I am not expected to employ the time assigned me, in the mere flattery of the farmers, as a class. . . . I believe there really are more attempts at flattering them than any other; the reason of which I cannot perceive, unless it be that they can cast more votes than any other.[3]

In the Illinois legislature, it is true, Lincoln supported the establishment of agricultural societies, served on a committee considering marks and brands, concerned himself with estrays, and favored a moderate bounty on wolves and the apprehension of horse thieves. He even brought to the floor the petition of an "old farmer" whose rights, "real and sacred," were trodden upon by the improvement system. Most important, he saw and presented his economic views as great boons to the business of farming. All the same agriculture was anything but his forte. As early as 1832 he honestly, but with uncharacteristic naiveté, excused himself in his platform from taking a stand on estray laws, among other things, because of "the great probability that the framers of those laws were wiser than myself."[4]

Lincoln saw advancement in life as all important, but working the soil as hardly the best road to it — whether for the individual or for the nation. It is not surprising then that on one occasion he came close to condemning agriculture as the most backward segment of the economy. More commonly he said the same thing by exalting it as the field with the greatest opportunity for improvement. Farming was a fact of economics, not a way of life for him. And since he had no use for Arcadian sagas, his views of the farmer could have turned out to be contemptuous had not equalitarianism been in his bones. Yet in spite of that equalitarianism he only once during a long career addressed specifically the subject of agriculture. Then he called for more scientific cultivation and "book-learning" with all their varied implications.[5]

Thus throughout his career Lincoln showed little interest in the special problems of farmers. Since politics in the West always attracted a goodly share of husbandmen, he could follow his inclinations without excessive pangs of conscience, although not without political risks. Occasionally, on minor matters, he ran into difficulties. At one of his stops during the 1840 campaign, he attempted to demonstrate the effects of deflation through the quantity theory of money. He used in illustration a horse he had seen a constable sell for $27 that morning. All due to the Democratic hard times, Lincoln explained, but if he had known more about livestock prices he would have remained silent. As it turned out, the constable was in the audience and presumably a Van Buren man, for he loudly protested that the low price was caused by the horse in question being blind in one eye. The Domocrats gloated over the incident and advised that Lincoln rest "his fame upon his printed speech."[6]

Although Lincoln either neglected farmers, or urged them to change their ways, as a rule he also possessed an uncanny sense of knowing when to stop. He provided the earliest important illustration of this when the Illinois legislature passed the so-called Little Bull Law.[7] The act has reached the proportions of legend in Lincolniana, for students assume it could have put an early end to his political career had Lincoln not opposed it.

The law prohibited bulls over a year old from running free, to "improve the breed of cattle." It was to permit selective use of good breeding animals, and provided for stiff fines. The proceeds were

to go to the owners of the best livestock in each county. Enlightened
as the act was, its passage was followed by an uproar that Governor
Ford believed largely accounted for the turnover in the next Assembly. "There has never been anything like this destruction of great
men in Illinois" but at one other time, he observed sardonically, and a
little nebulously, in his *History*. He concluded that the people were "in
favor of an equality of privileges even among bulls."[8]

Illinois' cattle were small, tough beasts, as visitors attested, inferior
to the livestock of the older regions. They were admirably suited,
however, to a country where domestic animals had to live off the
land, largely unattended. Most farmers were unwilling to spare
either labor or capital from their main business of bringing under
cultivation as large an acreage as possible. With inadequate transportation facilities preventing the marketing of good beef, only the
well-to-do husbandman tended to be interested in improving
breeds. This tendency was underscored by the absence of trees from
the prairie which made enclosures expensive, and also by the cost of
fodder, and the vexation generally caused by the attempt to fence in
young bulls.

Therefore, the "Little Bull Law" was declared undemocratic,
favoring the rich over the poor, and the stigma proved lethal. Although the law had been introduced as a progressive economic
measure, Lincoln's early opposition to it should not be a mystery.
The explanation for his stance can be found in his 1859 recollection
of "once being greatly astonished" by a demonstration of the very
high cost of "making and maintaining of inclosures." Thus, before
the popular uprising convinced many other lawmakers, Lincoln as
well as the rest of the Sangamon delegation had decided that the
cattle breeding act would be hard on the "poor," meaning average,
farmer. When Lincoln voted against his economic predisposition he
saved himself much trouble — thereby pointedly reinforcing his
political faith. The next legislature repealed the obnoxious statute
by a vote of eighty-one to four. Not for another generation did herd
laws for fencing cattle come to Illinois.[9]

Lincoln's allegiance to the "many" carried at times a distinct, politically selfserving ingredient, but even this could not overcome his
general inattention to the particular problems of farmers. This is

illuminated best by his lack of sustained concern with the question of public lands. His neglect flew in the face of a hunger for land that went back to the beginnings of civilized man's history and which in America itself had deep roots.

In the country's colonial centuries, land had been a great lure to immigrants, and British attempts to contain people in the East had helped bring disaster to the Empire in the New World. When the government of the new republic acquired huge Western lands and proceeded to guard them jealously, it became the target of the same resentment England had been subjected to in the previous decades. Although federal policy grew more openhanded as the nation matured, (by 1820 a settler could buy eighty acres from the public domain for $1.25 an acre,) laws on the whole favored the speculator. Whether the speculator was economically useful however, historians do not agree. In any case, in the 1820's the Democrats, led by Missouri's Benton, demanded liberalization of land laws through preemption and graduation, the legal confirmation of the claims of squatters and the periodic reduction of the price of unsold lands. Clay replied in 1832 with a bill calling for the distribution of the revenue from public land sales to the states, where much of it would be used for internal improvements.

The two Western senators represented not only rival land policies but also rival views of public finance, and indeed of economic life. Nationalist Clay aimed to maximize federal revenues through high land prices and by spending the money to induce commercial growth. He desired the government to find another source of revenue in the tariff which in turn would also encourage the creation of a commercial-industrial society. The ultimate goal was the internal improvement of the nation in a broad sense of the term.

Benton on the other hand, intended to derive indirect federal revenues through lower land prices that prompted settlement and consequent agricultural growth. Reduced land prices, together with allowing pioneers first choice of the land, also promised the opportunity to earn the purchase price of a farm by working it. Lincoln found much to admire in both sets of policies. Thus economic as well as political difficulties compounded his lack of interest in problems agricultural. He chose reticence as a result but the direction of his public land views are nonetheless reasonably clear.[10]

During the first years of his career the young legislator supported low prices, squatters' rights, and distribution, all at the same time. With unfailing economic logic he chose the combination that best suited the needs of the West and probably the growth of the whole nation as well. Had the Whigs been more the party of economic development and the advancement of the common man than they were of Eastern interests, such a program would have appealed to them. Certainly, reasoning based on economics placed no insurmountable obstacles before a program of preemption, graduation, and the distribution of the thus reduced land revenues. Government expenses could be met from tariff levies as the Whigs in fact desired. But as it was, party politics increasingly denied the legitimacy of Lincoln's stance and insisted on considering the propositions of Benton and Clay as the two rival systems of land policy.[11]

Lincoln continued to find room for maneuver, however. In election campaigns he spoke out only for Whig distribution, but he did not denounce either graduation or preemption. Even distribution (which meant a proimprovement stance in Illinois) could be given varying attributes. Revenues could be divided among states according to their populations, with only 10% thereby given to the Western states, where the lands were sold, as Clay had proposed. Or the percentage of revenues going to the public land states could be doubled, or more, as Lincoln had proposed in the Illinois House.[12]

Squatters' rights were more troublesome for Lincoln. On occasion he supported the policy. More generally he ignored the subject. In 1816-17 his family had been squatters in Indiana. But he did not approve of all his father's doings. He desired for all men the right to rise. But he did not see the unceasing expansion of the frontier as the best road to this goal.[13] Also, preemption often appeared to him more of a question of social order than political economy. He could not but wince when his party's "Gallant Harry" likened squatters to "club law men," "a lawless body." But as a state representative he would not countenance a proposal giving mere justices of the peace jurisdiction over squatter claims for improvements, not even those under $100. In Illinois, as elsewhere, land claims that would not stand up in a court sometimes spawned mob violence, not easily resisted by local justices. Lincoln condemned the lawless way.[14]

The issue, however, was not a major one in the state and Lincoln's near silence hid a divided heart and mind. In 1858 he returned to the topic for a moment and defined squatters as people "who squatted down in a country not their own . . . on a territory that did not belong to them . . . when it belonged to the nation." This was a bland statement neither praise nor denunciation and conveyed a sense of ambivalence. Yet a few years later Lincoln mentioned squatters in a rather positive manner.[15]

In the Democratic policy of graduation he found even less that was specifically objectionable than in preemption. At least once, however, he found himself uttering a few words in support of the Congressional Whigs's refusal to reduce public land prices. Willy-nilly he repeated Clay's reasoning, claiming that graduation schemes, instead of helping the needy settler, played into the hands of rich speculators. "Were the public lands to be put down to-day to a price of 50 cents an acre," Lincoln declared, "speculators would get the best of them before the poor men could get the news." He pointed to his own state's military bounty lands as an illustration of such abuse of good intentions.[16]

Recent economic scholarship gives this view some support, but Lincoln's words on its behalf amounted to lipservice. His negative opinion of large-scale speculation was earnest enough. He had brought himself to demand disproportionately high taxation of unimproved holdings, expecting that overburdening such properties would force them on the market and into cultivation. Like most Westerners he believed that speculation hindered economic growth. He also accepted, however, his party notwithstanding, the desirability of graduated land prices. Historians at times cite his above, Clay-like words, but in fact these words appear to have represented political artifice which he may never have repeated, and certainly never repeated on record.[17]

Lincoln spoke against graduation in 1839. That and the following year, however, displayed in great detail a much more authentic Lincoln via his important bank crusade. Opposing the independent treasury, he gave strong warnings about the reduction of the circulating medium of the country. Pointing to the increase in the real price of public lands which would follow such a reduction, he said:

Knowing, as well as I do, the difficulty that poor people *now* encounter in procuring homes, I hesitate not to say, that when the price of the public lands shall be doubled or trebled; or, which is the same thing, produce and labor cut down to one-half or one-third of their present prices, it will be little less than impossible for them to procure those homes at all.[18]

By proposing his land purchase plan in the Illinois House that same year, he further demonstrated that party development could not cripple his economic vision, aberrations notwithstanding. To help the state's finances and insure the continuation of some internal improvements, he recommended that Illinois obtain all the public lands within its borders. He thus fell in line with Calhoun's states rightist design for the cession of the national domain to the states. In fact Lincoln had debunked graduation in the very speech that defended his plan! It is not impossible therefore that his few words against lowered land prices were called forth simply by the need to assure his party colleagues that he still was a true Whig. Yet further a Whig could not fall from his party's land policies. There may have been some confusion in Lincoln about the public domain but that confusion did not reach very deep.[19]

By the early 1840's Lincoln was intently contemplating the routes leading to Congress. In the spring of 1843 when the Illinois Whigs began their preparations for the next year's elections with a conclave in Springfield, he played the leading role. He presented a set of resolutions and later a long address to the state, in effect a platform, discussing the party's principles and the means to victory. Preemption and graduation were not expressly mentioned in these documents but distribution was put on equal footing with other Whig policies more congenial to Lincoln. This platform provided the only recorded direct statement of his Whig years on the issue of public land disposal.

Lincoln's attention to distribution is explained by the special circumstances of Illinois at the time. The fall of the state's improvement system, and the debt left by it, made the people, as David Davis wrote East, "most interested" in the proposition. Never had distribution faced such favorable circumstances in Illinois, indeed in the nation as a whole. It is thus telling that even at this time Lincoln produced no more than a half-hearted apology for his party's land program and implied that graduation and preemption were more desirable policies. This, too, however, he did in his own Lincolnian way.[20]

Befitting his economic persuasion, as well as his distaste for constitutional disputation, he dismissed the "incomprehensible jargon" employed to prove the unconstitutionality of the national government handing out large sums of money. Instead he moved directly to his customary debating ground of economics. He pointed approvingly to the distribution funds awarded to their insolvent state, which were applied to reduce internal improvement indebtedness. He anticipated the charge that this kind of Congressional generosity tended to impoverish the Treasury by arguing that if the tariff became more necessary thereby, it was so much the better for the country. Indeed, it is implicit in Lincoln's views that his version of the American System allowed relatively easy terms for the acquisition of public lands and provided for internal improvements from the proceeds of high duties.

By not spelling out such details Lincoln kept the appearance of a good party man. In fact, with much justification, he considered the matter of the national domain as a sectional rather than a party issue. He explained that the older Eastern states wanted high land prices to prevent the loss of their population through migration. A new state that desired graduation, such as Ohio, by the time it became populous enough to carry weight in Congress had sold its public lands and accordingly was apt to act like "an old State." Thus the undeveloped West was a permanent minority. It was surprising that "so favorable" a bill as Clay's distribution had been allowed to become law. But the unsaid conclusion of Lincoln's reasoning was clear: the supposedly unattainable Democratic land policies were better than those of his own party. Under the circumstances it is not surprising that as he continued his preparations for the campaign of 1844, he increasingly neglected, as usual, the question of the public domain.[21]

The foregoing discussion suggests that Lincoln paid little attention to agricultural problems, such as the public lands, not only because his hopes for America led in a different direction, but also because of his distaste for Whig policies and his consequent political (and to a degree economic) perplexity. Yet of these factors, perhaps surprisingly, the first, ideology, was by far the most important. If in campaign utterances Lincoln understandably refrained from calling for the triumph of Democratic land policies, as a Congressman, when his stance carried more practical meaning, he supported liberalization. And when at last in his years as a Republican the homestead program made the espousal of more liberal views no longer contradictory to his party loyalites, he still ignored the matter almost entirely. Thus our conclusion must be that had the Whigs adopted a more open-handed land policy, matters agrarian would still have been very secondary to him.

In 1837 while Lincoln was becoming a leading bank and internal improvement champion in Illinois, Washington Irving praised the peaceful Creole villages where "the almighty dollar, that great object of universal devotion throughout our land, seems to have no genuine devotees." He added that unless some of this almighty's "missionaries" penetrated the quiet and built "banking houses and other pious shrines, there is no knowing how long the inhabitants may remain in their present state of contented poverty." Lincoln was a missionary, and in 1840 the Log Cabin campaign provided a sharp definition of his attitude. While the nation sang the jolly rhyme:

> But we'll have a ploughman
> President of the Cincinnatus line

Lincoln spoke of the virtues of centralized banking. Never in his long career did he change his priorities. He always saw himself as more than the representative of a small district. Even as a very young politician he often managed to think in national, even universal terms. It is possible that his unusually large ambitions were at the root of his outlook, but the end result was to help him develop a large vision.

Lincoln could sustain such a stance with much immunity, in part because his message was attractive to many, including farmers. Country lawyer that he was, he knew, better than Emerson did, that the Man With the Hoe was "covetous of his dollar." He presented his economic policies as opening the road of advancement to the farmer as well as others. He would not admit that there might be at least a short-term conflict between agrarian interests and those of commerce and industry. The heated debates of an earlier generation about the relative merits of agriculture and industry had died down by his day, and wisely, he did not disturb the peace.

Lincoln's success with his predominantly farming constituency (whether in Illinois or in the White House) stemmed also from his political ability. This ability was reinforced by both his sincerity and his appearance and ways. He seemed like a man of the soil with manure on his boots even if the manure was not there. When accused of siding with the aristocracy, as he was in 1840, he could ward off the charge rudely. In one debate when his opponent warmed up to such a haranguing Jacksonian performance, the Whig champion ripped open the good tribune's coat to reveal an opulent gentleman with ruffled shirt, vest, and gold chain. The People roared. Then Lincoln reminisced about the times when he had worked for eight dollars a month and about the single pair of buckskin breeches he had to his name:

> Now if you know the nature of the buckskin when wet and dried by the sun, it will shrink; and my breeches kept shrinking until they left several inches of my legs bare between the tops of my socks and the lower part of my breeches; and whilst I was growing taller they were becoming shorter, and so much tighter that they left a blue streak around my legs that can be seen to this day. If you call this aristocracy I plead guilty to the charge.[22]

There were not many who could doubt where Lincoln's allegiance lay. He was of the people, the Common Men whom Lincoln said God loved so and made so many of.[23] His knowledge of economics must have seemed deep enough to his fellow Illinoisans. When arguments failed, on occasion they still voted for him although not for the Whig policies. Economic development could not have had a better champion.

Lincoln often addressed his constituents in the language of the farmer: "My friends, to-day closes the discussion of this canvass. The planting and culture are over; and there remains but the preparation, and the harvest." As President he began his annual messages with thanks to Providence for health and the "bountiful harvest." Then as before he repeatedly affirmed the welfare of the farmer as being paramount.[24] But the economic viewpoint Lincoln espoused pointed toward a commercial-industrial society. He knew and argued that the farmer stood to benefit by such change, and over the long run he was right. Economic development did aid all, though over the short run the man on the land very probably carried a disproportionate share of the burden. Such, however, had nearly always been the necessary price paid by society seeking development.

Happily Lincoln did not have to face the problem squarely, as for example, the leaders of Russia and Japan had to in the twentieth century. The embryonic state of the political economy of growth allowed him an escape. He was fully convinced that the Whig policies on improvements, banking, and the tariff, smoothed the upward path of all, including the farmer. On the issue of public lands, where he had strong doubts, he set out to hew his own course. He believed that he did not discriminate in favor of the farmer nor against him, but rather served the interests of the whole nation. If Lincoln's view contained a degree of distortion, this was the bliss of ignorance, for his political faith could have become an immense obstacle to his championship of developmental economics. His Wisconsin address expresses his philosophy plainly:

> ... farmers, being the most numerous class, it follows that their interest is the largest interest. It also follows that that interest is most worthy of all to be cherished and cultivated — that if there be inevitable conflict between that interest and any other, that other should yield.

As it was, convinced of the fairness of his economics, Lincoln could pursue the swiftest road to the American Dream.[25]

In contrast to him, economists in the latter half of the twentieth century tend to minimize the importance of industry to economic development. Even though this basically Western view does not propose the perpetuation of exclusively agricultural societies, the countries most concerned with the problem, those which are relatively undeveloped, seem less than impressed by such favor as it shows toward agriculture. It is instructive to note that in the same way Americans sometimes lecture developing lands of the twentieth century, John Stuart Mill lectured them in the nineteenth. After Lincoln's pro-commercial-industrial policies became the official national policies, while he was in the White House, Mill complained that Americans believed that "a nation all agricultural — cannot attain a high state of civilization and culture."[26]

Whatever the outstanding economist of the age might tell her, in the end the United States chose the road which nations that would rise nearly always choose. Her ways began to change ever more rapidly. "The merchant is abroad," Hugh Legaré declared in Charleston, "civilizing, humanizing, and blessing mankind." In New York Greeley proclaimed the manufacturer the new constructive "king of men." America will never forget her fair rustic beau ideal with its sturdy yeoman hero. But before the nineteenth century reached its half-way mark, her people were already traveling the road to Calvin Coolidge's announcement that America's business is business. Lincoln confidently whistled them onward. It is not so much ironic as revealing (of how, through subterfuge, the nation endured the hardships of rapid industrialization), that in Coolidge's day a historian would find that the myths after Lincoln made the martyred President into a kind of agricultural deity.[27]

8
On the
Road to Paradise

IN THE MID-1840'S LINCOLN WAS FIGHTING FOR HIS PLACE IN the leadership of the Illinois Whig party and hoped, "very much," to go to Washington to the House of Representatives. It may have seemed a good omen to him that in the spring of 1843 in preparation for next year's presidential contest, a Whig conclave in Springfield, adopted his declaration of principles, and appointed him to write an address to the people of the state. These documents are significant for our purposes because they provide the earliest suviving attempt by Lincoln to define the specific policies his party stood for.[1]

In the Civil War era friends remembered an early Lincoln speech, from his first campaign for office (and the Clay-Jackson contest of 1832) which avowed: "My politics are short and sweet, like the old woman's dance. I am in favor of a national bank. I am in favor of the internal improvement system and a high protective tariff." The authenticity of these sentiments need not be debated. It is clear, however, that they tell more about what policies Lincoln's friends had associated him with in their memories than what he had said in 1832. And we have the undeniably authentic statements of 1843.[2]

Lincoln's Whiggery was mainly economic oriented, and not surprisingly his roster of party principles contained only economic statements. Others might speak, as Clay did, of "circumscribing the executive power" as the "first" and the "most important" tenet of the Whigs. They might emphasize the importance of governmental purity, a single presidential term, the sparse use of veto power, the evils of the spoils system, and so on. The Tyler years in the White House

93

lent themselves well to the enunciation of these attitudes. But Lincoln was not interested.[3]

His 1843 resolutions and his address to the state discussed the tariff, taxation, the national debt, the Bank of the United States, and the distribution of the proceeds of public land sales. Prudently Lincoln did no more than imply the need for internal improvements because the policy was *non grata* for the moment in the state. Since the country was still upon hard times and Illinois debt-ridden on account of her past efforts, the omission was not very meaningful.

It is understandable that the tariff was given first place in Lincoln's Whiggism by this time. He had been a high tariffite from the beginning, but only the 1842 repeal of the Compromise Tariff of 1833 opened a practical way for renewed discussion. In 1842 he may have composed and certainly signed a petition that contained the gist of his party's views on the matter. Then his 1843 statements, argued that protection was an absolute necessity "to the prosperity of the American People." They also gave evidence that he had studied the tariff problem at some length.[4]

Lincoln saw the tariff as a long-range policy but was willing to marshal short-term arguments also. The Whig disciples of Hamilton notwithstanding he decried the swift rise of the national debt, which was "reasonably to be expected [only] in time of war." He drew on the common analogy between the extravagant borrowing of an individual and the government, which his party brethren were wont to denounce as Democratic ignorance and which the followers of Lord Keynes would object to so strenuously in the twentieth century. The standard prescription for reducing debt, economy in government, did not appeal to him. In opportune moments he might point to such a remedy, but in defining principles he had to ignore it. Thus he pointed to the tariff and direct taxation as the sole sources of revenue, "one or the other must come . . . expenditures must be met." Of course, the public lands also produced funds, but Lincoln wanted these revenues shared among the states. Since only the most dogged Democrats were willing to champion direct taxation, outlining the question of governmental finances in this fashion made the least obtrusive case for the tariff. Underplaying thus the protectionist facet of import levies may have fitted the political needs of Illinois but not Lincoln's economic outlook. Soon he would go beyond so mild a stance.

Comparing the tariff and taxation as revenue measures, Lincoln correctly argued that the maintenance of customs officers was much less expensive than that of a host of tax collectors. He contrasted the relative painlessness of duty assessments with being "perpetually haunted and harassed by the tax-gatherer." But inevitably he carried his point too far by arguing that imposts would fall "chiefly" on those whom Thorstein Veblen would later condemn for conspicuous consumption, "those whose pride, whose abundance of means, prompt them to spurn the manufactures of our own country, and to strut in British cloaks and coats, and pantaloons." Thus under the American tariff "the substantial and laboring many" went free, while "the wealthy and luxurious few" carried most of the burden.

Actually Lincoln's case would have been an excellent one had the tariff been limited to the textiles he used an as illustration of how the protective system worked in general. By the 1840's effective protection among textile goods was only being extended to the finer quality cotton and woollen cloths. The coarse American manufactures had become export items. Thus with the particular examples Lincoln selected, the burden of higher prices in fact fell on the wealthier consumers whose demand for the better quality goods was less price elastic.

Employing such an approach, the import of Lincoln's message, as ever, become democracy, or rather its economic manifestation in government aid to the many. Yet, instead of making a broad, long-term case for economic development (as he had done in the Illinois legislature) for purposes of electioneering he had fallen back to simplistic, short-term demonstrations of the democratic virtues of Whig policies. This was not Lincoln at his best but, as we shall see, still above most of his colleagues.

His oversimplification of the tariff problem, which reflected campaign technique rather than ignorance of economics, is important primarily as a clarification of his understanding of democracy. This has two aspects. The first concerns Lincolnian political style. As we have noted in earlier chapters, he was ready to "plow around stumps," as he liked to say. This at times could mean the necessity of telling less than the whole truth, indicating that his extraordinarily deep faith in the common man was less than absolute.

The second point illuminated by Lincoln's tariff statement is economic. As his career progressed, he appeared more and more firm in his feeling that those "whose abundance of means" allowed should carry a graduated share of the "burthen."[5] He was merely one of thousands who voiced this feeling, though not yet so convinced of the justice of their view to abandon the ideal of "equal" (meaning proportional) assessment of all citizens. They were traveling on a road which led to the establishment of graduated taxation during the Civil War with the approval of the sixteenth President. Although the Supreme Court in the 1890's saw that act as strictly a war measure, it is plain that Lincoln, and others, were moving in the direction of the act independently of wartime needs. The Illinois Whig was perhaps sensing that what he now called "truly democratic" was a difficult goal to attain, and that changing times required changing means. And his conviction that he and his party represented the best interests of the people was totally real, "solemn" as he said. Thus he declared confidently (perhaps arrogantly) that in a real sense "the whigs are always a majority of this Nation."

Lincoln's list of principles included federal supervision of banking as well, although the thankless struggle of the early forties between President Tyler and Congress induced the Whig leaders, Webster and Clay included, to abandon this goal. There was justice in this retreat on the national scene, Illinois Democrats pointed out, for the Whigs, who made the BUS the prime issue in the state during the 1840 election, were beaten on it; whereas the national party, which won, had ignored the matter.[6]

Lincoln refused to accept defeat, however, and his 1843 platform gave a convincing, and more than ever historically oriented summary of his 1840 efforts — minus some campaign flourishes. This is not to say that he entirely ignored the lesson of that earlier contest, or national party developments; he gave less space to the Bank than to any other question.

In addition to favoring protection, a federal bank, and opposing a large national debt and direct taxation, Lincoln's declaration also gave some support to distribution (in positive terms internal improvements), as noted in the previous chapter.

But only the first part of his efforts dealt with such matters. The second part outlined, and recommended a tight political organization for the Illinois party, including nominating conventions. Thus

Lincoln attempted not only to define Whig policies but also to build the more practical means to the party's victory. In its division of interest Lincoln's work was symbolic. It reflected the local politician of 1843; but it also foreshadowed the President of 1863: a man of both principle and pragmatism.

In 1843 Lincoln argued for careful party organization with the words of the Apostle Mark he later made a byword of American history, that "A house divided against itself cannot stand." This half of his writing evinced both great political sagacity and understanding of psychology. Yet it brought down "thunder" on his head from his fellow Whigs, as he unhappily noted.[7]

It rather seems that on questions of broad party principles, which for Lincoln meant national economic goals, his at times individualistic leadership of the Illinois Whigs was widely accepted and followed because he had no real rivals in this sphere. But when it came to politicking, organization, and of course preferment, his rivals and would-be rivals were aplenty. It is understandable that at times he received no thanks for his labors in this area.

The "thunder," however, was also the consequence of Lincoln's understanding of Whiggery chiefly in economic terms. To others, political matters, the single presidential term or opposition to selecting candidates via centralized nominating conventions for instance, were the prime party principles. Lincoln's successful insistence on conventions in his state was good for the Whigs. But it probably cost him much support and contributed to the loss of the congressional nomination he fervently desired.[8]

Not only did Lincoln concentrate his public life on economic questions and consistently ignore (and sometimes combat) the non-economic principles of his party, but he also failed to measure up well to most noneconomic tendencies later scholars have diagnosed in that party. Thus when examining further his Whiggery we must note that his background was not Yankee but border state-Western poor white. He was not an evangelical Christian, indeed no formal Christian of any sort. It can be argued that he shared certain social values that can be broadly termed evangelical. Lincoln did speak on behalf of temperance, for example, but as with abolitionism, he was much too moderate a man to be one of the true faithful. In the

Illinois House, for example, he cast a decisive vote against prohibition which thus went down in defeat via a tie vote. Not surprisingly, when in the 1850's temperance became a telling political force and Douglas pointed out that as a young man Lincoln had kept a "grocery" (the frontier name for a saloon), Lincoln, after denying the charge, concluded that "I don't know as it would be a great sin, if I had."[9]

The moral tone of the Whigs and their devotion to building an ordered community appealed to Lincoln, yet in his public life this element received its prime manifestation via economic policies. When Whig morality became a demand for cultural homogenity (and during the Civil War a demand for remaking the South for the sake of Northern cultural supremacy and national uniformity) again Lincoln and his party leaned toward divergent roads.

Thus Lincoln did not partake of the nativist proclavities that contemporaries as well as subsequent students diagnosed among the Whigs (and eventually among the Republicans). Both in Illinois and in the White House he countered, with some success, anti-immigrant sentiments. His commitment to economic development was very important to this stance although one can not discount his humanitarian feelings or, however mislaid, his political hopes. Lincoln's attitude toward schools, another modern yardstick of Whiggery, was at best ambivalent. Nor did he see virtue in the antiorganizational bias that was so important to many of his party brethren and accordingly he helped remake the face of his party in Illinois.[10]

Richard Hofstadter, among others, has suggested that Lincoln was drawn to the Whigs by "the better sort" of people who led that party. Such conjectures were made before research revealed that little social gap existed at the leadership level of the two parties. (Impressionistic evidence, however, still indicates a Whig preference by "the better sort.") Whatever future studies will disclose about the political affiliation of the *créme*, it is significant that nearly half of the American voters also voted Whig. Perhaps they were attracted to "the better sort," but as for Lincoln in the 1850's he put in writing (in private) his own distaste for the "exclusive silk-stocking whiggery . . . the nice exclusive sort." It may well be that he was a Whig *in spite of* them. Indeed in 1858 he wrote with irony that the natural home of these folk was in "the great democratic party." And sixteen years before that he damaged himself politically (at least in Herndon's estimate) when he publicly chastised the respectables of Springfield for their disdaining to associate with drunkards who had reformed themselves.[11]

We should also note the spell Clay cast over Jacksonian America — including Lincoln. Although some of Lincoln's adulatory remarks about Clay were politically motivated, the attraction of the younger Kentuckian for the older one was real. This attraction, in some part, was that of one political moderate, a supporter of social order, towards another, and that of one antislavery man towards another.[12] But there was something more, deeper reaching here. Lincoln's 1852 eulogy of Clay celebrated the Kentuckian's rise in "the race of life" — from an "undistinguished" ancestry. (Lincoln's 1859 autobiography used the same term, "undistinguished," to describe his own beginnings.) Lincoln identified as Clay's "primary and all controlling passion" the "elevation" of the masses of people everywhere. "Subsidiary to this was the conduct of his whole life." We need not discuss here the historical accuracy of Lincoln's evaluation, or whether it was self-confessional, as one strongly suspects. It did, however, point out clearly what Lincoln found most admirable in a statesman.[13]

For many, Clay's name was synonymous with the American System. In the year Lincoln entered politics, Clay introduced into the language of the United States the phrase "self-made man." Fending off the Democratic charge that tariff protection was intended to create a hereditary aristocracy, he told the Senate that in "Kentucky almost every manufactory known to me is in the hands of enterprising self-made men, who have whatever they possess by patient and dilligent labor." It was for such men, he argued, not for an aristocracy, that the tariff paved the way.[14]

For Lincoln, devotion to Clay was inseparable from devotion to an economic vision. As Clay began to detach himself from his economic policies in order to satisfy his presidential ambitions, Lincoln's affection for him began to wane. At last, in the White House, Lincoln went on record, in private, charging that Clay's (and Webster's) personal ambitions and consequent abandonment of principle "contributed to the ruin of their party. . . ."[15]

But the time for such sentiments was not yet. In 1843 Lincoln boldly set forth his Whig policies, and also his enthusiasm for Clay. When the time of actual campaigning arrived, however, he characteristically focused on a single subject, in this case protectionism. In part a Lincolnian peculiarity produced this result. Long before he became the singleminded antislavery champion, he demonstrated that he was a one-issue politician on the stump, whether the issue was banking, internal improvements, or whatever. His thorough mind preferred to concentrate on one subject and dig deeply into it. The inevitable corollary of such scholarly, unpolitician-like, attribute was the need to limit the questions he would handle. A political ingredient, however, was probably also present, a self-knowledge that he was at his best when concentrating thus. Certainly his political effectiveness appears to have been enhanced thereby, somewhat in the manner of Cato the Elder's "Delenda est Carthago."*

Yet more than a mental trait, or its political ramifications, determined Lincoln's weapon for the 1844 presidential election. As the hard times continued in the United States, people's interest quickened in the supposed prosperity making properties of protectionism. This was true in Illinois, too. Of course the economic effect of tariff legislation does not lend itself to easy measurement because of the frequent changes it was subjected to and because of myriad other factors that modified its workings. Antebellum Americans nonetheless sincerely agreed that its potency was considerable, for good or for ill, depending on the vantage point of the observer. In 1832, for example, when Dixie expectations of reduced customs duties did not materialize, indignant South Carolina proclaimed the excellence of nullification. Both before, and after, the aura of sectionalism, and some of its substance, clung to the tariff, yet, on the whole, the political parties dominated its legislation. As the election of 1844 approached Congress proceeded to spar over protectionism. It did not become an important issue at the national level in the campaign, however. Vague statements both Whig and Democratic blurred the differences between the parties. As politicians scurried for the safe center, Lincoln remained unmoved, showing no more willingness to sit on the tariff fence than he had done four years earlier with the Bank.[16]

Perhaps there was an element of political gamble in this for his standing in the Illinois party was not as strong as it once had been.

*Carthage must be destroyed.

The congressional seat to which he aspired went to the younger, fast-rising John J. Hardin, who had opposed him both on the question of Illinois' internal improvements and on the issue of tighter party organization. In 1843 Hardin was nominated and elected by the Whigs. The following year Edward Baker, holding a similar record, was slated to succeed him.[17]

Thus for the first time since entering politics Lincoln fought through an election year without being himself a candidate for office. All the same he proved again that on the stump his voice stood out. He played a major role leading the Illinois Whigs into making the tariff by the spring of 1844 the most important issue of the contest. Although we can readily reconstruct this general picture, we can do no more than provide a rough outline of what Lincoln actually said.

The surface indication that as a Whig elector he did not research and write a "big speech" to map out his campaign, as he did four years earlier, is apt to be misleading. And yet, no long speech by him survives. Both the public and private reports of his frequent appearances are scarce and fragmentary and either generalize about his vast virtues or emphasize the most catchy aspects of his arguments.[18] When in 1860 as the Republican presidential candidate he was asked to document his early devotion to protectionism, he could only produce post-1844 evidence and an appeal to the memories of old-timers. An eyewitness, Jesse Fell, however, helped a Pennsylvania newspaperman produce early in 1860 a friendly, somewhat vague, yet on the whole remarkably authentic-sounding description of Lincoln's 1844 electioneering. It recalled that he "exerted himself powerfully" in Clay's behalf.

> The contest of that year in Illinois was mainly on the question of the tariff .... Mr. Lincoln, in these elaborate speeches, evinced a thorough mastery of the principles of political economy which underlie the tariff question, and presented arguments in favor of the protective policy with a power and conclusiveness rarely equalled, and at the same time in a manner so lucid and familiar and so well interspersed with happy illustrations and apposite anecdotes as to seduce the delighted attention of his auditory.[19]

A chief thrust of Lincoln's 1844 campaign appears to have followed the mainstream tradition of American protectionism and argued that support for young industries reduces the price of manufactured goods. Long-term arguments along these lines had been common in America. What newspapers found most fascinating in Lincoln's stump efforts, however, was his attempt to prove the same result for the short run as well. On one occasion he was reported to be so firm in his argument that he "promised to forfeit his 'ears' and his 'legs' if he did not demonstrate, that protected articles have been cheaper since the late Tariff [of 1842] than before. . . ."[20]

How duties affect prices had been under dispute in the English-speaking world since the seventeenth century. The claim to overnight results, however, did not make its American appearance until just before this election. Lincoln probably borrowed from other protectionists their selective statistics to substantiate his claim.[21] Indeed the law of 1842 might have encouraged some sections of the manufacturing community but could not have created cheaper products across the board in a year and a half.

It thus appears that the heat of campaign once again forced Lincoln to attempt to demonstrate the short-run merits of the economics he advocated. Larger goals were either pushed aside by him or, more probably, did not attract the attention of the press. Such short-term arguments amounted to bad economics but were good politics. Existing conditions favored Lincoln's effort. During 1843 the economic distress continued, but the decline of agricultural prices was slower than that of other commodities. The terms of trade in the Western states improved vis-á-vis the East. It was an easy next step to credit the tariff for the relatively low prices of goods farmers were likely to buy and then generalize the propostion. The price of raw wool in fact turned upwards, and as the product was important in Illinois Lincoln may have discoursed on the advantages of protection for sheepmen. Moreover, as selective signs of recovery appeared in 1843-44, a Whig could not be expected to resist pointing to the recent tariff and singing hallelujah.[22] The political considerations, and the less than sound economic reasoning (as it seems to our age), is not sufficient, however, to deprive Lincoln of the earnestness of his views. It should help put matters in perspective to note that scholars in the twentieth century could still reach Lincoln-like conclusions about the connection of the tariff and the business cycle![23]

The weak link of Lincoln's reasoning, as he sensed it, lay

elsewhere. The important question of the Illinois tariff debate was who carried the burden of the imposts? The alternatives were the producer, the merchant, and the consumer. Lincoln tried to argue for the first of these and made the British capitalist help support the American government. This was not a unique approach,[24] and the riddle of who paid the tariff tax was not readily solved. But, not surprisingly Lincoln's thoughts were muddled on the subject. In 1843 he had argued that the consumer paid the duty — even though it was the wealthy consumer of luxuries. After the Clay campaign he went along with the democratic compromise that manufacturers, purchasers, and middlemen carried equal loads. If much of this was hairsplitting, it nonetheless led to the acid test for any policy in the United States. To use the common words of a report on one of Lincoln's debates, was the tariff for the "benefit of the *rich* to the injury of the poor man?"[25]

Lincoln invariably excelled in controversies touching the core of his beliefs. Tying his economic views to democracy was his forte. Yet in the language of the twentieth century, the hard question here was whether the American import duties redistributed national income to the profit of manufacturers.[26] Lincoln chose to sidestep the issue via his compromises and confusions, and thus refused to admit, to himself or to the electorate, that protectionist policy might have an undemocratic ingredient. Instead he evoked his dream of a developed America toward which the tariff road pointed and which, he believed, would help lift up all Americans.

At one point he carried his campaign into Indiana to near his childhood home. His message there was summed up succinctly in the recollection of one of his listeners, a distant kinsman: "give us a protective tariff, and we will have the greatest country on earth." Fifteen years after that, when Lincoln returned to the area again, in a speech at Indianapolis he contrasted the undeveloped "wilderness" of the years of his youth with the "wonderfully different" conditions of 1859.[27]

Judged provisionally from the surviving evidence, Lincoln's tariff campaign appears to have been weaker in content than his bank campaign of 1840. It was probably still the high water mark of the Illinois Whig effort. At the largest rally of the election, for example, where some of the state's most outstanding Whigs gave patriotic speeches, Lincoln predictably spoke on the tariff. Presumably it was the incongruity between his eternal economics and the Whigs' eternal hoopla that enabled Jeriah Bonham to recall this speech four decades later. By then, of course, Lincoln's protectionism seemed "unanswerable," and its serious tone seemed to have qualified him for any office "from Congressman to the President of the United States."[28]

In 1844 Lincoln continued from earlier contests not only his economics oriented approach to politics but also the joint debate technique that had proved successful for him. He continued to put theoretical reasoning into local dialect and supplement it with both homely parables and precise statistics.[29] As in 1840 he worked hard to do his job. We do not know with certainty if his research went substantially beyond political literature, but we can conservatively venture that he read the current speeches by Senators George Evans, George McDuffie, Levi Woodbury, Congressman Andrew Stewart, Calvin Colton's "Junius Tracts," and Greeley's *Whig Almanacs*. Much of this had appeared in pamphlet form, and also in the local press. Political-minded Illinoisans read them all.[30] The economic sophistication of Lincoln's time — relative to available knowledge — was considerably higher than that of our own. And whatever he read, it took much learning to be an elector when one had Lincoln's mental traits and when debaters, as David Davis testifies, spoke for three or four hours at a time.[31]

The tariff notes that Lincoln completed before the end of 1847 began to germinate during the campaign. He had an assistant in his researches, a young law student at his office, and his future partner, Herndon, who considered himself an earnest student of political economy. Herndon " 'toted books,' and 'hunted up authorities' " for his mentor's campaigning, just as he normally did for his law cases. He also wrote to Washington for tariff materials. Later he regretted allowing the older man to mislead him into protectionism, but in 1844 they made a fine team.[32]

The only brief diversion Lincoln permitted himself concerned the Bank of the United States. On that subject, too, he presented "most able and conclusive" arguments, or so his supporters thought, and made "a clean shucking" of opponents. He went so far as to declare

that all state banks were Democratic institutions, for national banking was the Whig policy. Although he once signed his name to a local
rendition of the national Whig platform which spoke of "sound currency" instead of a Bank, he disdained to employ such euphemisms
on the stump. It was fitting, therefore, that at one huge party gathering in the old capital of Vandalia he should be greeted with the banner: "U.S. Bank Bill — J.J. Hardin, Cashier — Abraham Lincoln,
President."[33]

Lincoln's campaign was not challenged effectively until the middle
of 1844. By then, whether because the Democrats were "growing
sick" of the tariff question or because they were being beaten on it (as
Lincoln judged), or because a more attractive issue offered itself
after James K. Polk's nomination, they went on the offensive, stress-
ing territorial expansion. In a letter to Congressman Hardin,
Herndon gave voice to what clearly were also Lincoln's sentiments,
that if the "locos"

> could by any means keep the true issue from the people they will do it.
> They well know that their principles can not stand the test of an en-
> lightened public investigation and knowing and feeling this, they resort
> to Oregon to do battle for them.[34]

To consider expansionism as something less than a real issue took
a singular viewpoint. Lincoln's inward oriented nationalism, and the
unacceptability of Whig moderation on expansionism to the vast
majorities in Illinois, account for his attitude. But his resultant incomprehension of the ethos of Manifest Destiny is comparable only
to his inability to identify with the farmer, two forces which in
William Appleman Williams' view were firmly intertwined.[35]

Early in 1844 Lincoln announced that the annexation of Texas
was not then expedient and largely avoided the subject thereafter. It
rather seems that in the second part of the campaign his dialogue
with opponents evaporated. He observed contemptuously that the
Democratic platform was "nothing but Texas" and insisted that substantial subjects be discussed instead. Much as the country might
make Manifest Destiny the issue, he stubbornly went on talking
economics. Polk's partisan blustered at this, pressed increasingly
Texas on the Illinois electorate, and labeled Lincoln a leader of the
"British anti-Texas Junto."[36]

It is a measure of the Whig elector's hardihood and

singlemindedness that his counterattack came along the lines of the issue he had laid out for himself from the beginning. The tariff, too, lent itself to nationalism of the jingoist variety — second only to expansionism in the antebellum era. The American System made an eminent contrast to the "British System" that was free trade. Lincoln, however, true to character even in jingoism, avoided laboring the need for economic independence from depraved, decadent Europe. He made specific charges instead, proving "conclusively" that the English interfered in the election, supported the Democrats, and flooded the country with money and tracts against the Whig tariff. Their free trade association, the rumor was, appropriated £100,000 for the purpose. "*We all believe it,* & we are making the Locos believe it too," one of his audience enthused. Thus, not surprisingly, the Whigs, hounded long as disguised Federalists who now served the interest of the British on Texas and Oregon, began to speak of turning the "table on our old Federal Loco focos."[37]

Skillfully, if less than high-mindedly, Lincoln evaded the issue of territorial expansion and stuck to his economics. This, however, may have been a fatal mistake. The day would come when the majority of Illinoisans would lose interest in expansion, but not until it came to be synonymous for them with the expansion of slavery. The time was not yet.

In after years when Lincoln recalled this campaign he boasted of his many speeches on the tariff.[38] But if his campaign was not typical of the nation, it was not in as unusual a category as his fight for national banking had been in 1840. The Illinois Whigs received some encouragement from abroad, most importantly perhaps from the editor of the Washington *True Whig*, pamphleteer, economist, Calvin Colton. In Pennsylvania, of course, protection was the perennial question of politics. Even elsewhere a large number of Whigs found themselves emphasizing the tariff and downplaying Texas with Webster in their lead. In Illinois the annexation issue gained ground steadily as the campaign progressed, but the general opinion among Lincoln's followers remained unchanged: "the Whig Ship will sail well under Tariff colours." His protectionist efforts were seen as an "honor to himself and the Whig cause," and David Davis declared flatly that Lincoln was "the best stump speaker in the State."[39]

If the Whigs were well satisfied with Lincoln's performance, the opposition seemed to be equally certain that this "great Goliath" of protectionism had been slain over and over again by Democratic Davids. Yet that Polk's Illinois brethren were less than happy with the local tariff debate can be detected (quite apart from their emphasis on Texas and Oregon) in the tone of Springfield's *State Register*. At first it took a straightforward stand against "Lincoln's defence of the coon tariff." In time it backed down to proving Clay to be a weak supporter of the policy, or else Polk just as strong. It even cast doubt on the Whig pedigree of the Tariff of 1842 and pointed out that Democrats, too, had voted for it. In the final stretch of the campaign the paper occupied firm ground again but tied protection to a less acceptable policy with the justified claim that Whig economics had to be rejected in a package: "Bank and Tariff — One and Inseparable."[40]

Clay could "rejoice" at his fair prospects in the "Prairie State," as reported to him by one of Lincoln's close political allies, but what Lincoln's expectations were can only be surmised. As it turned out the Whigs lost the election. In most states the tariff played little part in the outcome but not so in Illinois, from whence came nearly one-third of Polk's popular majority. There, to quote Lincoln, the Whigs "got gloriously whipped."[41]

Later, Nathaniel Hawthorne, testifying to his artistic calling, and perhaps his political one as well, wrote in *The Scarlet Letter* "that neither the front nor the back entrance of the Custom House opens on the road to Paradise." For a season such became the bitter truth for Lincoln. And more. In the perspective of his twelve years of active political life, it seemed that all the great policies he had fought for, improvements, banking, protection, were buried in defeat. His national party sought a way out by abandoning tangible convictions. Many Illinoisans were ready to follow. Many of Lincoln's closest associates were so demoralized by Clay's defeat that they seriously considered disbanding the local Whig Party and starting anew under a different name and with different principles. In terms of political expediency, it can be argued their approach was very likely correct, but Lincoln would not go along with it. The affair is shrouded in mystery but a major Lincoln motive is clear: for however much he was a politician, his Whig principles were more than just a road to party victory. It is worth recalling his comment after the 1840 election: in the final analysis not the victory of a man or party was to create "happy effects, but the measures to be adopted" as a result. Therefore, to quote the hero of *The Pilgrim's Progress,* that favored reading of his growing years, "he resolved to venture and to stand his ground."[42]

Far off in the protectionist Keystone State of Pennsylvania in the midst of the campaign a young man went ahunting and shot an eagle. He brought the prize home to his uncle, who selected a fine quill and saved it for November — a gift for a new Whig Chief Magistrate. The good man had a sixteen year wait. Then he presented the pen to the sixteenth President of the United States.[43]

9

Foolscap Halfsheets

THE CAMPAIGN OF 1844 LEFT LINCOLN DISSATISFIED WITH THE RE-
sults, Clay's conduct and also his own. His mastery of the tariff question did not measure up to the high standards he set for himself. He
was ready to go back to study the subject and dig deeper. Such study
became all the more important because in 1846 he obtained at last
the nomination for the U.S. House of Representatives from his
Seventh District, by then known as the Whig district of Illinois.[1]

The Democrats in Washington were about to weaken the tariff
and reestablish the Independent Treasury and so his Illinois party
assisted him with a protectionist-antisubtreasury platform, no
doubt at his own request. Although the Mexican War drew
everyone's attention, in the first flush of patriotism it was not yet a
political issue. As usual, Lincoln seems to have campaigned only on
economic questions. And the Democrats gave up the contest early
although not without raising the issue of Lincoln's leadership of the
old internal improvement system. After his late summer victory the
Congressman-elect had to wait nearly a year and a half before he
could take his seat in Washington. He devoted much time during this
interval to studying economics, particularly the question of protection.[2]

While Lincoln was concluding his campaign in Illinois, Congress
drastically reduced the average level of import levies through the
Walker Act. For many this settled the matter but Lincoln declared
the tariff to be "in greater dispute than ever" and on eleven foolscap
halfsheets started writing notes for a speech. He used this method of
composition at other times, too. Herndon recalled that for the 1858

109

House Divided Speech Lincoln wrote his thoughts on "slips, put these slips in his hat, numbering them, and when he was done with the ideas, he gathered up the scraps, put them in the right order, and wrote out his speech." As it turned out Lincoln's tariff notes never became a speech. These incomplete and fragmentary scraps nonetheless provide the most extensive surviving evidence of his views on the subject. More important they indicate further the development of his thought.[3]

The notes begin with an introduction which remains in a bare outline form. As this was to be a summary of orthodox protectionist thinking (with the special Lincolnian emphasis, of course) there was no need to write it out in detail. It contained self-evident tariff truths. Lincoln either meant to speak from the outline or fill in his sketch as a last task. Thus there are only contours, but they are revealing.

They commenced with the assumption of a "great error in the mode" of past discussions: the tariff debate had concentrated too much on theory and not enough on the real experiences of the nation. The abbreviated notes do not name theory as the culprit, but Lincoln's meaning is clear. To condemn theory was a wise stance because classical thought demanding free trade ruled the scholarship of political economy. Protectionists, though they made some able efforts, had failed to construct an alternative system that was acceptable to the learned.[4] Leading tariff advocates often took the same antitheoretical tack, to which England's Common Sense School lent the authority of philosophy, and which Blackstone, too, reflected faithfully. In any case, Americans "loved the Real" — too much, Dickens grumbled in his *American Notes* — and Lincoln knew that the "test of *experience*," e.g. historical statistics, was likely to appeal more to his constituents than Adam Smith or Jean Baptiste Say.

Accordingly Lincoln proposed to display evidence that protected articles cost less "of labour" when duties were higher than when they were lower. This was his old battle ax from 1844 in considerably more sophisticated form. His desire to measure prices against wage rates implies an understanding of the concept of real wages — what wages would buy on the market place. It also illustrates his adherence to the classical axiom that the value of an article should be weighed by the cost of labor "embodied" in it, as Ricardo had explained. This labor cost theory of value was so widely accepted in America, and seemed so logical to Lincoln, as not to appear to be theory at all.

Still, his outline shows that he expected to go to some length defending the idea. Indeed he wanted to base his entire case on the labor theory, proving through this "single issue of fact . . . the *true* and the whole question of the protective policy." He selected the period 1816-1846 to demonstrate the verity of his contention. He thought the period suitable because it saw duty levies adjusted both up and down, it was one of peace, and it was "sufficiently long to furnish a fair average under all other causes operating on prices."

Such then was the freshman Congressman-elect's prelude to his case for protectionism. His approach was very different from his 1843 recommendation for an American policy that taxed foreign "wines, golden chains, and diamond rings." Lincoln had shown earlier that he could argue economics at several levels. But his consideration of the tariff during these years also demonstrated his capacity to learn and to grow.

The main body of his notes developed the following argument: if goods that were potentially manufacturable in the United States were protected, their prices would be reduced at a "no distant day." How this would come about he did not discuss because the infant industries argument was so commonplace. Lincoln simply took it for granted that his country was as good as any and would be able to produce manufactures as efficiently, in as inviting grade, amount, and price, as England or any other nation.

This was no small assumption, but it allowed him to go directly to an uncommon yet obvious path that led to the home market proposition. Transportation of imported articles, particularly large and heavy ones, was expensive. Under the heading of carrying costs Lincoln also included insurance and other service charges, the middleman's profits, and governmental levies. These expenses could be reduced by shortening the distance between manufacturer and consumer. Protection nurtured native industries, which in turn made goods locally, saving the price of conveyance from Europe. Manufacturers further aided the farmer by promising to create a demand at home for his produce which far exceeded that of the Europeans. Such a home demand also eliminated the expense of distant marketing of bulky agricultural goods. Moreover, having the city mart close by permitted extensive cultivation of perishable fruits and what the twentieth century came to call truck farming.

Lincoln hedged by allowing that, since labor was much cheaper in the Old World than in the New, in some instances the tariff might not be able to produce lower prices. To account for such a failure in the protective policy, he spoke of a wage differential in the ratio of one to four. This estimate, often heard among protectionists, was quite wide of its mark, but even less high wages would outweigh the tariff's effects on prices.[5] Also at stake was the creation of a stable home market for agricultural produce. In view of the paltriness and undependability of the European outlets, Lincoln thought this was very important to the farmer. That the interests of the urban laborers and industrialists were also involved was clear, but his surviving notes did not elaborate on this point. He spoke to the "many," above all the farmer and, at any rate, he was certain that urban segments of the population would fervently support high tariffs.

Lincoln carefully developed the argument of reduced transportation costs, devoting the bulk of his attention to it. He created two abstract case studies, one of which he worked out in two versions. Forever after when he voiced protectionist sentiments, he tended to turn back to them. His point made eminent sense. And by avoiding the important question of the potential of American industries to match those of England, it required only a single plainly academic prop, the labor theory of value.

Lincoln's defense of a variant of this theory began with his most powerful argument: labor created value and justice demanded that the fruit of toil should be the worker's. From this central classical assumption he moved on to even more sharply simplified economics. The "reward of labour" was "perfect," he said, when an article produced in a certain amount of time was exchanged for another that was made in an equal amount of time. Ignoring differences in skill and capital investment, he illustrated the point with the hypothetical trade of agricultural produce, that was the yield of a hundred hours of work, for the articles of the iron maker created in the same length of time. Whether Lincoln oversimplified for the sake of clarity in his illustrations we do not know. But the notion of labor cost measured by time was sufficiently popular in the United

States for Josiah Warren, for example, to establish his famed Cincinnati store, "Time Magazine," and exchange merchandise according to the time consumed in its making.[6]

What is significant here is that in purely economic terms the labor theory was not essential to Lincoln's argument. In terms of his overall vision, however, in terms of the American Dream, it played an all-important role. Lincoln's assignment of a fundamental role to the labor theory makes crystal clear that the moralist in him "never abdicated before the economist."[7] With this definition of value it was easily seen that the cost of transportation was paid from the laborer's just reward. The home market and home industries eliminated much of the *"useless* labour" of transportation to the benefit of *"useful* labour."* Lincoln's *"useless* labour" in this case was really a synonym for unnecessary transportation; and thus, while obviously derived from the more complex and less defensible concept of Adam Smith, it was not identical with it. In economic terms *"useless* labour" was the same as *"idleness,"* Lincoln explained. Thus, as always in his thinking, economics and ethics merged, and free trade turned out to be an unacceptable policy regardless of which of the two was the source of enlightenment.

"To [secure] to each labourer the whole product of his labour, or as nearly as possible, is a most worthy object of any good government," Lincoln noted. "But then the question arises, how can a government best, effect this?" Protection, which eliminated the useless labour of transportation, was one answer. And so Lincoln once again reached what was most essential in his economics. The tariff, like the national bank and internal improvements, was a policy to aid the laboring multitude that wanted to rise. To provide such aid was "a most worthy object of any good government." Thus it becomes plain why Lincoln's preface to his notes claimed that the labor theory contained the "single issue of fact . . . the *true* and the whole question of the protective policy."

Lincoln illustrated his thinking by clear, common examples. American cotton was sold in England, and the cloth made from it was carried back to be sold in the United States. He put the expense of what seemed like a pointless junket at 25% of the total value of goods involved, a very conservative estimate in view of his broad definition of transportation. The conclusion was self evident: why should cotton "not be spun, wove & c., in the very neighbourhood where it both grows and is consumed?" The farmer who raised cotton would thus receive 25% more for his product or buy cloth for 25% less.

Lincoln wrote his tariff notes after the Walker Act had reduced duty levels, and he considered the potential effect of such a "free trading" policy. To maintain his high tone of scholarly inquiry, however, he did not actually mention the Democratic sponsored law. He argued that abolishing protection would instead of cutting the prices of manufactures lead to a retrograde tendency toward a self-sufficient homespun and therefore constricted economy. His argument became a jeremiad with an elegiac description of the desolation of blighted industry: "All is cold and still as death — no s[m]oke rises, no furnace roars, no anvil rings." In effect he overode Ricardo's theory of comparative advantages and pointed to "constant employment," as he labeled it, as a more important goal.

Lincoln's rationale that the tariff created employment was to be found as early as 1767 in Sir James Steuart's *Inquiry Into the Principles of Political Economy*. The argument, like so many others, entered American thinking with the first Secretary of the Treasury. As the country grew more industrialized, the labor argument grew increasingly important. In 1842 Greeley proceeded to publish a monthly "devoted to the course of protection" that bore the name *The American Laborer*. By the middle of the decade, when Lincoln came to work on his notes, the argument was dominating the pro-tariff discussion. Therefore he, too, gave some telling blows with its help.[8]

Lincoln's tariff reasoning reflected a deeply nationalistic orientation. That duty walls could have repercussions on European income and employment which in turn could ricochet on America was beyond his horizon and that of most other protectionists. He applied his concept of transportation as unproductive labor only to regions beyond the borders of the United States; within them he advocated railroads and canals, quite as the outstanding economist Henry Carey would. That bulky goods, too, could earn foreign exchange, in spite of heavy transport charges, he likewise ignored, as did others from Hamilton on.

Lincoln accepted implicitly the dynamic infant-industry arguments, and explicitly the labor argument that made customs duties
the tools of full employment. He emphasized the savings that would
accrue from reduced transport cost through a tariff that brought
pressure for the shortening of routes. Free trade, he believed, led to
a low level of economic life and harmed all Americans. But the prime
beneficiaries of protectionist governmental policy were the "laboring many" whose right to the product of their toil was upheld.

Lincoln's technical expertise can be criticized. He believed that
American grain could never compete with European peasants' well
nigh unpaid for produce. He would champion the mechanization of
agriculture but could not see its potentially great effect on farm
prices. This was consistent with his refusal to acknowledge the same
factor of technological advancement when using statistics to prove
the tariff solely responsible for the reduction of the prices of industrial goods. For such was the protectionist mind.

Lincoln did not specify the products he wished protected, although his illustrations were selected with an eye to reality. He spoke
of cotton goods and coffee, the largest items among imported manufactures and raw foods, respectively, during the thirty antebellum
years. Recent scholarship might question his use of cotton to illustrate the virtues of protection, but he thus made clear that he kept in
sight the interests of the entire United States and not merely certain
regions. He did not indulge in the extremism of the Matthew Carey
variety that demanded agricultural tariffs oblivious to the lack of
necessity for American corn laws. His notes distinguished between
levies on iron and on coffee and thus by implication rejected the
British free trade argument that Alfred Marshall would satirize by
the beginning of the next century: that the same natural laws that
prevented the ex-colonials from raising oranges doomed their efforts to produce complex manufactures.[9]

Lincoln never got around to defining the length of time he expected import barriers to be maintained. At times he implied temporary duties but at others seemed to consider the tariff a "durable"
institution. Nor was he explicit as to the degree of protection. He did
express satisfaction with the measure of 1842, which placed the average percentage of duties at 34.4%, and four years later decried the
Walker Act, which reduced rates to 22.5%. But average rate changes

were not all important and could be offset by structural adjustments. Some of these questions may have received attention in fragments of notes which did not survive. At any rate Lincoln's task was to make a general case for protectionism in easily comprehensible terms. He was not framing legislation nor originating economic theory. His purpose was "to simplify this question," as he stated. This he did honestly and very convincingly. Thus, all in all, he should be no more condemned for technical vagueness than for concentrating only on the single point of "transportation" in the broad protectionist spectrum.

That point, small as it is, tells much about Lincoln's economics. Hamilton had already noted the American losses from the carrying of such bulky goods as cereals to Europe. Subsequent students expanded further his observation.[10] The argument, however, did not attain major importance until Henry Carey developed it fully in the 1850's. The Philadelphia high priest of the tariff shifted the emphasis of the protectionist case to the home market for the farmer and then focused it on the issue of transportation. The direction of his argument, like Lincoln's, presumably issued from a recognition that in a democracy the many ruled and had to be convinced of the virtues of any policy.[11]

In choosing to emphasize this reasoning, Lincoln identified himself with what was about to be the avant-garde of American tariff economics. He displayed his dogged independence as well, for he took a little appreciated skeleton of an argument, confidently developed it on his own, and based his entire case on it. He also furnished evidence of the Anglo-Saxon distaste for the theoretical. "Mr. Lincoln was a very patient man generally," Herndon once wrote, "but if you wished to be cut off at the knee, just go at Lincoln with abstractions. . . . Lincoln's ambition in this line was this: he wanted to be distinctly understood by the common people."[12] It may be argued that a politician could do no less, but few were as successful at the task as Lincoln. From amongst the myriad rationales for the tariff, the Illinois Whig could hardly have gone to his people with a plainer, more common sense argument than the one he chose for himself.

The desire for simplicity and clarity was only one reason for Lincoln's selection and development of the transportation argument. Another was a strong preoccupation, shared by many of his contemporaries, with the large role of transportation in economic life. His early championing of internal improvements foreshadowed his tariff reasoning. Although historians have been unable to provide an accurate evaluation of protection on the American economy, Lincoln's emphasis on the significance of transportation is proved fully justified. In the latter 1840's and in the 1850's the reduction of internal transport costs greatly improved the terms of trade of Western agricultural produce. The same end was furthered by the increasing productivity of eastern industries and the enlargement of the home market, both of which, rightly or not, Lincoln and other protectionists credited to the tariff. The result was the farmer's growing market orientation, along with higher living standards and social mobility — in short a step toward the American Dream.[13]

About a year after the tariff notes were written, Lincoln received a letter from his stepbrother, John D. Johnston, requesting seventy or eighty dollars. Not for the first or last time, Johnston professed a willingness to exchange his place in heaven for such a sum. By now it should little surprise us that Lincoln's reply not only breathed the spirit of his economic outlook but used the very terminology of his tariff notes.

It explained that Johnston's difficulty was that he was "an *idler*." Placed thus in the proper category within the Lincolnian economic framework, the solution was readily forthcoming: "go to work." The labor performed should not be useless, such as attempting to find gold in California (the date of the letter is 1848), but useful, performed right at home in Coles County, Illinois. "And to secure you a *fair reward* for your labor," Lincoln promised to match each dollar thus earned. This might allow Joe Johnston to get ahead in life.[14]

We have noted earlier that Lincoln's thinking also exuded nationalism. Nevertheless his case for a defensive wall of duties was made up of purely economic ingredients, ignoring not only jingoism but all political argumentation. On the one hand this reflected his developing political sophistication which enabled him to eschew the appearance of partisanship in his best efforts. On the other it took part of the tendency of protectionist thinking to move away from the politically oriented tariff policy of Hamilton and the generation that followed him, which had an air of apologia, a call to sacrifice, about it. If by the 1820's Clay came to base his case ever more on economic grounds, considerations of political independence, national welfare, the safety of the Union, and such, were still salient to his thinking. For Lincoln, and somewhat less so for his whole generation, the appeal to economic interest became the judicious stand. Indeed the abandonment of an economics whose ultimate goals were political, for one with frank socio-economic aims, constitutes the basic difference between his political economy and that of the old Whigs.

The economic revolution that came to the United States during the middle third of the nineteenth century, and which coincided with the growth of the nation's political security, produced this change in thought patterns. Americans developed an increasingly candid materialistic outlook even as the memories of the wars against England grew dim and a new emphasis on sectional loyalty arose in their stead. In the case of the tariff it was significant that the country developed a body of protectionist literature that dared challenge classicism. Lincoln thus met the free traders squarely on economic issues. On his eleven foolscap half sheets he did not once mention the name of either political party or allude to patriotism.

Lincoln thus displayed the depth of the training he had been receiving in economic thinking. In part because of that training, he developed a great propensity to see matters in terms of economic ingredients or interests. Never overshadowing his moral perception, and always hedged with persistent attempts to measure the politically possible, this propensity came to loom large when he turned his attention from economics, first to slavery, and later to making war and peace with the South.

For all that, it should be clear that Lincoln was not a systematic thinker on the subject of political economy and only attained an understanding of the outlines of the economic forces at work in his day. The same was true of Biddle and Greeley. But, like them, Lincoln made firm attempts to unveil these mysteries of the new age. Those who were foolish enough to confuse his folksy language with ignorance of economics would have profited from Leonard Swett's comments about Lincoln the lawyer: "Any man who took Lincoln for a simple-minded man would very soon wake up with his back in a ditch." Democratic-minded Secretary of the Navy Gideon Welles made that very mistake during the Civil War. And he had the displeasure of observing much of the Whig economic program enacted — in crucial instances under the President's direct stewardship.[15]

10
The Beautiful
Lonely Science

THE 1840'S BROUGHT LINCOLN TO ECONOMIC BOOKLEARNING, TOO. His tariff notes indicate this and so do the recollections of his law partners. The period of his greatest intellectual growth before the presidency is usually assigned to his years of semiretirement from politics, from 1849 to 1854. Such an emphasis is not unwarranted. Still, much more than periodization should, it contains a distortion of continuity — Edward P. Cheyney's first "law of history." It also ignores Lincoln's most assiduous years of economic study.[1]

John T. Stuart's recollections noted that his former partner "commenced carrying around with him on the Circuit . . . books . . . as early as 1844 and continued to do so down as late as 1853 . . . he read hard books. . . ."[2] Although works on political economy we can be certain constituted a goodly share of these "hard books," the enumeration of the authors that Lincoln studied is a hazardous scholarly undertaking. Such an attempt must fall short of total certainty since the ideas of various economists that he adopted, reshaped, and simplified could have come to him second- or third-hand. In the 1880's in a forlorn attempt to reconstruct Lincoln's reading list, Herndon remembered his partner having looked into James R. McCulloch, James or John Stuart Mill, or both, Henry C. Carey, and Francis Wayland. There were other economists whose names Herndon could no longer recall. Impressionistic as this list had to be four decades after the fact, the last two names mentioned ring very true.[3]

Carey is probably the outstanding protectionist thinker America has produced. The most original of his arguments for the tariff was the same as Lincoln's but was developed more extensively. He wrote much and often to Lincoln after the latter had become President. If Carey's 1835 *Essay on the Rate of Wages* came into his Illinois contemporary's hands, Lincoln found in it many of the economic concepts he later adopted. The *Essay* emphasized statistics; it demonstrated how wages of labor in dollar terms had not risen over the decades but real wages had, for food and clothing had become less costly; it contained the germs of the protariff transportation argument, and the thesis that the security of capital was all important to the advancement of the workingman. In other Carey works Lincoln could have seen demonstrated the identity of the interests of labor and capital; a high valuation placed on banks, particularly the national one; and the independent treasury proscribed. Above all Carey tied protectionism, economic development, and democracy into a knot that few mortals could dare try to undo.[4]

How much of the ponderous Pennsylvanian Lincoln read carefully we are not likely to know. In Springfield his law partner, who had a taste for political economy, owned the largest library in town and Lincoln freely helped himself to its contents. But he very rarely read books thoroughly. He had a tendency to skim; he "peeped into" things. Indeed he "read less and thought more than any man of his standing," Herndon declared somewhat nebulously. Yet when Lincoln did sit down to read a book through he made a study of it. As an old Illinoisan put it: "He didn't read many, but much." Once a challenging idea entered Lincoln's mind he attacked it with great earnestness, in his tariff notes working out a problem three times, until, as he liked to say, the thought was bounded east, west, north, and south.[5]

Lincoln's reading may have been on the whole limited and cursory, but the corpus of his works and also his contemporaries, speak of exceptions to the pattern: Blackstone, the Bible, Shakespeare, and for our purposes Wayland's *Elements of Political Economy*. It is remarkable that in 1886 his former partner still remembered Lincoln's special liking for this by then rather forgotten book.[6]

By the time Lincoln sat down to grind his way through that treatise he had spent a decade and a half studying, discussing, and practicing economics. His learning experience had been desultory, but his general outlook, and more immediately his legislative and electioneering duties demanded that he continuously investigate economic questions. Thus although it may have been true that "politics were his Heaven, and his Hades metaphisics," as Herndon metaphorized, politics had also made Lincoln into quite a political economist. *The Elements of Political Economy* capped his learning.[7]

President Wayland, as he was known to academia, at thirty-one the head of Brown University, was the prototype of the American intellectual, as Lincoln was in many ways of the American generally. In 1837 Wayland published the first edition of *The Elements,* and it rapidly became the country's most popular text in its field. It replaced Say's *Treatise,* which, as economic learning democratized, proved too subtle for the ever broadening audience. Wayland "was struck with the simplicity" of economic principles and accordingly reduced intricate matters to their plain elements. He was an "ideal textbook writer," Joseph Dorfman has noted. The Illinois lawyer and the Providence clergymen shared not only a love of clarity, but also some fundamental assumptions about political economy, and a common Whig faith. Lincoln could hardly have selected a teacher more suitable to him. It was little wonder that this partner saw him take to the Rhode Islander with great enthusiasm.[8]

At the center of Wayland's science was personal property. A logical American consequence of his outlook was the absolute necessity "that every man be allowed to gain all that he can." The book spoke of supply and demand, but the labor theory of value was a more dominant presence in it. Capital was defined as "pre-exerted labor." Wrote the preacher-economist:

> Labor has been made necessary to our happiness. No valuable object of desire can be produced without it. . . . The Universal law of our existence, is, "In the sweat of thy face shalt thou eat thy bread, until thou return to the ground."[9]

Wayland avoided the subject of slavery but allowed that any involuntary exchange between capital and labor, in either direction, was "robbery," and also that man's productive powers were at their highest when performing tasks he was happy with. Paper currency was useful, the BUS praiseworthy, and if banks in general were to serve the community they were not to be interfered with by legislatures. Banking institutions were particularly beneficial to the laboring man who was "improving his condition." The tenets of economic and moral philosophy were "analogous," so "that almost every question in the one, may be argued on grounds belonging to the other."[10]

All this, and more, was very acceptable to Lincoln. He rarely failed to make a moral argument for his economic positions. The importance of property and capitalism; their vitures for the man who wished to "make" something of himself; the benefits of industrialization, credit, and paper money; and hostility toward slavery — these were basic elements of his thinking that received systematic support from his study of Wayland. Several concepts in his tariff notes were in part or whole supplied from this learning: that labor created value, that it had a right to what was so created, that exchange value was influenced by various factors but over the long run it gravitated to labor cost, and that transportation expenses significantly inceased prices. Wayland spoke in his illustrations of goods that were bought with five days of labor, or fifteen, and also used letter symbols to denote different groups of people. Lincoln employed these techniques in his tariff notes and later when discussing slavery.

It is a credit to his mental acuteness and independent mind that Lincoln could "eat up, digest, and assimilate" *The Elements of Political Economy,* as Herndon said, make repeated use of what he thus learned, and yet reach some conclusions diametrically opposite from those of his tutor. There was a salient point of difference in their thinking concerning the role of the government in the economy. One was a classicist, opposed to both government-supported internal improvements, and the tariff, although with many qualifying exemptions and reaffirmations of the merits of industrialization and of a home market. The other subscribed fully to Greeley's "cardinal" Whig principle, "that Government need not and should not be an institution of purely negative, repressive usefulness and value, but that it should exert a beneficient, paternal, fostering influence upon the Industry and Prosperity of the People." Herndon, too, remembered this conflict and wrote that Lincoln liked Wayland's book, "except the *free trade doctrines.*"[11]

On this crucial matter it seems that Lincoln took academic comfort, if such was needed, from Carey. How many other works of political economy he "peeped into," or perchance studied, we do not know. He could hardly have escaped the elder Carey (Matthew) and

Hezekiah Niles of the *Register,* more propagandists than economists, the "Jachin and Boaz of the American System" guarding the temple of protection, as an Illinois newspaper scoffed. One also hopes, not unreasonably, that Lincoln came across a frequently cited work of the 1844 campaign, George Tucker's *Progress of the United States in Population and Wealth, in Fifty Years as Exhibited by the Decennial Census.* The title describes the statistical presentation of this antislavery Virginia Whig who favored the tariff and the national bank. The Illinoisan would have liked much in his writing.[12]

It is very likely that Lincoln read or sampled many other works on political economy. But an attempt to analyze the internal evidence of his speeches and writings and compare it with the works of economists popular in his day leads only to inconclusive results. As for the writers mentioned in addition to Carey and Wayland, by Herndon, on Lincoln's reading list, James Mill and J.R. McCulloch rewrote Adam Smith, and the younger Mill updated classical theory, making it more palatable. Lincoln probably looked into their works. But they left no distinctive marks on him. The "dismal science" of the Europeans, laden with Malthus and Ricardo, was not acceptable to an optimistic young nation. Not many economists and no politicians could preach industrialization in the United States and also accept, for example, an iron law of wages that doomed labor forever to a bare subsistence. The Americans, and few more so than Henry Carey, made political economy the "beautiful science." And so Lincoln "liked" this branch of learning, "the study of it," to quote Herndon again, but it was the native variety that left its impress on him.[13]

That such an impress was made, Lincoln's folksy ways and much celebrated pragmatism notwithstanding, is significant. After all few could afford to ignore abstract thinking as much as a Western politician. John Quincy Adams, to use an illustration, the man who personified the "professor" to Jacksonian America, was happy to express contempt for economic theory.[14] And yet Lincoln learned. He did so, in the final analysis, because political economy was important to his vision of the United States.

More immediately, the mid-1840's found him pressing his "old, withered" eyes, as he described them,[15] into textbooks because the

Whigs were developing an air of exigency. With Clay defeated for the third time, the Mexican War at its height, the slavery issue rising, the subtreasury reestablished, internal improvement bills vetoed, and the Walker Tariff passed, Whiggery seemed to many to be heading for collapse. To the faithful for whom economics were the party's raison d'être it seemed that Armageddon was arriving. It was time to gird for the good fight.

Going to Washington Lincoln transmitted such a feeling of urgency — not totally unwarranted, or unfathomable in an earnest freshman. The first of his lengthy tariff notes had declared starkly that "whether the protective policy shall be finally abandoned, is now the question." In his mind he may already have formulated the hard words he would speak on the floor of Congress: "the question of improvements is verging to a final crisis; and the friends of the policy must now battle, and battle manfully, or surrender all." Lincoln was so sure of the validity of his outlook. He saw the Democratic opposition ever so shortsighted. Wrote the Jacksonians' leading voice in Illinois: "The West is agricultural; it has no manufactures, and it never will have any of importance." Lincoln was rearing for battle. Some other economics-oriented Whigs shared the same urgency.[16]

Indeed, in purely economic terms, the tariff policy in particular seemed to have reached a decisive juncture. The indispensability of stable duty schedules had always been affirmed by protectionists. In 1842, however, levies were abruptly dropped by one-fourth, then ample amends were made a month later when duties were raised to the average level of more than 34%, and four years hence this rate was again reduced by one-third. For the sake of the economy it was imperative that a decision be reached about national policy. If the government hoped to foster development with its wide benefits the tariff could "not be a perpetual subject of political strife, squabbles, charges, and uncertainties," as Lincoln wrote in 1859.[17] Constant changes created a climate of precariousness and were a hindrance to the economy. If the Walker Act was to be struck down, it had to be done promptly or protectionism abandoned for many years.

The issue was clearly drawn. But in spite of this, in spite of the booklearning, in spite of the eleven foolscap halfsheets of tariff notes, if not more, Lincoln could not make a stand on the question in Congress. By the time he took his seat in Washington prosperity had fully returned to the United States. With Polk in the White House

and with a Democratic Senate the prospects for protectionist legislation was nil. Lincoln found even his Whig colleagues mostly unreceptive to tariff discussions. During his term he did vote for feeble
attempts to raise the schedule of 1846. But this was no more than
protest. The tariff issue had been settled for a season. To hold forth
on the subject under these circumstances took a man like "Tariff
Andy" Stewart. The gentleman from Illinois was of a more practical
disposition. He seems to have sent Stewart's speech to his constituents, but his own notes remained unused until 1860.[18]

Indeed on one occasion Lincoln voted for a resolution requesting
the Committee of Ways and Means to consider reciprocal reduction
of French-American duty rates. Like other Whigs, he abandoned
thereby a minute portion of his economic ground, but in 1848 this
was predictable. Below the surface of his economic beliefs was his
growing Dream, a love of democracy and the American way. Eighteen hundred forty-eight was a year of democratic revolutions in
Europe. The Congress of the United States hoped that its gesture
vis-à-vis the tariff would "afford some aid to the spirit of liberty
which was aroused in France." Lincoln perceived the symbolic import of the issue and there could be no doubt on which side his voice
would be heard.[19]

Reluctantly, and temporarily, Lincoln abandoned the fight for the
tariff. Predictably, however, he took up another economic issue. Indeed, even before he went to Washington at the end of 1847, he
became, once again, a leading Illinois spirit of internal improvements. Perhaps because the revived interest in the subject was nonpartisan in the state, he showed little uneasiness on account of his
past role in the System.

Of course the way of the 1830's could no longer be attempted.
Although the Illinois-Michigan Canal was pushed to completion
by 1848, a general renewal of state support was inconceivable. The
Illinois constitution ratified that year went so far as to prohibit completely aid to private companies. Even the vaguest concept of social
overhead capital seemed to escape the vast majority. Further mischief was wrought by practically banning banks as well, somewhat to
Lincoln's surprise. In spite of all, he took to battle for the state's old
improvement hopes.[20]

He contributed to appeals on behalf of the Springfield and Alton

Railroad, for example. These public letters demonstrated much economic and political sophistication, but the most remarkable element in them is an accurate prediction of future business organization. Lincoln and associates saw their railroad as "not merely a local improvement, but a link in one of a great national character," part of a "great chain of improvement" reaching from the prairie to Boston and New York. This "grand" railroad was to be a single business unit. In short, in 1847 Lincoln and colleagues spoke in terms of imminent concentration of capital in giant corporations that had its beginnings in the 1850's and came to dominate the railroad industry in the latter part of the century.[21]

The happy augury of the rise of a large railroad corporation connecting East and West reinforces earlier indications of Lincoln's totally innocent lack of foreboding on such a count. When the logic of efficient economic organization seemed to demand, he accepted the large corporation. No sharp lines existed over the issue either in Illinois or in the national parties. His brethren, Whig and later Republican, at best were only somewhat more favorable than were the Democrats toward corporations. In contrast Lincoln supported corporations unhesitatingly.[22]

"What is the passing [of] an act of incorporation, but the *making of a law?*" he had asked in 1839. His unrealistic attitude stemmed from the desire for economic development on the one hand, and on the other the demagogic attacks of the Jacksonians on the BUS, which obscured more than clarified the important questions arising from corporate organization. That an unbridled growth of large concentrations of capital might occur and either threaten or change the mode of the individual's chance to rise had not yet appeared as a *real* danger in Lincoln's eyes.[23] It is revealing that he did not even fear the influence of wealth on politics. In 1859, warning the yeomen of Kansas that slaveholders might wind up as their leaders, he naively explained that this could come about because planters, "by their greater wealth, and consequent, greater capacity to assist the more needy, perhaps [be] the most influential among you." That the wealthy might reach for leadership through more direct means did not seem worthy of consideration to this Western politician whose campaign chest for the senatorial contest against Douglas came to some hundreds of dollars. As for the Springfield and Alton railroad, by the end of the century it was part of a giant corporation headed by Edward H. Harriman. Lincoln's connection with it was long forgotten.[24]

Before going to Washington Lincoln also attended the Chicago River and Harbor Convention and made his first address to a national gathering on internal improvements in reply to the young David Dudley Field (who would become one of the most outstanding legal minds in America, and earn an international reputation). Although Lincoln's speech does not survive, what his views were, and therefore what he was likely to have said, should be no mystery. Over the decades his basic assumptions about improvements remained unaltered. Indeed, one reading of Field's speech should convince most students that Lincoln's speech on the subject made in the House of Representatives in the summer following was an expanded version of his earlier effort.[25]

The economic goals of the government, Lincoln believed, were never so exclusively "*general,* as not to be of some peculiar *local* advantage," and never "so *local,* as not to be of some general advantage." To illustrate this thesis in 1848 he turned to the Illinois-Michigan Canal, which reduced the price of sugar carried from New Orleans to Buffalo. Sugar, he explained, had formerly reached upstate New York via the Atlantic Ocean and the Erie Canal but now traveled the shorter Mississippi River-Illinois-Michigan Canal-Great Lakes route. The diminished transportation costs helped both seller and buyer, and thus "a benefit" accrued, "not to Illinois where the canal *is,* but to Louisiana and New York where it is *not.*" Although the Prairie State also profited enormously from the federally supported waterway, Lincoln's example of a "local" improvement, which was within the borders of a single state but nourished faraway places in the Union, was most attractive.

For strict constructionist Democrats like Field, or President Polk, such economic arguments were nullified by the unconstitutionality of national funding of local enterprises. Unlike them, Lincoln could not see liberty and democracy threatened by such aid — quite the opposite. Thus ignoring the question of the individual resonsibility of each President, he came to the same conclusion as in the case of the national bank and lesser matters, that economic merit should decide the issue of constitutionality. "I do think no man, who is clear on the questions of expediency, needs feel his conscience much pricked upon this." This, it can be argued, was a cavalier way to treat the fundamental law of the land and, as the nation was to learn, very Lincolnesque.

In some such way, we may infer, Lincoln met Field and then incorporated the material into his big improvement speech in the House, directing it against a president with Field-like views. The twenty-ninth Congress had passed two improvement measures. Polk vetoed the first — catalyzing the Chicago convention and Lincoln's appearance there. Polk disposed of the second bill via a pocket veto but insisted on explaining the action in a message to the following Congress[26] — catalyzing Lincoln's reply there. As above noted, Lincoln's speech debunked Democratic constitutional views as impractical, uneconomical that is. It then went on to challenge the Chief Magistrate's positive recommendations.

Polk attempted to bolster the legalist antiimprovement stand of his party with economic reasoning claiming that federal aid was not vital since tonnage duties could be used to prosecute works. Lincoln answered almost with contempt. He knew that user charges had proved to be valuable, and at one point allowed as much. But he wanted much broader and swifter improvement of the country than Polk, and that demanded national subsidies. Therefore, tonnage duties as a principal reliance would not do.

Another presidential proposal, that the states rather than Washington carry on improvement works, seemed to Lincoln nothing more than the passing of responsibilities. But Lincoln did pay special attention to the Executive's complaint that improvements tended to overwhelm the Treasury because of "undue expansion." He knew this to be the Achilles heel of the matter. He rejected Polk's exaggerated fears, however, noting that the $200,000,000 requested for improvements during the John Quincy Adams administration, cited by the Democratic chief, was not as meaningful as the $2,000,000 actually spent. "The subject is a difficult one," he admitted, but "the improvement of this broad and goodly land, are a mighty interest." It had to be met.[27]

Lincoln also offered a plan of his own. It was simple and

straightforward as his plans nearly always were. Whig or no Whig he refused for now to support a national debt, not even if improvements were the object. "I am against an overwhelming crushing system," he declared. Instead he proposed the adoption of a unified national strategy of improvement. At the beginning of each session he wanted Congress to determine the funds available for the purpose and appropriate no more. In order to allocate the money properly he called for the creation of a federal agency for collecting statistical information.[28] The data thus accumulated was to help legislators to select objectively the most essential improvement projects. He suggested that information concerning surplus products of the various regions, the capacity of each for greater surpluses, the existing transportation facilities and the potential of their improvement, and damages and losses occurring during transportation, and their causes, would be "among the most valuable statistics." In effect he was proposing a plan of national improvement, with a budget, and based on careful statistical evidence. To South Carolina's Robert Barnwell Rhett, who balked at "counting all the pigs and chickens in the land" Lincoln gave short shrift. He could "not perceive much force" in such objections.[29]

It was inevitable that in his discussion of improvements Lincoln would speak of his central ideas. He admitted that there was some truth in the Democratic criticism that Whig economics was a "burthen to the many, and benefit to the few." But he also insisted that the subject be viewed not in selected individual instances but in broad perspective. "The true rule, in determining to embrace, or reject any thing, is not whether it have *any* evil in it; but whether it have more of evil than of good. There are few things *wholly* evil, or *wholly* good." This was particularly true of government policies. Appraised thus, internal improvements served all the people. With a pragmatic man like Lincoln economic policies generally showed more concern with increasing the opportunities of Americans to rise in life than with making certain that those opportunities be exactly equal. He judged that, on the whole, the entire nation benefited thus. But this was one of the rare times during his thirty-three years of public life that he came close to admitting as much.

The Congressman closed his hour-long talk with words that could be included in a text book on developmental economies:

let the nation take hold of the larger works, and the states the smaller ones; . . . what is made unequal in one place may be equalized in another, extravagance avoided, and the whole country put on that career of prosperity, which shall correspond with it's extent of territory, it's natural resources, and the intelligence and enterprize of it's people.

The *New York Tribune* noted the speech and the Illinoisan's great height and concluded that his "intellectual endowments" matched his physical one. The historian, too, must judge that Lincoln presented an able case for improvements.[30] He did not place the President's views in a favorable light, but neither did he misrepresent them. He was totally practical, refused to be drawn into constitutional arguments, or philosophical ones, and ignored Polk's point that government involvement with improvement economics was imprudent on principle. Even when Lincoln stooped to voice a common Whig calumniation concerning the Chief Executive's supposed dawdling, it fit his theme (and proindustrial orientation) and condemned what he saw as Democratic hairsplitting over the Constitution: "An honest laborer digs coal at about seventy cents a day, while the president digs abstractions at about seventy dollars a day. The *coal* is clearly worth more than *abstractions*. . . ."

Lincoln underscored his proimprovements stand by presenting to the House land grant petitions for railroads in his state. He was active in the nonpartisan efforts by the Illinois delegation on behalf of his favorite Northern Cross and other roads. He helped in the attempt to secure rights of way through the public domain. He wrote to an anonymous colleague of his "great personal" interest in the subject, but to no avail.[31]

Lincoln also participated in a determined legislative game over the subject of improvements. The Whigs attached to the general appropriations bill an amendment providing for the removal of obstructions from the Savannah River in Georgia. In the face of a certain veto enough Representatives relented to relinquish the rider, but the gentleman from Illinois was not among them. As a grand gesture the House even passed a new river and harbor bill although its fate was foreordained. Presidential elections were coming up. Politicking became the unabashed order of the day. But again, more was involved. The economic Whigs, however limited their numbers by 1848, were wholly in earnest in wanting to take away from the Chief Magistrate the important decision concerning federal support of improvements and turn it over to the people in a national election. For some, certainly for Lincoln, politics continued to be not only self-seeking but ideal-serving as well.[32]

Such politics formed a main motivation behind Lincoln's improvement speech. In making it he hoped to influence his colleagues, too, but the *New York Tribune's* judgment that his "very sensible" discourse "succeeded" in doing exactly that was too enthusiastic.[33] The central fact was that no amount of talking would pass improvement bills over executive vetoes. The way out of the difficulty was through the upcoming election.

In addition to federal aid for building transportation, lesser economic matters were also considered at the Thirtieth Congress. Lincoln made his maiden effort, "by way of getting the hang of the House," in the interest of administrative frugality, and in opposition to some influential members of his own party.[34] He spoke and voted for economies on other occasions also; dealt with financial matters in his committee work; and listened to protracted discussions of governmental appropriations.[35] He heard David Wilmot of Proviso fame propose direct taxation of personal property, stocks, and money at interest, and predictably voted nay. Yet because this tax would have been levied on slaves also, some Northern Whigs favored it. During his service in the House Lincoln received his first strong indications of the possibility that the question of slavery might disrupt his party.[36]

The potential of the public lands, political and economic, also held some attraction for him. The Mexican War had brought bounty land legislation at the previous Congress. Now, rather aggressively for a freshman, Lincoln maneuvered to have his name attached to the liberalization of these laws. Never forgetting the self-made man, he prepared a "carefully drawn up bill" to assure that officers who began as privates also received lands. He wanted to make the veterans of the War of 1812 eligible, too, and allow the location of an allotment in parcels. He introduced only part of his bill, but others were adopted, too conservative to please Lincoln fully. Not until its next meeting did Congress include in its coverage the soldiers of 1812. In later years it added further extensions.[37]

The close-fisted Whig policy on the public domain never had

Lincoln's allegiance. For some time now he had read Greeley's pleas for free homesteads and during his second session he saw the difficult New Yorker introduce legislation to that end. Andrew Johnson and Elisha Embree of Indiana, too, produced free land bills. Only one resolution, that of Lincoln's old Democratic foe John McClernand, required a recorded vote:

> *Resolved.* That the present traffic in the public lands should cease, and that they should be disposed of to occupants and cultivators on proper conditions, at such a price as will nearly indemnify the cost of their purchase, management, and sale.

Here, too, was a long step toward the homestead concept, and it was accordingly tabled. But Lincoln voted nay.[38]

All the same he retained his preferences that subordinated matters agrarian and was ready to compromise his support of low land prices for federal aid to improvements. The question of granting alternate sections of the public domain for railroad use and then doubling the price of the reserved federally owned sections as a compensation to the government was debated repeatedly in the House. Many Westerners, like Caleb B. Smith of Indiana, Chairman of the Committee on Territories, opposed such an arrangement because they wanted uniformly inexpensive land. Not Lincoln. He realistically reminded his future cabinet officer that

> . . . the question appeared in a different aspect to persons in consequence of a difference in the point from which they looked at it. It did not look to persons residing east of the mountains as it did to those who lived among the public lands.

He himself favored low prices. Yet if Congress demanded the opposite for reserved sections in exchange for donating alternate sections, Lincoln would go along. Not that he acquiesced in the justice of this, for internal improvements enhanced the value of the retained public lands, too, to the considerable profit of the Treasury. More important, the national government gained "by the general good which the people derived" from such works. But Lincoln would rather bargain with the old states than reform them; he thought chances of success infinitely greater thus. And he was willing to pay a logical Eastern price for federal aid to improvements.[39]

At the second session of the Thirtieth Congress Lincoln had the pleasure of voting for the establishment of the Department of Interior. He also continued, in spite of his lame duck status and lack of success, to work for federal aid to internal improvements, including the Illinois Central Railroad.[40] When Vinton of Ohio, husbanding the traditional Whig land policy, assailed a railroad grant bill on the grounds that the states might often leave such allotments unused and allow speculators to take them over, Lincoln was hard pressed not to show scorn for this leader of his party. In the end he tried patient reason: since they were considering a bill that made railroad surveys prerequisite to grants, he explained that no state would suffer the large expense involved in such work unless it had serious intentions. State governments functioned like businessmen, and like "men who have money were disposed to hold on to it, unless they could see something to be made by its investment." "That was all he desired to say," and even that, as so much of his Congressional labors, was for naught.[41]

Lincoln charted a clear record in Washington on economic questions. He favored a substantial protective tariff even though, as the Democrats repeatedly pointed out, this deterred the building of railroads somewhat.[42] He opposed direct taxation, a large national debt, and a free hand for the government in its regular expenditures. At the same time he desired large scale internal improvements, federally directed, at federal expense. On the question of the public domain he continued to follow his own liberal views. Yet just as he would suffer slowing the progress of internal improvements in order to obtain the varied benefits of the tariff, so he would give ground on the public lands to obtain federal backing of improvements. Thus he provided a fair measure of his economic priorities. Federally supervised banking, perhaps through a Bank of the United States, was the only policy close to him that he did not speak out on. His private notes, however, indicate that he was merely waiting for a propitious occasion.[43] Finally, Lincoln stood for free labor and against slave labor — a fact that, as we will consider shortly, was becoming increasingly important to his fundamental faith that he served the laboring many of America. Yet, for the moment, perhaps the most startling development of this, his first stay in Washington, was a substantial change in the priorities of his politics. The United States were at war.

11

God's Political Economy

UNTIL LINCOLN'S ARRIVAL IN THE NATION'S CAPITAL IN THE WINTER
of 1847 the enticing promises of political economy made up the central interest of his political career. He never abandoned the fundamental assumptions of that interest, democracy, economic development, the right to rise. But in Congress Lincoln began to shift his
attention from specific questions of economics. The shift was ac-
tuated, in conjunction with the constant influence of ever changing
politics, by the rise of an overriding issue of morality. This factor,
tempered with practicality, had always occupied a pivotal role in his
thought. There is much truth in Herndon's estimate that his partner
"stood bolt upright and downright on his conscience."[1] It was on
such basis that Lincoln championed his economic policies, but they
were generally long-term policies, and when a more immediate
question with a large moral ingredient had to be settled, economics
took a back seat. The first time this occurred during the Mexican
War.

Lincoln's opposition to the war was propelled by a complex array
of factors that need not be examined here.[2] He voiced that opposition in purely moral terms, objecting to his country provoking an
unnecessary war and attempting to aggrandize itself at the expense
of a weak neighbor. He did not speak of any of the other ingredients
of his antiwar position, and matters economic were included in his
silence: their partisan hue of long standing would have weakened his
exclusively moral stance.

Yet those matters could not but play a considerable, if somewhat
curious, role in Lincoln's thinking. Expansion promised major

137

economic benefits. These he failed to acknowledge. The failure was independent of the moral and political imperatives that precluded his support of expansionism in the Mexican War. Americans may have seen in the conquest of the West a "sublime spectacle of God's political economy," as William Alexander Caruther's Nathaniel Bacon did in *The Cavaliers of Virginia*. But this god of economic interest and Manifest Destiny spoke not to Lincoln.

It is not impossible that his attitude had roots in his personal history. He had seen his father track West, ever further West, and fare ill again and again. Although thus Lincoln too was a Westerner, he showed no great admiration for his country's gigantean westward movement. When stepbrother Johnston wrote in 1851 of his latest plans to move, Lincoln replied in an almost angry tone that the "notion is utterly foolish." He could not see the necessity of following the setting sun:

> If you intend to go to work, there is no better place than right where you are; if you do not intend to go to work, you can not get along any where. Squirming & crawling about from place to place can do no good.

Lincoln made America's Protestant work ethic and her westering lust into antipodes for his stepbrother and opted emphatically for the former. When a few years later he read in George Fitzhugh how "in forty-eight hours laborers may escape to the West and become proprietors," he knew from personal experience that the Virginian was wrong. Even in the White House he retold common anecdotes with the moral that moving three times was worse than having one's home destroyed by fire.[3]

Whatever personal experience had to do with Lincoln's lack of enthusiasm concerning the relentless movement West, his economic outlook carried an aura that sharply clashed with expansionism. Unlike a majority of his countrymen, he did not confuse geographical and social mobility. Tariff, central banking, internal improvements, even his blurred stance on the public lands, bespoke an inward-looking orientation, a desire for internal instead of external development. Perhaps he was not as much against territorial expansion *per se,* as he was in favor of concentrating the people's energies *within the country,* to make *it* flower, to build *it* up. Major L. Wilson spoke of this Whiggish attitude as support for "vertical development in time" and contrasted it to the Democratic hunger for "horizontal development in space." His phraseology is especially happy when applied to a mind which was developing a central allegiance to the right to rise.[4]

One of Lincoln's early arguments for protectionism and against excessive importation illustrates well this frame of mind. He announced categorically in 1843, as the United States stood flexed on the threshold of another gigantic leap westward, that the country was already "extensive enough . . . to answer all the real wants of its people." And in 1860 he exulted to New Englanders, having seen the fruits of the economics he had been preaching: "You have a soil that scarcely sprouts black-eyed beans, and yet where will you find wealthy men so wealthy, and poverty so rarely in extremity? There is not another such place on earth!"[5]

Two Lincoln tutors, Wayland and Carey, spelled out, among others, the harmful effects of too speedy expansion on industrialization and development. The Illinoisan accepted their learning when it came to Manifest Destiny, even though he refused to go as far as his party and apply it to public land policies. Yet even for the farmer he favored intensive cultivation instead of the prevalent practice of working larger and larger acreage. Speaking on the subject to a Wisconsin audience, he forecast in 1859 that "ere long the most valuable of all arts, will be the art of deriving a comfortable subsistence from the smallest area of soil." These were the words of a man who took small part of the expansionist ethos.[6]

If Lincoln's outlook was, to an extent, a reflection of the inward-oriented Whig mind, as such it was exceptionally steadfast. In Illinois the other outstanding Whig leaders, like Hardin and Baker, could be readily quoted on both sides of the expansion issue, depending on the political exigencies of the moment. On the national level Webster, for example, looked with interest to California, and J.Q. Adams and Seward cast covetous eyes beyond.[7]

Lincoln understood the unacceptability of his sentiments to much of his state and said little on the subject. Yet in the 1830's he ignored Texas, Alamo and all, except for labeling it, once, a foreign land "where a villain may hope to find refuge from justice." In the following decade, while expansionism mounted to frenzy in Illinois, he explained that he was "never much interested" in the Texas question. In 1844 he opposed annexation. In 1846 he refused to support a forceful stand on Oregon. In 1848 he took an advanced position against the Mexican War and realizing that some land acquisition was unavoidable, labored to minimize it, and then tied it to the aggravation of the slavery dispute. When Democrats accused him of wanting to return to Mexico the bounty of the Treaty of Guadalupe Hidalgo, he made no denials. In 1858, when pressed by Douglas, Lincoln declared he was not against "honest acquisition of territory" in principle. This was as close as he ever came to appearing to endorse in plain words expansion. But as there no longer seemed to be any would-be purveyors of unoccupied land on the continent, except perhaps in Alaska, to meet his standard of "honest acquisition," and there had not been any since early in the century, his concession was meaningless. In 1859 he made a bittersweet attack on Manifest Destiny and ridiculed Jackson's notion of the "extension of the area of freedom." In 1860 when Duff Green visited the President-elect to urge sectional compromise, one of the reasons for his refusal was the fear of renewed attempts to annex Mexico. And when a Canadian envoy came to his White House to measure annexation pressures there, he came away so reassured about the President that he felt justified shelving his concern about Secretary of State Seward. Thus during the Civil War, when Francis Blair, Sr., proposed to reunite the country via a joint Union-Confederate attack on Mexico, he could hardly have selected a less sympathetic listener than a Chief Executive who sent former senator Thomas Corwin, of Mexican War protest fame, as his minister to Mexico.[8]

Lincoln's lack of enthusiasm about expansion may have been shortsighted in economic terms, but in 1848 it was propped up by the connections Whigs saw between their economic principles and the Mexican War. Justin H. Smith has argued that the opposition to the war was concocted in part to delay military measures and force Polk to return to a higher tariff.[9] There indeed was a widespread Whig fear that Southwestern encroachment would seal the fate of the party's policies and of the party itself. Lincoln could carefully digest Webster's remarks concerning the "timely" appearance of Texas senators at the Twenty-ninth Congress. They tipped the balance and overthrew the tariff of 1842, "the best system of revenue ever established in this country." The Bay State senator warned that in the future colleagues from California and New Mexico might present themselves to assist in the economic ruination of the nation, and if necessary, the Mexican provinces of Sonora, Tamaulipas, and who knows what might be enlisted.[10]

Greeley went further in the discovery of evil designs and added internal improvements to the tariff as one of the real targets of the Democratic warmakers. It was equally plain that if the United States were to move again in the direction of centralized banking, the representatives of New Mexico, or perchance Sonora, were not likely to help. Such Whig alarms at times became bipartisan when the war was identified with large-scale land speculators whom Lincoln had combated since the beginning of his career. To some the Mexican War was an extension of what Greeley had called the "Texas iniquity." When the first shots were fired, Democratic Senator John A. Dix threw up his hands and moaned: "The whole thing is the work of speculators and bankrupts."[11]

Lincoln strongly desired immigration into Illinois and was unhappy about emigration from there. The annexation of Texas had already brought groans that the best of the Illinoisans were leaving for the new country. The historian of the state's agriculture for this period saw farming as the caricature of what it might have been because of the "foot-looseness" of the population. One may go further and see the Mexican War to some extent as the fruit of the ethos of the American farmer, as William Appleman Williams does. Lincoln did not share that ethos, nor did he fully understand it. It was consistent therefore that he opposed its manifestation in the war. It is also possible to look upon expansionism as an expression less of destiny than of classical economics. Williams argues thus by identifying Adam Smith's lesson about the division of labor and the extent of the market place with geographical growth. To the degree Lincoln might have perceived matters in such light he again had to say no. [12]

Economic development demanded peace. It also required England's friendship, which was sorely threatened by America's expansionist penchant. Lincoln knew the importance of British capital. He was appealing for investments in the Sangamon and Alton Railroad as Scott marched on Mexico City. Indeed many business men, rightly or wrongly, were not enamored of America's martial exploits. Thus there were plentiful specific, short-term economic reasons, too, for Lincoln's pacific posture, even the discourse in Wayland's text on the vast wastefulness of war. In the House the gentleman from Illinois sat on the Committee on Expenditures in the War Department and could mull over these matters. In the end, however, he left the economic arguments all unsaid, and took his stand on more universal and unimpeachably nonpartisan moral grounds. His stance was both good politics and a good intellectual decision.

Thus, in opposing the Mexican War, for the first time Lincoln left his politics of economics for another substantial road. He could console himself with the belief that his war opposition was consistent with his economic convictions. Still, his stand demonstrated that the proper moral stimulus could redirect his politics — if not his underlying moral assumptions. And although Lincoln also hoped to distinguish himself thereby, he was fully justified in subordinating economic matters to his antiwar stand. Not very surprisingly, however, what followed was a sharp, less justified, and at first only half-conscious, subordination of these principles to political expediency as well.

Eighteen forty-eight was a presidential year, and Lincoln's candidate was Zachary Taylor, old soldier and no politician. Lincoln settled on him not because of vain notions that he would make an outstanding president, but rather on account of what the Democrats derided as the "General Availability" of the Hero of Buena Vista. Greeley for one felt the party could not "with any decency support Gen. Taylor," and it was realistic to see the Whig military boom as the yielding of principle for expediency. But Lincoln refused to see matters thus.[13]

Lincoln had a strong devotion to principle and also a strong desire to be victorious and came to see the nomination of "Old Zach" as the only way to neutralize the war issue. He saw much justice in catching the war hero as his party's candidate. He believed that the Democrats had provoked the Mexican conflict in part for political reasons, and the Whig gambit, he wrote Herndon, turned "the war thunder against them. The war is now to them, the gallows of Haman, which they built for us, and on which they are doomed to be hanged themselves."[14] Such ingenious solution would also allow devoting the canvass to the real issues of Whig economics instead of to explanations of an antiwar stand.

Lincoln realized that the old soldier was quite apolitical and reluctant to speak out on issues. But he also had reasonable assurances that his candidate supported Whig economic policy and would be persuaded to take up their defense. Preparing for the Illinois stump, or perhaps merely idling away time, he started jotting down thoughts for suitable Taylor pronouncements. In these notes he used the suggestive format, "were I president."[15]

The vast majority of Whigs firmly believed that the tariff was not then a viable cause, but the national debt bred by the Mexican War quickly rekindled Lincoln's hopes and that of some others as well. To have Old Rough and Ready rekindle protection was just too good an opportunity to forego. And so Lincoln decided it was best for Taylor to take a firm stand and announce upward tariff adjustment with "due reference" to home industries as "indispensable."

Lincoln faced a more troublesome matter in the national bank. He knew the extent of Jacksonian success on this issue. He did not have to wait until the Philadelphia convention to know that his own party could not be made to champion the centralization of banking. Indeed the only banks that would be mentioned in the Whig platform were the green banks of the Mississippi River. Therefore, he compromised some, noting that he would not urge the "reagitation" of the question by Taylor. He nonetheless expected his party's standard-bearer to declare squarely that the first and second Banks of the United States had been constitutional, and should Congress establish another such institution the Whig president would say amen. In view of his party's complete abandonment of the Bank, to the point where the name itself had been banned from the Whig language, Lincoln's unpolitican-like devotion to principle deserves emphasis.

On the problem of expansion, too, he thought a Taylor declaration in order. In the Mexican peace "we shall probably be under a sort of necessity of taking some territory," he wrote. So much should not be taken, however, as to "agrivate the distracting question of slavery."[16]

The Congressman-stand-in-for-president did not finish his notes. At some point before he reached the discussion of internal improvements, the issue he judged most suitable for the 1848 campaign, he came to realize that Taylor would be committed only to the principle of the sparse use of the veto, and no more. Economic policies, the substance of Lincoln's Whiggery, would be ignored. By the time Lincoln perceived what kind of candidate he had espoused, he had thoroughly committed himself to Taylor both in Illinois and in Washington. Backing out would have been well nigh impossible. Lincoln no doubt felt like Seward, who bemoaned the emasculation of "the virtue of our party" but, like his future Secretary of State, he toed the line and went to the work at hand. Even holdouts like Greeley and Webster came around, at least halfheartedly.[17]

Lincoln knew that when Clay had been the Whig candidate four years earlier principles had been upheld only weakly. Since the Great Compromiser had helped his party onto the road of no principles, Lincoln may have even seen a measure of retribution in the Taylor nomination. At any rate, he could take satisfaction in vice-presidential nominee Millard Fillmore. This New Yorker seemed to be a solid economic Whig: the father of the Tariff of 1842, backer of the Tyler aborted Fiscal Bank of the United States, and delegate to the Chicago River and Harbor Convention.[18]

In the face of Taylor's silence and the Philadelphia nonplatform, Lincoln fell back on the views of his friend A.G. Henry, who argued that asking an avowed Whig to endorse specific policies "implies a distrust of his honesty and sincerity." "No Whig can be opposed" to protectionism, internal improvements, a sound currency, and economy in government. Lincoln had already subscribed to this specious reasoning in the fall of 1847 while biding his time until Taylor came out fighting for Whig principles. When the General refused to budge and the party ratified his silence, Lincoln made the temporary expedient do for the entire campaign.[19]

Lincoln's stand was not a mere matter of lusting after the rewards of politics, although that was part of it. Paradoxically, precious principles were involved, too. The economic policies he fought for were sorely endangered and much needed presidential acquiescence. Even from the vantage point of principle the General was a better man, as Lincoln wrote, "than Polk, or Cass, or Buchanan, or any such creatures, one of whom was sure to be elected" unless Taylor was. Yet such thinking sadly implied that the Whigs had failed to get their message across, that their policies were not viable enough to be carried to victory by party regulars, at least not in 1848.[20]

Thus when Lincoln went through with his support of the old soldier, he finally succumbed to the Whig disease of attempting to bring their principles to triumph through the back door. Not unreasonably he thought the front door could be opened more easily from inside the White House. The doughty bank champion of 1840, the upright tariff Whig of 1844, had been mellowed by defeats. For the first time since he had entered politics Lincoln embarked on a campaign almost empty-handed.

The Congressman made a fine internal improvements speech on the floor of the House and condemned in it not only Polk but the new Democratic nominee Lewis Cass as well. But alas he dared not mention Taylor's name. He perhaps hoped that his speech would become the keynote of the Illinois campaign, but it took another full-hour, pamphlet-length effort to defend Old Zach's reticence on "the prominent questions of Currency, Tariff, internal improvements, and Wilmot Proviso." In this speech Lincoln insisted that his candidate's announced refusal to veto economic legislation made Whig principles safe, by no means an entirely unreasonable assumption, as long as the party's sentiments held sway in Congress. He characterized Taylor's stand as straightforward and censured Cass's reluctance to elaborate on the anti-improvement plank of the Democratic platform. He charged that the Michigan Senator "well understood he was to be claimed by the advocates of both sides of this question," but he remained silent to "retain the benefits of that double position." Lincoln's analysis was no doubt correct, but it took considerable gall to acclaim Taylor and condemn Cass in the same breath for the same sin.[21]

The wily campaigner also managed to mention the national bank, in an offhand fashion but not without Whig effect: to illustrate the importance of the conservative use of presidential power, he cited Washington's refusal to veto the First Bank. He considered slavery and the Wilmot Proviso only to amplify Cass's vacillation. He raised the specter of a spendthrift administration even while implying that the Democratic aspirant was comparable to a "listless ox." The highlight of the effort came with the mockery of Cass's military career, this much to the amusement of the House, and earning the *Baltimore*

American's appraisal that his was the "crack speech of the day."[22] Thus Lincoln descended to the lower levels of empty stump politicking, which he had mostly avoided until now. It was the ultimate consequence of his acceptance of Taylor's nomination. Yet what is most noteworthy about this, in so many ways uncharacteristic speech (the weakest in substance up to this point in the surviving Lincoln corpus), that many later scholars took it as a display of the quintessential Lincoln before the slavery controversy.

Once Lincoln left Washington the campaign trail breathed some fresh life into him. He succeeded in putting more solidity into his speeches without straying from the Taylorian confines. It was no inconsiderable feat to uphold Whig principles while having to rely on the platform of a disinclination to use the veto. Lincoln generally attempted this via the earnest censure of the Democratic abuse of power that struck down laws passed "for the good and prosperity of the country." That his full meaning was not lost on the audiences was illustrated when after a talk he was characterized as "a high protective Tariffite."[23]

The Congressman's invitation to Massachusetts for a speaking tour provided the first wider recognition of his ability to communicate with folk of strong moral leanings. In the Bay State the movement for free soil had split the Whigs between the conscience and cotton factions, threatening the loss of the region for the party.[24] Lincoln's speeches marshalled a two-pronged attack aimed at defectors. On the one hand, he argued that the Whigs were still the same old party that he liked to think they had always been. The tariff, bank, and other orthodox principles could be carried to glorious fruition with Taylor in the White House. Those who felt the magnetism of Whig economics were thus bid to stay within the fold. On the other hand, and more importantly for New England, and increasingly for Lincoln, too, he affirmed that his party opposed the expansion of slavery as firmly as did the Free Soilers. A vote for Taylor he saw as a true, meaning "practical," antislavery vote; that for the new party as mere protest and an aid to Cass and slavery's extension. He pointed out that Van Buren, now the Free Soil nominee, was an old foe who had only one right principle, that on slavery. The implication was plain: the ex-Democrat had the wrong view of economics. It was in such fashion that Lincoln managed to adopt the central Whig argument of the campaign, that the support of Van Buren actually succored Cass, to his economics-oriented Whiggery.[25]

The exigencies of the times prodded him into a new definition of his party's faith. Whigs were those, he said, "who wished to keep up the character of the Union; who did not believe in enlarging our field, but keeping our fences where they are and cultivating our present possessions, making it a garden." The government, of course, would have to be devoted to these purposes which aided the people, the many. This was as good a Whig platform as Taylor's candidacy would bear. It stood against both the extension of slavery and expansionism, and endorsed positive economic action, at least to those who wished to find such policies in the party. It might have served the Whigs better than the nonplatform adopted at the Philadelphia convention that nominated the General.[26]

Lincoln went home for the last of the campaign, "can not something be done, even in Illinois?" he asked, and, though he really did not think so, served as an assistant elector. He continued to show, as one newspaper reported, "that the peace and prosperity of the country, and the limitation of slavery depended upon the election of a Whig Congress and Gen. Taylor."[27] In one debate his Democratic opponent asked him why did he not simply come out for the Free Soilers? Lincoln replied that he would not mind doing so were it not for "other questions" of disagreement between the two parties. Pressed for an amplification of these differences, and hampered by Taylor, he still implied that internal improvements were one such matter. This obviously hurt the Democrats in Illinois, for his adversary immediately raised the question of Lincoln's antiwar stand. And thus the canvass came to an end. The Congressman's "noblest Roman of them all" triumphed, but as he suspected, nothing could be done in Illinois.[28]

Lincoln only made a temporary concession in 1848 to the Whig malady of weak attachment to principles. But that had long-term results. Since Taylor's sole avowed position was a disavowal of the overuse of the veto power, Lincoln had to fit his economic policies into such a framework. The effort changed the substance of his Whiggery. It may be that he had always shared to an extent his party's antagonism to the broad use of presidential power that began with Jackson. One suspects the contrary, however. The concept of a sharply circumscribed executive, a central doctrine of the Whig faith, did not attract him sufficiently before 1848 so much as to pay lip service to it even once as far as the record indicates.[29] Indeed in 1849, writing about minor matters to Secretary of State John M. Clayton, Lincoln revealed, in private, a major political tenet of his own when he warned against "fixing for the President the unjust and ruinous character of being a mere man of straw. This must be arrested, or it will damn us all inevitably." He even committed the ultimate sin for a Whig by pointing to the lesson about strength to be learned from the arch enemy. " 'By the Eternal;' 'I take the responsibility.' Those phrases were the 'Samson's locks' of Gen. Jackson's."[30]

An economic aura, above all had attracted the young Lincoln to the Whigs, not their wails about the terrors of King Andrew I. But in 1848, with Taylor the Whig nominee, the only route he saw open to upholding economic principles was through a *partial* support of his party's attitude toward the presidency. Lincoln's marriage to this Whig policy was thus one of necessity, but he was an earnest man, had always been one, and always would be one. He could not espouse any policy unless he managed to convince himself of its wisdom. As a consequence his marriage to the Whig view of the presidency became also one of conviction, which he kept on nurturing through the antebellum years. The large fruits this bore became evident after 1861. Even when Lincoln became the strongest executive since Jackson, indeed perhaps in all of American history, in his relationship with Congress and his Cabinet he remained exceedingly reserved. In effect he became in part what David Donald perceptively called "a Whig in the White House."[31]

The presidency was still far off. Now, with the election and his own congressional career finished, he went home to handle the chore of patronage. He tried hard to be fair. But applicants often realized that he might give special consideration to those in need. Accordingly, aspirants for his favor were wont to stress that they were poor, out of health, or excessively prolific — although these qualifications did not always secure appointments. If the Whig lawmaker helped some of these men more than their due, it was not only a reflection of his humanity but also of his conception of an active government whose duties include charity.[32]

Lincoln himself made a hesitant try for the office of land commissioner and was supported, among others, by Congressman "Tariff Andy" Stewart. Lincoln's economic persuasion, however, made him ill-suited for the job. Nor had he changed his derisive view of, specifically, the land offices, which in 1839 he labeled "the great gulf by which all, or nearly all, the money" in the West was "swallowed up."[33] As it turned out another got the office. The governorship of Oregon Territory was offered to him, but Lincoln had done all the westering he would, and his wife felt that way too. They stayed in Illinois.

He was now a discontented man. He had gone forth from Illinois to make his mark, well prepared to fight for Whig principles as he understood them. Instead he had fought against an aggrandizing war and then for "Taylorism," as he called it, Whiggery camouflaged in a military coat. He thought this was still the same old party, with the same "black cockade federalism," as he jested. Economic beliefs were still the heart of his allegiance. Yet in 1848 he had found himself beginning to speak, in Illinois as well as in Massachusetts, mostly about slavery. Slowly he began to focus on the relationship between this institution and his developing Dream for America. God's political economy had wrought changes indeed.[34]

War, election, distribution of spoils, party infighting all consummated in due course, Lincoln was eager to get back "on grounds of *measures* — policy — where," he wrote, "we can unite & rally again." But he had to add: "At least I hope so." Room for doubt there was plenty. A correspondent of Judge Davis noted pensively:

> As you say queer things are being developed these days. I *phrophicy* a total loss in the fog soon of the old Whig and Democratic parties — "old things will pass away and all things become new."[35]

Lincoln's platform in 1848 — his party had none — stood for the containment of slavery and for Whig economics. After one of his speeches which thus held the fort a Massachusetts Free Soil newspaper concluded its report by outlining clearly a new political program: to stop slavery, it argued, the North must unite; to do so old party lines had to be erased; such goals could not be attained "unless every man is willing to sacrifice his attachment to minor questions and make opposition to slavery the leading idea."[36] This Lincoln was quite unwilling to do, unwilling because of party loyalty, because of fear of the slavery issue, and also because the "minor questions" to Free Soil were major ones to him. He had dedicated his entire career to them. They were intimately tied to his conception of what the United States was and would be. He was not ready to abandon his economics.

Retired from Congress his disheartenment grew. By the early 1850's Herndon saw him undergo a personal crisis. Both in Lincoln's face, and underneath, he saw the emerging of a "changed man." In retrospect the younger lawyer explained the transformation via his partner's opposition to the Mexican War. Lincoln's stand had proved so unpopular in Illinois as to appear to put an end to his political aspirations. It thus brought on his reformation — away from politics.[37]

What Herndon espied on Lincoln's dark face (in addition to the mental change perhaps all men go through with age) was defeat, real defeat, albeit not so direct a one as he believed. One of its major sources was the changing tone of American politics that made Lincoln's life-long cause, and his party allegiance, seemingly ever less viable. Related to this was a second matter. Until his term in the House of Representatives his career had spiraled, with fits and starts but steadily upward. Congress turned out to be an unsatisfying experience, reaching a humiliating climax in the futile pursuit of spoils: a federal office. And so at last, after two decades of no small personal progress, Lincoln had to acknowledge the bitter truth that in politics he could rise no higher.

The Senate of the United States was attractive to him and perhaps the governor's chair, too. Yet no Whig had ever been victorious in a state-wide contest in Illinois. There were no longer even false glimmers of a prospect for change. Lincoln saw the Dream as a central quest not only for his people but also for his own self. His 1860 statement that "I hold the value of life is to improve one's condition," was both a declaration of national policy and a personal confession. In the early 1850's, however, he saw no attractive road open to join in the work. Blocked from further advancement, he turned to the legal profession "more assiduously than ever before." Law offered room to rise in; public life did not. As the years went on, he even began "losing interest in politics."[38]

Law was one of the decisive battlefields of the nineteenth century on which the partisans of economic development conquered their tradition-minded foes. When Lincoln reached a seeming end in politics, it might be assumed that he had the choice of continuing his long labors in his profession. Law appeared to offer "a superior opportunity" not only to be a good, peacemaking man, as he wrote, but, more importantly for the purposes of this study, also the opportunity to help accommodate the country's legal system to a growing new economy.[39]

Lincoln's practice, coupled with a deep commitment to economic development, taught him the need for a law that was evolving. He noted while preparing a railroad case: "*Legislation* and *adjudication* must follow, and conform to, the progress of society." His entrance in earnest into his profession coincided with the heightening in Illinois of the legal battle for the release of the economic energies of the people. Yet inviting as this road was it could not be taken by Lincoln.[40]

The workings of his mind account in part for this state of things. Lincoln was not a consciously innovating, or an abstract thinker — qualities demanded by the role of the creative attorney. Reinforcing such a lack was the fact that his true calling was politics. Law was a road to it and to a living. As a young attorney he had to work hard to make ends meet. By the 1850's it had been thoroughly ingrained in him to accept any case that had a legal foot to stand on. This, at any rate, was the common ethic of lawyers. Nearly all worked for fees instead of the triumph of personal convictions. Thus Lincoln's wonderful bias toward morality did not always receive free play in the courtroom, nor his strong impulse to promote his economic vision. Had he possessed the prerequisite mental make-up, it would still have been a formidable task for him to change his ways in the 1850's.

If most of Lincoln's notable courtroom successes that had economic bearings came when his client's case and his own convictions coincided, this is not surprising. He was only human and more sensitive than most. Some of his suits helped move the United States, in small ways, in the direction he wanted her to move. He repeatedly defended the greatest internal improvement of his region, the Illinois Central, sometimes in very significant lawsuits, and at times when it was not the popular thing to do. He established the right of railroads to restrict their liability in Illinois, thus reversing common law precedent. He set another local precedent by forcing a delinquent railroad stockholder to pay up on his stock although subsequent to his purchase the road's route was changed to his disadvantage by the state legislature. Lincoln also nullified the first known successful attempt in Illinois to circumvent the rule of competitive bidding. He helped establish the right of railroads to build bridges over navigable rivers without having to face nuisance judgments. In these and in lesser cases he contributed to the creation of what Willard Hurst described as a dynamic American consensus, "that it was common sense, and it was good, to use law to multiply the productive power of the economy."[41]

Lincoln's study of political economy was useful in his legal practice, and vice versa. His suits gave him a close acquaintance with many of the day-to-day problems spawned by the economics he advocated. On occasion his exalting vision of the future could be given employment at his trials. Yet he also gave the devil his due. He opposed railroads regularly, including the Illinois Central, and sometimes did so over startling issues. Once, for example, he argued with some success that building a bridge over a navigable river was a nuisance and a hazard to water traffic, his case running totally contrary to his own economic convictions as well as another one of his suits, aforementioned.[42] Thus, although his legal work at times reveals a mastery of the beautiful science, it gives no witness to his dreams.

After Lincoln became a Republican, and his party came to power in Illinois in the late 1850's, he advised the state government as an attorney on various economic issues. He provided opinions on banks, taxes, on the state's internal improvement debt, and on other matters. He demonstrated fully that his basic views had remained intact. Had his work been in the public eye, it might have caused considerable political controversy. But it was not, and otherwise it had little intrinsic significance. A few years earlier such work would have been very important to him. It was no longer so. The United States had entered a new era — what later historians would call the Age of Lincoln. The conflict over slavery became the order of the day.[43]

Book Two

12

The Fruit of Labor

AS THE MISSOURI COMPROMISE WAS SWEPT ASIDE, SO WERE THE Whigs and their economic policies, in the language of the Bible, "as corn blasted before it is grown up." In place of the old party a powerful new organization was created, dedicated to a single immediate goal: preventing the extension of slavery. Lincoln not only acquiesced in this movement but also became one of its important local leaders. His relative readiness to be unwhigged seemed to belie the sincerity and depth of his attachment to the ideals to which he had dedicated twenty-two of his thirty-three years of political life. But skepticism is not in order.[1]

The events of 1854 convinced the majority of the Whigs and a minority of the Democrats that slavery had grown aggressive. The proof, the Kansas-Nebraska Act, came like Jefferson's "fire bell in the night." It irresistibly forced Lincoln to the exchange of his Whig economics for antislavery. It was clear that no amount of improvement or banking legislation could build the American Dream, and the way of life it stood for, if the whole nation became a slave society. To put up an effective front against encroaching slavery, a Whig-Democratic coalition had to be created. The principal price of the new alliance was submerging the economic differences between the two old parties. Lincoln was willing to pay that price because of his sharp perception of both the moral and the practical realities of the 1850's.[2]

In his mind the roles of slavery and Whig economics were thus completely reversed. For the first period of his political life economics provided the central motif. Antislavery was also there but

155

was pushed far in the background with its triumph placed at a very distant day. After 1854 antislavery became Lincoln's immediate goal, and the economic policies that he continued to esteem highly and work for when possible were relegated to the background and to a future triumph. Political expediency had much to do with both the first and second compromises of his beliefs. His underlying assumptions, however, his moral underpinnings, remained unchanged. Indeed, when Lincoln embraced the antislavery cause, he raised his Dream to its highest plane. The challenge of this moral ascent, in turn, inspired him to enunciate more clearly and more beautifully than ever before the ideals he stood for.

If the menace of slavery dwarfed for the moment the importance of traditional economic policies, more purely practical considerations also pulled Lincoln toward Republicanism. In 1859 when a Pennsylvanian inquired about his tariff views, he replied with a reaffirmation of faith but also with the observation that "we, the old Whigs, have been entirely beaten out" on the question. He could have included in his statement the remnants of the party's economic program as well.[3]

In Illinois the national political situation was reflected with even greater severity. By 1852 the Whigs well nigh abandoned all serious efforts for the presidential contest. As an elector Lincoln made some speeches on behalf of nominee Winfield Scott, among other things repeating his old thoughts on the tariff and internal improvements. But his activity was perfunctory. Neither victory at the polls, which excited him, nor triump for Whig economics, which gave substance and inspiration to this excitement, was within the realm of possibility.[4]

Had the slavery dispute not intervened, Lincoln might have gone on agitating for what he believed, and forever would believe, to be the economics of prosperity, freedom, and thus democracy. This is not likely, however. His talents lay not in the way of the reformer. In his banking speech of the Harrison campaign he had sworn "eternal fidelity to the just cause, as I deem it," yet by the 1850's he was losing interest in politics. He was ripe for a more realistic political allegiance. The Kansas-Nebraska Act gave him high grounds for moving from a position now on the fringes to one that allowed active participation in shaping the course of American life. Thus the

Republican road beckoned to Lincoln not only because his ultimate loyalty was to a world view and not a party, but also because by the 1850's he found himself in an exceedingly tight political corner. To sum up matters, perhaps it is not improper here to use the words of Harry V. Jaffa: Lincoln's message in the fifties was "the phoenix risen from the ashes of the old Whig call for internal improvements" — the last phrase connoting the broadest meaning.[5]

This chapter will not attempt to analyze anew Lincoln's opposition to slavery and its extension. Instead it will emphasize the continuity in Lincoln's thought before and after 1854 by pointing to manifestations of his economic orientation in his antislavery discussion. Such a continuity can also be detected by focusing on his religious, or stylistic development; or by limiting the inquiry to his expressions concerning political processes.[6] Economic matters were Lincoln's main political concern, however, during the first and much larger part of his career.

Writing his autobiography in 1860, Lincoln recalled his first protest against slavery, made in a very lonely minority of two in the Illinois legislature of 1837; it "briefly defined his position," and as far as it went "it was then the same that it is now." The brevity of the Lincoln protest prevents an evaluation of the accuracy of this recollection. His 1837 judgement, however, that slavery was based both on "injustice and bad policy," the combination of moral and practical grounds, remained a constant in his antislavery stand.[7] If one ventures beyond this first protest to Lincoln's other pre-1854 speeches and writings, the rough outlines of more detailed elements of his post-1854 stand can be recognized also.

Politics had to be moral, therefore, important political judgements in the final analysis had to be moral judgements. Moderation, which seemed so often to so many through the ages irreconcilable with morality, was the only successful route to moral victory. Broadly defined, these were Lincoln's ends and means. A job of the politician, and hence of government was to create the best conditions for the laborer to secure the fruit of his labor so that he might get ahead in life. This was the task of an America which was the "fondest hope, of the lovers of freedom, throughout the world." Slavery was a relic of barbarism and in taking away the natural rights of black men it potentially threatened the rights of all men. The institution, however, was dying a "natural death," and the duty of the federal government was to aid this process. This was to be done by preventing the expansion of slavery, which could reverse the natural dying process, and by supporting gradual, voluntary, and compensated emancipation wherever possible under the Constitution. The freedmen were to be colonized in Africa whence they had been "forcibly torn." Displaying a profound awareness of history, Lincoln also saw that an American Emancipator would have eternal fame, greater than Washington's, and that a man powerful enough for such a deed could also endanger the Republic.[8]

It is not surprising that in his first fully recorded speech on slavery, made at Peoria in 1854, the Illinois Whig tied all of these strands together but for the last mentioned one.[9] As the antebellum years drew to a close, he shifted his emphasis slightly, primarily to meet political challenges, but in essentials he did not deviate from his stand until the Civil War made a revolution. Yet the fundamental consistency of Lincoln's thought should not obscure the fact that via the slavery controversy, and with the leaven of collective Republican thought, he not only organized, clarified, and provided detail for his thinking, but also focused more sharply on the virtues of the open society and placed a greater stress than before on morality.

The *"central idea"* of America was equality, Lincoln noted in 1856, taking his stand squarely on the Declaration of Independence. Whether his historical judgement was accurate is open to question. But we can be certain that the meaning he gave to Jefferson's famed words was scarcely identical with Jefferson's. Whatever equality meant to the Virginian and his age, Lincoln, crowning the work of the Jacksonian generation, extended its meaning to equality of opportunity to get ahead in life. This was his *"central idea."* One may dare to suggest that this is one of the most important metamorphoses of an idea in American history. Auden's song of Yeats fits here:

> The words of a dead man
> Are modifed in the guts of the living.

The poet's words particularize for our purpose the historical lesson that in a changing society the transmission of ideas is, inevitably, also their transformation.[10]

In the 1850's Lincoln defined again and again his central idea as "the principle that clears the *path* for all — gives *hope* to all — and, by consequence, *enterprize,* and *industry* to all." Richard Hofstadter could therefore venture that Lincoln's most "vital test" of democracy was economic. In the absence of previous research he could not explain that this was the fruit of the Illinoisan's economic orientation and of the orientation of the age which spawned him and which eagerly accepted this new definition of equality.[11]

Recognizing the all important role Lincoln assigned to economic opportunity is not to diminish his devotion to other manifestations of democracy. He made war on slavery, for example, from many directions. He could point out that "according to our ancient faith" the power to govern derived from the governed and the "relation of masters and slaves, is *PRO TANTO,* a total violation of this principle."[12] Yet he failed to make this his main avenue of attack. After all he had devoted his career to an economic vision. Moreover, to effectively use the demands of political equality as the avenue of peaceable elevation for the black man would have been well nigh impossible. It was not through default, however, that he made the Dream the central idea of the Republic. His choice was the result of long considered judgement in which principles and pragmatism met. As important and necessary as the right to vote was, for example, it was not so important to him as the right to get ahead in life. Thus he insisted that a black man in America was entitled to the fruit of his labor as much as a white man, but refused at first to concede the suffrage to him. Women working outside of the home indeed were treated thus by society as a whole. How good political theory this made is debatable, but it did play a pivotal role in the rise of the black man from slavery.[13]

Since the central idea of America was economic, the measure of the nation's success had to be economic, too. "We made the experiment," he wrote in 1854. "We proposed to give *all* a chance." "The fruit is before us. Look at it — think of it. Look at it, in it's aggregate grandeur, of extent of country, and numbers of population — of ship, and steamboat, and rail. . . ." The nation's prosperity proved the American experiment a success. It proved that clearing "the *path* for all" was the road to greatness. As in the past so in the future the country's goal had to remain the same, ever widening the path, "constantly spreading and deepening its influence."[14]

Lincoln was unabashed in offering an economic definition of American democracy. He also insisted, however, that immeasurably more than a question of "dollars and cents" was involved. Although in his United States for the first time in the history of Western man, the measure of virtue became material, virtue was still the goal. Thus Lincoln saw the right to rise transcending material aspirations and becoming a spiritual goal: the standard for a free society. The industrial revolution had made the triumph of material values inevitable. Lincoln's intellectual achievement was the successful tying of this materialism to democracy for the common man at a time the former might conceivably have engulfed the latter.

Giving a moral direction to the material values of the age can be seen as a subversion of reality. Lincoln's political religion can be seen, to borrow the phrase of Marx, as another "das *Opium* des Volkes."* A more realistic valuation, however, places Lincoln at the head of those who uplifted America's coarse materialism and gave it a spiritual dimension. His devotion to democracy and economic development, coupled with his belief that politics is a moral occupation, prepared him for the task of updating the Declaration of Independence to meet the needs of a society exploding economically. There were countless others (appreciably more of them Whigs and later Republicans than Democrats) whose outlook was much like his. Yet no one else reached his high eminence and placed the Dream so clearly on the highest pedestal as the *central idea* of the Republic. He spoke of it eloquently, insisted on its reality persistently, and lived it fully. More than any other individual it was he who made the Dream, in the highest sense of the words of John Greenleaf Whittier, "the moral steam enginery of an age of action."

Lincoln's presentation of the idea was totally unselfconscious. The view that his apparent artlessness was supreme artfullness cannot be evaluated at the present stage of applying psychology to history. In the case of his central idea all acceptable evidence indicates that he was unaware of his creative approach to Jefferson's Declaration. Indeed he saw himself as the priest of orthodoxy. Even his "new birth of freedom" meant the rebirth of freedom the Fathers had created "four score and seven years ago." This artless innocence, exempting Washington, singular among America's greatest leaders, gave

*The opiate of the people

Lincoln the most direct access to his countrymen. It allowed him to perform one of the supreme creative acts in the making of American ideology and play a *central* part in providing what still appears to be a *central idea* of the nation.

The identification in folklore of the sixteenth President with the American Dream meets the test of scholarship. The ideal of the open society where, to use the words of the Bible, a "man's gift maketh room for him," was probably as old as civilized man. Its modern Western seeds were planted with the Renaissance, with the rise of capitalism in Europe, and with what Max Weber chose to call the Protestant ethic. In the New World its development can be traced from the early settlers through Benjamin Franklin to the civil rights movement of the 1960's. John William Ward and others clearly detected a great surge of this ideal in the election of Andrew Jackson, the first "self-made" President. John Cawelti suggested that a largely economic definition of the open society emerged about the same time and (at least in rhetoric) was accepted by both parties. Eric Foner argued that by the 1850's the Republican Party made this ideal the main plank of its platform.[15] Thus Lincoln neither invented nor produced its triumph single-handedly. But like Jefferson, who inscribed the Enlightenment concept of equality on the banner of his new-born nation, so Lincoln would nail the Dream to the mast of the Union. Thus, *summa summarum,* Abraham Lincoln, more than anyone else, helped institutionalize the American Dream — made it perhaps the most *central idea* of the nation. And more than anyone else, he set the country on the road to including blacks in that Dream.[16]

Identifying the right to rise as the central idea of the United States, Lincoln placed it above the Constitution and the Union.[17] This is implicit in all of Lincoln's thinking. Only rarely, however, did he express it explicitly, and then most clearly in notes jotted down for his private use. This is understandable. Since he identified the Union and self-government with the open society, it was not important to emphasize a distinction that was meaningless in practice. In the 1850's he would have judged making such a distinction bad politics, too much like Seward's higher law. When the opponents of the open society, as he saw, attempted to destroy the Union in battle, making such a distinction would have been suicidal. Thus Lincoln upheld the Union as the all important goal, particularly during the war, when it became the common denominator upon which almost all consequential political blocks in the North could combine. But as he repeatedly explained, he meant not merely the "integrity" of the Union's "territorial parts" but more significantly the "purity of its principles" — in most central terms, the American Dream.[18]

Slavery of course subverted the Dream, and so its eventual extinction had to be ensured. Although it was protected by the Constitution, it was not meant to be protected indefinitely, according to Lincoln. He saw indications of the long-term intentions of the Fathers in the Northwest Ordinance, the provision for the eventual constitutional prohibition of the African slave trade, and lesser matters. Most decisive in his thinking, however, was the belief that the Dream itself was the Fathers' creation.

Lincoln made his stand on the issue of the extension of slavery, as was the case with most antislavery men, and it was an inflexible stand. Once, in 1854, he allowed that he would rather see slavery extended than the Union dissolved, for a "GREAT evil" was preferable to a still "GREATER one." But never again did he let such words escape him. And that one time it is reasonably clear that his words, general though they sounded, were tactical and referred to Kansas which appeared headed for slave statehood, and to the antislavery element which therefore threatened disunion.[19]

In the midst of the defeats of 1862 Lincoln told Horace Greeley, having already drafted the Emancipation Proclamation, that he would save the Union with or without slavery, but even then he would not consent to the extension of slavery. Such extension implied slavery triumphant in material terms, which in turn measured for Lincoln and his generation a moral triumph as well. Although he never said it directly, the implication of his thought was clear: the Union without the Dream was not "worthy of saving." In his answer to the Prayer of Twenty Million" he posed a theoretical choice for the nation between the "Union as it was," in November 1860, with slavery dying, or the Union as it soon would be, with slavery dead. In his mind he no doubt gave careful consideration to saving the Union with slavery expanding, but he rejected this option. That he thought the problem through is certain. And he "would *accept* war" rather than let the only nation in the world dedicated to the Dream perish.[20]

Lincoln's opposition to slavery was expressed in moral terms, and he raised the moral ingredient of politics perhaps to its highest level in the dominant stream of American politics. Under the all-important moral superstructure, however, he often buttressed his thought with economics — not surprising for one who had placed the good science at the heart of his efforts for more than two decades. Lincoln perceived the interest of the slaveholders in slavery as almost exclusively economic, "an immediate palpable and immensely great pecuniary interest."[21] His statements occasionally suggested a limited awareness of other factors, political, social, even psychological, and led to the admission of the complexity of the slavery problem and to a sense of puzzlement as to how to deal with it. More characteristically he managed to take firm ground by relying on what approached economic determinism for the slaveholder. The planters saw their peculiar institution "through 2,000,000,000 of dollars," was Lincoln's recurring image, "and that is a pretty thick coating."[22]

If in his eyes economic interest motivated the Southern defense of slavery, the same was true of slavery expansion. He made no beginnings at a sophisticated analysis that would culminate in the second half of the twentieth century with Marxist oriented historian Eugene Genovese. Simplified economic determinism sufficed for him. The opening of new lands to slavery perhaps "quite *doubles*," at any rate substantially increases, the value of this property, Lincoln explained. How he arrived at this figure can only be conjectured. He was certain, however, that without expansion slavery was "naturally" dying and that a great deal of money was involved.[23]

Lincoln did not think it necessary to specify why contained slavery would die, perhaps in a hundred years, why it was like "starving and famishing cattle." This was a self-evident truth to him, implicit in his entire economic thought, and had little to do with soil depletion or other less fundamental factors of which he was also aware. American prosperity, the greatest in the history of man, was the fruit of social mobility, of the clear path to all. The absence of this principle caused economic decline. Deprived of the artificial and by definition temporary stimulus of expansion, the slave economy had to decline. Since the planter, too, desired prosperity, he then would turn out of self-interest to the free labor system. Thus the unprofitability of fenced-in slavery would bring about the moral regeneration of the South.

Even in his own time Lincoln saw the "slave-masters" having "a conception" of incentives improving the productivity of their man-property. Therefore the perpetuation of slavery was only a "temporary self-interest" of the slave owner. His long-term interest, in harmony with other Americans, was in the creation of a free society. Even in economic terms then, slavery was a case where "one man ruleth over another to his own hurt," to quote *Ecclesiastes*. Emancipation was in the interest of the South, however hard it was for Southerners to see this. Having issued his Proclamation freeing the slaves in 1863, Lincoln looked forward therefore to the extension of the "material prosperity" of the already free North to the South.[24]

If the Southern defense of slavery was motivated primarily by a shortsighted view of economic interest, the Northern opposition to slavery Lincoln saw, above all, as moral. The North stood upon the principles of an ever developing open society which transcended mere matters of materialism. Lincoln could get so consumed with the moral vision of his cause that he could declare that the North would not "gain a dollar" by restricting slavery. Even over the long run he said his section had "only *slight,* and *remote* pecuniary interest added." The moral goal of the Dream alone was important.[25]

At other times, to be sure, he fell in with the masses of Republicans in his region and pointed out that the North had a materialistic interest involved, too, which was neither slight nor remote. By keeping slavery from the territories the land was reserved for free white people. "In this we have . . . a deep and abiding interest," Lincoln said, meaning, as nearly always when he used this word, economic interest. Yet this interest was not a major ingredient of his argument, however important it might have been to his Illinoisans.[26] He minimized the influence of this line of thinking in part because his Whiggish mind had not yet integrated fully the public domain into his economic thinking nor could see expansion into the territories as important *per se.* In the same time he recognized that emphasizing materialistic self-interest weakened his high moral tone. To avoid this pitfall he indeed tried to raise his territorial argument to the level of the Dream by insisting that the land was to be "for poor people to go to and better their condition."[27]

Lincoln was certain that over the long run the superior economics of free labor would put an end to slavery, but over the short run he saw the danger of an opposite result. He did not explain the mechanics of this failure of free labor to compete successfully with the "unpaid workman" system. But theoretical explanations were unnecessary in the presence of living proof: the South. "Slave states are places for poor white people to remove FROM," not to get ahead in — this he knew since childhood.[28] Thus since the free labor system was desirable but could not be obtained in open competition over the short run government interference was in order. This conclusion came readily to a Whig. The same was not true of Democrats. Those who turned Republican from Jackson's party had to make their major ideological concession on this point and, as many of them feared, it proved to be a costly concession: the Whig doctrine was quickly turned again to the more ordinary matters of economy.

The federal government had to stop slavery expansion because free labor could not do so over the short run, and over the long run, free labor might disappear. Thus the building would have had to begin anew, the noble labor of generations lost. Lincoln did not believe that climate could put a "natural limit" on slavery. His disbelief in turn became the prosaic heart of the Revisionist historians' condemnation of him. These scholars, accepting the isothermal theory, saw in Lincoln's demand that the federal government exclude slavery from the territories a demand about "an imaginary Negro in an impossible place."[29] They tended to explain his uncompromising stand by the political preferment that fell to him because of it. Since Lincoln's stand led to the Civil War, by implication he was made into the worst criminal in American history, although no Revisionist scholar dared follow through this thought. Their message still sits heavily on scholarship and thus one as far removed from them as William Appleman Williams can look upon the Illinoisan's antislavery motivation as "chilling." It is important therefore to understand that Lincoln's rejection of the natural limits thesis, like that of other young Republicans, was rooted in a progressive economic outlook.[30]

Lincoln saw man not as a victim of economic forces but their creator. His study of the problem of slavery gave some pause to this optimism, and later the war presidency may have significantly tempered it. Throughout much of his life, however, he believed that man could make prosperity or unmake it; make panics and depressions, or stop them; in short, man could "dig out his destiny."[31] In life generally, and much more so in mundane economic matters, he saw broad horizons before humanity. Where there was a great interest involved — and the expansion of slavery he saw as a billion-dollar business — natural limits had little potency. In such a case only unbendable laws, and more importantly the spirit they indicated and further inspired could do the job.

Lincoln's attitude was not only the product of Enlightenment influences which indeed were shared by the entire nation, but much more importantly, also of his own experiences. As a young man he had fought for internal improvements in Illinois, and when the great plans failed they were judged to have been a hopeless dream. Yet by the 1850's he saw the state well on its way to building the transportation arteries envisioned twenty years before. In the early 1840's Governor Ford, leading a large chorus, had declared that the Prairie State could not run a safe banking system, but a decade later the bankers proved him wrong. As late as 1846 the leading Democratic newspaper of the state had declared that Illinois could "never" have any industries of importance, even as Cyrus McCormick was preparing to move to Chicago. Then the 1850's saw Illinois climb toward the top of the national census in the production of manufactured goods.

With the rise of the slavery controversy Lincoln had to listen to politicians argue that one might as well try to raise oranges in Siberia as to try to establish the peculiar institution in New Mexico. This could not but sound to him like the old British free trade argument that Americans could no more have complex manufactures than orange crops. Within his lifetime the United States had not only developed complex industries but, after acquiring new territories, was producing oranges. The lessons of the first half of the nineteenth century were plain. Natural limits could be both surmounted and outflanked.

Even what many saw as mere accidents of history had to be taken into account. In the briefest of time spans the discovery of gold remade California, Lincoln pointed out. He knew and preached that there were "more mines above the Earth's surface than below it. All nature — the whole world, material, moral, and intellectual, — is a mine." He sang like a poet. Every man is a miner. Lincoln looked around with his Whig eyes and could not find any God-ordained line that separated free and slave labor and which man in his ingenuity and cupidity could not overcome. Indeed, by 1852, *De Bow's Review* could bespeak, in a different context, a fitting epitaph for natural limits. Lamenting the railroad-inspired fall of New Orleans from economic primacy, it pointed North, to the "enemy:"

> Armed with energy, enterprise, and an indomitable spirit, that enemy, by a system of bold, vigorous, and sustained efforts, has succeeded in reversing the very laws of nature and of nature's God, — rolled back the mighty tide of the Mississippi and its thousand tributary streams, until their mouth, practically and commercially, is more at New York or Boston than at New Orleans.[32]

It is not surprising that to an older generation of Whigs and to the majority of Democrats, the natural limits thesis seemed more acceptable. Webster could allude to the cotton gin as the instrument that revolutionized slavery, but he failed to generalize the thought and see similar instruments helping make new revolutions in the future.[33] Thinking in terms of a permanent economic revolution was second nature to many of the Whigs of Lincoln's generation but not to those of Webster's, though they, too, were fond of speaking of great transformations. What they seemed to have lacked was having experienced the industrial revolution as young men when their minds were still deeply impressionable. Although as Jaffa felicitously noted, "the 'natural limits' to slavery in 1790 were totally destroyed before the year 1791 was out" by the cotton gin,[34] and like revolutions shocked other spheres of American life, much of Webster's generation managed to feel safe behind the shield of an isothermal line.

If there was a division in Whig thinking, the dominant Democratic mind functioned apart from both these factions. Thus Salmon P. Chase, for example, rather a moderate on economic matters at that, could also contemplate the cotton gin but without finding it necessary to admit that it was primarily responsible for the revitalization of slavery. He preferred to see the growth of the Southern institution as a result of dark, nonmaterial and political influences.[35] Lincoln, too, looked at Eli Whitney's invention. He saw in it an illustration of the revolutions man could make and how the material world could remake moral values thus making the former all the more important. He spoke often of the cotton gin bases of slavery. And he took for granted that the future was full of great advances, which when applied to slavery could handily overcome limits that others, who were less the children of the industrial revolution, could sincerely see as God's incontrovertible will.[36]

Stephen Douglas, who became the chief champion of the natural limits thesis, must be classified with the entrepreneurial wing of Jackson's party in spite of idiosyncrasies. Although he and Lincoln had disagreed over economic policies throughout the 1830's and 1840's, in broadest terms their goals of economic development tended in the same direction. Lincoln knew that his rival, too, had an appreciation of the economic changes of their times and their import for the future. It was Douglas who had declared so alluringly that the application of steam to transportation put the twenty-six states of the Union of 1845 closer together than the original thirteen had been. It may well be that one of the reasons for Lincoln ascribing hypocrisy to the Little Giant, indeed "covert *real* zeal" for slavery, was in this. For Douglas, too, should have admitted the unreliability of the isothermal theory.[37]

While the economic orientation of the first two decades of Lincoln's public life continued to play a considerable role in his thinking during his final decade, his arguments during that last period concentrated on the issue of morality. He tended to neglect economic questions *per se* even when they were closely related to the slavery problem. Thus he never speculated in public about the ways the "peculiar institution" might jump across its "natural" borders; perhaps he thought it foolish to try specific prophecies. But he did not confuse salvery expansion with the expansion of cotton cultivation. He called "ridiculous" the Douglas charge that he rang the alarm about the danger of cotton grown "upon the tops of the Green Mountains" of Vermont. As he saw, the danger was in the free farmer and the free laborer being "elbowed" by the slave "from his plow or his anvil." Speaking of the 1860 strikes in the shoe factories of New England, Lincoln warned that the danger was that the "free labor that *can* strike will give way to slave labor that *cannot!*"[38]

This is not to suggest that he knew much about the industrial employment of slaves in the South or that he gave careful consideration to the potential of such employment in the North. Indeed his ideas about the factory system, like that of most of his generation, were hazy. His abstract faith in the equality of men and his personal experiences, however, left him with no illusions concerning the ability of blacks to handle complicated tasks. Lincoln knew that the Negroes' "intellect" had been "clouded by Slavery," by having been "systematically oppressed." Yet he believed that blacks were "capable of thinking as white men." He took care of the real estate problems of William Florville (Fleurville) of Springfield, for example, the man who "came closest" among blacks to "being a personal friend of his," to quote Benjamin Quarles. Lincoln probably knew that the saline lands of Illinois Territory had been worked by border state slaves who had hired themselves out with the acquiescence of the local legislators. In Washington he had heard congressmen speak of the great profits to be had from slave labor in the mines of the territories. Thus in Lincoln's view slavery was eminently expandable to both the agriculture and the manufacturing of the North even if there were no new cotton gins to make new revolutions.[39]

It may be true that as late as 1850 for most American leaders the employment of slaves in industries was not a real possibility. One suspects that either these men had not been truly penetrated by the idea of economic development, or they had prejudices concerning the ability of black men that ran much deeper than Lincoln's. As the last antebellum decade wore on, however, the link that many planters saw between the industrial uses of slaves and the institution's expansion was also recognized by Northern leaders. This was certainly the case with the "corporation lawyer" from Illinois. It could hardly have been otherwise for a man who spent the larger part of his life championing the economics of development.[40]

Lincoln's own brand of Whig mind could see the Southerners' interest in slavery as almost purely economic, their object as being to control slave property "as other property," in short to "make the most money" with it. At the same time he thought it very important to deny that slavery was just another species of property like hogs and cattle, or, as he said in more humorous moods, "upon a par with onions and potatoes." If this was not done, if Douglas and lesser men were allowed to stand uncorrected, the federal government would certainly come to support the object of the slaveowners. This would only be right in Lincoln's view, for ordinary property was a positive good deserving governmental aid. Thus the nationalist former Whig could foresee a future for slavery as ordinary property that most conservative states-right oriented Democrats could never admit.[41]

As a start, Lincoln believed, the African slave trade would be revived, for it was thus that the "commodity" could be purchased most advantageously. In the 1840's he had labored valiantly, but with no great popular success, to prove that to *"buy cheapest"* was not the best long-term economic policy. In the 1850's his fight for the tariff was clearly in his mind when he foretold a similar battle over the importation of slaves. The only economic argument he could see against buying slaves where they were the cheapest was *"protection* to home production." An ex-Whig whose party had been "entirely beaten out on the tariff question," however, was not about to rely on such defenses even if they had been acceptable on other grounds. This was all the more true as Lincoln did not carry his tariff analogy far enough and mistakenly assumed that in the case of slavery "the home *producers* will probably not *ask* the protection." On this as on other points his antislavery arguments showed a remarkable similarity to his earlier economic arguments, not only in their underlying spirit but even in the specifics of their language.[42]

Lincoln was certainly capable of building his case against slavery via purely economic reasoning. His failure to do so, his emphasis on moral rather than economic arguments, was more than a reflection of the relative values placed on the two kinds of reasoning by the traditions of Western civilization. As his tariff-slave trade analogy further clarifies, it was also the fruit of the realization that there were no narrowly economic forces in the nation, nor reasoning based on them, that could stop slavery. Only the moral sense of the people could do the job.

Thus the spirit that opened the territories to slavery by looking at the problem as a matter of property rights would in time revive the importation of slaves. The next step, Lincoln believed, was likely to be the passage of a federal slave code to deal with the "peculiar institution" in the territories — a just demand, as he saw it, if only a question of protecting property was involved. The culmination was to be the legalization of slavery in all of the states, for it was wholly unreasonable to forever prevent all Americans from enjoying this "positive good." To the nationalist Whig, oriented toward economic growth aided by the federal government this process had an inherent logic of its own.[43]

Lincoln's conviction, that the advocates of slavery, in spite of their states-rightist-strict-construction ideology, would over the long run follow the nationalizing course he believed their economic interest dictated, may or may not have been correct. But in American terms, he was clearly thinking Whig. Because he and so many other Republicans were also talking Whig, pledges concerning the enforcement of the Constitution and a lack of desire to impose the free labor system on the slave states sounded hollow to Southerners. Indeed it was with much greater justice that they could ascribe nationalizing tendencies to Lincoln's party than vice versa.

The Illinois Republican for one could declare that slavery was not "distinctly" and "expressly" affirmed in the Constitution. In contrast, like countless nationalists before him, he noted that the Constitution "expressly charged" the federal government "with the duty of providing for the general welfare." And he added:

> We think slavery impairs, and endangers the general welfare. Those who do not think this are not of us, and we can not argue with them. We must shape our own course by our own judgment.[44]

All this did not add up to emancipation for him; indeed he hastened to reassure slaveholders about all their rights, exempting the expansion of their peculiar property. Yet at times even his assurances sounded ominous. "I say that we must not interfere with the institution of slavery in the states where it exists, because the constitution forbids it, and the general welfare does not require us to do so." But what if Lincoln came to the firm conclusion that the general welfare did demand emancipation? Would he still see prohibitions in the fundamental law of the land when, as he pointed out, slavery was not so much as named in it? He went even further:

> The thing is hid away, in the constitution, just as an afflicted man hides away a wen or a cancer, which he dares not cut out at once, lest he bleed to death; with the promise, nevertheless, that the cutting may begin at the end of a given time.[45]

Could the Southerner trust Lincoln's assurances then? And even if he could, and the Republican President-elect faced with civil war did go along with the proposed Thirteenth Amendment, which would have forbidden federal interference with slavery in the states, could the Southerner trust Lincoln's successors? If fencing in slavery would not have produced its "natural" death abolishing the interstate slave trade might have. Before the Whig mind the economic arsenal of the national government was potentially unlimited.

Lincoln could perceive America only through nationalist eyes. He thus saw that the forces of economic nationalism if applied on behalf of slavery would make all of the United States slave. He could not conceive these forces lying idle or being voluntarily checked by people who could wield them and so immensely benefit by them. He also saw that if these forces were applied on behalf of free labor they would make all of the country free. States rightists could argue in all sincerity that these were not the only alternatives, that the nationalizing forces could and must be limited; or the nationalist could argue that the conflict was truly irrepressible. As Lincoln saw it, the nation was to become either free or slave, one or the other. And so, as he said, the "tug" had to come. Calhoun and others had noted early that the Whig attitude toward the federal government and the economy posed a danger to slavery. Some three decades later it was the Whiggishness of Lincoln's background and thought, and that of the majority of the Republicans, more than any other factor, that made their antislavery stand a real and potentially total threat.[46]

Lincoln's arguments about the American Dream were addressed to the white people of Illinois and of the North, people whose votes were necessary to uphold his views. He probably also shared to some extent the confusions and prejudices of his people about the black man. His speeches, especially when he was pressed by a rather blatant racist like Douglas, reflected this. It is to Lincoln's eternal credit, however, that when it came to what was most essential about his America he insisted on including the black man.

There was a finality to Lincoln's announcement that in the Negro's "right to eat the bread, without the leave of anybody else, which his own hand earns, *he is my equal and the equal of Judge Douglas, and the equal of every living man.*" In his estimate the man who robbed the black man of the fruit of his labor was on par with, and in a sense was worse than, the man who robbed the white man thus. He tempered his views by disclaiming any desire for the social and political equality of blacks. He also suggested that they, "perhaps," were not the equals of whites "in moral or intellectual endowment." He suggested that God may have given "little" to them and thus their achievements were likely to be little. They were not going to be dangerous competitors of the white man in the "race of life." Behind the disclaimers, however, as Douglas correctly pointed out, and as Lincoln began to spell it out even before the war, there was a mighty meaning. The blacks too were to be allowed to rise in America as high as their ability could take them. "I want every man to have the chance," Lincoln announced.

> And I believe a black man is entitled to it — in which he *can* better his condition — when he may look forward and hope to be a hired laborer this year and the next, work for himself afterward, and finally to hire men to work for him! That is the true system.[47]

Lincoln helped institutionalize the Dream for the white man of America but he also helped open the gate, both by word and deed, for the same institutionalization of the Dream for the black man which, one may say, came at last a century later. And in the final analysis it was above all he, to cite the words of Quarles, who gave blacks "the feeling that they could make their way in America. . . ."[48]

Beyond ideology, and beyond political calculations, Lincoln sympathized and, to a degree, identified with the downtrodden black man. As with most of the abolitionists, his personal acquaintance with slavery was minuscule. Yet he could speak of the bondsman with an empathy that few whites could match. In doing so he perhaps laid bare some of the psychological roots of his ideology.

In 1841 Lincoln took a trip on the Ohio with Joshua Speed, and saw on their boat "ten or a dozen slaves, shackled together with irons." Although these men seemed happy, leading Lincoln to philosophize about the ways of God and man, the memory of the sight, he recalled in a letter fourteen years later, remained a "continual torment" to him. Slavery, he confessed to his oldest friend who now defended it, had "the power of making me miserable." And he defined the institution as "stripes, and *unrewarded toils*."[49]

Years later black abolitionist radical Frederick Douglass, who sharply differed with Lincoln on substantial issues, conceded that the President was "the first great man that I talked with in the United States freely, who in no single instance reminded me . . . of the difference of color." Douglass could find an explanation for this puzzling absence of prejudice only in both he and Lincoln being "self-made men." What appealed to Lincoln was "the similarity with which I had fought my way up, we both starting at the lowest round of the ladder." And as if to bear out Douglass's impression, the Chief Executive told John Eaton, so the latter recalled, "that considering the conditions from which Douglass rose, and the position to which he attained, he was in his judgement, one of the most meritorious men in America."[50]

☆ ☆ ☆ ☆ ☆ ☆ ☆ ☆ ☆ ☆ ☆ ☆ ☆ ☆ ☆

13
In The
Shadow of Slavery

ONLY SEVEN MONTHS HAD PASSED SINCE THE REPEAL OF THE MIS-
souri Compromise when the *Philadelphia Public Ledger* observed that
the tariff issue was "as dead politically as a United States bank."[1] The
new politics of slavery had conquered Pennsylvania, the stronghold
of protectionism and the entire nation as well. Lincoln's abandonment of the economic debate was part of a national pattern. Although as the decade wore on, prosperity faltered and the old issues
began to revive, they never attained more than a supporting role.
The focus of the political stage remained on the confrontation between free and slave labor.

Lincoln's public silence on economic questions was understandably even deeper than that of his party. In ideological terms
slavery was the supreme issue for him because he feared that its extension would strangle the American Dream. Tacking economic
policies, however complementary, onto his antislavery principle
meant to him, as to the radicals, "lowering the Republican Standard"
and diluting its moral authority. This stance was buttressed by the
mental trait that made him into a single issue candidate at most
junctures of his career. Furthermore, in political terms Lincoln saw
slavery not only as the one issue that could keep intact the Republican coalition of former Whigs and Democrats, but also as the sole
issue that appeared important to voters. There was no profit, he
advised a friend in private, in "magnifying other questions which the
people just now are really caring nothing about."[2]

Between 1854 and 1860 Lincoln scrupulously observed in public
his self-imposed silence on matters specifically economic, but he did

not always do so in private. Also his discussion of slavery indirectly elaborated on some of his economic views, most meaningfully those on free labor. He considered the subject of agriculture, too, in a "nonpolitical" speech. There is an element of distortion in all of his economic arguments, for he now viewed all matters with his focus on slavery and pictured free labor almost solely as the antithesis of slave labor. Theoretical consistency, never a main concern to him, he now perhaps neglected more than ever. Still, this period also produced advancement and clarification in his thought. And, at its end, the presidency was waiting.

Labor had always played a central role in the development of Lincoln's outlook. His definition of labor, however, was broad and imprecise, like that of his age. He could speak of labor as including all who did productive work, the lawyer and the merchant as well as the farmer and the mechanic. At other times he excluded the middle classes, limited labor to those performing physical toil, and showed a vague uneasiness about the moral position of those otherwise engaged.[3]

Labor, defined one way, or the other, was to Lincoln the creator of all value. Like the classicists, his tutor Wayland among them, he saw capital as the "fruit of labor." This theory of value led him to conclude that in economic terms labor was the "superior — greatly the superior — of capital." The political implication of the theory for him was that labor's interest preceded other interests. His democratic faith independently produced the same conclusion, that "working men are the basis of all governments . . . for the reason that there are more of them than of any other class." If a conflict arose between their welfare and that of "any other, that other should yield." Thus justice, arrived at through both classical economics and the political theory of democracy, dictated that labor and its interests be considered preeminent.[4]

The opposite of labor was capital, and Lincoln, once again in step with the economists of his age, often spoke of this contradistinction. Although he refused to find the antagonism in this relationship that European political economy found, and followed the American branch of the science which emphasized the harmony of interests, he did not entirely deny an element of conflict. He divided "our whole species" into "three great classes — *useful* labour, *useless* labour, and *idleness*," and in the 1850's by implication placed the capitalist in the last category. His capitalist, however, was not the man who ran the average industrial shop of the antebellum peiod with less than ten employees (half as many in Illinois), and who worked himself. Nor was he the landowning farmer who hired hands. These men were in their own eyes, as in Lincoln's, part of labor whether broadly or narrowly defined. Lincoln's capitalists (even more loosely defined than labor) were the very rich, who did not work and as such were somewhat suspect, and who lived from the labor they hired with their capital.[5]

Lincoln conceded the right of some to "save themselves from actual labor," but it was axiomatic to his thought that their number and influence would be limited. "It has so happened in all ages of the world, that *some* have laboured, and *others* have, without labour, enjoyed a large portion of the fruits," he mused in 1847. This was "the great, durable, curse of the race," he added in 1859. By then he was directing his thoughts to the slaveholders, whom he placed, in a less than conscious way, in nearly the same class as the large capitalists. The desire to escape from physical labor was akin to the desire to be idle and was a disease of which lawyer Lincoln admitted not being entirely free of. In ancient times, he noted, educated people did not work at all, and "this was not an insupportable evil to the working bees, so long as the class of drones remained very small." This class, however, had to be small to be tolerable.[6]

The ideal, the most productive society was the one in which the laborer obtained the whole product of his labor, "or as nearly as possible." This implied that the workingman was to own his own tools of production, whether land, shop, or machinery. A large capitalist class owning most of the means of production would prevent labor from obtaining the whole product, thus limiting both its economic mobility and productivity. The "true system" was that where the

> penniless beginner in the world, labors for wages awhile, saves a surplus with which to buy tools or land, for himself; then labors on his own account another while, and at length hires another new beginner to help him. This, say its advocates, is *free* labor — the just and generous, and prosperous system, which opens the way for all — gives hope to all, and energy, and progress, and improvement of condition to all.[7]

Although too big a capitalist class would stultify the system, it also had a role to play. It provided employment to the needy, thus helping them to rise. Its status was the just reward of earlier labor, and it served as an "encouragement to industry and enterprise." Lincoln did not desire a large class of this kind but thought preventive governmental action unnecessary because he did not see that class becoming overly large or overly powerful. This confident outlook he shared with much of the Republican Party, including its leading economist, Henry Carey. Since Lincoln saw no inherent problem, he saw no need for laws "to prevent a man from getting rich; it would do more harm than good."[8]

The self-made man that Lincoln admired was not the business tycoon (who in time came to usurp this American symbol) but any man who improved his standing in life. Lincoln believed that it was generally the able who advanced, but in his overly democratic mind most men were able. That there could be but small room at the top mattered little. Indeed, to repeat, one was to be suspicious of the John Jacob Astors of this world.

The reverse side of the self-made man ideal, the poor, did not receive Lincoln's contempt — as it did with so many of his party brethren, whether Whig or Republican. Some might fault him, however, for being too simplistic in emphasizing prudence, industry, sobriety, and honesty as the keys to success. Indeed, in 1859 he *once* blamed "improvidence, folly, or singular misfortune" and the "dependent nature" of some men for their failure to get ahead. Although he had spent decades attempting to improve the system and fighting shortsighted policies that he believed even made depressions, he could declare that if some failed to reach beyond the state of wage earner, that was "not the fault of the system."[10] This extreme stance, however, represented an aberrant note in his career, called forth only temporarily by the shrill proslavery argument that denied the worth of free society and touted bound labor as superior to the free. His 1862 words about advancement summed up his lifelong views: "Success does not *as much* depend on external help as on self-reliance." Indeed, the heart of his Whig party allegiance had been the belief that the government must give Americans, to as large an extent as possible, this needed "external help."[11]

Nonetheless, as the occasional self-righteous utterance suggests, by the 1850's in certain ways Lincoln was no longer as forward-looking as he had been in the earlier decades. Lincoln was somewhat unrealistic even in terms of his own days, although it is not clear to what extent. He overestimated, for example, the size of the independent middling classes and saw wage earners as making up no "more than one-eighth of the labor of the country." Later he considerably moderated his claim by becoming less specific, speaking only of "a large majority" of the North as being "neither hirer nor hired"; and by broadening his already broad definition of labor, which included working employers, to embrace "men, with their families — wives, sons and daughters," who labored "on their farms, in their houses and in their shops." Although historians face a huge task yet in measuring levels of employment and mobility, it is safe to conclude that Lincoln made the system appear much more open than it was.[12]

After one of his speeches a Democratic newspaper in Chicago attacked him savagely, stating that he was no advocate of the workingman. Not all laborers could advance in America, its argument went. Probably not more than one man in ten could become an employer. Others had to remain hired wage earners, mechanics, farmhands and such. "Mr. Lincoln's assault upon labor and laborers," the article concluded, was disgraceful.[13]

Lincoln and his Republicans dismissed the Douglasite fusillade as proslavery slander. They were absolutely confident of their self-estimate: Republicans were the champions of labor and the proslavery element was the enemy of the workingman. The historian must agree in essence with their judgment but must also note again that underneath this stupendous fact the Democratic accusation contained a growing component of truth.

Thus, if the slavery controversy helped clarify Lincoln's thinking in many respects, in others the opposite was the result. The menace posed by labor in bondage concealed other dangers by shrinking them to insignificance. It shifted his emphasis from seeking improvements in the economic system to affirmation that the free system was good. In the 1830's and 1840's Lincoln had been more aware of the developments taking place in the American economy than were most of his contemporaries. In the 1850's, however, he failed to prepare adequately for coming to grips with the changes industrialization was bringing. The United States greatly needed the sharpening of vision: people had to understand the changing relationship of capital to labor if the Dream was to remain healthy. But the best men of the nation were almost totally engaged in the fight over slavery. Thus some of the failures of the Gilded Ages can be traced back to the shadow which the "peculiar institution" cast over the perceptions of men in the 1850's.

Lincoln's absorption in the slavery issue also put an end to the advancement of his economic self-education. "There is a difference of opinion among political economists" about the role of labor, he noted in 1858, but there is no evidence to indicate that he went to their works to investigate the question, as he had done earlier. Books on economics continued to come into his hands, like Edward Kellogg's *Labor and Other Capital,* and he may have looked into them. His reading, however, like his interests as a whole, shifted rather fully to slavery. He continued to read works that contained much political economy, such as Helper's *Impending Crisis* and Fitzhugh's *Sociology for the South,* but the economics was incidental to his main purpose. Moreover, the economic apprehension of these authors, too, was greatly weakened by the distortion of slavery. They helped Lincoln little toward a better understanding of the problems then brewing.[14]

After recognizing the Lincolnian failures, it should still be emphasized that to the end of his life Lincoln continued to move toward the future — sometimes quite alone. The essential part of his thought was improvement, the advancement of the *independent* farmer-workingman-entrepreneur was only the chief means. The latter's inevitable eclipse, we know now, did not have to diminish the right to rise. On the contrary. As industrialization entered a stage with which Lincoln had little first-hand familiarity, as factories and increasingly mechanized farms came to dominate the land, new opportunities opened up. Mobility in the direction of economic independence was replaced by mobility toward higher standards of living, and higher positions in the management scale, in a wage-earning society. Lincoln's understanding of this coming change was very restricted, but it permitted him to maintain his support of economic development unwaveringly. Indeed, the assumption that development increased mobility was so fundamental to him that by the late 1850's, with most of his political career behind him, it is no longer enough to say that he favored development and expanding productivity because it helped people to rise in life. He also favored the right to rise because it led to development.

Thus in spite of his eloquent support of the small, independent producer that dominated his America, Lincoln could continually adjust his sights to the changing world around him. A specific, early indication of this was a certain willingness to accept the concentration of capital for the sake of economic efficiency. He had always supported corporations and in the mid-1840's already cheerfully predicted the coming of gigantic railroads. His intimate business association with the Illinois Central in the 1850's indeed thus takes on a symbolic significance.

Lincoln's related love of machines, proverbial among his friends, pointed in the same direction. He accepted the factories, too, if perhaps only as a somewhat peripheral part of the system. Yet, in the White House, when told that Gordon McKay's machine could sew around the sole of a shoe in thirty seconds, his reaction was clearsighted and anticipatory. Go home and prepare, he told his informant, the mayor of the shoe manufacturing town of Lynn, Massachusetts. As far as that industry was concerned, Lincoln judged, "the day of the little country shop is coming to an end. Shoes will be made in big factories in cities."[15]

Lincoln did not shrink from the economic world he helped create. And his attempts to come to terms with some of its problems, without changing the heart of his beliefs, is most fully illustrated by his approval of labor strikes. By the time he spoke out on this very difficult subject, it had received decades of consideration from both economists and politicians. The thinkers generally displayed negative attitudes. Wayland, for example, spoke of the "tyranny of trade unions," and Carey was not much more forebearing.[16]

One basis for such condemnation for many economists was *laissez-faire* philosophy. Thus, a little curiously, it was not uncommon to decry usury laws and labor unions in the same breath. Lincoln had no difficulty rejecting those arguments. The same cannot be said of the other fount of antilabor-union attitudes, the concept of harmony of interests, which denied any conflict between capital and labor. This outlook Lincoln shared to some degree. But he did not embrace it totally. He did not see the working class as a well-defined stratum with its own special interests because he did not see any permanent classes in America. Yet he did acknowledge some tension between labor and capital, and he placed the former above the latter. And since he conceded an important and growing place to such forms of production as the "cotten fabrics from Manchester and Lowell," or the railroads, he also came to endorse strikes. He thus admitted the right of the wage-earning class, however temporary he saw its membership to be, to act jointly in defense of its interest against capital.

In the political sphere the issue of trade unions was a matter of slowly increasing, but non-partisan, concern in ante-bellum America. It might be pointed out that an able scholar can refer to the Democrat Andrew Jackson as a "strikebreaker" and that the landmark decision of Commonwealth v. Hunt in 1842, growing out of a Massachusetts shoemakers' strike and upholding the right of labor to organize, was handed down by a panel of Whig judges. Yet Webster, a Whig leader, denounced unions, and so did the younger Greeley, repeatedly, in the pages of the *Tribune*. The latter thereby also gave voice to the dominant Republican position. Thus Lincoln's support for labor unions was the product of his own mind, not that of his party.[17]

Lincoln had to reach his position also in the face of a yet confused Illinois. The reaction there to the 1859 work stoppage in the building trades of London, an event sufficiently removed geographically to permit coolheaded objectivity, illustrates the point well. The newspaper which tended to pay attention to strikes, the Republican *Chicago Democrat*, reported factually on the London affair in its daily edition and concluded that the workers would fail. It implied that the strike was foolish. The weekly edition of the paper, however, flatly declared that "notwithstanding various objections to trade unions, they have, no doubt, on the whole proved beneficial to the workman." It then noted that in the specific case of the London strike the laborers' demands seemed "unreasonable." Finally it concluded by hoping for their success, for that would "strengthen the power of labor as opposed to capital, the world over."[18]

Workingman's actions closer to home were given similar coverage, as was the case with the New England shoe strike early in 1860 (which elicited Lincoln's support and Greeley's condemnation.) The laborers' goal, the *Democrat* thought, "would have been better accomplished by less violence of language and action." As to local strikes in Illinois, the most newsworthy occurred at the beginning of 1859 on the Chicago & Alton Railroad, and it received the usual equivocal treatment by the organs of both parties.[19]

Lincoln made his strong argument for self-education for labor at about this time and pointed derisively at those who opposed the idea. They, he said, desired workingmen who would not "tread out of place, or kick understandingly." The implication, however faint, was that at times labor did have to kick.[20] Then in the spring of 1860, touring New England after his appearance at the Cooper Union, Lincoln took a strong stand on strikes. Having first made a written outline of what he would say, he declared: *"I am glad to see that a system of labor prevails in New England under which laborers CAN strike."* His commitment was absolute, and he repeated it. He further suggested an awareness of the international nature of the problem: "I would to God that such a system prevailed all over the world." Thus one is prepared for his earnest White House inquiries about the labor systems of Mexico and Russia, and his affirmation that "the strongest bond of human sympathy, outside of the family relation, should be uniting all working people, of all nations, and tongues, and kindreds."[21]

It is futile to see Lincoln's words as "little sermons in socialism," but equally so to dismiss them as meaningless. The interpretation that he had merely endorsed the laborer's right to quit a job and seek other employment is also untenable.[22]

Lincoln's stand was called forth by a specific well-organized strike in New England. The area was the center of boot and shoe manufacturing in the nation, and the industry was beginning to enter the factory stage. The workers struck on Washington's birthday in 1860 in two Massachusetts towns, primarily for higher wages; the stoppage soon spread to nearly all of the region's shoe industry. By the time Lincoln spoke out, perhaps twenty-five towns and twenty thousand laborers were involved. There were pledges, marches, police, headlines, and even demonstrations by women, thus setting a shocking precedent. George Rogers Taylor called the action "the greatest strike in American history before the Civil War."[23]

With his typical modesty Lincoln "didn't pretend to be familiar with the subject" of the shoe strike but, of course, he could hardly have escaped the controversy surrounding it as he traveled from New York to Rhode Island, through Massachusetts to New Hampshire, and back through Massachusetts and Connecticut. His speeches do indicate that he had discussed the issue with local people. And his support of strikes fits well into his evolving economic outlook. Lincoln made it clear that he did not advocate "war on capital." His loyalty to the laboring man, however, was very real: his concern was keeping the path of opportunity open to all, including the wage earners. He wished, as he said endorsing strikes, "to allow the humblest man an equal chance." Interestingly, not long after his speeches, wage demands by the strikers were met.

The significance of Lincoln's stand should not be overestimated, however. The wide separation between capital and labor was present only where the factory system was coming into being, and with the railroads, and his commitment to trade unions was presumably limited accordingly. It must also be repeated that slavery played a large, confusing role in his labor thought. The leading intellectual of the South, George Fitzhugh, saw strikes and unions as symptoms of the failure of the free labor society. His *Sociology*, Herndon recalled, "aroused the ire of Lincoln more than most proslavery books." Fitzhugh and his disciples thus helped prompt Lincoln to tout the right to strike as a virtue, not a failing, of free society. Indeed the central point of his New England comments was the contrast between "free labor that *can* strike" and "slave labor that *cannot!*"[24]

Still, the slavery dispute only covered up the differences between the developing outlooks of Lincoln and his party. The Republicans offered the homestead policy as the cure for the problems spawned by industrialization. Charity for the poor, or strikes by workingmen, were therefore unnecessary in their eyes.[25] In contrast, Lincoln's enthusiasm for the homestead idea was tempered with realism, in part because he was an economic oriented Whig and in part because he knew firsthand the hardships of the poor on the frontier. Accordingly, he believed that "charities, pauperism, orphanage" were governmental responsibilities, and that the right to strike was allied to the right to rise.[26]

During the Civil War several delegations of striking men from the Machinists and Blacksmiths Union of New York visited the White House, whose occupant thirty odd years earlier had considered becoming a blacksmith himself. Lincoln reminisced to them that "having been raised in a rural district, he had never participated in a strike." The only major strike he had seen personally was in Massachusetts and there, he explained, the "shoemakers succeeded in beating the bosses." The labor representatives took great comfort from their interview, reasoning that although their employers refused to deal with them, Lincoln received them. "If any man should again say that combinations of workingmen are not good," they concluded, "let them point to the Chief Magistrate." They even quoted the President as saying "I know that in almost every case of strikes, the men have just cause for complaint." It is rather likely that the union men quoted Lincoln correctly.[27]

★

Posterity exaggerated Lincoln's commitment to the economic independence of the individual. It is suggestive that agriculture, the field *par excellence* for such economic organization, interested him little. Farming, of course, however independent, was not the best road to rising in life. And not surprisingly, the sole speech of Lincoln's career to consider agriculture, made at the Wisconsin Fair of 1859, tried to point out ways to improve that road.[28]

The address provides Lincoln's most extensive meditation on free labor in an open society, the subject discussed in the early part of this chapter. It also reveals clearly the basis of his willingness to move beyond a mere defense of independent livelihood. A discourse on farming created a fine opportunity to exalt its independence, yet the way Lincoln went about this task underlined further the fact that his ultimate loyalty was not to independence *per se* but to advancement in the world.

By the 1850's the prairie sprouted large estates worked by hired labor. The condemnation of land barons in terms of Jeffersonian ideology became an everyday occurrence.[29] Understandably, Lincoln's speech, too, made a bow to popular opinion in implying, but not directly stating, that the small-holding community, whether in farming "or any labor," was a guarantee against "oppression in any of its forms. Such community will be alike independent of crowned-kings, money-kings, and land-kings."[30] But this atypical Lincolnian statement (however often it has been quoted) is the only such in the corpus of his works. In Wisconsin, too, the rest of his argument characteristically showed that he preferred intensely cultivated small holdings, over larger ones, because they made the best economic sense.

Lincoln made his customary disclaimers about his ignorance to his Milwaukee audience, too, and then proceeded along the thinking of agricultural reformers. Abundance of land had made for wasteful cultivation throughout American history; so, leaning on his trusted statistical approach, he focused on the disparity between the usual farm yields and yields that were obtainable when the soil was pushed "up to something near its full capacity." With the staples of the Northwest as his illustration, he argued that intensive cultivation could raise wheat production from eighteen bushels an acre to fifty, and corn from twenty bushels to a hundred. (In the absence of reliable data the sources for his figures had to be informal and, in time, his predictions proved to be unrealistically optimistic.)

The price a farmer would have to pay for the increased crops was "more labor to the *acre*" but not "to the *bushel*." Lincoln assumed that the same labor input produced about the same yield in both extensive and intensive farming (no small assumption) and then went on to enumerate the advantages of the latter. The blights that regularly cut down crops could be brought under control more easily. The investment in land, a "great item" which he warned "grows greater . . . as the country grows older," could be reduced. Smaller farms could also make substantial savings in the erection and maintenance of fencing. Finally the work could take place on a more manageable area and thus more efficient use could be made of energy, human, animal, and machine.

Interestingly, Lincoln singled out the effect of what he called "thorough farming" upon the farmer's mind. He treated his Wisconsin fair goers to a fine piece of elementary business psychology:

Every man is proud of what he does *well*; and no man is proud of what he does *not* do well. With the former, his heart is in his work; and he will do twice as much of it with less fatigue. The latter performs a little, looks at it in disgust, turns from it, and imagines himself exceedingly tired.

Intensive farming, he concluded, being good farming, would produce both satisfaction and profit.

Lincoln made an excellent case but also continued to display incomprehension of the farmer's expansionist ethos. For the historic American pattern was, and on the whole would remain, extensive agriculture that, on a continent of abundant arable land, emphasized productivity per man hour rather than per acre. Lincoln showed his bias further by ignoring speculation which permitted many farmers to find their best gains in buying up the largest possible acreage and selling out at the right time. Although Lincoln was correct that "the ambition for broad acres leads to poor farming," he may have been wrong in deducing that it therefore also led to poor profits. Still, the dearth of firm data for the 1850's precludes fully trustworthy conclusions. And more than a century later scholars could still argue that mechanization (which Lincoln advocated) not western expansion was the essential ingredient of the American growth in agricultural productivity.[31]

Intensive farming to Lincoln meant machines. It also meant such techniques of scientific cultivation as deep plowing, draining and irrigation, soil analysis, and new kinds of manures and seeds, new hedges and fences, the use of botany, chemistry, and the "mechanical branches of Natural Philosophy." The "natural companion" of his husbandman was "book-learning." All this fitted well into his economic thinking. It not only tied sophisticated commercial farming to industrial development but by minimizing soil depletion also eased the pressure for expansion into new territories.

Lincoln's timing was good. He knew personally many of the Illinois land barons and he knew the hard times that followed the Panic of 1857 were especially hard on them. Thus he could underscore his argument with the all important "test of experience" and speak of the ill fortune of the large estates. "I scarcely ever knew a mammoth farm to sustain itself," he told the Wisconsin audience. They were "like tools or weapons, which are too heavy to be handled. Ere long they are thrown aside, at a great loss." The forces of rational development were a central part of Lincoln's American Dream and, as ever, the conclusions he reached were optimistic.

The unfolding economic realities of the mid-century made Lincoln's case for "thorough farming" into a sound one. The policies he advocated helped the farmer adjust to the ending of geographical expansion and brought him within the market economy. As empty land became scarcer and speculation increasingly sophisticated and difficult, the farmer's reliance on it as a source of income became less needful. As for farming itself, given the technology of the period, wheat and corn came to be most efficiently produced on the family-sized unit. Thus after the 1870's the kind of intensive cultivation that Lincoln had championed in fact broke up the swollen holdings.[32]

Over the long run, however, the road led toward the larger economic unit. Mechanization in particular, which made agriculture an occupation in need of ever increasing capital outlays, grew into a major threat to the family-size farm. Lincoln's total identification of economic development with mobility, as well as his fascination with machines and inventions, had made him oblivious to any danger from this quarter. In his Wisconsin speech, immediately after dismissing large-scale agriculture as economically unfeasible, he went on to urge mechanization. He discussed in some detail the steam plow which had captured the imagination of the nation and prompted the Illinois press to proclaim that "steam had conquered the face of nature." Interestingly, however, although Lincoln, too, saw the harnessing of this power, "a *desideratum*," at least for the steam plow the technical difficulties he perceived forced him to conclude with strong, and as it turned out prophetic, reservations.[33]

Lincoln's speech, as much as his acceptance of factories and labor unions, testifies that he favored the small producer much more because of Whig-Republican economic than Jeffersonian sociopolitical reasons. His small producer embodied more the chance to get ahead via ever greater productivity and economic development than independence. Such an outlook in turn implied for him, and for like-minded Republicans, a substantial potential to accept economically inspired social change in America, in some ways perhaps in spite of themselves.

Lincoln's antipathy toward farming had considerably lessened over the years. He may have never quite made his peace with the life on the land, yet as the span separating him from his early days widened he mellowed. This change was hastened, to quote the somewhat pompous words of Calvin Coolidge, by Lincoln's learning to "vision agriculture as one of the learned professions." The economics he championed began to ameliorate Greeley's "life for an ox." By 1859, therefore, Lincoln spoke in a half-conscious fashion of the "business" of farming.[34]

This Lincolnian speech on economics suggests that his old fire was still there, intact, and that it must have taken a substantial effort to keep it away from the public eye. It helped hold his Whig urges under control, even as the old economic debates were reviving, to engage in private Whiggish activities through Illinois' Republican government (which, however, reveal nothing new about his views); or to give nonpolitical lectures on discoveries and inventions.[35] The Wisconsin Fair address itself performed a similar sublimatory function. Although Lincoln believed it to be nonpartisan, for such befitted the "occasion," it was that only in a superficial sense. He had selected from a variety of agricultural subjects one that supported his political-economic message fully. Lincoln became partisan when speaking on an economic question perhaps in spite of himself. So it was well that he avoided the subject in the political arena.

There he did not cross the bounds he had set for himself since 1854. He felt that he could not do so as a moral man — or as a political man whose party was marching toward the White House. Even after the homestead plank found its way into Republican platforms, indeed, became an important part of Republican ideology, he remained silent. Three months passed after his election to the presidency before at last he voiced his approval, saying laconically that "every man should have the means and opportunity of benefitting his condition." Internal improvements, also ever present in his party's declarations of principles, a policy needed, as the 1858 Illinois platform stated, to maintain "the rights of labor," did not receive even that much of an endorsement from him. Although he permitted his local followers to declare their position on these relatively noncontroversial economic issues, which came to be almost equally espoused by the Illinois Democrats, he himself would not speak of them. Lincoln had made up his mind what the all important political issue was and seemingly no earthly power could divert him.[36]

In private he might muse for example that "the legitimate object of government, is to do for a community of people, whatever they need to have done, but can not do, *at all,* or can not, *so well do,* for themselves — in their separate, and individual capacities." The logical conclusion of his Whig thought was that "the best . . . governments are necessarily expensive." But he no more allowed himself to publicly voice this general economic statement than to voice his specific policies.[37]

Lincoln's silence was supported, largely, by both his party and a prosperous economy — at least until the Panic of 1857. As it happened, a few months before that Congress had reduced the tariff. Thus when the Panic came protectionists were once again provided with a signal demonstration of the import of their policy. Here was a "terrific free-trade crisis," Carey declared. In the political world Greeley's *Tribune* and Pennsylvania spearheaded the old Whigs' high-tariff attack. As among newspapers the *Tribune* was the most influential, so among the states the swing vote of Pennsylvania was the most coveted one. The tariff issue posed a serious threat to Republican unity.[38]

In Illinois, Chicago became the vanguard of protectionist agitation. Some "Republican papers of old Whig proclivities," to quote the bitter words of a Republican paper of old Democratic proclivities, grew insistent in their tariffism. As the hard times continued, banks became a focus of controversy also. If former Whigs rejoiced in the new-found demand for their policies, a former Democrat like John Wentworth declared that banks created panics and that tariff taxation was "oppression." With much justice, another Democrat-turned-Republican concluded, in a letter to Senator Trumbull who had traveled the same route, that the Douglasites were using the economic crisis to bring back these old issues and break up the Republican Party.[39]

In the end, caution prevailed among Illinois' Republicans and the germinating economic debate was throttled. Lincoln's role in this is not clear, but where he stood is. His Whig spirit was stirred by the Panic. Replying to a private protectionist inquiry from Pennsylvania, the leader of the 1844 tariff campaign in Illinois stated flatly that his "views have undergone no material change on the subject." In public, however, he set an example of steadfast muteness on the question.

When the *Chicago Journal* tried to introduce the issue into the Great Debates, he turned a cold shoulder towards it. He refused to mention the subject even when the occasion seemed to call for it. When he was urged from Pennsylvania to speak out for protection, his negative reply was firm. In the spring of 1860 on his Eastern tour he acknowledged that the tariff, internal improvements, financial affairs, and the public domain all had prime significance. But he insisted that "just now, they cannot even obtain a hearing, and I do not propose to detain you upon these topics, or what sort of hearing they should have when the opportunity shall come. For, whether we will or not, the question of Slavery is *the* question, the all absorbing topic of the day."[40]

To justify to himself, and to others, his refusal to speak out on economic issues, Lincoln did not merely point to the overriding importance of stopping slavery. In the case of the tariff he argued, in another letter to Pennsylvania, that the country was not politically ready to fully accept protectionism. In economic terms this meant that even if high levies were passed, they would be "a perpetual subject of . . . uncertainties," thus doing more harm than good. He believed, however, that the obvious need for protection would in short order "force" many of its opponents to change and establish a "more firm and durable" tariff. In private moments, it appears, he already foresaw his Republicans turning into an openly Whiggish party.[41]

First, however, the slavery question had to be settled, the institution placed where men's minds could "rest in the belief that it is in the course of ultimate extinction." In the meantime an undivided Republican Party had to be preserved. The economic issues of the Jacksonian period were a threat to that unity, although Lincoln saw, probably correctly, deviant antislavery views as a still greater threat. His goal, he wrote to Schuyler Colfax, and others, was "to hedge against divisions." The Indiana Congressman replied that the man who could unite the antislavery ranks would truly be "worthier than Napoleon or [Victor] Em[m]anuel." Whatever Lincoln thought of those historic models, he knew that a man who would be a Republican President had to do just that.[42]

The impropriety of raising economic issues was so clear to Illinois' favorite son that he underestimated their strength within his party. He expected no trouble on this count at the Chicago convention, although on its eve he thought best to repeat to his Pennsylvania correspondent, in attendance there, that "the Tariff question ought not to be agitated." He conceded that protectionists, among whom he counted himself, would justly wish for some guarantees. These could be obtained, he suggested, by nominating a man "whose antecedents give assurance." He meant assurance about Whiggishness, although he could no longer use that name, assurance about a man who would neither force nor obstruct the tariff work of Congress. "Just such a candidate," he concluded, "I desire shall be put in nomination."[43]

Lincoln's public silence helped keep the eyes of his party, and of the nation, on the main challenge of slavery. It enhanced Republican chances in Illinois and in the country as a whole. It also helped him to his selection as his party's standard-bearer. Historians agree that, apart from shrewd political maneuvering, Lincoln's nomination for president was the triumph of availability, the triumph, to quote his own words, of a man who "was not the first choice" but towards whom no one had "any positive objection." His silence on economics increased his availability to some factions of his party without weakening him with others. It made him acceptable to former Democrats who in 1860 still had a voice in Republican counsels that was far out of proportion to their numbers. His Whig antecedents also made him acceptable to the majority of the party. His private assurances to Pennsylvania, which saw the tariff as indispensable and whose support to Lincoln was indispensable, served the same end. The radicals, who resisted adulteration of their crusade with economic matters, felt a kinship for his singleminded emphasis on slavery. Yet moderates and conservatives saw Lincoln as one of themselves. By contrast Seward was too outspokenly Whiggish in his economics for the taste of many former Democrats, and so was ex-Democrat Cameron, at least on the tariff issue. Chase, on the other hand, was not trusted by protectionists, and Bates failed on the immigrant issue. Lincoln's stance on economics thus was a supporting element in the complex equation that added up to his nomination.[44]

Yet, in a more significant if less tangible manner, Lincoln's economic persuasion played a central role in his nomination. Whereas the radicals of his party tended to denounce slavery on purely moral grounds, the conservatives did so largely on general grounds of economics.[45] For Lincoln these two grounds had always been the same: his political economy was an intensely moral science. This inner unity, with its moral-economic antislavery, more than his conscious efforts to bridge the gaps between his political brethren, put him at the very center of his party. It made him the most natural choice as the standard-bearer of Republicans.[46]

☆ ☆ ☆ ☆ ☆ ☆ ☆ ☆ ☆ ☆ ☆ ☆ ☆ ☆ ☆ ☆

14
The Whig in
The White House*

Part I

PRESIDENT LINCOLN "BELONGS TO THE OLD WHIG PARTY, AND WILL never belong to any other." Radical Kansas Congressman Martin F. Conway's denunciation was bitter. His ire had been aroused by White House restraint in the matter of slavery. Yet with equal, if equally limited, justice he might have been speaking of Lincoln's attitude toward all ordinary functions of the executive branch of the government.[1]

Purist Whig theory of the presidency, born out of despair over the might of Andrew Jackson but having colonial roots, narrowly circumscribed the exercise of executive power. By the time Lincoln first expressed in writing, with whatever element of jest, the possibility of his own occupancy of the White House, he had come to accept his party's view of executive duties. "Were I president," he wrote in 1848.

> I should desire the legislation of the country to rest with Congress, uninfluenced by the executive in it's origin or progress, and undisturbed by the veto unless in very special and clear cases.[2]

Having repeatedly expressed this principle from one end of Pennsylvania Avenue, he reiterated it on his way to the other, after his election to the presidency. He explained that under the Constitution the executive may recommend some measures, veto others, and may also employ "certain indirect influences to affect the action of congress." But, he added, "my political education strongly inclines me against a very free use of any of these means." As Donald has pointed out, Lincoln lived up to this political education.[3]

---

*With acknowledgement to David Donald who first used this title for an enlightening essay in Graebner, ed. *The Enduring Lincoln*, 47-66.

195

One must recognize that the role demanded by the Whig theory of the executive was not congenial to the sixteenth President. He was a strong person. Indeed, all in all, he performed his White House functions with extraordinary vigor. Nevertheless he largely limited his activity to what he conceived to be purely executive rather than legislative fields. If these ranged far, it was, as he wrote in his Emancipation Proclamation and elsewhere, "by virtue of the power in me vested as Commander-in-Chief . . . in time of actual armed rebellion." Thus the war permitted him to satisfy his desire to be much more than a "mere man of straw," without forcing him to abandon a reserved presidential role in the functioning of Congress or even the Cabinet. One can only wonder to what extent he would have shed this slowly acquired aspect of his Whiggery had there been peace instead of war in his time.[4]

As it was, Lincoln made few large departures from his conservative road, and these reluctantly. And slavery, rather than the more narrowly economic questions, provided the major instances of this. Even on the slavery question when in the spring of 1862 he recommended compensated emancipation to Capital Hill, he could write to editor Greeley that "I do not talk to members of congress on the subject, except when they ask me." Soon he abandoned this attitude. Historians see him by 1865 as playing a decisive part in the congressional espousal of the Thirteenth Amendment abolishing slavery. Yet even then he acted apologetically. He told the solons: "I trust . . . you will perceive no want of respect to yourselves, in any undue earnestness I may seem to display."[5]

It is true that he also clashed with Congress over another much publicized issue, Reconstruction, but this he did in defense of what he assumed to be presidential war powers. He intended no encroachment on the lawmakers' prerogatives, although on this issue he was pushed to exercising the veto — the only time he did so over a weighty question. On ordinary legislative matters, including most of the important economic issues, he acted out to a fair degree the part of the light-handed Whig executive.

Nor was this difficult. First the slavery controversy, later the war, curtailed the relative significance of purely economic policies. Even if this had not been so, there was little call for Lincoln to pressure

Senators and Congressmen, to use those "certain indirect influences," on behalf of "sound" economics. For by the 1860's the Republican Party had largely adopted these policies for its own. Those in the fold with Democratic antecedents had little chance to resist, for the organization of military victory seemingly required centralized, nationalistic economic legislation. "Sir," said Senator John Sherman with finality: "we cannot maintain our nationality unless we establish a sound and stable financial system. . . ."[6]

Lincoln thus had the pleasure of signing into law much of the program he had worked for through the better part of his political life. And this, as Leonard P. Curry, the historian of the legislation has aptly written, amounted to a "blueprint for modern America." The present and the following chapter will briefly catalogue the President's role in the creation of this blueprint and also in related matters of political economy.[7]

The man Lincoln selected for the sensitive position of Secretary of Treasury, Salmon P. Chase, was an ex-Democrat, but of the moderate variety on economics, one whom Joseph Dorfman could even describe as "a good Hamiltonian, and a western progressive of the Lincoln stamp in everything from a tariff to a national bank." This he was not when he took office, although by the time he left the Treasury he had almost earned the description.[8]

Such an end result was the upshot of war, and the President-elect could not have foreseen it at the time he picked his Secretary. Quite a ferment had arisen from the Treasury appointment, and it had a strong flavor of discord over economic policy. As Lincoln said, the "Iron and Coal men" of Pennsylvania wanted Simon Cameron, or at any rate a protectionist. Free traders preferred Chase. Yet the issue was not clear-cut, and the nation's two leading high-tariffites, Carey and Greeley, for example, were both opposed to Cameron. The President-elect himself saw rather too little real economic significance in the matter because he expected Congress to provide economic direction. However others felt about the powers of the Treasury portfolio, he believed that his Cabinet-making could safely proceed as primarily a political maneuver.[9]

And yet, to some extent, his choice of Chase indicates that the Republican victory of 1860 on a platform that emphasized economic issues, in addition to antislavery, did not change Lincoln's priorities. His eyes remained set on one foremost goal: stopping slavery extension in the name of the American Dream. More narrowly economic ends were important, but not on the same plane as this goal. The existing Republican coalition had therefore to be maintained. He had held this ground since 1854. Early in 1861 he was still holding it.

The war at first did not rearrange matters. The President's earliest message to Congress, in the summer of 1861, all but totally ignored economic questions, although Chase prepared a careful financial report for use in the message. If anything, the civil conflict made Lincoln increase his labors to attract Democrats into the ranks of his supporters.[10] Yet, before a year had passed, he took up a Whiggishly circumspect championship of almost the full range of his old economic policies. He felt free to follow such a sharply new course because to the country it could appear as part of the war effort. His calls for economic legislation, which generally underscored recommendations from his Cabinet or were tied to earlier work by Congress, became a regular if limited feature of his annual messages. And although he consistently pleaded war necessity, he also fully understood that the program he advocated had, on the whole, long-term goals.

The President thus departed from a cardinal practice of his early Republicanism, but outside the annual messages he rarely attempted to exert a direct influence on the economic work of the lawmakers. They in turn appreciated his attitude. In mid-1861 Sherman, a leading economic light of the Senate, wrote to him for example: "I venture with reluctance to trouble you about any matter — especially one not connected with military operations. . . ."[11]

Whig conservatism characterized Lincoln's relations with his Cabinet, too. His first outstanding biographer, J.G. Holland, noted perceptively as early as 1865: "His heads of departments were heads of departments indeed."[12] When the President did decide to champion a cause brought forward by one of his advisors, he continued the practice of his more leisurely younger years and digested thoroughly the material at hand. Of course in this he had to be quite selective. A comparison of his Cabinet ministers' annual reports with his own indicate that very few of their recommendations were even seconded. The Lincolnian mind that required thoroughness thus also helps explain his Whiggery in the White House.

As a rule he refused to be drawn into economic battles. Sometimes he used his old subterfuge of claiming ignorance. He would brush off Chase by announcing: "You understand these things. I do not." The ex-Democrat Secretary appears to have expected at first to work closely with him and, unlike the members of Congress, was often less than grateful for being given so much independence. Although he accused his chief of many offenses, an inability to understand economics was not one of them. Indeed instead of accepting the President's plea of ignorance he complained about the lack of executive support in his struggles with the legislators.[13]

The President's attitude was enhanced in the case of the Treasury Department by its tradition of direct links with Congress. The one sharp break in this tradition came under Jackson, and although Lincoln more than half admired him it was hardly for this reason. Harrison, the first Whig in the White House, had gone so far as to criticize the nation's founders for not making the Treasury "entirely independent of the Executive." His party talked about amending the Constitution to rectify the error. By 1870 Henry Adams would speak of the portfolio as "one of real authority, rivaling the President."[14] Lincoln followed, and thus further secured, this American path. Yet on a few occasions he did descend from his high Whig presidential chair to promote economic legislation. The most important instance of this came when he joined the battle for the national banking system.

Historians generally credit Chase with the reorganization of banking along rather centralized, Hamiltonian lines, and with much justice. Students of the sixteenth President, however, have overlooked the fact that he, too, made a substantial contribution to this cause. In December, 1861, the Treasury Secretary's first suggestion for banking reform on the model pioneered by New York fell on deaf legislative ears. Not until a year later, when Chase reiterated in some detail his proposal and Lincoln came to his aid, did Congress begin to move.[15]

The President was not one to demand credit for himself in any field of endeavor. But he did claim a share of the laurels for the creation of the national banking system. In private he explained to John Hay how he "generally delegated to Mr. C. exclusive control of those matters falling within the purview of his dept." Banking, he went on to say, was an exception. His words, that Chase "frequently consulted him" on this subject, focus attention on the fact that the 1862 administration proposal was rather more consistent with the President's notions on economics than with his Secretary's. The exact nature of Lincoln's contribution, whether it was substantive or only political, is likely to remain a mystery. But we do know that he had a long and clear record on the issue reaching back to his first political efforts in 1832.[16]

The earliest public intimations of his views from the White House came in the summer of 1862 when he handed down one of the three direct vetoes of his career. This thwarting of a relatively unimportant District of Columbia banking bill probably originated with a subordinate in the Treasury, but its language was notable and its thinking Lincolnian. The President warned against making laws that were not enforceable. The purpose of banking leglislation, he said, was to protect "honest trade and honest labor." "During the existing war it is peculiarly the duty of the national government to secure to the people a sound circulating medium." In this one local case he recommended legal tender, but his overall goal was to "furnish to the people a currency as safe as their own government."[17]

Then, at the end of the year, in his annual message Lincoln went on record in favor of the Chase plan for banking associations. He was satisfied to reproduce in its entirety the Secretary's very able summary of his longer report to Congress. It conceded the utility of U.S. legal tender notes which met temporarily, and to a certain extent, the long-felt need for a uniform circulating medium. Over the long run, however, it was difficult to envision that such notes, redeemable in specie, on demand, and in large enough quantities for the wants of the country, could be safely maintained. The best available solution was in the organization of banking associations.

Banks would be issued uniform circulation notes by the government. This money's convertibility into specie would be secured through U.S. bonds purchased by the banks and deposited in the Treasury. The new currency would not only protect all against bad moneys and facilitate commerce, but, by creating a steady demand for government bonds, improve (the greatly weakened) public credit. Newly organized banks as well as the already existing institutions were to be welcomed into the system.[18]

With both the President and his Secretary of the Treasury firmly committed to bank centralization, Congress was plunged into heated discussions. In a short time there followed what Bray Hammond characterised as an *impasse*. It was then that Lincoln openly cut loose from his Whig theory and sent identical messages to both Houses, pleading in strong language of his own for the new banking system. He repeated in essence the annual message but now stressed that the measure was needed to carry on the war. He lamented the mounting inflation and explained, as he had when debating over banking in his early Illinois days, that he wished to protect the interests of labor and also of the "whole country." And as in 1837 he even interjected a slightly antibank tone that Senator Sherman later capitalized on in shepherding the banking law through his chamber, by arguing that moneyed institutions, too, should be made to help carry the burden of war.

It is possible that Lincoln's attempt to smooth ruffled Jacksonian feathers by picturing long-term economic policy as a war measure improved the popular support for the banking bill. It misfired, however, as far as many of the lawmakers were concerned. Congressional discussion indicated that they had found his argument less than convincing. And presidential interference in their business was totally unacceptable to many of them. For Lincoln the subject was "so important" that he felt "bound" to speak out on it. But the Senate, contrary to custom, did not order his message printed, and the House did so only reluctantly. *The New York Times* reported that even his friends judged his action "injudicious."[19]

The contemptuous treatment of the Chief Executive's epistle no doubt reinforced his Whiggish view of his office. The centralization of banking, however, was too much his "special interest," as he told Hay, to stop now. Chase, and to a lesser degree Interior Secretary John P. Usher, continued to work openly on members of both Houses. The President, on the other hand, made his tactics more subtle while he kept a careful eye on the progress of the measure. As the final Senate vote approached, and both sides claimed victory, he sent one of his private secretaries, William O. Stoddard, to convey gently his views to two crucial Senators. Speaking to Timothy O. Howe of Wisconsin, who had denounced federal meddling with banks, Stoddard remembered saying: "The President, Mr. Senator, is always cautious, and rightly so, about saying or doing anything which can be construed as Executive interference with the independence of the legislature." Stoddard then went on to explain that the man in the White House felt very "deeply" about the pending bill. Whatever else was said, or perhaps promised, when the upper House passed the bank bill on Lincoln's birthday, by a vote of twenty-three to twenty-one, the gentleman from Wisconsin voted yea.[20]

Stoddard had also spoken in like manner to a second senator, although he could no longer recall the lawmaker's name in his reminiscences. There is considerable likelihood that he was Michigan's Jacob M. Howard. Having spoken against the bill the day before the final Senate vote, he surprised all by casting a "yea" with the majority. He explained that he changed his mind with great unwillingness and only to support the administration.[21]

Perhaps the most crucial, and also most reluctant, convert to the cause, however, was the titular leader of the Senate Republicans, the Chairman of the Committee on Finance, Maine's William Pitt Fessenden. Without his acquiescence there would have been no new banking system. But Fessenden opened an easy passage for the bill, though later remarking that it was anything but a "favorite" with him and that he had supported it because of the demands of the Secretary of the Treasury and the President.[22]

It is possible that the Chief Magistrate also let his "indirect influences" be felt by some members of the lower chamber of Congress. It was certainly so rumored. The day before the final showdown Chase wrote an urgent note to him about Illinois Representative William Kellogg who appeared "disinclined" to support the bank bill. Kellogg had received "more favors" from the White House, to quote Lincoln's earlier words, than "any other Illinois member," and accordingly the Treasury chief now asked the President to "secure" Kellogg's vote. Whether he did the Congressman, too, voted "yea" as the Republican House leaders railroaded the act through. Lincoln received the good news immediately from Chase who lobbied on Capitol Hill to the last moment and then wrote about the act: "It needs your approval only. . . ."[23]

The Chief Executive signed the measure and thereafter refrained from touching upon the subject, except briefly in successive annual messages. In addition to diehard old Jacksonians seeing in the national banking association a revived Bank of the United States, many bankers also were unhappy with the reform. At the end of 1863 Lincoln still spoke of it as primarily an instrument to aid the war effort. A year later, however, he dared to be more explicit. The "national system," he said, was to be a "reliable and permanent influence" and a "great benefit" to the people.[24]

Perhaps atoning a little for past indiscretions vis-á-vis Congress, or mollifying the New York financiers who came to Washington to protest the new system and were told: "Money, I don't know anything about 'money,'" Lincoln now allowed that whether the banking association needed further strengthening was for "Congress to determine." He thus again returned to being the cautious Whig, much to the displeasure of Chase, who entreated him to use his sway on behalf of new legislation. The Chief Magistrate's Whiggishness did not go so far, however, as to prevent him from making it clear in the semi-privacy of his Cabinet that the law indeed required reinforcement, that the private bank notes competing with the national currency "must be" taxed out of circulation.[25]

The majority of the lawmakers soon demonstrated the wisdom of the President's approach; executive pressure was no longer needed to move Congress along the precharted route. And Lincoln's concluding remarks on the subject, in his 1864 message, showed how far the United States had traveled under his stewardship. For as the end of the war approached, he could assume that it was "quite clear" to all "that the treasury cannot be satisfactorily conducted unless the government can exercise a restraining power over the bank-note circulation of the country." Alexander Hamilton or Nicholas Biddle could not have said it as well.[26]

Early in 1862 Oliver Wendell Holmes observed that "our people are worked up to the *paying* point," which he took to be also the fighting point. In fact fighting was to come easier than paying. Lincoln knew this full well. Whatever methods were to be used to support the war effort, they were not likely to be popular. Taking refuge in his Whiggishness, he therefore allowed the most important short-term economic question facing his administration, war finance, to be handled largely by others. He operated on the assumption that so long as

Congress and the successive secretaries of the Treasury were able to wring the wherewithal of war from the people, there was no need for executive interference.

In annual messages he praised the "signal success" of the Treasury operations and also the "patriotism of the people" that made such a success possible. "By no people were the burdens incident to a great war ever more cheerfully borne," he rejoiced. He also requested, citing Chase, the "most diligent consideration" and "best reflections" of the solons on how revenues could be raised "without injuring business or overburdening labor."[27]

Twice only did he make specific policy recommendations, acting in both cases independently of his Secretary of the Treasury. Once he suggested that the government accept the liberation of slaves in lieu of taxes. Rather than a project to increase revenues, this was an attempt to facilitate the gradual abolition of slavery, since the value of the Southern property vastly exceeded the assessments levied against the region.[28]

Nor was his second proposal designed primarily to fill the Treasury. Lincoln called for tax exemptions and freedom from debt seizure for bona fide purchasers of government bonds. This was to be a limited privilege and one properly guarded against abuse. He intended thus to "enable every prudent person to set aside a small annuity against a possible day of want." A further advantage of his plan was to distribute widely the national debt. The political significance of such democratization of finance was "obvious." "Men readily perceive that they cannot be much oppressed by a debt which they owe to themselves." Thus had the war taught him anew of the virtues of the public debt, and he spoke of it now as a "substantial branch of national, though private, property."[29]

The free hand given to the Treasury by Lincoln was viewed with skepticism by Chase most of all when it came to raising taxes. It also incited the Secretary's political ambitions. To an Ohio ally he wrote: "I fancy that as President I could take care of the Treasury better with the help of a Secretary than I can as Secretary without the help of the President." In the end, after he resigned for the last time, he explained his action, in part, by mentioning the absence in the White House of an "active and earnest support" he felt "entitled to." He specifically indicted the Chief Executive for his refusal in the gloomy summer of 1864 to intercede with Congress, "notwithstanding my appeals," on behalf of "sufficient tax bills."

Thinking thus, Chase did not take into account (or perhaps did) the likely effect of tying Lincoln, during an election year to higher taxes, through a public, or semi-private, appeal from the White House. To say this is not to question the ambitious finance minister's sincere desire for higher taxes nor the soundness of his economics on this point. Indeed he appealed in all directions. If on the day on which he resigned he wrote on the subject to his chief, the day before he also had written to Thaddeus Stevens, Chairman of the House Ways and Means Committee, and not long before that to Senator Fessenden. Yet it is pertinent to note that to his *Diary* he confessed, what the financial history of the next months was to prove, that "even if taxes are not increased a tolerable showing can be made."[30]

In place of Chase, Lincoln first nominated former Ohio governor David Tod, whose moderate Democratic economic leanings happened to resemble those of Chase. The selection suggests that Lincoln saw virtue in having a Democrat give sanction to Whig legislation. The Tod selection, like that of his predecessor, also indicates that Lincoln, as he told Hay, felt that "experience in government finance" was no prerequisite to success at the Treasury. In the midst of war, however, Congress disagreed with him, and when Tod declined, the President chose Fessenden for the post. Not until 1865 did he reach, in the view of the *New York World*, "sufficient mental enlargement to go outside of the walks of politics for a Secretary of Treasury" and appoint banker Hugh McCulloch, after Fessenden resigned and Senator Edwin D. Morgan declined. But the non-politician thus chosen then still appeared to possess a most important Lincolnian requisite that politicians tended to have: flexibility. McCulloch had nicely displayed this for the President when he changed from firm opposition to support for national banking and greenbacks.[31]

In December, 1864, safely reelected, Lincoln at last was ready to "concur" with his Secretary that tax assessments should indeed be "further increased." This became all the more important because with Chase out of the way, the Chief Executive made the decision to pull out all stops in the way of military spending. He personally determined, to quote the recollection of Assistant Secretary of the Treasury George Harrington, to supply General Grant "to the fullest extent" with "men and material."[32]

The President's publicly laconic approach to finance was thus not matched in private. An occasional inadvertent reference to taxation also seemed to indicate that his mind wandered to the problem more often than surface signs indicate. At certain junctures, particularly early in the war, he was seriously worried about the state of the federal purse. At times he kept in close touch with Chase. Once he proposed to the Secretary a scheme to increase the sale of bonds. At another time he refused to sign a fiscal measure because of an error — though quite likely it was not he who had caught the lawmakers' slip. He also listened to advice on how to avoid the repeating of the "Jackson Crash" of the 1830's or why Bullion Benton's views on money were correct. He repeatedly held conferences with well known or less well known financiers. With Chase, ex-Treasury chief Robert J. Walker, and lesser folk, he plotted to destroy Confederate credit. He helped steer Fessenden toward reengaging Jay Cooke as the agent for selling bonds, disregarding the clamor against the brilliant banker. Some of the stimulus for his extensive involvement in the trade in Southern cotton stemmed from the view that federal finances were "greatly involved in the matter." He suggested a plan for the government to purchase all available cotton, resell it for gold in New York, and then to "buy up its own greenbacks."[33]

The greenbacks played a major role in financing the war and later, when they became a prime political issue, the martyred President was claimed by all sides. In fact there is little in his record to strongly commit him to any extreme. He approved of the legal tender act, which originated in the House, in large part, to support the war effort. He appears to have helped remove Chase's doubts about its constitutionality — as it turned out, only temporarily. When the first greenbacks came off the press, his friend Lamon found him "in high spirits . . . happier than I had seen him for a long time."[34]

It was important to him that for the first time in American history a national currency was created. This saved for the people very considerable sums, he explained. That these noninterest bearing notes could not, for the moment, be made redeemable in specie he saw as unavoidable. He looked, however, for a return to the gold standard. In his second annual message he explained in a noncommittal manner that most likely carried an import different from Chase's, whose words he used on the occasion, that resumption should take place "at the earliest period compatible with due regard to all interests concerned."[35]

That Lincoln did not expect a return to specie payments

immediately upon the war's end may be inferred from one of the reasons he gave for his appointment of Chase as Chief Justice at the end of 1864. He believed, he told among others George Boutwell, his first Commissioner of Internal Revenue, that the man who was ridiculed as "the foreman" of his "green printing office," would uphold the legal tender act. Lincoln even admitted that specie banking was not the sole road to a sound currency. Before the war he may have familiarized himself with the thought of Edward Kellogg, who, after the war, became one of the apostles of the "people's money." Yet, to sum up the matter with words the President saw fit to borrow, he doubted that greenbacks could be "permanently, usefully and safely maintained" as the currency of the United States.[36]

Lincoln was concerned about the inflation produced by the ever increasing issues of paper money. He warned of "disastrous consequences," at least while seeking a national banking system. He seems to have been particularly angry with gold speculators; his hope was to reduce currency fluctuation "to the lowest possible point." He held conferences with financiers to plan strategy to this end. The painter Francis B. Carpenter, who lived in the White House for a spell, even quoted him as wishing, with clenched fist smashing on the table, for every speculator's head to be shot off. This is doubtful — even if he was unapprised of the fact that some of his Secretary of State's funds (without Seward's knowledge) were invested in gold speculation. We do know that the President rejected a proposal for the arrest of the speculators. He is on record in a different case, however, making a sharp reference about those who in their economic self-serving disregarded "all questions of country."[37]

Lincoln noted that the inflation hurt both labor and business and also that "for every hard dollar's worth of supplies we obtain, we contract to pay two and a half hard dollars hereafter." "We can live through it at all events," he assured a general, but demanded "an earnest effort" by all to improve the situation. On the whole, however, he allowed others to make these efforts. In the matter of the gold speculators he refused the request of Chase to promote a Congressional act that attempted to control them. Once the measure passed he signed it without comment, and likewise signed its repeal after the law had failed.[38]

Lincoln kept an eye on the stock market. As early as 1860 the *New York Herald* reported as much. During the war Chase sent him market summaries at times. After the preliminary emancipation proclamation he wrote disgruntledly to Vice President Hannibal Hamlin that the "stocks have declined" and implied that they, and Army enlistments, were better measures of public confidence than the views of newspapers or "distinguished individuals." He took some satisfaction at gold speculators taking a beating, yet he is remembered giving advice, at least once, to Thomas C. Durant, Vice President of the Union Pacific, saying "it's a good time to sell."[39]

The revolution brought by the Civil War reached the nation's public finances, too. A people whom Adam Gurowski is supposed had "an inborn hatred of taxation," learned to accept the common fate of mankind. Although the graduated income tax that Lincoln signed into law did not immediately become a permanent feature of American governance, the base of national finance was permanently shifted from the public land and customs revenues to internal sources. As if by a "common instinct," James G. Blaine later wrote, the United States turned to lean on its internal strength. But the President firmly limited his involvement in this movement. Indeed he often joked about finances, distressing Chase by telling him to give his "paper mill another turn." And this levity for once may have masked no deadly anxieties. For in the final analysis he believed that in his materially "favored land" these matters would somehow be taken care of.[40]

When his Treasury minister recommended war finance through Southern wealth, the draft of the proposal, instead of finding its way into Lincoln's annual message, was buried among his papers. When Congress nonetheless placed a vast potential source of funds at his disposal in the form of confiscation legislation, he largely ignored it for reasons of policy. There was truth, too, in the Chase complaint about the administration's spending: "The spigot in Uncle Abe's barrel is made twice as big as the bung hole. He may have been a good flatboatman and rail-splitter, but he certainly never learned the true science of coopering." To the end there remained in the President something of the young politician of 1832, who had championed overly sanguine plans for internal improvement and sidestepped matters of finance. Thus in the midst of a stupendous war he could still cheerfully call various public work projects to the lawmakers' kind attention.[41]

One of the essential sources of revenue during the antebellum period was the tariff. Since it was also a salient tool of Whig economic policy, Lincoln became something of an expert on it. The tariff was also the one economic question on which he broke his silence after being elected to the presidency. He did this, very gently, early in 1861, in Pittsburgh, thus acknowledging the electoral support he had received in Pennsylvania on account of his protectionist views.[42] The former Whig pleaded his ignorance of the subject, "especially as to details," which was no doubt true enough as far as the specifics of the Morrill bill then before Congress were concerned. He also explained that it was the job of the legislature, not the executive, to determine pertinent policy. He nevertheless repeated, in a mild way, one of the protectionist arguments he had adopted long ago. And he summed up masterfully the difference between the Democratic and the Whig-Republican outlooks. "One party insists," he explained, that protectionism "oppresses one class for the advantage of another; while the other party argues that with all its incidents, and in the long run, all classes are benefited."

In the White House, however, Lincoln followed his "political education" to the point where he managed not to directly mention the tariff at all in official messages. He did not have to. Congress passed tariff increase after increase and he signed them into law. Rates reached unprecedented and previously unimaginable heights. They were made frankly protectionist. The revenues thus collected helped finance the war. But the lawmakers were also shaping industrial America. The time indeed had come, as Lincoln had predicted it would, when protection was placed on a "firm and durable basis."[43]

He desired a protectionist policy, as he said in Pittsburgh, which stemmed from "an enlarged view" and which, "so far as possible," was "just and equal to all sections of the country & classes of people." But he did not attempt to influence the work of Congress, however open it was to pressures from local interest groups. He saw the nation moving toward the right direction and, harrassed and overburdened as he was, felt justified to seek refuge in his Whig theory of the executive. Only once did he impose his will over a Cabinet officer in a question involving domestic industries and international trade. And military needs were uppermost in his mind when early in the war, though not early enough, he overruled protectionist Simon Cameron, his first War Department head, by beginning large purchases of European arms for the Army and Navy.[44]

Yet if the President largely avoided either dealing with or discussing these issues, he did not neglect making political use of the historically symbolic subject of the tariff in his defense of the Union. During the secession crisis he spoke about offshore duty collection as a way of showing federal authority over the Southern states. Later, more importantly, as part of a strong economic argument for the Union, he conjured up a mournful picture of a secession-ridden country severely divided by internal tariff walls. He toiled not unlike the Fathers had in the divided days of the Articles of Confederation.[45]

In the old American System internal improvements were the necessary companions of protection. The Republican Party did not explicitly continue this direct link between the two policies, yet it did support them both. The prime improvement project of the period, the Pacific Railroad, was endorsed by its successive platforms. Lincoln himself, even before his election to the presidency, received from Francis E. Spinner, whom he later appointed the Treasurer of the United States, volumes of surveys for the road. In spite of his fascination with the subject, from the White House he tried to allow free hand to Congress. In the process, however, he had to make some weighty decisions, do some soul searching, and withstand considerable political pressure.

He thus, with little leeway, designated Omaha and Sacramento as the two terminals of the road. He appointed directors and an examiner to represent the government. He selected companies to handle some of the railroad's business and approved the first hundred miles of the proposed route. Once he even recommended, as he had done in the Illinois legislature, a competent engineer acquaintance for a job with the railroad. His sole, immediately controversial act was fixing the gauge of the road at five feet, perhaps making thereby an economic appeal for the Union, for that gauge was widely used in the South and in California. On this, however, Congress promptly overrode him.[46]

In private Lincoln discussed the railroad work enthusiastically. Hay, for one, spoke of the Tycoon's "profound" interest in the enterprise. Lincoln may have even given serious consideration to the unrealistic proposal of simultaneously building three separate lines to the West Coast. Among his papers there is a pamphlet on the subject with many passages underlined, including a sentence that berated the opponents of such a gigantean project for "want of confidence in our ability as a government."[47]

After the enactment of the 1862 Pacific Railroad bill Lincoln expected the "earliest completion of the road." By early 1863, however, he, like others, reached the conclusion that more aid would be required to bring the plans to fruition. He demonstrated his own liberality by fixing the Western base of the Sierra Nevada so as to include the foothills with the mountain. This decision of the ex-Illinois surveyor, which overlooked a California Supreme Court verdict on the subject, increased the Central Pacific's federal subsidy by three quarters of a million dollars. Among those who claimed having helped him decide was California congressman Aaron A. Sargent who is supposed to have quipped later: "Abraham's faith moved mountains."[48]

More important was the President's conversion, with the aid of General Grenville Dodge, to the view of the Union Pacific promoters that, to succeed, the railroad must have the first lien on the company's property and the government loans second. Lincoln's opinion may have been used by the railroad lobbyists to obtain the acquiescence of Congress. Not that Capitol Hill required overly much prodding. The lawmakers not only gave the corporation the first lien but also doubled their land grant in 1864. The Chief Magistrate approved their work and reported at the end of that year that "the great enterprise . . . has been entered upon with a vigor that gives assurance of success. . . ."[49]

A less mighty Civil War internal improvement plan that also greatly interested the President was the enlargement of the Illinois-Michigan Canal. His old friend, and later biographer, Isaac Arnold, acted as the chief legislative promoter of the measure. Arnold was not only a Congressman from Illinois at the time, but also an attorney for the Canal that the young Lincoln had worked hard to have built. Arnold evidently obtained the Chief Executive's discreet support for the new venture very early. The 1861 annual message to Congress spoke of the military need for navigation improvements and specifically mentioned the Great Lakes region. A week later the Illinois Representative, whom Noah Brooks would characterize as one with "undying faith in Old Abe and the Great Western Ship Canal," started the legislative machinery on behalf of the improvement.[50]

Arnold ran into difficulties and appealed to the White House. Aid came forth once more from a President engaged at the time in planning both military strategy and emancipation. Supporters of the Illinois bill had decided on logrolling and therefore presented him with a memorial in favor of a New York canal project, the enlargement of the Erie and Oswego. This permitted Lincoln to circumvent his Whig compunctions. He forwarded the memorial to the lawmakers, strategically timing his action to coincide with the reporting of the Illinois-Michigan bill in the House. In a covering letter he explained that he had not the "leisure" to investigate the proposal in detail but its "great importance" seemed to him "obvious and unquestionable." Soon after, an appropriation for this work was coupled with the one for Illinois.[51]

The double canal bill, although second in importance only to the Pacific Railroad among the improvement proposals before the Thirth-seventh Congress, faced much opposition. Lincoln conferred with various people on the subject, including the old transportation building war horse Samuel Ruggles, Seward, and Illinois Governor Richard Yates. At the end of 1862 the annual message came to the project's strong support. The Chief Magistrate tied the waterways to the already approved Pacific Railroad, as did earlier its congressional supporters. He spoke of the canals "as being of vital, and rapidly increasing importance to the whole nation, and especially to the vast interior region" which he described as the economic heart of the nation. He transmitted an evaluation of the military significance of the works that he had ordered made. And he promised to have further statistical information prepared on the subject.[52]

In spite of the presidential effort, political and commercial foes blocked the appropriation for the canals. The final decision was reached about the time Congress voted to establish the national banking system. Lincoln had intervened directly for the latter reform, but there is no evidence that he did so on the much less momentous canals bill. It was one thing to break the bounds of Whig theory and risk the displeasure of Congress in order to overturn the great Jacksonian decision of the 1830's on banking; another to subsidize the Illinois-Michigan Canal, useful as the project was, and however sentimental an attachment he may have had to it.

The Canal supporters however would not accept defeat and in mid-1863 organized a national convention in Chicago. They thus imitated the internal improvement convention Lincoln had attended seventeen years earlier. Vice President Hamlin presided at their meeting, and the President laid its memorial before Congress. "This interest is one which, ere long, will force its way," he told the lawmakers in his annual message at the end of 1863 — in a language reminiscent of his words on the tariff. By then, however, he had fully retreated behind his Whiggery and left it to legislative "wisdom" what could be done during the war. Still, as late as 1864 he furnished information that he had had prepared on the subject. He did not live to see peace bring the desired improvements.[53]

The supporters of both the Pacific Railroad and the Illinois and New York canals laid claim to war necessity, among other arguments, and the Chief Executive went along without showing much conviction. He used the same rationale, but in earnest, to recommend to Congress three other improvement projects. The first was a railroad from Kentucky into East Tennessee, clearly a "military measure," to quote Lincoln, but "also a valuable permanent improvement, worth its cost in all the future." Nothing came of this.[54]

A second plan he espoused called for the extension of the Pacific Railroad into a guerrilla-infested region of Missouri. In this case "the military necessity" was "not so patent, but that Congress would try to restrain me," he mused. Therefore, he appears to have bypassed the legislators entirely and procured federal aid through the War Department.[55] Lincoln also wished to see the rail communication into the capital improved. It is revealing, however, that in presenting to the legislators, early in 1863, a Washington memorial calling for such a work, he mentioned its "great practical importance," but would go no further. Whiggishly restraining himself, he deleted from an earlier draft the following:

I deemed it proper to note that it must be apparent to all, that the Nation in time of peace, will derive great advantages from these Roads, and they will be invaluable to the government in time of war. Their want has been, and is severely felt in suppressing the present rebellion.

Congress, here, too, refused favorable action.[56]

It is worth noting again that although at times the vast problems of war finance distressed Lincoln, and he deplored inflation, he also maintained a very large measure of confidence in the ability of the United States, both the government and the economy, to underwrite improvement works while engaged in a great war. Although as the conflict grew longer, he moderated his demands a little, it was his Whig view of the executive, and the benefits he derived from it, that played a major role in stopping him from endorsing even more projects than he did endorse. Thus the President illustrated the hazards of the faith for those who believe in the activist concept of government.

☆ ☆ ☆ ☆ ☆ ☆ ☆ ☆ ☆ ☆ ☆ ☆ ☆ ☆

15
The Whig in
The White House

Part II

LINCOLN CONSIDERED AGRICULTURE THE MOST BACKWARD AREA OF economic life and thus, in theory at least, the most in need of governmental aid. His first annual message noted that although the largest interest of the nation was farming, it received scanty assistance from Washington. He sensed that any call for change would raise the ire of the idolators of yeoman independence, and having decided to seek such a change, he spoke in an un-Whig-like, Jeffersonian language. He applauded farming, which was "so independent in its nature as to not to have demanded and extorted more from the government." He went further and disclaimed any desire for making detailed suggestions for modification. Nonetheless, ever so gently, he broached the decades old subject of creating an independent governmental bureau of agriculture.[1]

Congress was slow to respond even to this moderate presidential initiative. "We are engaged in a struggle for national existence," objected one Senator. "We need all our energies devoted to that object . . . ." Fessenden of Maine added, no doubt with some truth, that not one farmer in a hundred desired a new agency.[2] Yet even as the clamor about Washington robbing the husbandman of his self-reliance grew, lawmakers who agreed with the President came to his aid. A House committee chaired by Illinois' Owen Lovejoy produced a strong report that began by citing Lincoln's views. Its tone was such that one able student mistook it as coming from the man in the White House.[3]

In the end the Lincolnian view prevailed. After much trouble in

215

the Senate a separate sub-Cabinet level department was created. To its head the President appointed Isaac Newton, a self-made man whom he had befriended and who had a scientific bent that befitted one with such a distinguished name. The new Commissioner's predisposition toward scientific agriculture must be emphasized for it played a pivotal role in his selection. He was not a well known agriculturist and as a department chief alternately showed both ability and blundering. He proved to be a controversial political figure, too. All the same, he soon had a botanist, a chemist, an entomologist, and a statistician working for him — all very able persons. He also started an agricultural library and a museum.[4]

Newton's first report read much like an exposition of Lincoln's views, indicating perhaps both consultation with the President and the currency of his ideas. It explained that the goal of the agriculture department was to " 'make two blades of grass grow where one grew before.' " Later a historian of the department saw these words as the organization's *raison d'etre* over the decades, and cited them as the title for its history. He, like others, failed to note, however, that the direction the department took fully reflected the Chief Executive's outlook, too. It is even pertinent to recall Lincoln's 1859 words to the Wisconsin Agricultural Society: "Every blade of grass is a study; and to produce two, where there was but one, is both a profit and a pleasure."[5]

By the end of 1862 the President could report with enthusiasm on the new agency's research work "at home and abroad"; its study of "recent improvements in agriculture"; its "introduction of new products"; its collection of statistics, and its future plans. He felt confident that the Agriculture Department would serve the best interests "of a large class of our most valuable citizens" and over the long run, "all our people." It was, as he later said, "peculiarly a people's department." In time he got pulled into some of its administrative and monetary problems although he tried manfully to resist. And it is interesting to note that he valued, in terms of dollars and cents, the services of an able agricultural chemist considerably higher than did Congress.[6]

The idea of an independent agricultural agency had not originated with the Civil War Executive. President Taylor had already recommended such a body in 1849. Some farmers' organizations had advocated it before that. In 1861 Lincoln may have taken up the cause, in part, because of the report of his Secretary of Interior, Caleb B. Smith. Still, in view of the reluctance of the Senate, it was probably important that he did so in his official capacity. He certainly helped set the direction of the new arm of the government. For whatever faults Lincoln's Commissioner of Agriculture had, ever after the Department would follow, to quote Paul Gates, "new lines of statistical enquiry, experimentation, and scientific activity. . . ."[7]

Championing a new Department of Agriculture, the Chief Magistrate followed his Whig inclination in favor of intensive, scientific husbandry. In economic terms less Whiggish, but still Lincolnesque was his stance on homestead legislation. He did not ask for such legislation and avoided intruding on the lawmakers while they redeemed this major Republican campaign pledge. But once Congress accomplished its work, providing one hundred and sixty acres of public domain for settlers, he expressed his support. Some ex-Whigs still bemoaned the squandering of the national heritage, but Lincoln's historical overview of land policy contained little comfort for them. He spoke of the "early settlement and substantial cultivation" of the public lands as being cherished by "some of our wisest statesmen," and illustrated the dominating influence of their viewpoint with a number of historic examples. And he summed up his sketch by declaring that the policy received "its most signal and most beneficent illustration" in the Homestead Act.

Though some later historians would question the success of the 1862 public land legislation, Lincoln, like the majority of his contemporaries, saw it as an achievement. It was to provide an "opportunity" for people to improve their condition. Following his Secretary of Interior, he advised amending the law to assure that soldiers, too, would receive its full benefits, and Congress acted on the recommendation. But he did not desire "essentially changing the general features of the system."[8]

The President, and perhaps a large segment of the Republican Party, saw Civil War economic legislation as promoting the "material growth of the nation" and the rise of the "many." In his first annual message Lincoln repeated, verbatim, his ringing 1859 defense of free labor before the Wisconsin Agricultural Society, enlarged it, and repeated it, yet once more to a Workingmen's Association in 1864. He thus cautioned against "the effort to place *capital* on an equal footing with, if not above *labor,* in the structure of the government." He again argued that since labor created value it "deserves much higher consideration" than capital. Although the juxtaposition of free and slave labor continued to blur the clarity of his economic vision, to which now was added the almost insupportable burden of war, he issued a remarkably strong, forward-looking warning to working people:

> Let them beware of surrendering a political power which they already possess, and which, if surrendered, will surely be used to close the door of advancement against such as they, and to fix new disabilities and burdens upon them, till all liberty shall be lost.

Thus again, however much Lincoln and his party agreed on broad outlines of economic policy, there was a measurable difference between the two. The House, which was unwittingly laying the foundations for the economics of the Gilded Age, did not even refer to a committee, as was customary, the part of Lincoln's message about labor. They acted in sharp contrast to the view of the President, who saw *only* this section of his address as worthy of discussion in the Cabinet. Congressman, ironmaster, and radical Republican, Stevens explained the action of his colleagues: "There is no appropriate committee on metaphysics in the House. . . ." Copperhead Clement Vallandigham readily agreed: "I presume it will go then to the Committee on Unfinished Business." And so, as a historian added, "unfinished business it remained for the rest of the century."[9]

Lincoln's very real loyalty to the workingman was expressed, within the limits of the Civil War and a Whig perception of executive powers, only through small activities. These nonetheless carried immense symbolic value. His numerous pardons provide, at least in part, a case in point. He specifically objected, for example, to the punishment of withholding soldiers' pay for "it falls so very hard upon poor families." At times he appeared to be running a White House employment agency for the needy, this quite apart from the office seekers, whom he came to resent bitterly. "I am always for the man who wishes to work," he wrote in recommendation for one laborer, and wrote in behalf of a young boy seeking work, "He must have a chance." He helped some to start small businesses. The largest number of his beneficiaries, however, were women.[10]

George Bancroft's 1866 judgment carried much truth that "the laboring classes everywhere saw his advancement their own." They sensed that Lincoln's praise of labor was genuine. He could mention in an annual message, for example, that the heroic performances of the Navy were "scarcely more wonderful than the success of our mechanics and artisans in the production of war vessels." He entertained workingmen's delegations and replied to their addresses in a fraternal fashion. If he saw the congratulatory letter sent to him by Marx and the First International, which depicted the war as one for the rights of all workingmen, he would have been pleased by much, although not all of it. Seward replied through Charles Francis Adams for the Chief Executive, at his direction, as the Secretary of State explained, and in so friendly a fashion as to make Marx exultant.[11]

Accepting honorary membership in the New York Workingmen's Association, Lincoln took the occasion to deplore the 1863 riots in that city. Some of his words could have come from the very mouth of Marx, illustrating the extent to which these ideas were part of the Western intellectual currents of the time:

> The most notable feature of a disturbance in your city last summer, was the hanging of some working people by other working people. It should never be so. The strongest bond of human sympathy, outside of the family relation, should be one uniting all working people, of all nations, and tongues, and kindreds.

The President had something fairly specific in mind. "The most notable," certainly the most unhappy feature of the draft riots was their racist overtone. White workingmen had hanged black workingmen. In 1862, even before Lincoln fully came to face the fact that black colonization was a will-o'-the-wisp, he had already made some efforts to convince the white worker that the black man was no threat to him. In 1864 his call for the "uniting of all working people" had, above all, this same end in view. His comment, coming as slavery was passing away, gave promise of readiness to face the real problems of labor once the confusing shadow of bondage was removed. And, in specific political terms, Lincoln's words implied a slowly stirring hope that black and white laborers might be awakened to their common interests.[12]

On a few occasions the President directly intervened on behalf of labor groups. A petition of Philadelphia working women, accompanied by a letter of Pennyslvania Governor Andrew G. Curtin, complained of inflation reducing wages below "the price of living." It requested increased pay at the government arsenals, employment of more women, and the regulation of war contractors so that they would have to pay the same wages as did the government. These were not small requests and writing to Secretary of War Stanton, the President confessed that he did not know how much the government could legally do. He added emphatically, however, that "it is certainly true in equity, that the laboring women in our employment, should be paid at least as much as they were at the beginning of the war." Although the exact meaning of his words is not clear, he directed the Secretary to provide as much relief as the law and public interest allowed.[13]

In a similar case, a committee of working women from Boston visited Lincoln and reported that he was "deeply impressed with the tale of their sufferings. . . ." He told his Quartermaster General that government contracts should provide "remunerative wages." Another Massachusetts group, the employees of the Watertown Arsenal, petitioned him against having to work longer hours than those in force at Navy yards. A presidential note to Stanton, requesting "early attention," got quick results. The working day was reduced.[14]

By late 1863 Lincoln began to be worried by labor stoppages, at times in important war-related industries. A joint Army-Navy movement against Charleston, South Carolina, for example was weakened because, as Secretary Welles explained to him, "strikes in the Shipyards had thrown the completion of vessels back." The President's own home state practically outlawed strikes. Elsewhere, without his knowledge, generals used federal troops to break strikes. In the most notable of such cases, St. Louis shipbuilders, tailors, and printers petitioned to him for help. They reminded him of his 1860 words and paraphrased them: "Thank God we have a system where there can be a strike." Labor meetings in other parts of the country seconded this call for assistance. Soon thereafter, the military withdrew, having been ordered not to "interfere with the legitimate demands of labor." The workers felt certain the order had come from

Lincoln and they were probably right. At any rate, the deed grew into legend in the labor movement.[15]

From the presidential chair Lincoln faced a cruel dilemma over such an issue. On the one hand he saw the Confederacy warring "upon the rights of all working people," as he wrote to a New York labor group. Its defeat had to come before all other matters. On the other hand he had strong sympathies for the laboring men, and visiting union leaders could quote him as saying that almost invariably strikers had "just cause" for their action.[16]

In these circumstances Lincoln's prolabor attitude was remarkable. On at least two occasions he received in the White House the leaders of striking unions whose members walked off jobs on Navy contract projects. At the same time the employers of these very workers were announcing their opposition to "every combination which has for its object the regulation of wages." The President explained that he could not step into disputes between labor and employer, and even said let "the best blood" win. Yet through such a passive stance, which included an insistence that contractors meet original project deadlines, the government in fact sided with the strikers. For all his evenhandedness Lincoln made clear which side he thought had "the best blood." "I know the trials and woes of workingmen," he told one delegation of strikers. "I have always felt for them."[17]

One manifestation of the President's broad view of how to serve the interests of the "laboring many" is his attitude toward immigrants. The nativist leanings of the old Whigs he never shared. In 1844, after he brought his Illinois party to a strong condemnation of nativist mob action, the Democratic press could not but report that the "most benevolent feelings toward foreigners . . . were . . . the sincere and honest sentiments of *his heart*" — even if they were "not those of *his party*."[18]

His attitude had a political ingredient, but one made up of future hopes much more than of contemporary realities. Few immigrants appear to have been attracted to his party until it became Republican. Much more important were his central economic beliefs. On the one hand he bade "God speed" to immigrants "if they can better their condition by leaving their old homes;" on the other he identified, correctly for his time and place, the growth of population with economic development. Although his humanistic outlook stopped him short of a Henry Carey who valued immigrants at $1000 a head, and declared instead that men are "better than gold," he, too, saw men as important — the most important of any country's "natural resources."[19]

The Civil War not only diverted hosts of Americans from civilian to military pursuits, it also drastically reduced immigration. At first the Lincoln administration tried to meet the difficulty through unofficial State Department efforts, and by aiding the work of state agents, with the President taking an interest in the matter. By the end of 1863 he decided to do more and extended governmental activism to still another area of economic life.

His annual message requested Congress to devise a system for encouraging immigration. It spoke of the inflow from the Old World as a "source of national wealth." It pointed to the labor shortage in both agriculture and industry and to the "tens of thousands of persons, destitute of remunerative occupation" who desired to come to the United States but needed assistance to do so. The conclusion showed that in spite of slavery and war, Lincoln could still be a perceptive observer of the American economy, for it was in such a context that he said:

> It is easy to see that, under the sharp discipline of civil war, the nation is beginning a new life. This noble effort demands the aid, and ought to receive the attention and support of the government.[20]

Congress responded favorably to the presidential request, and immigrants, in time, contributed in a very major way to the making of the American industrial revolution, "beginning a new life" not only for themselves but also for their adopted country.

Contrary to Charles A. Beard and his disciples, industrialists at first were rather suspicious of government fostered immigration. Nor could labor be friendly. Lincoln fully recognized the effect of labor supply on wages, once discussed it in some detail. Yet he saw no inconsistency between his devotion to the workingmen and his support of immigration. He was certain that mineral discoveries and the Homestead Act would attract legions of men to the West and perpetuate, if less painfully, the labor shortage of the war. For America, with the economy ever growing, the problem had never been a glut on the labor market — quite the opposite.

Lincoln consulted Seward on the subject, who also had pro-immigrant sentiments that earlier had set him apart from the mainstream of Whiggery. In the spring of 1864 Seward had drafted an immigration bill which the Cabinet approved, except for the un-reconstructed Democrat Welles, who grumbled about governmental meddling. This draft may or may not have contributed to the even-tual act that permitted immigrants to mortgage future wages, up to a year, in exchange for passage to America. The law also established the office of the Commissioner of Immigration. Europeans who dis-liked the martial calling were promised freedom from service so long as they refrained from voting or declaring their intention of becoming citizens. The Chief Magistrate signed the bill on July 4, 1864.[21]

Five months later his last annual message solicited the legislators to improve the design of "this great national policy." He wanted the government to protect immigrants from frauds that denied them the freedom to choose either a vocation or a place of settlement. Looking to the future Lincoln explained: "I regard our emigrants as one of the principal replenishing streams which are appointed by Providence to repair the ravages of internal war, and its wastes of national strength and health." But the Republicans who went along with him in recognizing immigration as an integral part of their de-velopmental policy would not go all the way by providing the new-comers with "the effective national protection," that he demanded. It was ironic, and sadly presaged the future, that the contract labor law, as it became known, which was meant to benefit the nation, in-cluding the workingmen, was used among other things to import strikebreakers.[22]

If Lincoln's demeanor indicated a special deference toward the laboring man, the same can not be said of his meeting with John Jacob Astor for example. Certain big businessmen he called "respect-able scoundrels." When during the secession crisis William E. Dodge begged him to save the country from economic disaster and declared that the President-elect had to decide "whether grass shall grow in the streets of our commercial cities," Lincoln replied coolly that "If it depends upon me, the grass will not grow anywhere except in the fields and the meadows." But he would not accommodate the capitalists and compromise his central beliefs, "let the grass grow where it may."[23]

Lincoln could not be quoted, not even in private, impugning businessmen as a class in the manner of a John F. Kennedy. He did, however use a technique that in the later man's epoch came to be called "jawboning." Thus in 1862 Samuel Ruggles had to report to New York Governor Edwin D. Morgan the President's "marked displeasure" with the rise in railroad and canal charges in that state after Confederate forces cut off rival transportation routes further south.

Ruggles had gone to Washington to promote the chances of federal subsidies for the enlargement of the Erie and Oswego Canal. Faced by Lincoln's anger he explained that the laws of economics, supply and demand, had created the higher prices. He offered other defenses, too, with equally little success. The Chief Executive, when he wanted to, showed that he understood economics. Now he insisted that he was facing a "grievous imposition" by the Empire State's carriers on the Western food producing states. He spoke of reaching a point of danger where the New York facilities "would practically become the regulators of the prices of transportation." And he added "quite emphatically that adequate measures would be adopted to terminate this abuse. . . ."

Not surprisingly, Ruggles, backed by Secretary of State Seward, urged businessman-governor Morgan that the canal board and the railroads reduce their charges and make clear to the West that "no undue or needless burthen on their products should or would be permitted." It is revealing of Lincoln's political methods, and reminiscent of his handling of emancipation about the same time, that even as he told Ruggles that "he should feel but little inclined to exert his influence and authority" on behalf of federal aid to New York, he had in fact already included a strong paragraph to that effect in his annual message.[24]

Lincoln insisted on protecting, to the best of his understanding, the interests of the common man but his willingness to stand up to capitalists did not indicate active hostility. Indeed he recognized

the importance of business and was ready to aid it. Nationally supervised banking, tariff, subsidies for internal improvements, and other
policies that many historians and nearly all Jacksonians regarded as
probusiness, he did not see as such. He did, however, consciously
and repeatedly intercede on behalf of businessmen.

He announced bravely that the "government can not afford to
accept services, and refuse payment for them," and facilitated the
settlement of the claims of many — from undistinguished citizens
through the Illinois Central Railroad to states of the Union. On
occasion he was rewarded by grumbling about presidential interference.[25]

Friends, or strangers, eager to make money, took advantage of
Lincoln. He became concerned with corruption, war profiteering,
and his administration came to be tainted with minor scandals that
were lost from sight in the whirlpool of war. He gave firm, if Whiggishly covert support to the House committees monitoring war contracts. At the same time he could be lenient toward wrongdoers, in
the well publicized case of the Smith brothers of Boston annulling
the verdict of a military court. His leniency stemmed from charity,
political expediency, and in some cases may have had policy implications. It also showed an understanding attitude toward business; he
noted with resignation "There is powerful temptation in money."[26]

The President paid some attention to commercial treaties (using
those with Haiti and Liberia to establish diplomatic ties with the
black republics); agonized over privateering; and sounded
thoroughly genuine in regretting his inability to devote time to matters such as industrial exhibits, a subject "so interesting in itself, and
so extensively and intimately connected with the material prosperity
of the world."[27] At moments he was forced to contend with the pet-
tiest economic matters, at others he spent considerable sums for
ends he thought necessary, but which were not the ends the money
had been appropriated for by Congress.[28] The important postal re-
forms accomplished under him received only his cursory attention.[29] The telegraph, however, firmly captured his imagination
and his constant support.[30]

The same was true of mining, but to a larger degree. Typical of his
outlook is an incident from 1864 when, having listened to Bishop
Simpson mention in a sermon beneficial discoveries, Lincoln com-

plained: "But, Bishop, you did not 'strike ile.' " Samuel Drake had
drilled the first oil well only a few years earlier.[31] Lincoln spoke with
deep enthusiasm of the "enterprising labor" in the mines of the Rock-
ies and California, indicating that at last he had fully accepted the
fruit of antebellum American expansion and had integrated it into
his Whiggish vision of internal development. He wanted the "immense" resources "developed as rapidly as possible" and recommended "extraordinary measures" by the government — but to no
avail. Here, as elsewhere, in advocating expenditures he spoke of
war needs, but his eyes were plainly fastened on long range goals.[32]
As the war was ending his interest quickened. He planned to develop
the mineral regions by channeling immigrants to them. He also saw
mining as a source of employment for returning soldiers and as a
tool which would help reduce the national debt. He sent a fine message to the miners through the Speaker of the House Schuyler Colfax,
who wrote his words down a day later:

> I have very large ideas of the mineral wealth of our Nation. I believe it
> practically inexhaustible . . . its development has scarcely commenced . . .
> I am going to encourage that in every possible way.

This was on the evening of April 14, 1865, and the message was
Lincoln's last to the public. It bespoke both his past and future
hopes.[33]

During his four years in the White House Lincoln presided over a
revolution that also changed the government's role in the economy.
The Democratic charge that his party struck down "at one dash all
the labor of Gen. Jackson" contained much truth. Lincoln was the
first nineteenth-century president with a strongly nationalistic
economic outlook who did not face a hostile Congress. This dominant Democratic past of the nation played a large role in urging the
majority of the Republicans into a revolutionary pace of change.
Senate leader Fessenden, who nurtured doubts about the vast
masses of economic legislation, conceded in 1863: "I cannot say that
the wiser course was not to make the most of our time, for no one
knows how soon this country may again fall into a democratic
slough." A year later the President could report, while calling for the
succor of immigration, that the nation was "beginning a new life."[34]

And yet Lincoln did not organize or direct this revolution. He repeatedly applied what appears to have been a crucial touch. His acquiescence was *sine qua non* and made a sharp contrast to the record of Andrew Jackson, and lesser presidents, who had frustrated Whig economic policies. Over some issues, such as "jawboning" businessmen, or exalting labor and giving moral support to strikers, his activities were, and long remained, unmatched in American history. And because of the magnitude of the economic change that was mapped out during his administration, even his more cautious contributions outweigh the more noted work of other chief executives.

Nonetheless Lincoln's stance can be best conceptualized as one of restraint. At the root lay his attachment to the Whig theory of the executive and lack of necessity to violate that theory. More was, however, involved in producing the Whig in the White House. He entered office as a new party's minority president, and he might also be considered the first in the nation's history without any executive experience. Whatever natural advantages he had, he was not the top leader of his party, but a compromise candidate who ran behind the state tickets. Thus his power was sharply restricted. At any rate, he appeared to have a temperament that found little satisfaction in ordinary administrative chores. By contrast Congress, and the Cabinet, abounded with old and tried talents. Taking leadership away from them in the normal business of government would have been a formidable task even if Lincoln had desired to do so.

After his position grew more consolidated he may have been beset by more temptation to deviate from his road, but he succumbed less. There were many reasons for this. His Whiggishness helped cultivate the goodwill of Capitol Hill. Lincoln understood that the average solon was more likely to take offense if the executive arm denied certain economic benefits for his constitutents, than if it took upon itself the direction of Reconstruction for example. Indeed, giving Congress a free rein on the one hand probably gave the President a firmer grasp on the other, where for the moment the more substantial issues were.

Keeping himself at arm's length from his Cabinet had advantages, too. When a group of bankers descended on Lincoln and argued him "blind" (to cite his lament), opposing the legal tender act, it was a relief to insist that they go see the Secretary whose job it was to deal with such questions. Similarly, when Congress showed unhappiness with executive direction, the separation between the President and his official family often diverted the legislators to attacking the latter. With the Cabinet absorbing much of the fire, the White House could often escape unscorched. It was more than just to anecdotal effect that Lincoln complained about his lack of influence with "this administration."[35]

The Chief Magistrate thus deprived himself of the benefit of a unified administration, but he knew that there was strength at the top in division below — as did the second Roosevelt in the following century. Lincoln also appreciated the value of having his Secretaries compete against each other. When one of them, Chase, decided to compete against the chief himself, Lincoln nodded with measured approval. He told with relish the story of the Illinois farmer who let a large chin fly bite his horse — it only made the animal pull the harder.[36]

Whiggish correctness actually allowed the Executive more control than appearances indicated. Some important issues with vast ramifications, such as emancipation, he reserved for himself, treating his Cabinet, to quote David Donald, "as an unnecessary nuisance."[37] In other cases he remained fully in command without seeming to be so. Not desiring strong enforcement of the congressional laws of confiscation, he assigned the task to his conservative Attorney General. Bates opposed the policy strongly enough to tell Stanton, who professed an eagerness to go far on behalf of confiscation, that in certain circumstances the Secretary of War would be "subject to be hanged." As a consequence the Attorney General, not the President, sustained most of the bitter onslaughts which followed. Bates later judged that his boss was "beyond question the master-mind of the Cabinet."[38]

To illustrate further, Lincoln wanted a policy that firmly supported cotton trade with the South. He even helped work out treasury regulations to that end. Yet when at a crucial juncture Chase brought to him the completed plans for discussion and approval, all he got was a signature and a presidential comment about not understanding the details of the subject. Once again Chase, and later Fessenden, much more than the President, carried the brunt of the hostile reactions.[39]

Lincoln's Whiggishness toward Congress also created for him, to some extent, the image of a statesman above partisan politics. This may have contributed to the building of his "Union" party. More narrowly, it permitted lawmakers to turn over power to him on a number of issues, particularly when they faced potentially violent and divisive disagreements among themselves. It was the Executive who thus determined the terminals of the Pacific Railroad for example, and it was he who regulated trade with the enemy. And his appointive power helped give shape to economic policy in the Agriculture Department and elsewhere, too. To the "tariff region" of the Treasury, for example, Lincoln appointed — originally to counterbalance Chase — a disciple of Henry Carey.[40]

The President's use of his annual messages to push selected programs, legitimate within the Whig framework, carried considerable influence in Congress, as Senators Fessenden and Howard testified. His support was eagerly sought by Chase, Governor Morgan, Congressman Arnold, and many others, and it became the condition for Fessenden's acceptance of the Treasury post. Carey badgered Lincoln for some protectionist declaration (which, under the circumstances was quite unnecessary), and failing tried to use Justice Swayne of the Supreme Court to persuade the President.[41] The Whig in the White House knew when to apply his theory of the executive, and also when to discard it — as he did in the case of national banking.

It may be argued that Lincoln should have involved himself much more than he did with the economic legislation of Congress. A man who declared his goal to be "no less than National" in all things, could have done much to countervail the often parochial, special-interest-oriented attitudes of the solons. Yet he was an old politician who felt that in the end it was most equitable to let the lawmakers bargain their way to their compromises. And he was the Whig who already explained in 1848 that he saw no wisdom in taking legislative tasks from the members of Congress, who, coming from "all the various localities of the nation . . . understand, with minuteness, the interests of the people." He opposed giving those tasks to one man "who does not, and can not so well understand" them.[42] This was the facet of the Whig theory of government, with its circumscribed executive, which made it fully compatible with democracy, in spite of a demand for centralization of power in Washington. So Lincoln trod lightly vis-à-vis Congress in most cases.

On the whole his way worked. If special interests were repeatedly given extra benefits, if the tariffs and taxes were not as equitable as they might have been, if perhaps the same was true to a degree of bank, railroad, homestead, and other legislation, on the whole the potential of his administration's economic achievement was magnificent. It is not likely that Lincoln speculated that his Whiggishness might accelerate substantially the weakening of presidential power, begun in the 1850's, and might pave the way toward post-war congressional dominance. Had he thought about this trend, he would have approved it, without foreseeing its future excesses. For whatever he desired for himself, he wanted a restrained executive for the United States.

Thus many factors went into the making of the Whiggish President, but the most important was the war itself. Circumstances forced the man who, at least according to his theory of politics, was "unwilling to go beyond the pressure of necessity in the unusual exercise of power," to become the most powerful president in the nation's seventy-five years of history. The painful details are familiar enough. And even if we postulate that at a certain level of consciousness he may have thrived on the wise use of power, the wielding of vast new forces, involving life and death for hundreds of thousands, was an anguishing trial. In time Lincoln confessed that inside himself he carried a very tired spot. Nothing could touch that spot.[43]

Thus even if the President had desired to play a truly major part in the Civil War economic revolution, and even if Congress had acquiesced in this, we can be reasonably certain that he could not have mustered the psychic energy for the task. Time he could have found. But economics was an important field of endeavor for him and would have required a major commitment on his part. This he could not give.

We can be equally certain that only the failure of war finance would have moved Lincoln sharply off his Whig road. This much is indicated through his assumption of the direction of the military facet of the Union war effort. In April, 1861, having made some decisions about the army, he told Hay that "this was the last time he was going to interfere in matters of strictly military concernment." As it turned out instead he resurrected, and then used more fully than any one before or since, the commander-in-chief clause of the Constitution.[44]

But beyond theory, beyond the immediate practical benefits he derived from adhering to it, beyond even the energy draining of war, there was something more making Lincoln into the Whig in the White House vis-à-vis economics. In ordinary times the economic legislation of his administration would have carried a supreme significance for him; the war dwarfed them to insignificance, and with much greater urgency than the attempted extension of slavery had done before. To borrow the farmer's language that he was fond of using, economics became for the moment "small potatoes and few in a hill."[45] Therefore during his years in the White House he devoted his deepest resources to a search for peace and to the waging of war. And thus Lincoln provided the most profound testimony to his economic persuasion.

☆ ☆ ☆ ☆ ☆ ☆ ☆ ☆ ☆ ☆ ☆ ☆ ☆ ☆ ☆ ☆

16

The Business of Peacemaking

"Le veau d'or . . . . . est tou-jours de-bout!"

"CLEAR THE WAY FOR THE CALF OF GOLD!" MEPHISTOPHELES'
aria about mammon filled Washington's Grover Theater. In a box sat
the presidential party, Mr. and Mrs. Lincoln and Secretary of State
Seward, probably all in formal dress for it was an "Extra Grand Toilet
Night." The date was December 5, 1864. The Chief Magistrate's annual message had been composed and he was relaxing at the performance of Gounod's new opera, Faust.[1]

Lincoln was attending Faust for the third time that year and whatever drew him hither, one suspects that the song of the Calf of Gold,
both its melody and its message, played a part in it. The interaction
of man and money interested him, like it did his age. "God and
mammon" were opposites, he declared with biblical fervor at the
commencement of his antislavery crusade. "Whoever holds to the
one, must despise the other."[2] He condemned the slaveholders for
serving mammon, yet hastened to add that he himself did not neglect Southern economic interests, that over the long run these
would fare best with free labor. For, if throughout his life Lincoln
tried to serve God, if this is an acceptable way of describing his highest motives, he also felt that mammon must have its due, too. More
than that, his work testifies that the peace he made with man's material longings was full indeed.

233

The economic orientation that Lincoln brought to the White House manifested itself on a grand scale under the pressure of the Civil War presidency. These manifestations were multitudinous and pervasive, from everyday routine to the most significant actions and state papers. They illuminate the economic aspect of his outlook more fully than does his attitude toward specific economic problems. Among them, a major road he chose in search of peace is one of the most revealing.

Lincoln defended the Union on many occasions and in almost as many ways, but by far his most extensive and determined defense was a largely economic argument. "Physically speaking we cannot separate," said his inaugural address in 1861. He provided an indication of his deeper meaning, in his first annual message, as he discussed the great growth of the nation's population and wealth and pointed to the "promises of the future." The year 1862 had to come and nearly go, however, before he fully clarified his thinking.[3]

The United States could not be broken up, the President's annual message declared, because it formed an indivisible economic unit. It was indivisible because only its unity produced prosperity. He summed up an argument he had first advanced explicitly during his debates with Douglas, that the economic diversity of the country was in fact a cement binding it together through the aid of "steam, telegraph, and intelligence." Summoning thus the spirit of economic Whiggery, Lincoln reached the astounding but logical conclusion that even if military success came to the rebellion, the desire for prosperity "would, ere long, force reunion, however much of blood and treasure the separation might have cost."[4]

With more parochialism than he would have owned up to, he went on to single out his own region, defining its borders broadly, as the heart of the Republic. The other sections, East, West, and South, he described as "but marginal borders" to this center. He qualified himself as speaking "territorially," that is of geography, but his discussion and later direct admission indicated that in fact he was speaking about economics. He pointed to his region's vast economic strength, its "undeveloped resources," the large growth in population it expected, and concluded that the "magnitude of prospects presented" was truly overwhelming. This central area of the country could not exist without the Union, he declared. Modifying somewhat his inland Whig outlook under the combined pressure of disunion and his national office, he announced that the interior region must have access "to Europe by New York, to South America and Africa by New Orleans, and to Asia by San Francisco." He thus wound up sounding more than a little like that antitariff and antihome market Illinois Senator, Sidney Breese, who had declared in the 1840's that his state needed "the market of the world."[5]

Lincoln was not, like so many before him, arguing that the brute facts of nature decreed the Union. Although he used with flourish (and perhaps to a degree shared) his countrymen's exaltation of Nature, he did not truly worship with them. His Union had been decreed not by nature alone, but, to cite him again, by a nature harnessed by "steam, telegraph," in short, by man's economic might and intelligence.[6]

The President's defense of the Union was the kind Wendell Phillips derided as having "the clink of coin — the whir of spindles, — the dust of trade."[7] In the 1862 message it formed the introduction to a grand peace plan which was to end the rebellion and place the Union on secure ground. He had begun to formulate this design at the commencement of hostilities. He presented it in full to the nation at the end of 1862. And although in time his faith waned in its prowess, he did not cease advocating it so long as the war continued.

The plan, coming after the preliminary emancipation proclamation, had two parts. Lincoln devoted most of his attention to the first section, which formed the heart of his proposal: the nominally voluntary emancipation by the states, to take place gradually over as much as thirty-seven years if necessary, with the federal government compensating the slave owners. As a recognition of the growing reality of self-liberation by slaves, and both as a prod to the South and a bid to the radicals of the North, Lincoln added that slaves freed by the fortunes of war must remain free — but again with compensation to the loyal owners. The second part of the plan was to be put into effect later: the voluntary colonization of the freedmen, this, too, with federal aid. He had first espoused both of these large policies during his Illinois years. But he did not provide them until now with more than piecemeal support.[8]

Brief summaries of these familiar policies will suffice here. They envisioned large-scale federal-state cooperation and carried the

Whig understanding of government to a new height. The compensatory feature of emancipation turned out to be an enormous misjudgement of the political realities, one that historians see, somewhat mistakenly, as springing from Lincoln's reverence for property rights. The gradualist and voluntary aspects of the plan were the products of his moderate outlook and, as J. G. Randall had pointed out, reflected a recognition of the economic realities of the South. They, too, however, were to be proved ill-conceived. Both appealed to the economic cupidity of men — in this case Southerners.[9]

By 1862 Lincoln was convinced that slavery would be a casualty of the war and thought that "the signs of the times" should be intelligible to all. For the Southern states he saw a choice between abandoning the institution through procedures of their own selection and with compensation, or losing their property without any mitigation. Perceiving matters thus, he was confident, or professed to be so, about the section's eventual choice. Therefore he devoted himself to a more practical task at hand, the persuasion of a reluctant North, "those who are to pay, and not to receive." Such an appeal was also needed to convince the Southern people of his sincerity.

Lincoln began by explaining that his proposal was "both just and economical." Compensation was just, he said, because "in a certain sense the liberation of slaves is the destruction of property" and because North and South were equally responsible for the existence of the evil institution. Having established the morality of his cause, he devoted the bulk of his time to proving his plan practical — good economics, that is.

The expense of paying for slaves would be a large one, the Chief Magistrate conceded, but not so large as the cost of continuing the war which, as he saw it, was the alternative to compensated emancipation. Equally important, the payment was to be made later and much more easily since abolition was to take place gradually, over a long period of time during which the population of the country would triple at least. Because the choice was between two large debts, for either war or emancipation, it was imperative to decide on the one which would cause less hardship. Not surprisingly, in the latter part of the twentieth century an economist, using sophisticated techniques, developed a like argument but without being aware of her illustrious predecessor.[10]

Lincoln mentioned in passing the saving in blood that his plan promised and then formulated his main proposition as a law: "time alone relieves a debtor nation, so long as its population increases faster than unpaid interest accumulates on its debt." He developed this point in careful statistical detail. He computed the average growth rate of the country's population between 1790 and 1860, found it varying so little as to speak of another law, the American "law of increase," and projected a like rate of growth well into the twentieth century.[11]

Characteristically, Lincoln illustrated his argument from history with the national debt contracted during the Revolution. He calculated that if not a penny had ever been paid on that debt, and instead it had been allowed to run "at six per cent. per annum, simple interest," it would still have amounted to less money per capita in 1862 than it had in 1783! In his war message to Congress he had already used a similar quantitative comparison with the Revolution to justify his huge request for military appropriations. Thus, a little incongruously, the same economic argument had bolstered his case for both war and peace. The analogy between the Fathers' war and the Civil War he felt was altogether fitting because in both struggles the central idea of America was at stake.[12]

The population statistics that Lincoln provided to justify compensation for liberated slaves measured for him, above all, prosperity. Men, as he later said, were "the most important branch of national resources." His understanding was shared by Westerners in general and somewhat less so by the entire nation. Increasing the population was synonymous with increasing the "wealth of the country." In the end thus his blueprint for peace and the glorious future of the Union merged into one. And his entire message can be summed up in the explanation that "the national authority" would be restored because it would restore "the national Prosperity."[13]

Lincoln's message reveals how much remained unchanged in his thinking since his years in the Illinois legislature — both in fundamentals and in details. To appreciate this it is not enough to note his continued preference for gradualism and compensation. He had first used population growth as a measure of economic growth in the 1830's. It was in the Illinois Assembly that he had first argued for large appropriations (for internal improvements) with the economic rationale that the giant investment would lead to a giant increase of the population which in turn could repay the original outlay readily. As in the Illinois House, so now he drew firm outlines of the finances of his plan but left particulars, such as aggregate sums to be spent and actual interest rates to be paid, to the experts. (Most probably he underestimated both the cost of war and the value of slaves.) His horizons had grown, keeping pace with changing circumstances. In the 1830's he had labored for greater prosperity and expanding opportunities for Illinoisans. His 1862 plan promised the same for the whole nation, plus relief from the evils of both slavery and war. Above all, there remained in Lincoln, unchanged, that firm, moral-materialistic core.

The President thus put forth the most ambitious plan of an ambitious lifetime. Momentous as this step was, it did not of course mean leaving politicking out of his calculations. Among other things, with his plan he tried to take away some of the initiative from the radical elements in Congress. He also hoped to appeal especially to the border states and to the middle of the road and the conservative portions of both parties. And, in any event, he knew that his plan would help prepare the general public for emancipation.

For Lincoln did recognize that as little use as he had for revolution the Civil War had become one. Accordingly he issued the Emancipation Proclamation on January 1, 1863 — to be discussed further. But he intended the peace plan and the proclamation to be complementary, the former to be made more attractive by the latter.

Lincoln's commitment to his peace plan was remarkable. He did not discard it although success did not stray close to it. As long as life seemed left in slavery the border states refused to cooperate with his design. Democrats made it into a salient point of attack, charging that he wanted to tax white people to buy Negroes. Within his own party he had no illusions about the radical faction, but even the conservatives showed little appreciation, his friend Senator Browning labelling his plan a "hallucination." And we must conclude that Browning was right.[14]

What caused the pragmatic President to hallucinate so? Why did he persist with his plans to the very end? Why the intensity, the uncharacteristic bitterness, shown in his rejoinder to the 1864 serenade that Marylanders gave him on the occasion of their state choosing emancipation? He congratulated the celebrants but saw fit at this joyous moment to regret that such action had not been taken two years earlier, when he had recommended it! He was sure that such a step "would have saved the nation more money than would have met all the private loss incident to the measure."[15]

Earlier he had urged his thinking on members of Congress even in private meetings, thus making another rare break with his presidential Whiggism. He persevered in the face of the most discouraging response from the lawmakers. The House appropriated a totally inadequate ten million dollars for the cause, with specific reference to Missouri, and without showing much enthusiasm. The Senate doubled the amount, the two chambers disagreed, and there the matter ended.[16]

Lincoln continued to see his peace plan as a useable instrument, however. In part his mental makeup accounts for this: once committed it was difficult to change his course. More important, on this matter his mind had been made up for a lifetime. The basic solution to our riddle is Lincoln's profound belief in the power of economic forces.

Whatever expectations he may have had of the Confederate leadership in Richmond were quickly, but never wholly, dissipated. He did not lose faith in the Southern people as a whole, however. He was sure that the common folk "would be ready to swing back" to their true interests within the Union if given the opportunity.[17] This confidence, delusion perhaps and so often ignored by historians, was at the roots of both his war and reconstruction efforts. The planters, he felt needed more persuasion: they had to be *shown* that their true interests, too, lay within the Union. So through arguments and policies he appealed to their economic interests. He tried to weaken their allegiance to the rebellion and strengthen their ties to the Union. Through them he hoped to influence the course of the Confederate government itself. With driving military blows on the one hand, and the attractive forces of economics on the other, he expected to make peace.

At the same time Lincoln may have hoped to lay the foundations for a post-war Republican Party of the South — as Kenneth M. Stampp has argued. Indeed the Lincolnian declarations about the Unionist majorities in the South resembled his earlier statement that in a real sense "the whigs are always a majority of this Nation." But if in fact his peace efforts were aimed not only at the rebuilding of the Union but also at the strengthening of his party, the two objectives no doubt appeared to him as mostly the same.[18]

Lincoln expected the North to acquiesce in his plan because, peace and nonmaterial considerations apart, it offered prosperity and a reduction of burdens. The equally mandatory acceptance of the slave interests was to be motivated by compensation for property worth billions, which otherwise would be lost outright. For one who saw Southern interest in slavery as primarily economic, it was logical to put forth such a proposal. Since "all knew that this interest was . . . the cause of the war," as he later said, it was logical to anticipate that the appeasement of this interest would restore peace. An economic problem demanded an economic solution.

The President gave the nation some of his most beautiful, and later most often quoted (but as the context here shows, misquoted) prose in behalf of his plan: "The dogmas of the quiet past, are inadequate to the stormy present . . . . We must disenthrall our selves . . . . Fellow-citizens, we cannot escape history . . . ." He was absolutely certain that his plan, almost exclusively economic as it was, offered a major key to peace. "We know how to save the Union," he declared firmly. For him the main question was if the representatives of the people would act, and pay, according to the plan he outlined. "We shall nobly save, or meanly lose, the last best, hope of earth," he said, and meanness connoted shortsighted miserliness more than anything else. The road was clear, it "could not fail."[19]

The intense materialism that underlined this peace plan was typical of mid-nineteenth century Western civilization. Its optimistic variant was American, and it was not only shared but carried beyond ordinary limits by Lincoln. This, perhaps more than any other of his qualities, justified James Russell Lowell's evaluation of the President as "the first American." He was ahead of his times. He saw the reach of material prowess as potentially unbounded. It could even play a giant role in bringing peace to a war of brothers.

Surely, Lincoln was also a highly moral, indeed spiritual, being. Yet this characteristic was thoroughly intermingled with his materialism and while cleansing it, also strengthened it. This materialism carried his America along an often glorious and beneficial road into the twentieth century.

We now see that the road was also at times one of folly. It would be comforting to conclude that in "the fiery trial" of war Lincoln, or his nation, learned that the materialistic outlook, even when tempered with morality, had sharp limitations. But the lesson was only partially heeded at best.[20]

The President refused to abandon his plan despite its lack of success in the South and the hostility to it in the North. But if he showed a perseverance fed by an ideological commitment to the materialistic road to peace, he also evinced pragmatism. Thus in 1863 he pushed emancipation and moved the grand peace plan into the background — waiting for the appropriate moment to bring it to the fore again. He did however reply to the Democratic charges that he wanted to tax the North to free the slaves, saying that his goal was to save the country from "greater taxation" stemming from the prolongation of the war.[21]

Lincoln tried purely political measures, too, to entice Southerners back into the Union, most notably the ten percent plan for reconstruction. Issued at the end of 1863, it reflected, in part, the lack of success of the economic road. In its psychology, however, it fit the broad Lincolnian prescription for gaining peace by appealing to Southern self-interest.[22]

With the economic peace design held in the background, Lincoln looked not only for political tools but, as we shall see, also for economic ones that would emphasize the immediate material benefits of peace and Union. Still, he never let his grand peace plan out of sight and kept probing with it. Thus came the Northern peace missions that began to crop up in the second half of 1863. Some of these missions had a large publicity ingredient for Northern consumption, but it is a mistake to completely dismiss any of them as empty political activity. Certainly the efforts that were in the limelight carried the least real meaning. And the Chief Executive was his "shut-mouthed" self in all of these dealings. Nonetheless even the publicized ventures contained a serious message. While insisting on Union and emancipation, they promised "liberal terms on other substantial and collateral points."[23] Lincoln thus continued on the one hand to hold out the basis of a genuine peace settlement, and on the other tried thereby to bring peace closer through weakening the Confederacy.

In more private efforts the President dared to extend the generosity of his terms beyond those he outlined in public. After the victories at Gettysburg and Vicksburg he sent to Richmond Dr. Issacher Zacharie, his chiropodist, who had Southern connections, apparently to convey a Northern willingness to assume the Confederate debt or at least part of it. The doctor dealt with both officials and leading private citizens. Since Lincoln's Cabinet was not much more enthusiastic about his economic-oriented peacemaking than Congress, he excluded it from knowledge of the scheme, excepting only Seward. Chase, who found out about the project by accident, lodged a stern protest. Nonetheless, fragmentary as the picture is, it is possible that as late as the fall of 1864 the Zacharie mission was still alive. By then enough of Lincoln's unofficial efforts leaked out to spur the radicals to protest in the Wade-Davis Manifesto his Amnesty Proclamation's silence on the illegality of Rebel debts. How right the protestors were is clear from the persisting European delusion — that Seward could bemoan as late as the spring of 1865 — that these debts would be paid "as a condition" for the American peace. In short, Lincoln's well meaning maneuvering to use the Confederate debt to break down the Confederate war effort may have helped finance that very war effort.[24]

In 1864 he began to stiffen his peace conditions. This is clear from two other missions. One involved his old Illinois acquaintance Thomas Yeatman, Charles Francis Adams, then Minister to London, and an English businessman; the other James Jaquess, an Illinois preacher-soldier, and J. R. Gilmore, a writer-diplomat. Lincoln still offered the benefits of the 1862 plan, plus the repeal of confiscation legislation, and financial aid to the Southern states. But he no longer would have anything to do directly with the ever growing Confederate debt. He thus tried to signal to the South his earnestness, that there were strong political pressures in the North opposed to his liberality, and that his commitments could not be open ended in time.[25]

The President's faith in the power of economic incentives led him down some very strange paths. It may well be that the claim about one of his secret peace missions supposedly directed into the rich cotton growing region of the Red River is true. There may have been a project there involving a combination of military threat with economic spurs, the latter in the form of allowing planters to sell their cotton to the government for a good price. Indeed Lincoln's belief that the South could be seduced into peace via the economic charms of the Union is the predominant factor behind the inordinate amount of time he devoted, and the undeserved importance he attached, to the subject of trading with the Confederacy, especially in cotton.[26]

The good Whig Lincoln saw commerce as a glue that bound the Union together. Throughout the war he showed much more leniency toward trade across hostile lines than did Congress, not to mention the military. Immediately after the firing on Sumter he acted to stop European intercourse with the Rebel states, but he did nothing at first to hinder Northern trade with those same states — this in spite of the popular clamor for stringent measures. Even after Congress met in the summer of 1861 and specifically authorized presidential action, he waited for five long weeks before bringing himself to prohibit commerce with the Confederacy and thus bringing his weight down on the side of the law. Still later he did his best to ease restrictions, indeed went so far as to circumvent statutes to that end. His old tutor Henry C. Carey agreed with him and wrote to Lincoln in support of "large, direct and rapid intercourse between the loyal men of the northern and southern sections." Without that, he said, the Union was "the merest rope of sand."[27]

When in 1862 August Belmont suggested that the Confederacy could be weakened and demoralized through the cotton trade, he was told that that, too, had been under presidential advisement for some time. Indeed Lincoln explained to an Illinois friend that even the blockade, however ineffective at first, would work in a similar way, causing enough disruption, while allowing much normality, to make Southerners disgruntled and eager for the advantages of peace and Union. This hope indeed was central to his entire peace design.[28]

As Lincoln shifted the tactics of his peace work in 1863, cotton came to play an increasing role in his thinking. He tried to be careful, recognizing inherent dangers in his policy, fearing an atmosphere where "profit controls all," even the army. Nonetheless by early 1864 he prepared a careful program with the aid of Chase, and others, that invited Southern planters, for three years unable to freely market their cotton, to take the oath of allegiance and sell their product to government agents for twenty-five percent of its market value. They were to receive the rest of their purchase price after the war, provided they had remained loyal to the United States.[29]

This scheme did not bring the hoped for results, and in the summer of 1864 the President helped devise a new arrangement which attempted to reach far into the Confederacy. It not only allowed Treasury agents to pay seventy-five percent of the New York price for cotton, but also to send merchandise in return, right into enemy lines, up to one-third of the cash value of the transaction. Since Lincoln realized that the exhaustion of the South's resources was a sure way to military victory,[30] we have an indication of the importance he attached to his design.

The Chief Executive never made an official announcement of the aim of his policy. Publicity would have undercut its effectiveness with Southerners. Even among his own associates few shared his faith in the prowess of economic persuasion. After one of the presidential trading schemes came to require the aid of the Navy, Seward (the only Cabinet member Lincoln confided in) explained to Welles that through cotton "important persons in the Rebel cause were to be converted." The President, he said, "had been very confidential and secret in all that was done," and believed, even if his Secretary of State did not, that "there would be results." As if to explain his policy, Lincoln's 1864 message to Congress noted Jefferson Davis's irreconcilability and added confidently: "What is true, however, of him who heads the insurgent cause, is not necessarily true of those who follow. Although he cannot reaccept the Union, they can." *Le veau d'or est tou-jours de-bout.*[31]

For the benefits of skeptics, the President most frequently defended the cotton trade "for its bearing on our finances," obtaining thus the cooperation of Chase, among others. Lincoln spoke, with good reason, of cotton's positive effect on the nation's gold reserves, its tempering of inflation, and its reduction of the real national debt. In his own mind, however, these had limited significance. He not only issued with some freedom a type of trade permit that in effect reduced the government's revenues, but also admitted frankly, even while arguing in favor of cotton commerce, that "we can live through" the war "at all events." Most revealingly, early in 1865, he used one of his extremely rare vetoes to prevent legislation that might have increased the cotton flow to the North but at a price of reduced presidential elbow room for maneuver. Massachusett's John Murray Forbes groaned: "old Abe had pocketed our grand bill — I could have wrung his long neck!" And he spoke, uncomprehending, of the influence of speculators over the President.[32]

International relations were also among the considerations that entered into Lincoln's cotton policy. His first annual message summed up Confederate diplomacy as based on the hope that the European powers "would act solely, and selfishly, for the most speedy restoration of commerce, including, especially, the acquisition of cotton. . . ." He did not think it "just to suppose" that England and France in fact would so act, but just in case he hastened to assure them that in the long run their commerce would fare better with a restored Union. In the meantime it made eminent sense for the North to provide the Powers with as much of the Southern staple as was feasible. It did not, however, suit Lincoln's peacemaking purposes to allow direct European trade with the Rebels, as Seward proposed. Thus the middleman role was the solution. Later in the war, the Red River campaign, which had a large cotton ingredient, also showed a diplomatic facet that Lincoln appreciated and that was aimed at the French influence in Mexico.[33]

The President knew that Northern industry needed cotton as well as the Southern market. Edward Atkinson, a New England mill owner, even sold him a bit of specious reasoning which led to the theoretical conclusion that, to paraphrase Lincoln's words, it was better to give the Confederates guns for cotton than to let them have the vital staple. The Atkinson logic began with the true premise that the blockade kept enough cotton away from Europe to drive up the price of the remainder which Southerners ran through the U.S. lines. It limped on falsely, however, to argue that the Rebels obtained thus as large funds as they would have received for a full, peacetime crop. Thus the Confederacy had all the money it could expect to have with which to buy European supplies, while a large segment of its land and labor, normally engaged in producing cotton, was released to support the war. To prick the bubble all the federal government had to do was to create as free a market as possible for the

Southern staple. Its price would then go down, Confederate land and labor would have to be once more devoted to it, and the Rebel war economy would be crippled while the North thrived.

That Lincoln would reproduce such a reasoning for the benefit of one of his anticotton generals, and at a time when the blockade was closing the last Southern ports, indicated not so much that he could be deluded by economic sophistry, as that he had thoroughly committed himself to trying to help make peace with economic weapons. Cotton was to aid in saving the Union.[34]

The Chief Magistrate's delusion concerning the peacemaking properties of the Southern staple was akin to the widespread American faith of antebellum days that cotton was king. No doubt many profit-minded souls played on his delusion without sharing his patriotic motives. Atkinson wrote to him: "We want the product and we want to bring the owners to their allegiance by an appeal to their personal interests." Atkinson had some very fine qualities, but one wonders which goal was uppermost in his mind. In any case the by-product of Lincoln's thinking was to help provide speculation with an air of respectability. Many responsible Northerners came to be involved in the cotton trade. Stanton, and other opponents of intercourse with the enemy, might look upon this business as "trading in the blood of our soldiers." But Lincoln's friend Ward Hill Lamon, Marshall of the District of Columbia, hoped (but failed) to get rich via cotton, justifying all with the understanding that he was carrying out the presidential policy of thus breaking "the backbone of the Confederacy." Similarly, another Lincoln friend, the estimable Orville Browning, Civil War United States Senator, later Secretary of the Interior and acting Attorney General, and in 1864-5 an investor in the cotton trade, could see himself as making "some money" and at the same time doing the "Country some service."[35]

One of Browning's projects, which also involved Senator Morgan among others, and which received the President's support, sent Illinois politician James W. Singleton to Richmond to deal in peace and cotton. This ex-Whig, now a Democrat, talked with Jefferson Davis, General Lee, and others. While he thus sounded out the Confederate leaders, he bought up the cotton of their constitutents with U. S. legal tender. Browning explained the rationale for the cotton part of the operation: "every Treasury note we put into the pocket of a rebel makes him, to that extent, interested in this government and its friend, and will become one of the means of destroying the confederacy."

This, too, was hollow reasoning, as much as Atkinson's. Instead of holding on to their greenbacks, Southerners were likely to buy supplies with them, perhaps nonbulky ones, such as drugs, which could be easily smuggled across the lines. Only strong bias could make such an argument seem adequate. As it was, the Chief Executive was enthusiastic and wanted to pump into the Confederacy "all the Green backs he could."[36]

Earlier, using the same rationale, Lincoln had forbidden investing in cotton any Rebel scrip owned by loyal men. He did this although he desired the cotton. Furthermore, the Kentuckians, for example, who had petitioned for such a permission, and whom he generally went out of his way to accommodate, thus faced huge, unfair losses because during a hostile raid, Rebel money had been forced on them in exchange for supplies. In face of all this Lincoln defended his course unflinchingly: for the government had to do all it could to prevent "giving currency" to Confederate moneys.[37]

Historians have noted that the President handled his trade permits as a form of political patronage. This was not the cause of his cotton policy, as some suspect, but a byproduct of it. Indeed, that policy involved having to permit Chase, with his rival ambitions, to reap much of the political profits of cotton operations. Furthermore, when Lincoln did exercise his prerogatives he showed a remarkable soft spot for old Illinois friends, most of whom had no real political weight. He likewise provided trading permits for such as a widowed relative, or a businessman whose ties with the South had been cut off by secession and was thus nearly bankrupted. Even his more clearly political patronage, for Thurlow Weed and cohorts for example, in the end served more meaningful goals for which the Republican Party was the vehicle. Some of Lincoln's permit holders were well known Southern Unionists, and some, after the war, became champions of the New South. The President also showed partiality toward those who pioneered in paying wages to their former slaves. And of course his New England manufacturer-supporters publicized the free labor aspect of what was, after all, a seamy business.[38]

In the end the cotton component of the grand policy of making peace via economic incentives failed, too. Indeed (as did Lincoln's flirtation with the Rebel debt) it probably prolonged the war, for the Confederacy needed the fruits of the trade much more than did the North. The trade, no doubt, turned some Rebels into Unionists and even into supporters of the free labor system. Their numbers could not have been large, however. It may to some extent have demoralized the Confederacy, as some Southern leaders fretted, but it did much the same in the North. There, indeed, Ludwell Johnson concluded, "men who were often powerfully assisted by President Lincoln . . . corrupted the war."[39]

The Chief Executive did expect some inevitable crookedness in the application of his scheme and accepted the "fierceness" with which cotton profits were sought. He explained that "if pecuniary greed can be made to aid us in such effort, let us be thankful that so much good can be got out of pecuniary greed." He did not, however realize at first, and never fully admitted, unless at the very end, what vast corruption went hand in hand with his plans. Those plans thus are indefensible.[40]

We thus have an illustration of a thoroughly camouflaged *hubris* that only men very close to him, like Herndon and Hay, noticed. Lincoln came to agonize over the problem of corruption, particularly when it tainted the military. At times he was discouraged, at other times angry. Our surviving Lincolniana contains a calling card of his textile consultant from Massachusetts with the President's note on it: "Mr. Atkinson: I can not think of any cotton question to ask & I am really very tired. Will Mr. Atkinson excuse me?" And we have the recollections of a preacher who two decades later still appeared startled as he remembered witnessing a rare loss of temper by Lincoln, after a businessman insisted on pushing a scheme on him. "No!" the Chief Magistrate exploded. "Do you take the President of the United States to be a commission broker?"[41]

Lincoln's cotton peacemaking failed, in part because it was so incompatible with military operations both in spirit and in practice. Never in the history of men had trade and war mixed well, although the mixture had continually been tried. The two elements had rarely served the same ends. The Red River campaign exemplified the problem well. When the Commander-in-Chief permitted Banks to embark on the operation, one suspects that cotton played a decisive role in his thinking. The General had first proposed the action, in part, because it would show the planters how Union rule meant money for their pockets and so wean them from the rebellion. Once the operation got under way, however, and planters started to bring their cotton to the federal forces at the river, Admiral David D. Porter, who later explained he "never understood" the goal of the campaign, simply had it confiscated. In the end the Navy even awarded prize money to the sailors![42]

However much effort Lincoln put into the cotton business, and however false his hopes may have been, he never quite lost his sense of proportion. He allowed department commanders to veto trade operations. He repeated again and again on *this count* that the general on the spot had to be "judge and master." Indeed he permitted Grant to suspend completely commerce with the enemy "South Eastward of the Alleghenies," in March 1865. Yet he never admitted that the underlying assumption of his policy had been mistaken. This was given a final illustration during his visit to his general-in-chief at City Point, where he listened to reports from occupied Charleston and Savannah. He was told about planters bringing their products to the market. And he remarked with satisfaction: "I reckon they'll accept the situation now that they can sell their cotton."[43]

With the war ending, when cotton no longer had any more supposed Union-saving properties, the President was ready, indeed eager, to divest himself of his unwieldy peacemaking tool. At the last Cabinet meeting, on the day of his assassination, he asked the Secretaries of War, Navy, and Treasury to take full control of the cotton business. He said he "should be satisfied" with whatever decisions they would reach. Later that day, when George Ashmun of Massachusetts came to him to plead a cotton claim, the President told him with unusual heat that he was "done" with such ventures and spoke of persons cheating the government of the United States.[44]

Lincoln's use of economic incentive to engineer peace appears to have been also at the heart of his weak enforcement of the confiscation laws of Congress — his "Guarding Rebel property," as one observer saw it. To say this is not to minimize other factors in his thinking, especially the deep respect for property rights that he shared with most of his countrymen. In 1861 he asked Browning: "Can it be pretended that it is any longer the government of the U.S. . . . wherein a General, or a President, may make permanent rules of property by proclamation?" After the New York riots of 1863, which brought much destruction, he lectured in his most conservative tone about the virtue of property and the dangers of the "houseless" foolishly pulling down the house of another. General Grant he directed to confer with General Lee on "a mutual discontinuance of house-burning and other destruction of private property." And to a Baptist delegation he exclaimed: "When brought to my final reckoning, may I have to answer for robbing no man of his goods. . . ."[45]

The prizing of property rights thus helps explain the Chief Magistrate's failure to exploit the potential of the Congressional laws of confiscation. His doubts about their constitutionality, as well as his personal magnanimity, must also be taken into account. He spoke of the policy's impracticality, too, for it was almost inseparable from constant "temptation" and "gross abuse."

Yet, we must remember that he supported cotton trading despite the abuse that went with it. He suspended the right of *habeas corpus,* among other things, the Constitution notwithstanding. And he could completely ignore property rights when it came to the "peculiar institution," telling Browning in one case, if his friend's diary recorded the words accurately, that he would "rather *throw* up" than order payment for some seized slaves. Certainly by the second year of the war he appears to have accepted the principle of confiscation. "By the law of war," he declared, "property, both of enemies and friends, may be taken when needed." Thus something more is required to solve the riddle of what Stampp labelled the presidential "sabotage" of the law of the land.[46]

Lincoln saw economic persuasion as a very important peacemaking tool, although he tried to use all available means. Selective confiscation was one such potential tool but an extremely awkward one. On rare occasions it had "a very salutary effect," the President said, particularly when used as a countermeasure to depredations on the property of Union men in the border states. As a general rule, however, it only planted "thorns in the bosom of society." Therefore the occasion that most frequently brought Lincoln's attention to it was the need to suspend the military's attempts to put the law into effect.[47]

Confiscation could be enforced only in areas that came under federal control. Had the President permitted broad enforcement, the reestablishment of Union authority would have come to mean in the Southern mind the process of being turned into paupers. This was the diametrical opposite of the notion Lincoln was trying to implant. Retribution he was not interested in. His government would not have the "motive of revenge," the "purpose to punish for punishment's sake." And more important than improving Washington's finances by commandeering the wealth of the South was the hope of enticing her people back into the Union. It is true, via emancipation Lincoln departed from his road to peace, but that was a special case and even there he worked for compensation to the very end. Otherwise, the most important employment he gave to confiscation was as a threat (or, when he paid lipservice to the policy, as a way to placate radicals).

Proclaiming amnesty at the end of 1863, Lincoln promised the "restoration of all rights of property," excepting of course slaves and cases with legal complications. Later, too, he spoke of remitting appropriated property. By early 1865 he warned that unless the Rebels laid down their arms, their property would have to bear the cost of war. But one wonders if he meant what he said. For in his view general confiscation was a self-defeating policy.[48]

Lincoln made the above threat at the Hampton Roads conference which he attended reluctantly. Yet once there, he again brought forward his 1862 peace plan. The Confederates were still not interested. He nonetheless prepared a new message to Congress, urging the appropriation of four hundred millions of dollars for the purpose. He repeated his "dollars and cents" argument, that the amount saved by shortening the war would pay for the liberation of the slaves. In the privacy of his official family he also explained that such a sum would help not only to revive the Southern economy but also to reduce the Southern war debt! And it should have been self-evident to all that the payment in government bonds would provide bond holders with a vested interest in loyalty to the United States.

Lincoln's proposal failed to reach Capitol Hill because his Cabinet *unanimously* disapproved of it. After the fall of Richmond, however, he still clung to the vestiges of his original design. He suggested to former Supreme Court Justice and Hampton Roads conferee John A. Campbell that if Virginia ceased resistence immediately, he would put an end to the congressionally ordered confiscations of property. It took him a lifetime, until three days before Appomattox, to reach the point at which he would admit: "I do not think it is very probable that anything will come of this." And this was also the epitaph for his plans for peace through economic inducement.[49]

Three years before this end, drafting a message to Congress, the Chief Executive had suggested that it would be wise if he were provided with the power to remit confiscations of property. He wanted, as he wrote, to leave the Rebels "some motive for returning to the Union." Even for Lincoln this explanation had too much of "the clink of coin" to it, to cite Wendell Phillips again, and he deleted it. Yet the offending sentence summed up well the underlying assumption of his peace works, whether via cotton, nonconfiscation, or compensation for slaves. All were, as Chase was remembered to have said of them, attempts at "buying peace" and also emancipation.[50]

The President refused to see matters thus for, excepting rare cynical moments, he found pure raw materialism unpalatable — however much he relied on it in his attempts to lead men. Life had to have deeper meaning and he was unwilling to admit, even to himself, that Unionism, even in its Southern variety, could be measured in dollars and cents alone. He preferred to see his labors, and thus to a degree made them into, acts of morality and statesmanship that revolved around basic interests of man. His methods were Hamiltonian; his morals and fundamental goals were not.

Lincoln's peace design never had a chance and he had to settle for fragments. Had Southerners acted according to their best economic interests they would have accepted his overtures for peace. They did not and Lincoln's unpragmatic persistence in hoping that they would change indicated, above all, the limitations of too much faith in economics. In the final analysis his peace efforts foundered on the fact that his opponents, too, had firm ideological commitments and hence did not always act in a practical manner in favor of Union and material prosperity.

In the end the President did obtain both peace and emancipation, but only after victory had been gained on the battlefield. Property had to be expropriated and this, most importantly the abolition of slavery, could not come gently "as the dews of heaven." The historian

can judge with reasonable certainty that peace and emancipation
could be reached only the way they had been, through a war of revolution. Yet it tells very much about Lincoln that he kept hoping that
they could be attained through economic persuasion, and as Senator
Sumner marveled in 1862, his "whole soul" could be "occupied" by
the attempt.[51]

☆ ☆ ☆ ☆ ☆ ☆ ☆ ☆ ☆ ☆ ☆ ☆ ☆ ☆ ☆

17
The Most Difficult Question

"TOWERING GENIUS DISDAINS A BEATEN PATH." IN NINETEENTH-century America a man of action, and of such genius, could reach great renown by either "emancipating slaves, or enslaving freemen." The rising young politician of Illinois who thus analyzed history in 1838, issued the Emancipation Proclamation twenty-five years later. Then he confided his feeling that his stature depended on that act.[1]

Lincoln was not only aware of the historical significance of emancipation, but was also capable of fashioning some of the greatest state papers in the history of the English speaking peoples. Yet the man who created the Gettysburg Address and the Second Inaugural also produced the mundane Emancipation Proclamation. However inspiring that document was to many at the time, it is much less so when read by posterity. Indeed Marx's judgment comes to mind: Lincoln's great work carried the odor of "the mean pettifogging conditions which one lawyer puts to his opposing lawyer."[2]

Why the meanness in a generous man? Tolstoy for one noted that Lincoln wanted to be "great through his smallness." Marx himself had added elsewhere:

> Where another man, acting for the sake of so many "square feet of land" declaims about "the struggle for an idea," Lincoln, even when he is acting for the sake of an idea, speaks only in terms of "square feet of land."

The Europeans thus recognized a major component of the American's appraisal of democratic statesmanship.[3] Historians in turn spelled out further the pragmatic facet of the Emancipation Proclamation. The largely nonmoral language protected the Constitutional basis of the act. It also reduced the hostility of Northern and

255

border state conservatives who, at best, listened only to the anti-slavery argument of "military necessity." In this chapter we must add still another element to the emancipation mosaic. For the President's approach to peace making via economics, the thinking which led to the plan of 1862, which promoted the cotton trade and so largely eschewed confiscation, which seemed willing to legitimize the Confederate national debt, also helped produce the unhallowed language of Lincoln's most momentous public paper.

Emancipation by itself ran counter to the President's policy of enticing Southerners back into the Union through economic means. Lincoln knew that no Rebels were likely to *choose* the expropriation of billions of dollars worth of their property. He nonetheless took the emancipation road because, over the long run, it was inherent to the American Dream, and therefore slavery he saw as the root evil. More immediately there seemed to be "military necessity": blacks formed the indispensable labor force of the Confederacy, a mainstay of her war effort. The North needed that force. It is also difficult to believe that the Chief Magistrate entirely escaped the sin of *hubris,* which tempted him to the greatness awaiting the emancipator. Radical political, European diplomatic, and lesser pressures, entered his equation, too. Finally, we should add his perception of the will of God. Thus ultimately the Emancipation Proclamation testifies to Lincoln's pragmatism: he did not follow blindly the path of economic incentives. And yet it is revealing that incongruous in some ways though the attempt was, he tried hard to mold even emancipation to his understanding of the materialistic ways of man.

Lincoln's preliminary proclamation of September, 1862, was a threat. It was aimed only at those areas that continued in rebellion after a specified future date: January 1, 1863. In effect it stated that within the Union slavery would be protected. If and where involuntary servitude was "voluntarily" abolished, compensation was to follow. In contrast, outside of the Union slavery was to be ended without further ado or mitigation. The London *Spectator* summed up matters thus: "The principle asserted is not that a human being cannot justly own another, but that he cannot own him unless he is loyal to the United States."[4]

True to this approach, the final proclamation touched neither the loyal slave states nor the federally occupied Confederate areas. Lincoln interpreted his rule for these exemptions "generously" enough to leave the chattels of contested Tennessee in bondage (and thus drive another wedge among the Confederate states). On the occupied Sea Islands, off the coast of South Carolina, however, where there were no whites to be made loyal (they had left *en masse*), only blacks to be made free, the proclamation stood.[5]

The President did not intend to help perpetuate slavery — on the contrary. Yet he hoped that at least some conservative Northerners and liberal Southerners would so understand his proclamations. Indeed, the first concrete effect of his preliminary proclamation on the South was to start a bustle, in Union held areas, about sending representatives to Congress in Washington and so qualify for absolution from emancipation. Democratic Representative Daniel Voorhees of Indiana accordingly declared, with some justice, that the Republican chief's strategy of incentives was "the grossest and most outrageous assault upon the freedom of the elective franchise." Of course he failed to take into account that this, as all the executive attempts to influence Southerners, was brought on by a vast civil war.[6]

Still emancipation by itself did not fit the economics of the Lincolnian peace scheme. In conjunction with the grand peace plan of 1862, however, issued between the preliminary and final proclamations, emancipation did fit to a surprising degree. During 1862 slaveholders failed to recognize "the signs of the times" and refused the freedom of slaves in any form. With the Emancipation Proclamation Lincoln made "the signs of the times" unmistakable. Among other things it put teeth in his peace efforts; it was to make the *gradual, compensated* ending of slavery at last attractive, to the border states first, then to the whole South as well.

The high hopes, the "soul" (to quote Senator Sumner and Justice Davis again) that Lincoln's peace plan carried, and never quite gave up, were unrealistic. But we still have to measure whether they were entirely misplaced. For it is possible that the presidential efforts weakened significantly the spirit of the rebellion. We do know that, after the war, Jefferson Davis had to defend himself against charges that he might have obtained a better peace, including compensation for the expropriated slaves.[7]

★

Congressman George Julian, like many of his comtemporaries felt that without projects for colonizing blacks outside of the United States, Lincoln would not have gone ahead with emancipation. Indeed, one suspects that most Northerners agreed with the young men of Tammany Hall who declared their opposition to emancipation — "unless on some plan of colonization."[8] And indeed the details of Lincoln's 1862 peace plan also included colonization.

This facet of Lincoln's thought has been intentionally ignored in this account up to now. The President's talk of colonization was more than a political ploy to expedite emancipation by assuaging Northern fears of being overrun by former slaves. But his espousal of the policy, however sincere, was superficial. It had little deep, long-term significance for him. For Lincoln approached colonization at two levels of consciousness. At one he favored colonization; at another he understood that it could not be implemented but he avoided the realization of this truth until circumstances made it acceptable.[9]

What true attachment Lincoln had to colonization stemmed from a difficult dilemma: along with his conviction that the right to rise should not depend on color, he also had a full awareness of the practical obstacle to it in white prejudice. This situation, he believed, injured both races because the denial of the central idea of America to some undermined it for all. Colonization was the way out: the creation of a New America in Africa or Latin America by black Americans.

Lincoln made numerous efforts on behalf of voluntary, federally-aided emigration. He attempted to demonstrate that the policy made good economic sense. Blacks would be able to improve their condition, and the country as a whole would not suffer, for the departing men's place would be taken by European immigrants. His activity in support of the policy, however, contained a large element of ambiguity, and very rapidly, perhaps as soon as politically feasible, he conceded its impracticality. The concession came readily, difficult as his dilemma was, since colonization ran contrary to major elements of his economic persuasion.

One may point to a word here, a suggestion there, and argue that the President had grown away some from an antiexpansionist Whig outlook — but not overly much. All in all as in his early years, internal, not external, development remained his object. Colonization, particularly, in Central America, was, to many, the beginning of an American empire, "the pivot on which to rest our lever," as Francis Blair, Sr., explained to Lincoln.[10] But in his younger years the President had shown that he had little use for continental expansion. Notions of an American India, or empire building, only repelled him more, for they also clashed with his devotion to political democracy.

We should note that there were some who foresaw near and faroff lands, settled by blacks, joining the Union on an equal basis. These folk may be called colonizationists, but not in the sense Lincoln used the term. They offered no solution to the American dilemma. Instead of being an empire builder, therefore, he was, as a Congressman angrily complained, "a hinderance and a calamity" to those who were. For Lincoln lacked "any belief in the superiority of northern civilization, or its right to rule this continent."[11]

Permanent territorial acquisition was perhaps not an unavoidable corollary of black colonization; the losing of population, one-seventh of the census of 1860, was. For one who had devoted much of his life to economic development, one who considered people the most important natural resource, it was totally incongruous to send a large part of the country's laboring force away — as Secretary Seward, for one, pointed out in the Cabinet. Such a plan, to quote another congressional critic, was "political economy run mad." Lincoln's gradualist approach to emancipation reflected, in part, his recognition of Southern realities, to cite Randall again. Colonization reflected a total disregard of them.[12]

The Chief Executive's gradual abandonment of the policy sheds further light on his pragmatism. When, at first, he supported colonization, he saw the problem he attempted to solve as stemming from race, the "physical difference" between blacks and whites. This difference, which he did not think possible to separate from the mental attitudes it bred, was insurmountable. It provided the rationale, as he told a black delegation, for "why we should be separated." As the political situation changed, as emancipation became acceptable to the country, as the need to ease the fears of whites about freedmen swarming over the North lessened, he began to allow the economic implications of colonization to penetrate his thinking. He began to face the fact that colonization was not a viable notion and accordingly began to redefine the problem it supposedly would have solved.[13]

His 1862 annual message still proposed a constitutional amendment to permit federal financing of colonization, an amendment that was as un-Lincoln-like in its view of the Constitution, as its goal was un-Lincoln-like in its economics. This same message, however, devoted much more space to his budding opinion that no harm would come to whites if the blacks remained in the country. To be able to argue thus he changed his problem from one of race, which appeared insoluble, to one of economics. Blacks, he assured his countrymen, could not "displace any more white labor by being free, than by remaining slaves." On the contrary, "very probably, for a time" the freed people would work less than before, creating a greater demand for the services of whites. This in turn would lead to higher wages. "Labor is like any other commodity in the market," the President concluded; "increase the demand for it, and you increase the price of it." That questions of social adjustment, and of race, were still likely to be central in the minds of white laborers he now chose to ignore and promised instead higher wages.[14]

In the 1850's when the complexity of the slavery question threatened to engender paralysis in Lincoln, and spawned comments that "if all earthly power was given" to him he still would not know what to do, he found in part a way out by defining the problem in terms of its economic facet. In the 1860's at times he did the same, reducing the overwhelming problem of race to one of economics. Political economy was a refuge for Lincoln, a field he understood, where solutions could be found. To the extent such simplification allowed positive action, it was beneficial. But we have no evidence to show that Lincoln sensed that this tendency to foreshorten issues to their materialistic ingredients also held grave dangers over the long run.

The President's support of colonization helped to bring about emancipation, but there was a price to be paid for his temporary attachment to the unrealistic idea. Having made a black exodus part of his master plan for the reconstructed Union, he could not turn away from it, overnight, as the situation demanded. Even if peace would have come sooner, he could not have brought his full faculties to bear on the problem of providing a place for the black man in the American peace. Doing so would have meant an acknowledgment of bad faith vis-à-vis both himself and his people. Therefore, just as the impossibility of the colonization idea dawned on him gradually, so alternative solutions appeared only slowly. At the time of his death they had not yet emerged to their full extent.

It is very probable that the President never gave up hope entirely that emancipation for the majority of the slaves could be made gradual, over a "comparatively short" period, and thus benefit all involved. This is true even if at times he paraded his gradualism as a concession to the South. He was convinced that the masses of both blacks and whites needed to be "better prepared" for their new relationship, for "a total revolution of labor," and it appears that he was thinking as much of blacks as of whites. He believed that Southern white cooperation for nurturing black freedom was both indispensable and obtainable. He also knew that these whites, particularly the former Whigs, might be more amenable to slower emancipation. However, the recognition that bondage had "clouded" the intellects of blacks was perhaps closest to the center of his gradualist approach. One may question the sociological soundness of his thinking, and even its political wisdom, and history tells us it was not implemented. We should not question its sincerity and good will, however.[15]

Perhaps the most important result of Lincoln's attitude was that it tended to concentrate his thinking about the place of the freedmen in reconstructed America on that portion of blacks whom he judged ready to stand on their own feet. This, over the short run, favored "the few" not "the many" among blacks, but he saw such an approach to be the most practical for benefiting over the longer run all blacks — and thus whites. This black elite he swore never to subject to any gradual emancipation process; indeed he hoped by 1864 to enfranchise them immediately. He defined the group as "the very intelligent," counting among them those who escaped from slavery during the war, and "those who have fought gallantly in our ranks."[16]

Lincoln appreciated the need for an economic base for the former slaves. While still promoting colonization at Chiriqui, in Central

America, for people "capable of thinking as white men," he enumerated the economic assets of the area, laying his greatest emphasis on the rich coal deposits that were supposed to be there. These mines were to be "the means of self-reliance" for the settlers. It is telling that the two men most intimately associated with him professionally in the White House, his private secretaries Nicolay and Hay, later recalled that the main reason for the "Tycoon's" discarding the Chiriqui scheme was in his realization that the coal there had "little or no commercial value."[17]

The Ile à Vache emigration project, in which he interested himself next, was similarly founded on what appeared to be a reasonable economic basis. Lincoln carefully considered the plan that made each colonist to some extent a "joint stock proprietor," gave each a house, a job, and, after four years, guaranteed landownership.[18] Even before he cut himself off from the the last vestiges of the colonization idea he approved the experiment promoted by Chase which provided very rich twenty-acre plots on South Carolina's Sea Islands for the heads of black families, at a nominal price of $1.25 per acre. This gave the freedmen, as he explained in 1863, "an interest in the soil" — in the United States. These black yeoman were to be selected with care from the same class for whom the Chief Magistrate was to request the ballot, who "will be examples of moral propriety and industry." A squatter scheme for the same area seemed to have less attraction to him.[19]

Although in the absence of a clear plan for the future the historian must grope impressionistically, Lincoln's notions about the masses of freedmen can be outlined, too. To the end he seems to have hoped for a grace period, as he saw, during which both these blacks, and also the masses of whites, could be apprenticed into their new relationships. The transformation could perhaps best begin with an actual period of apprenticeship for the former slaves, resembling somewhat the status of aspiring craftsmen prior to the attainment of independence — but with "no power of the national Executive to prevent an abuse" abridged.[20] Apprenticeship was to lead next to the establishment of a wage-based employer-laborer relationship between former master and slave, and finally to property ownership for the freedmen.

For slaves liberated by the circumstance of war the President abandoned the first stage and, beginning in late 1862, moved to foster a wage system wherein for the first time, as he believed, the black man would receive the reward of his labor — would march toward the American Dream.

To General Butler in New Orleans Lincoln wrote that he was "much interested" in the wage arrangements made by Louisiana planters. To Congress he affirmed his certainty that the freedmen would "gladly" work thus, and in his Emancipation Proclamation recommended that they "labor faithfully for reasonable wages." The military he ordered to "facilitate the introduction and carrying forward, in good faith, the free-labor system." He used his patronage powers to encourage the policy. He also supported the leasing of abandoned plantations (most often to Northerners) so that "the blacks can be provided for via jobs." It was on this count that John Eaton remarked that "the President's grasp of the situation was astonishing." It is significant that within a month after a delegation visited the White House soliciting that the pay of black and white laborers by equalized, the War Department issued an order to that effect.[21] It is also significant that on the sensationalized issue of equal pay for black soldiers Lincoln acted with great caution.[22] The contrast places in sharp relief both *his* leanings and what he judged to be the leanings of the American people.

The employment of slaves helped relieve the army's burden of taking care of refugees and also reduced Northern fears of black invasion. Most fundamentally, however, it transformed the slave into a wage-earning free laborer.[23]

The free labor system was developed under the War Department, primarily in Louisiana and the Mississippi Valley where Union victories permitted an actual ending of slavery. The War Department's system gave the freedmen a choice of employment at times, but more generally encouraged their hiring on their home plantations. Contracts between laborers and planters were signed for a year and were strictly enforced. Whether this arrangement served the best interests of the freed people was sharply questioned by radicals. Whatever the case was, in 1863 and 1864 Lincoln's most urgent goals were elsewhere. He wanted military victory on which the freedom of the slaves, too, depended; and he wanted to show without risking any chance for failure that the free labor system was workable in the South.

At the Treasury, representing more radical desires, Chase hoped to create a rival system that paid better wages, leased lands to the freedmen, and tried to induce landowners to sell land to the former slaves. Lincoln saw this approach as "well intended," the presidential ambitions of its sponsor notwithstanding. But he also feared that it was unworkable, that it "would fall dead." We are not privy to the details of his reasoning but know that in 1864 he opted to allow the military, rather than the radicals, to exercise control over the employment of the freedmen. Yet by 1865 he approved a wide-ranging plan in the establishment of the Freedmen's Bureau and with it, to cite La Wanda Cox, the "promise of land" for the masses of former slaves, or at least the germs of a promise that had potential for growth. He also allowed General William T. Sherman to go ahead with a similar proposal of land reform to be sponsored by the army. In short, Lincoln had a preferred road but with the freedmen, too, he showed his farsighted pragmatism which was shared neither by Andrew Johnson nor by enough of the congressional politicians who, after Lincoln's death, came to dominate reconstruction legislation.[24]

Ultimately, how and to what length the President might have gone to promote the economic welfare of the freedmen one cannot safely conjecture. He carried the burden of a deep sense of justice, the pain of knowing of "the bond-man's two hundred and fifty years of unrequited toil." This sense received support from his humanistic Whig outlook that gave a large economic role to the government and which saw economic rights as more fundamental than political ones. Yet Lincoln's Whiggery also indicated congressional leadership in economic matters. As for his thought, it carried a hard individualistic component, too. The contrabands, he insisted, should be "set to digging their subsistence out of the ground." At the Hampton Roads conference, when Confederate envoy R.M.T. Hunter expressed doubts about the blacks' ability to stand on their feet, the Chief Magistrate replied with an anecdote about an Illinois farmer who instead of feeding his hogs made them dig potatoes from the soil. The moral of the story was "root, hog, or die!" He repeated his tale with relish to several people, explaining that he had told the Southerners, or so it was later recalled, how "whites and blacks alike will have to look out for themselves; and I have an abiding faith that they will go about it in a fashion that will undeceive you in a very agreeable way." In the end then, how Lincoln would have faced up to the problems of the freedmen — had he lived — would have depended to a considerable degree on how he would have faced up to the coming Gilded Age.[25]

In his lifetime he failed to come to grips fully with the needs of the masses of blacks. This resulted from a convergence of factors. There was, first of all, the war which demanded the best of his mental powers and which subordinated the need "to provide for blacks" (the problem he once said troubled him the most)[26] to military necessity — or what seemed like military necessity. There was also his initial support of colonization which, however necessary politically, and perhaps psychologically, clouded his vision. There were his hopes for gradual emancipation which created an illusion that time was still available. There was the fact that the basic step of abolishing slavery remained contested to the very end. There was his Whiggish view of executive functions. Finally, although he never admitted, perhaps not even to himself, he also appears to have continued to harbor vestiges of the suppressed feeling that "if all earthly power was given," the problem would still be too large for human solution.

It may well be significant that the five-year delay in emancipation that the President proposed at Hampton Roads would have passed the issue to another administration. He desired to reconstruct the Union with "charity for all," both for white and black. But deep down he may have feared this could not be done. The Freedmen's Bureau bill that he signed into law in the spring of 1865 — an agency which he had wanted to create since 1863, recognizing its "great magnitude and importance"[27] — envisioned ceding land to blacks from properties confiscated from whites. Was Lincoln going to execute the law? Was he going to ignore confiscation — as he largely did during the war — so as to continue pacifying the Southern majority? Was he going to implement the policy by procuring compensation for former owners?

The forces that helped deform the language of the Emancipation Proclamation were bound to affect Lincoln's whole approach to blacks. He felt that he had to appeal to "the many" of the South, the whites, and this, at times, could only be at the expense of "the few," the blacks. His belief was unshakable that the black man's labor should be rewarded. But on that road to fair reward for all how lightly was he likely to tread — or how heavily? How much could a leader accomplish in a democracy where the majority ruled? "With malice toward none; with charity for all," Lincoln said. But he became a martyr, as Richard Current added, "before he had a chance to realize the full dimension of the dilemma."[28]

The President's untimely death leaves the historian with many questions. Still, we can not but look with sympathy on his belief that the interests of the two races could be reconciled, that there was only one South and one nation, and blacks and whites were "attached . . . at all events." And one fact we can note with certainty, Lincoln was sure that the end of slavery would bring an unheard of prosperity to *all* in the South. "The central act of my administration and the great event of the nineteenth century," as he called the coming of black freedom, was to make the American Dream a more fully Southern dream, too, and a dream that was reaching toward triumph in the world.[29] His almost mystical faith in the power of this idea — for black and white, and for man everywhere — points of course both to his strength and limitation. In the 1850's he already looked forward, as did other Northerners, to a time when the well-being of the free North would be extended to an equally free South. During the Civil War his hope grew and it gave him strength.

One of the places in which the Chief Executive found refuge from his White House labors was the Treasury. There he would chat with clerks and officers, and the talk often turned to political economy. Often Lincoln spoke and the others worked on. On one such occasion he produced "a half-soliloquy," "a magnificent outburst," as the Register of the Treasury, Lucius Chittenden, later recalled. The President created a "word-painting of what the South would be when the war was over, slavery destroyed, and she had had an opportunity to develop her resources. . . ."

Subsequent to the war a new breed of Southerner arose, preaching economic development and advocating a New South. Listening to one of these missionaries, more than twenty years after the above episode, Register Chittenden experienced a flash of memory. It came with "the vividness of an electric light," he wrote, "as I recognized the word-picture of Mr. Lincoln. . . ."[30]

☆ ☆ ☆ ☆ ☆ ☆ ☆ ☆ ☆ ☆ ☆ ☆ ☆ ☆ ☆ ☆

18

The Backwoods Jupiter

"SOME WELL-MEANING NEWSPAPERS ADVISE THE PRESIDENT TO KEEP his fingers out of the military pie," John Hay's diary noted in the fall of 1863. "The truth is, if he did, the pie would be a sorry mess." After the passage of more than a century, the devoted secretary's necessarily provisional judgment is increasingly confirmed by historians. "The old man sits here and wields like a backwoods Jupiter the bolts of war and the machinery of government with a hand equally steady & equally firm," Hay wrote. Few descriptions of the Commander in Chief are as meaningful as this poetry by the young scribbler in the White House.[1]

Lincoln's way to peace, intended both to shorten and end the war and to reconstruct the Union, was to be adopted by a South chastened by the blows of Northern arms. However complementary thus peace and war efforts were in the President's mind, of the two military victory was more important because, if less desirable, it was the more certain route to a reconstructed Union. Therefore in terms of time, and probably in terms of mental intensity, Lincoln's most demanding task throughout his tenure of office was the direction of the Union military effort. Such was the ironic fate of the man who had devoted his life to economic development, to building things up, for the war protestor who had once decried "military glory — that attractive rainbow, that rises in showers of blood." For him, and the nation, the time had come when it had to be said that upon "the progress of our arms . . . all else chiefly depends."[2]

For four bloody years the Illinois politician had to act, to quote T. Harry Williams, "as commander in chief and frequently as general in chief." Taking office in 1861 he was untutored in the book-learning of war and had no real experience in its practice. In his younger days political economy had been at the heart of his interests. The presidency forced the less beautiful science of war to the center of his work. But the economic outlook he developed as a statesman of the backcountry he blended thoroughly into his new task. He characteristically protested that, "of course," he did not "pretend to understand" martial matters yet he gave sufficiently able direction to the war to permit later historians to seriously discuss his "military genius."[3]

During the war Lincoln was the only man in a position to bring Whig-Republican economics to bear on military policy. His civilian advisors, Cameron and Stanton, did not share his economic vision. Nor did probably any of his top generals and, in any event, they were too educated in the military science to reach for fundamental revisions of military ideas via strange, nonmilitary routes.

In contrast, the military neophyte Lincoln had to search deep inside himself to provide new strategic concepts that would lead to victory. That he did this, successfully, historians acknowledge. But first even this student — seeking exactly such manifestations — was startled by the extent Lincolnian strategies reflected Lincolnian economic views. The Civil War President's presumably often unconscious combination of two different fields helped produce a fresh mixture which, as frequently is the case, is labeled genius. A summary examination of this combination, with its ordinary as well as revolutionary results, illuminates not only his way in war but also the significance of his economics — both for Lincoln and his United States.[4]

In April 1861, after calling out the state militias, Lincoln's first important military act was essentially economic: the proclamation of a blockade of Southern ports. Former Whigs Seward and Bates, and others too, shared in making this policy, but the President made the final decision. It was he who ordered the blockade pushed forward "with all possible dispatch." The adaption of economic policy to military strategy, thus begun a few days after the fall of Sumter, continued to Appomattox.[5]

It took various forms. The technological bent of Lincoln's mind that welcomed innovations in weaponry and overrode the foot-dragging of ordnance men has been clearly revealed by Robert V. Bruce. It is easy to recognize in the warmaker who played a major role in the adoption of the breechloading rifle, and supported vigorously John Ericsson's plans for ironclad vessels and T.S.C. Lowe's experiments in military aeronautics (reconnaissance balloons), the Whig political economist who had advocated the mechanization of farming, delivered lectures on discoveries and inventions, and considered in all seriousness the protection of patents of equal value to humanity with the discovery of America. Indeed the President was conscious of this interconnection. As the end of the war approached he spoke enthusiastically to a *Scientific American* reporter about the application of inventions not only to war but also "to the industrial arts in general." His ultimate goal in war and peace was the same and technology was a prime mover toward it: the improvement of the condition of man.[6]

Similarly the Westerner who had championed railroads since early youth now perceived their military significance. From the first year of the war he emphasized that new factor in the equation of battle. He also fully appreciated the meaning of Northern superiority in this respect. His understanding was thorough enough for him to suggest to one general the modern notion that guerrilla raids against railroads are best countered with like action. He was thinking militarily, but a good part of his rationale was economic. "It would trouble them more to repair railroads and bridges than it does us."[7]

Again, historians single out for praise the Commander-in-Chief's Western strategy. They point to its brilliant recognition of the strategic importance of the Mississippi Valley. Here, some argue, the war in fact was won. Various political and military factors contributed to Lincoln's decision to give priority to having "the Father of Waters" go once more "unvexed to the sea." But its ultimate intellectual source was his unshakable, albeit parochial, belief that the Mississippi Valley was the economic heart of the Republic.[8]

Perhaps even weightier evidence of Lincoln's military genius is his contribution to the evolution of a unified command system. This was a fundamental advance in military science. It went hand in hand with his championship of a central, overall plan of strategy. These two innovations did much to bring victory to the Union, and both were the products of a Federalist-Whig-Republican mind forced by circumstances to function in a military capacity. The Lincoln who had demanded from Congress a centralized and coordinated American system of internal improvements in the 1840's in the 1860's was making like demands upon his generals for centralization of authority and coordination of plans. The North as a whole acceded to him, because, in part as a result of the war, its dominant ethos was rapidly conforming to his ethos. The war was now imposing system on Lincoln's America. In contrast, as Williams has pointed out, the states-rights Confederacy was unable to achieve either a unified command or a centralized strategy and indeed, with its parochial traditions, insisted on defending every one of its localities. It thus hastened its own demise.

The most original and probably most significant, of Lincoln's military contributions was his insistence that the true objective of the Union forces should be destruction of armies, not the conquest of territories. "Destroy the rebel army, if possible," became the Chief Executive's refrain to General McClellan and later to his successors. "I think *Lee's* Army, and not *Richmond,* is your true objective," he telegraphed point blank to "Fighting Joe" Hooker. The President's idea appears to have stemmed from two related elements. The first was his Whig reluctance to value territorial acquisition for its own sake; the second was the contrasting importance he assigned to internal economic strength, for which in his eyes population was the most meaningful index. Men, not miles, were the measure of might.

In the good old days of peace he had already warned the South:

> You will never make much of a hand at whipping us. If we were fewer in numbers than you, I think that you could whip us; if we were equal it would likely be a drawn battle; but being inferior in numbers, you will make nothing by attempting to master us.

If any military man heard Lincoln's argument in 1859, they no doubt thought it naïve, uneducated in military science. When as Commander-in-Chief he proposed his strategy of destroying men instead of occupying territory, his generals were equally unreceptive. The idea ran contrary to all they had been taught, and they probably felt its execution required not soldiers but a butcher. This analogue of the "dismal science" was dismal indeed.[9]

Of course, generals unwilling to follow Lincoln's proposition lost

multitudes of men anyway. After the battle of Fredricksburg the disappointed but undaunted President expounded the grim economics
of his strategy to his secretary, Stoddard, who later mused:

> We lost fifty percent more men than did the enemy, and yet there is a
> sense in the awful arithmetic propounded by Mr. Lincoln. He says that if
> the same battle were to be fought over again, every day, through a week
> of days, with the same relative results, the army under Lee would be
> wiped out to its last man, the Army of the Potomac would still be a mighty
> host, the war would be over, the Confederacy gone. . . .[10]

In 1861, the President, in his war message, having tried to carefully calculate manpower and financial needs, concluded that "the
evidence reaching us from the country, leaves no doubt, that the
material for the work is abundant." Three and a half years later, in
his last annual message to Congress, he enthusiastically reported on
the economic growth the country had continued to enjoy in spite of
the war and contrary to his own earlier expectation. Addressing
North and South alike, he declared:

> The important fact remains demonstrated, that we have *more* men *now*
> than we had when the war *began*; that we are not exhausted, nor in proc-
> ess of exhaustion; that we are *gaining* strength, and may, if need be, main-
> tain the contest indefinitely. This as to men. Material resources are now
> more complete and abundant than ever. The national resources, then,
> are unexhausted, and, as we believe, inexhaustible.

In essence the President argued, as would Richard Current a century later, that the North had to win the war because, more than
anything else, economic might determined the outcome of war. As
for other, less readily measurable factors, such as the quality of soldiering or of civilian leadership, it was safest to exclude them from
the equation. Of course, Lincoln tried to get the better of the Confederates in these matters, too. But his ultimately successful strategy
that aimed at armies rather than territories was, most fundamentally, the fruit of the above understanding.

The Commander-in-Chief's steadfast advocacy of what in the soldier's jargon came to be called cordon offense, advancing on the
enemy on all fronts, was also the product of this line of thinking.
Such a strategy matched unceasingly all Northern resources against
all Southern. For Lincoln it put the final outcome of the war beyond
doubt.[11]

The same appreciation of the economics of war helped lead the

President to the most fateful military decision of the contest: the recruiting of black soldiers. He had resisted the step for long. He may have harbored doubts about the soldiering qualities of former slaves and, in any case, under the circumstances of the Civil War the step had too much of the substance of the "remorseless revolutionary struggle" he warned against. He went ahead in the fall of 1862 and the spring of 1863 because of what he called in an interview the "arithmetic" of war which was increasingly appreciated in the North. His policy worked "doubly," he explained. Since most of the black troops came from the South, they weakened the Confederacy to the identical extent to which they strengthened the Union.

Lincoln's decision gave the black men a new, and by most whites previously unimaginable, importance. In the war-weary land these fresh, deeply motivated troops came perhaps to hold the balance of power. By 1865 almost one hundred and eighty thousand wore the U.S. uniform — two-thirds of them Southerners — and the Commander-in-Chief saw fit to declare that if they had been thrown into "the battlefield or cornfield against us," the struggle would be lost. Here was, he said, a "physical force which may be measured and estimated as horse-power and steam-power are measured and estimated."[12]

The President attached equal significance to the economic might of the North and the weakness of the South. At first, indeed, he had underestimated secessionist tenacity and expected a quick end to the disturbances. He learned. In 1864, even in an optimistic mood, he spoke of fighting for three more years if necessary. His annual message that year, as quoted above, spoke of maintaining the contest "indefinitely." His second inaugural address, in early March, 1865, held out "high hope for the future" but "ventured" no prediction concerning the termination of the war.

Nevertheless, two weeks later, Lincoln suddenly glimpsed the end, at last, and on economic grounds. The military situation had not changed significantly in those two weeks. Lee seemed as strong as ever in Petersburg. Yet Lincoln burst with optimism because of the news he had of the Confederate Congress' coming within one vote of authorizing the use of black soldiers. He was jubilant. He joked about sending to Richmond his own favorable vote to decide the question. Blacks "cannot fight and work both," he said in an exultant

speech. "One is about as important as the other." "We must now see
the bottom of the enemy's resources. . . . They have drawn upon
their last branch of resources. . . . I am glad to see the end so near at
hand."[13]

Lincoln understood the importance of clarifying his thinking not
only to his military commanders, and in a more general way to both
North and South, but also to Europe. In a realistic reckoning the
power of the Old World had to be weighed, too. Accordingly, in the
fall of 1863 the President and Seward sent Samuel Ruggles overseas,
to an international statistical convention, charging him with dem-
onstrating that the United States possessed the *resources* to maintain
the Union.[14]

There remains one other major manifestation of Lincoln's
economic persuasion in his military policy. Secretary Stoddard, to
whom in 1862 Lincoln had unburdened himself on his strategy
aimed against men, "the most important branch of national resources," noted with the benefit of retrospect, that "no general yet
found can face the arithmetic [of the President], but the end of the
war will be at hand when he shall be discovered." In time Lincoln
found his general in U.S. Grant, and the end of the war was at hand.
But the way he found that general, indeed the way he handled his
top commanders, has drawn harsh criticism from many students of
military history.[15]

On the Eastern front, in a period of two years, the Commander-
in-Chief replaced the general in charge seven times! Elsewhere
changes were less drastic but the pattern was similar. The President
is blamed, above all, for failing to support his generals in defeat.
Without engaging in the details of this controversy, it should be observed that Lincoln's actions reflected a core aspect of his economic
outlook which under the pressure of war became extreme. He conducted an often ruthless campaign of pushing the successful of the
lower ranks to the fore. It is worth emphasizing that his commitment
was not to rough equality, but to rough equality of opportunity. If
some good men were lost in the process, the system nonetheless
worked. By the end of the war, very good soldiers usually — one is
tempted to say, the best — had risen to command.

The President's view that in the Civil War one side stood for an
"open field" for all, and the other against it, thus receives more than

symbolic corroboration on this count. In the Confederacy the men who had the chief commands early in the war, were again there when Appomattox came. Even if Jefferson Davis made a relatively fortunate initial selection of top generals, it is startling to note that the one exception to the above was the gallant Albert Sidney Johnston and he was dead. In contrast, there was not a single general commanding a main army in the Union service of 1865 who had held high command at the beginning of the struggle. In this respect, Lincoln's American Dream had triumphed on the battlefield, too.

☆ ☆ ☆ ☆ ☆ ☆ ☆ ☆ ☆ ☆ ☆ ☆ ☆ ☆

19
Watchman,
What of The Night? *

"THIS IS ESSENTIALLY A PEOPLE'S CONTEST." THUS ABRAHAM LINCOLN defined in 1861 the war he was to lead for four ever more painful years.

> On the side of the Union, it is a struggle for maintaining in the world, that form, and substance of government, whose leading object is, to elevate the condition of men — to lift artificial weights from all shoulders — to clear the path of laudable pursuit for all — to afford all, an unfettered start, and a fair chance, in the race of life.[1]

The President repeated that definition many times thereafter without substantial variation. Yet he also spoke of the war in terms more political than economic, as a war for the Union, or democracy, and — less frequently — as a war for free constitutional government, or justice, or the rights of the people. Indeed, elsewhere in the very address quoted above, his first to Congress as Chief Magistrate, he spoke of the conflict as a test of the idea that "a government of the people, by the same people" was practical.[2]

Historians generally resolve the seeming ambivalence, or at least duality in Lincoln's thought, with good instinct but poor logic, by ignoring some of the evidence. The majority of them take his expressions about the Union as stating his fundamental war aim. If we focus on Lincoln's presidential years in isolation a fair case can indeed be made for such an approach. But if we scrutinize his life as a whole, and thus see those final, crowning years of conflict in the perspective of this book, we should speak — awkward as this is — about Lincoln's War for the American Dream.

An earlier chapter has explained that Lincoln in fact placed his

---

*An early version of this chapter was published in Sidney Fine and Gerald S. Brown, eds., *The American Past: Conflicting Interpretations of the Great Issues* (2 vols., New York, 1976).

central idea of the Republic even above the Union, but, being a politician rather than a philosopher, he treated the two concepts as identical. The difference between the two was the kind he liked to dismiss as "a merely metaphysical question and one unnecessary to be forced into discussion."[3] What has been said of the Union may also be said of democracy and of the less frequent formulations of the President's war aims. The American Dream, Union, democracy, liberty, all became interchangeable in his utterances.

Lincoln made many attempts to define democracy, and some of these appear curious to the political scientist. "As I would not be a *slave,* so I would not be a *master,*" his most often quoted version begins. "This expresses my idea of democracy. Whatever differs from this, to the extent of the difference, is no democracy." Lincoln knew, of course, that the absence of slavery was no foolproof criterion of free government. Neither England nor continental Europe practiced slavery, yet he knew they were not the best hope of democracy; quite the contrary. When Czar Alexander II abolished serfdom in Russia, that country still remained, as Lincoln said earlier, a land "where they make no pretence of loving liberty . . . where despotism can be taken pure, and without the base alloy of hypocrasy." He also knew, as he declared from the White House, that "we cannot have free government without elections," and he thus mentioned what even in his troubled days was a more generally recognized attribute of democracy than the mere absence of slavery.[4]

And yet Lincoln's definition of democracy in terms of slavery, however questionable as political science, cut to the heart of his thinking. It was certainly more than a mere political device; indeed he never appears to have used it in public. It becomes fully meaningful only if one recognizes that after 1854 slavery became the most direct antithesis of the American Dream in his thought, the diametrical opposite of the central idea of the Republic. If his definition of democracy is restated as follows, it still remains questionable political theory, but it will express his meaning in more accurate terms: As I would not want my *chance to rise in life* obstructed, so I would not want to obstruct the chance of others to rise. This expresses my idea of democracy. Whatever differs from this, to the extent of the difference, is no democracy.

For Lincoln, unobstructed upward mobility was the most important ideal America strove for. Although there had to be "yielding to partial, and temporary departures, from necessity," he explained repeatedly during the war that this ideal was "the leading object of the government for whose existence we contend." Mobility was the ideal and slavery its antipode. But as the Dream was not perfectly attainable, thus perhaps was almost a symbol, so slavery, and its dangers, had degrees, and thus it, too, grew to be a symbol in Lincoln's thought.

When he raised the threat of enslavement before the white laborers of the North, (a threat the reality of which historians reject) he was using slavery as the symbol of a loss of mobility. He did not wish to argue, as later students and presumably many of his contemporaries understood him that free labor faced an immediate and total loss of mobility, that is literal enslavement; but that the degree of its freedom might be diminished by the expansive tendency which was totally antithetical to mobility. For slavery was the principle that "You work and toil and earn bread, and I'll eat it."[5]

Attempting to define liberty in 1864 — not democracy this time — Lincoln spoke of the same fundamental idea, of the opportunity "for each man to do as he pleases with himself, and the product of his labor." About half a year later he wrote on a piece of cardboard a few sentences, which he humorously labeled "The President's Last, Shortest, and Best Speech," but which he valued sufficiently to procure its immediate publication. The cardboard essay criticized a religion which set men to "fight against their government, because, as they think, that government does not sufficiently help *some* men to eat their bread in the sweat of *other* men's faces. . . ."

Ten years earlier he had already indicated that he saw the Dream, most fundamentally the right to the fruit of one's labor, almost as a law of nature, and had said triumphantly "you still cannot repeal human nature." About the same time he wrote:

> The ant, who has toiled and dragged a crumb to his nest, will furiously defend the fruit of his labor, against whatever robber assails him. So plain, that the most dumb and stupid slave that ever toiled for a master, does constantly *know* that he is wronged. So plain that no one, high or low, ever does mistake it. . . .

This in turn harks back to his definition of 1847, or earlier, that a "most worthy" object of good government was the securing "to each labourer the whole product of his labour, or as nearly as possible. . . ." Indeed, if we accept Lincoln's own 1861 recollection, his faith was as old as his ability to think seriously, and probably older. Whatever ideal he held to, whatever stood for America in his eyes, in the most basic sense was embodied for him in this faith.[6]

If the shock of the great rebellion against the "best, hope of earth" made the President brood much more than before about the political aspects of democracy, about majority rule, about the appeal to arms and other matters, his central concern remained unchanged. This explains why in its defense he was more willing to make temporary sacrifices of certain *political* liberties — the right of *habeas corpus* for example — than were others who did not share his predominantly *economic* definition of democracy. Thus he defended the Union, expatiated on the futility of appealing "from the ballot to the bullet," but also explained with clear pragmatism why he spoke thus, why such a doctrine was essential, why the laboring many had an immeasurable stake in America. Union, democracy, the free constitutional government of the people — in the final analysis all meant the same thing in his usage. They were all identical to, or indispensable means to, the American Dream.

These concepts had always been interchangeable to an extent in Lincoln's mind. During the war they became ever more so. Once, in 1861, he even used his distinctive expression, "the central idea," to describe American political democracy — if Hay's diary recorded his words accurately. Scholars are therefore correct when they see no contradiction in Lincoln's various explanations of the Civil War. In the most fundamental sense, even when he was not explicit, he was speaking always about the same thing. As he told the soldiers of an Ohio regiment in 1864, the war was a quest for "an open field and a fair chance for your industry, enterprise and intelligence; that you may all have equal privileges in the race of life . . . ."[7]

To recognize Lincoln's variations on his great theme helps to clarify his thinking. Reviewing his life, nearly at its end, he stated that he was "naturally anti-slavery" and that he could "not remember" when he "did not so think, and feel." Many scholars question the truthfulness of his reflection, rather unjustly even if his words are taken literally. But some of the doubts can certainly be dispelled if Lincoln's words are interpreted in the light of what has been said. Looking back from the vantage point of the Civil War, his lifelong struggle towards the American Dream appeared to him the same as a lifelong struggle against the bondage of labor. In a very basic sense his view was correct, although it is fair to note that he may not have been fully conscious of the supreme significance of the antithesis of the Dream and slavery until 1854.

Lincoln avowed similarly that "I have never had a feeling politically that did not spring from the sentiments embodied in the Declaration of Independence." Once more his affirmation becomes meaningful only if we recall that to Lincoln the essence of Jefferson's Declaration was its preamble, which in turn meant, as he explained repeatedly, "that *all* should have an equal chance," that there should be a "progressive improvement in the condition of all men everywhere."[8]

If before secession Lincoln placed his central idea above the Union, secession did not change his mind. This is not to deny that the President often appeared to thrust the Union, simple, unadorned with special meanings, onto the highest pedestal. His 1862 reply to Greeley's "Prayer of Twenty Million" declared for example:

> My paramount object in this struggle *is* to save the Union, and is *not* either to save or destroy slavery. If I could save the Union without freeing *any* slave I would do it, and if I could save it by freeing *all* the slaves I would do it; and if I could save it by freeing some and leaving others alone I would also do that.[9]

Historians appeal most frequently to these words to illustrate Lincoln's supreme devotion to the Union. Yet if we recognize that the Union, simple, unadorned, was the one war aim on which nearly all the powerful political forces of the North could unite, the Chief Executive's words are transformed into a manifestation of his political prowess. The reply to Greeley thus becomes much less an oath of allegiance to the Union than a stratagem addressed to people whose support was indispensable to ending slavery. Indeed, the object of Lincoln's statement was to build up his credentials with those who would oppose the freeing of the slaves at all cost, except at the cost of the Union.

To understand this maneuver we must recall that he had decided to issue a proclamation of freedom more than a month before the letter to Greeley. He had presented his decision as an unalterable fact to his Cabinet (and politely asked the members' advice as to language and timing). Thus, contrary to appearances, the letter to the *New York Tribune* editor was not aimed to any substantial degree at the radicals who were demanding emancipation, but at the constituency which had voted for Douglas in 1858 and 1860. The letter suggested (without actually saying) that the President, in his official capacity, did not care whether slavery was "voted up or voted down" — the very crime he had accused his opponent of in the Great Debates — that he was one of the Douglasites. Of course he was not. And remarkably, that very moment some abolitionists fully fathomed his meaning, that he had announced in the Greeley letter "the destruction of Slavery."[10]

Lincoln could use the Unionism of his countrymen so successfully because he not only understood it fully but also largely shared it. But he did have some all important reservations. The second significant fact about the letter to Greeley was noted elsewhere: that it did not really surrender Lincoln's principles. It indicated his willingness to save the Union with or without slavery, but *not* his consent to the extension of slavery. It posed a choice for the nation between the Union " 'as it was' " at the time of his election, with slavery confined and hence (as he believed) dying; or the Union as it soon would be with slavery dead. Had he been willing to accept the Union with slavery expanding (and thus, as he saw it, slavery triumphing both materially and morally) there probably would have been no Civil War.

Thus, politics notwithstanding, the President's emphasis on the Union was fully compatible with the supremacy of his central idea. The common view, shared by layman and scholar, that he saw the Union as absolute ("perpetual," as he preferred to say) is appropriate. For practical purposes this was the logical consequence of his outlook. Yet in Lincoln's theory, if so cold a term can be applied to his feeling, the Union was not an end but a means. It was to be upheld so long as it upheld "that thing for which the Union itself was made." The Union was the ship, he explained in 1861, and the American Dream its cargo: "the prosperity and the liberties of the people." And "so long as the ship can be saved, with the cargo," he added, "it should never be abandoned." There is no evidence to show that he ever changed his mind.

Without the ship the cargo would go down and therefore it was senseless to emphasize a distinction between the two. Yet this imagery implied that had there been another equally seaworthy ship available, Lincoln might have been satisfied with transferring the cargo. But there was no other ship, the idea itself was beyond the realm of his practical thought. And so there had to be a war, to save the ship, yes, but to save the ship so that the cargo could be saved.

A plausible case can be made that in his obsession with the Dream Lincoln approached what in others he at times called monomania. The religious mysticism that Edmund Wilson and others perceived in him was there, above and beyond a strong rationalism. But it is not enough to say, indeed to a degree it is inaccurate to say, that it centered on the entity of the Union — the ship. The *right to rise* — the cargo — was Lincoln's central ideal. It was for this, more than any other, that the war had to be fought. It was this idea that made the "right result . . . worth more to the world, than ten times the men, and ten times the money" which he asked from the nation.[11]

This distinction, however unimportant it might have appeared to most Americans at the time, held fateful meaning. The idea of the Union is essentially national, that of the Dream is universal. One view prizes the Civil War, to quote Francis Lieber, as "a war for nationality." It makes Lincoln into "the Great Nationalist" of the modern historians, a man who had a religious faith in the Union. The other cherishes him as an American Moses or Christ, one who spoke to mankind.[12]

At the same time, paradoxically, the first view denies the uniqueness of the United States. It values Lincoln as a New World counterpart of Cavour and Bismarck whose highest goal, to use the German's expression, was "*Staatsbildung.*" Without gainsaying the achievements of the Europeans, we must note that their degenerate twentieth-century descendants in the worship of the nation as an end in itself were Hitler and Mussolini. In contrast, Lincoln's Dream helped lead America to the nationalism of Theodore Roosevelt, Woodrow Wilson, and Franklin Delano Roosevelt.

If for Lincoln the most "central idea" of the Union war effort was the preservation of man's right to rise, the "central idea of secession" was a monstrous hybrid of anarchy and despotism. In using such a description he appealed to the deep American attachment to law and order that he himself shared. Indeed, enlarging on this, he pointed to the Rebels's subversion of political democracy. But that there was something more behind his renewed use of the words "central idea" grew clear when he later spelled out that by Southern "despotism" he meant that the ultimate Confederate aim was closing down "the door of advancement" before the common people. Or, as he explained still later, "at the bottom" of the rebellion was the desire to overthrow the central principle of the Declaration of Independence.[13]

It bears repeating that although we are justified in considering Lincoln's Dream as economic in substance, it was always much more to him. In the torment of war it grew in his mind to primarily moral dimensions. It is revealing that his second annual message, which developed his economic argument for the Union, did not, in so many words, refer to the Dream at all.

It was his perception of the moral truth that the President tried most incessantly to communicate. In nearly all of his important speeches he made allusions or direct references to it. He built the Gettysburg Address on "the proposition" he believed the United States had been founded on, "that all men are created equal." It was this, Jefferson's Declaration, which Lincoln saw as the first enunciation of the American Dream, for which his soldiers "gave the last full measure of devotion." They had died, he also said, so that the "nation might live," and they had died so that the "government of the people, by the people, for the people shall not perish from the earth." The Dream, the Union, democracy — these three Lincoln held up before his people through the darkness of war. They, not unlike the Trinity, were one and the same and also different. But of the three, for him and one suspects in a fundamental sense for his people, the greatest was the Dream.[14]

Lincoln was "happy to believe" that the "plain people" understood his message. He professed to be certain that they saw, as he did, the all important stakes of the war, that none were "so deeply interested to resist the present rebellion as the working people." He found myriad proofs of the people's clear perception. In his first message to

Congress he contrasted the military aristocracy, the large number of officers who had resigned their commissions, with the common people in uniform, of whom "not one common soldier, or common sailor is known to have deserted his flag." (Presumably, he did not realize that enlisted men were rarely given the privilege of resigning.) Later, too, he emphasized that "no classes of people" were so devoted to the cause as the common "soldiers in the field and the seamen afloat." In numerous ways he emphasized the common people's loyalty, using the term "common" with great pride. He pointed to the national debt that financed the war, much of which, he said in 1861 had been taken by "citizens of the industrial classes."[15]

The President was deeply imbued with the belief that the American Dream had a worldwide significance, and it must have been heartening for him to receive the congratulatory message of the workingmen of Manchester, England, in 1863. This spoke of America as "a singular, happy abode for the working millions" and of Lincoln as the leader who decisively upheld the great belief that all men are created free and equal. Here was evidence for Lincoln that the laboring folk not only of his nation but also of the entire world understood the meaning of the Civil War. He sent a long reply, commending the Manchester cotton-mill workers for their "sublime Christian heroism" in accepting unemployment and privation for the great cause of all workingmen.[16]

Although Lincoln consistently maintained that the plain people "understand, without an argument" what the conflict was about, he could not but have some questions which he did not entirely keep to himself. Certainly elections were hotly contested in the North; there were even riots against the "government of the people." Rather lamely he explained such matters as the fruit of "prejudice, working division and hostility" among the laboring man, and he also spoke of "ambitious and designing men." Later he added to his store of explanations the inexplicable workings of the divine will.[17]

More important than Northern divisions was the overwhelming Southern support of the rebellion, at least among whites. This Lincoln was slow to admit and, indeed, never admitted fully. Such an admission would have challenged his basic faith in the good sense of the common people. After more than two years of war he could still declare that force, the Confederate Army, was Jefferson Davis's only hope, "not only against us, but against his own people. If that were crushed the people would be ready to swing back to their old bearings."[18]

It had all begun long ago with a poor boy's conviction — in a time and at a place which nurtured such convictions — that a man should receive the whole fruit of his labor so that he might get ahead in life. The boy became a man and a politician, and worked through the better part of his life to the end that government might always be dedicated to that proposition. Both politics and political economy were moral enterprises for him, and so his goal, which we call the American Dream, was a moral goal. When he, and the majority of the nation, took a stand against slavery, the moral ingredient of his faith assumed exalted proportions. Then the war came and he accepted it to save the nation of the Dream — this "light to the world," to quote the words of Isaiah that the President knew by heart. Lincoln felt that as the men of 1776 did *"fight,* and *endure"* for the central idea, the great hope, of America, so must their descendants. And they did as he bade them — for four long, bloody years.[19]

Early in 1861, on his way to Washington, Lincoln spoke in Trenton, New Jersey, about the Revolutionary War and the battle there in which Washington defeated the Hessians. His thoughts went back to his first childhood readings in history:

... you all know ... how these early impressions last longer than any others. I recollect thinking then, boy even though I was, that there must have been *something more* than common that those men struggled for. I am exceedingly anxious that *that thing* which they struggled for; *that something* even more than National Independence; *that something* that held out a great promise to all the people of the world to all time to come; I am exceedingly anxious that this Union, the Constitution, and the liberties of the people shall be perpetuated in accordance with *the original idea* for which that struggle was made, and I shall be most happy indeed if I shall be an humble instrument in the hands of the Almighty, and of this, his almost chosen people, for perpetuating *the object* of that great struggle.

It was perhaps the emotion born of the remembrance of his own beginnings that so possessed Lincoln's mind that he did not then explicitly define *"that something," "the original idea"* of America, which he believed the nation's founders had already struggled for. Or perhaps it was the fault of the *New York Tribune* reporter that the President-elect's reflections in Trenton remained incomplete.

A day later, however, speaking in Independence Hall, at Philadelphia, Lincoln continued his Revolutionary theme. He still spoke with "deep emotion," and now the press reported his completed thought: "It was that which gave promise that in due time the weights should be lifted from the shoulders of all men, and that *all* should have an equal chance."[20]

One suspects that remembering "away back," Lincoln exaggerated the clarity of his youthful ideas. Nevertheless their seeds must have been there early, in the "earliest days of my being able to read," as he recalled. Indeed, for a moment, we must reach beyond these early days, to a toddler in Kentucky.

It was cornplanting time in the valley where the Lincolns made their home. Children had to be taught to work very young. Little Abe was beginning his lessons, walking behind his father, dropping pumpkin seeds into the hills made by Thomas's crude hoe. Two seeds in every second hill, in every second row. Then the Sabbath came and with it a great cloudburst up on the hills above them. It did not rain in their valley but the water came swirling down from the hills, washing away corn, pumpkin, and topsoil. The fruit of their labor was lost. This was the earliest memory, earliest pain the grown man Lincoln could recall. Almost half a century later he told another Kentuckian, Cassius Clay: "I always thought that the man who made the corn should eat the corn."[21]

Lincoln's ideas matured slowly, over decades. They came to full growth through the interpollination of his own unique mind and the mind of his age. Although further study of both is needed, it is clear that what he taught his nation was not learned from Parson Mason Weem's *Life of Washington,* as Lincoln appears to have believed, not from the other histories he reputedly read as a boy, not from the general literature of those times. Few saw the Dream as *the* "central idea of the Republic." The role Lincoln gave to man's right to rise through the reward of labor was in no small part of his own making. And as he reminisced on the threshold of the presidency, his faith in that central role had become unshakable. The United States had to be saved *with* that Dream. "If this country cannot be saved without giving up that principle," he declared, "I would rather be assassinated. . . ."[22]

Lincoln had the fortune, so very rare, to live his dream from childhood to the last full measure of his days. Preaching the right to rise, he preached also by example. In a sense, he preached himself to the nation. If this contained an element of inherent egotism, as does perhaps all great work, it was so far below the surface as to make one hesitate to label it as such. In his first annual message he told the country: "No men living are more worthy to be trusted than those who toil up from poverty." Humble man that Abe Lincoln was, he could speak thus in praise of his own triumph because of an unawareness of the all important self-generated aspect of his thought.[23] He believed that he was preaching America to America, not Lincoln to America. When he had accomplished his life's work, the two indeed were the same thing. If the world came at last to identify the man from Illinois with his nation, it is inspiring to know that the first to have done so was the child Lincoln himself.

As the Civil War reached its climax and end the President's concept of the American Dream also reached its ultimate heights. In the spring of 1865 he summed up for a final time the Rebel cause, as he saw it: "It may seem strange that any men should dare to ask a just God's assistance in wringing their bread from the sweat of other men's faces." But he added now: "let us judge not that we be not judged." Even for one of his legendary fortitude the "nation's wounds," and those of the men who had "borne the battle, and . . . his widow, and his orphan," proved too much to endure by reason alone. As his years of trial were about to end, he turned for support from a central idea that was the law of man, perhaps the law of nature, to that same idea as the law of God. Not surprisingly, for such is the way of man, Lincoln had found that the purpose of his Maker was like his own purposes.

"Fondly do we hope — fervently do we pray," he told his countrymen "that this mighty scourge of war may speedily pass away."

Yet, if God wills that it continue, until all the wealth piled by the bond-
man's two hundred and fifty years of unrequited toil shall be sunk, and
until every drop of blood drawn with the lash, shall be paid by another
drawn with the sword, as was said three thousand years ago, so still it must
be said "the judgments of the Lord, are true and righteous altogether."

Unrequited toil, unearned and bloodstained wealth, war as judgment. The denial of the Dream had to be expiated. The extorted
labor of two and a half centuries had to be paid for. Lincoln's American Dream had become the will of God.[24]

Appendix A

A Historiographical Essay
LINCOLN: MAN AND GOD

Dedicated to my Forebears in the Field of Lincolniana
— in spite of my critical words —
With a Deep Sense of Gratitude

All these you are, and each is partly you,
And none is false, and none is wholly true.

So how to see you as you really are,
So how to suck the pure, distillate, stored
Essence of essence from the hidden star
And make it pierce like a reposting sword.

For, as we hunt you down, you must escape
And we pursue a shadow of our own
That can be caught in a magician's cape
But has the flatness of a painted stone.

Never the running stag, the gull at wing,
The pure elixir, the American thing.

Stephen Vincent Benét, *John Brown's Body*

I. REVIEW OF HISTORIOGRAPHY

The quantity of Lincoln literature in the English language is said to be second only to the writings about Jesus. By contrast, the attempts to examine this literature are few. Systematic analytical probes into the historians' conception of Lincoln are even fewer. Only two scholars, David M. Potter and Don E. Fehrenbacher, tried such an endeavor, and interestingly, both did so in lectures delivered in England, in 1947 and 1968, from the Harmsworth Chair at the University of Oxford.[1]

In 1947 Benjamin P. Thomas provided in his *Portrait for Posterity* a faithful, information-packed narrative of the at times trivial controversies of three generations of Lincoln students. About the same time David Donald analyzed the growth of "The Folklore Lincoln," and also touched on the subject, repeatedly, in *Lincoln's Herndon* (1948). Thirteen years earlier, in *The Lincoln Legend*, Roy P. Basler traced the growth of the popular, in the main literary, images of Lincoln.[2]

At various junctures scholars also paused to assess the state of Lincoln studies. J. G. Randall's 1936 essay, "Has the Lincoln Theme Been Exhausted?" was the first such significant effort. Paul M. Angle, Clyde C. Walton, and Robert W. Johannsen followed in 1954, 1960, and 1968, respectively. Angle returned to the subject in 1967 in a pessimistic piece that bespoke the anguish of the conscientious student who faced the mountains of often "incompetent," or even "dishonest" writings. "The Lincoln theme, if not exhausted, is becoming very, very tired," wrote this student, then sixty-seven years old. Yet, as if to contradict himself, he outlined an enticing interpretive program for the coming generation.[3]

The present essay will aspire to find the historiographical ancestry of *Lincoln and the Economics of the American Dream*. Its perspective is circumscribed by its goal. It thus focuses on many, but not all, of the outstanding scholars of the Lincoln field, with no general evaluation of their works intended. The main theme is the development of the double image of Lincoln, and how this, and other factors, prevented researches into his economic persuasion.

II. CONCEPTUAL SCHEME:
THE POLITICAL RELIGION OF A NEW WORLD

. . . breathed by every American mother, to the lisping babe, that prattles on her lap — let it be taught in schools, in seminaries, and in colleges; — let it be written in Primmers, spelling books, and in Almanacs; — let it be preached from the pulpit, proclaimed in legislative halls, and enforced in courts of justice. And, in short, let it become the *political religion* of the nation; and let the old and the young, the rich and the poor, the grave and the gay, of all sexes and tongues, and colors and conditions, sacrifice unceasingly upon its altars.

Lincoln in 1838[4]

When the Christian Church was young, when crucial values had to be defined, the most heated controversies centered around Jesus. To resort to the broadest of outlines, on one end were those who, like the Gnostics, leaned toward the worship of Jesus the God, choosing to ignore that he was "the son of man," of flesh and blood. On the other end stood those who, like the learned Arius, foully murdered for his beliefs, emphasized Jesus' humanity. Jesus the God or Jesus the Man? It took the Church centuries of striving to be truly catholic before it reached firm ground in the middle. It then insisted on both the humanity and divinity of the one from Galilee.

In our own post-Christian era, to adopt Arnold Toynbee's definition, man still needs to worship — and to scoff. In the United States, where democracy is the unifying religion of the land, Lincoln has been shaped into the central figure of the nation's faith. He is loved, to repeat Clinton Rossiter's citing "someone," the American Everyman, as "the martyred Christ of democracy's passion play." He has his temple, modeled after the religious architecture of the ancient Greeks, the founders of democracy. And he has his name cursed, often in the shadows of the dark and with shame. Like priests and theologians of old, the historians of this later day argufy about him — to find him for what he truly was, or to find him for what a troubled people needs. Not surprisingly, the disputes about him in this young United States resemble a little the disputes in the young Church about Jesus. Some envision Lincoln as a common man of Illinois; some see in him divinity.[5]

III. THE COMING OF THE MAN

By 1870 William Herndon, "myth maker and truth teller," as Donald summed up his work, gave up the notion of writing the life of his former law partner. He had developed, however, some strong ideas on how such a book should be written. He wanted the biography to show the rise of "Lincoln the unaided, uneducated, Lincoln the penniless barefoot boy," to the presidency. He wanted to "applaud" the democracy which made such a life possible and point to Europe where it could not have been lived. And he wanted to hold the story "up to the young in this world for all coming time." The central motif of Lincoln's life was to be in a "bold contrast" between *"low origin* and *high end*."[6]

Herndon's conception was not original insofar as it pictured the rise of a self-made man. This American idol had been in the native forge for a long time. Lincoln's earliest campaign biographer, whose name remains a mystery, and who knew no better than to spell the hero's name as "Abram," knew enough to introduce him as a workingman whose story was "the true offspring of democracy." "No where else in the world," this author wrote, "could such things be, and be normal and natural." Herndon's contribution thus was not the recognition of a prime source of Lincoln's appeal, but the recognition of the virtues of shaping Lincoln's *entire* life around a sharp, dramatic contrast between "*low origin* and *high end*," between a "stagnant, putrid pool" and apotheosis.[7]

Yet because Herndon felt that he could not write the great biography, he sold his laboriously collected materials to Ward Hill Lamon. After that he gave generously of his advice, too. He told Lamon, this burly Lincoln friend whom Potter characterized as "more stalwart of body than of mind," that the above theme must be followed "if you want your hero to shine." What Lamon's views were we shall never fully know, but in Chauncey F. Black, who in fact wrote Lamon's *Lincoln,* Herndon found at least a partially receptive soul; Black, too, saw a dichotomy in Lincoln's life and spoke of the "dunghill" and the "diamond."[8]

Of the projected two-volume Lamon-Black history, the first, *The Life of Abraham Lincoln from his Birth to his Inauguration as President,* appeared in 1872 and emphasized the hero's "*low origin.*" Although the book showed courage, and contained much new information, mostly Herndon's, it was, at best, second-rate biography. The public received it as something much worse than that and Lamon's inept attempt to write the sequel alone failed miserably.[9]

Thus Lamon's *Lincoln* largely presented the "dunghill" thesis and there was no "diamond." On the eve of his first presidential bid Lincoln had said after sketching out his own life that "There is not much of it, for the reason, I suppose, that there is not much of me." Twelve years later Lamon-Black tried to show this timely campaign utterance to be a substantially accurate enduring truth.[10]

In the 1880's, when Herndon himself finally embarked, with Jesse W. Weik, on writing the *True Life,* he brought both more knowledge and a greater love of Lincoln to the task. His conception of what the biography must say remained unchanged, however. Because his book, too, considered the prepresidential years, with only a single chapter on the White House, its message was quite like Lamon's. Although the quality of Herndon's work was incomparably higher, at first the book-buying public received it with only slightly more enthusiasm than they did Lamon's.

Herndon had a certain respect for the pioneer folk from amongst whom both he and his partner had risen. Historians accurately count him, and with somewhat less justification Lamon as well, among the harbingers of Frederick Jackson Turner. Still, *Herndon's Lincoln: The True Story of a Great Life* (3 volumes, 1889), the title notwithstanding, showed no glimmer of the towering qualitites of the man from Illinois. An "honest account by an honest man," Samuel Eliot Morison was to write of the book in the 1920's. But he had to add: "I do think that something about Lincoln which made him great was missed by Herndon."[11]

IV. THE TRIUMPH OF THE GOD

As Lincoln's old partner bequeathed to the nation his masterpiece, the President's wartime secretaries, Nicolay and Hay, produced *Abraham Lincoln: A History* (10 volumes, 1890). They displayed the Chief Magistrate "on dress parade," as one reader put it, and they were wildly successful before the public. And deservedly so. If Herndon's work was perhaps the most interesting biography written in that generation in the United States, Nicolay and Hay's was one of the best histories.[12]

One pictured Lincoln the man, a down-to-earth, typical Westerner; the other, the great leader whose perfection partook of divinity. They created dissimilar images in part because of dissimilar proportions. In Herndon's three volumes only one chapter dealt with the presidency. In Nicolay and Hay's ten volumes two-thirds of a volume seemed sufficient to cover the years before the slavery controversy broke in 1854. One became the epitome of what might be labeled the "Lincoln the man" school, the other that of "Lincoln the god."

The battle of the two Lincolns, repeatedly noted before this and likened by Donald to "a religious war,"[13] has never quite ceased. Yet for more than two generations after Good Friday, 1865, the godly school overwhelmingly carried the field. The idealized image of the Great Emancipator and the Savior of the Union dominated both popular and scholarly endeavors because it filled a deep need, one that has been revealingly discussed by Lloyd Lewis in *Myths After Lincoln* (1929), by Basler, by Donald, and by others. Indeed the image created a large world-wide effect. By the turn of the century Lev Nikolaevich Tolstoy found in the Caucasus tribesmen speaking of the American mother to whom "angels appeared . . . and predicted that the son whom she would conceive would become the greatest the stars had ever seen." Tolstoy himself concluded: Lincoln "aspired to be divine — and he was."[14]

In the United States this image of popular divinity first came to life among blacks. Exalted a freedman in 1865: "Lincoln died for we, Christ died for we, and me believe him the same mans."[15] Whites, too, turned rapidly to the engaging image which, in a more or less muted version also entered the historical literature. By the time the gospel according to Nicolay and Hay appeared, a clear historiographic channel had been charted for it by a host of earlier works. Most important among these were J. G. Holland's 1866 *Life of Abraham Lincoln* and Isaac A. Arnold's several books: *The History of Abraham Lincoln and the Overthrow of Slavery* (1866), *The Life of Abraham Lincoln* (1885), etc.

After Nicolay and Hay came a large number of able books set in the same mold of near hagiography. Ida M. Tarbell assimilated the essence of Herndon's information and yet managed to show only romantic greatness in her influential books. Among these *The Life of Abraham Lincoln* (2 volumes, 1900) was the most important. The same was true, in a different manner, of Carl Sandburg's 1926 masterwork. He dared to devote two long volumes to the *Prairie Years* without tarnishing the image of the folk-god. Well-written apotheosis ruled Lincolniana.

V. BEVERIDGE

The hagiographic age of Lincoln scholarship came to a rather sudden end during the second decade of the twentieth century, after only moderate warnings from Lord Charnwood and Nathaniel Wright Stephenson: *Abraham Lincoln* (1917) and *Lincoln* (1922). As a rule the writing of history is hardly dramatic. The work of Albert Jeremiah Beveridge, however, had that effect. The senator-turned-historian possessed one of the most brilliant minds in the extraordinary galaxy of a century of Lincoln scholars. Although fate did not allow him to finish his work, the volumes he completed were pivotal points of Lincoln historiography: *Abraham Lincoln, 1809-1858* (2 volumes, 1928). Charles A. Beard did not exaggerate when he wrote, having read the manuscript at an early stage, that it was "a revolutionary piece of historical writing" which revealed the young Lincoln in "a blinding light."[16]

Beveridge breathed new life into the image of Lincoln the man with such unprecedented force and scholarship that its vitality has not failed to this day. Inevitably he thus strongly influenced attitudes toward the Civil War and the image of Lincoln the god as well. Although it is readily demonstrable that here was an idea for which the times were hospitable, and also that the techniques to uphold such an idea had been perfected at last, the fact remains that Beveridge, well-nigh single-handedly among Lincolnists reversed the dominant trend of Lincoln scholarship.

In the young Lincoln Beveridge found an average mortal even more than had Herndon, who had looked upon his partner's warts six months out of the year for more than fifteen years. Surface signs indicate that Beveridge had expected to find a great figure long before the White House. When he was disappointed, he was disappointed cruelly. Being the first to examine carefully the abbreviated records of the Illinois General Assembly, he understandably met considerable difficulties in discovering any intelligible message in them. He called the documents "a morass," a "muddle," "this wilderness." These "vital years never have been touched at all," he groaned with astonishment. Indeed he never managed to find much light in the musty records. But he saw enough of an outline to dislike what he saw: a Lincoln "of narrow partisanship and small purposes." In private he wrote even more emphatically: "I wish to the Lord he could have gone straightforward about something or other."[17]

Actually Beveridge did appear to recognize, for a moment, an important thread and wrote to Beard that "from the very start the economic element is almost predominant." Soon, however, he lost the thread in the "morass" of the Illinois political record. Moreover, in his book Beveridge tried to refrain from all interpretations. And, in any event, as a Progressive he had little sympathy for the chief business of Lincoln's early years, the championship of budding capitalism. As so often befalls even the finest historians, the message of the present proved too much for the past. Judging the 1830's with the values of the 1900's, Beveridge misunderstood the Illinois legislator's stance as "firm support of vested interests."[18]

Tracking Lincoln to Congress made things worse. Once again Beveridge was the first to comb through the legislative documents. Is not that "astounding"? he asked friends. His discovery provides an indication of the quality of studies of the early Lincoln before him. He complained bitterly of "this boundless and uncharted morass" but went on to uncover an opportunistic politician who opposed his country's just cause in the Mexican War. Although all of Lincoln's public and private statements on the subject spoke otherwise, Beveridge explained to his historian colleagues, and demonstrated in his book, that the congressman "was not bothered very much about convictions."[19]

Yet the worst was still to come. With the rise of the slavery controversy, Beveridge began to rewrite not only the Lincoln story but increasingly also American history. Indeed, he became a founder of the Revisionist school which dominated Civil War scholarship during the generation that followed. him, and which laid a heavy portion of war guilt on the opponents of slavery. If in the 1840's the Illinois representative's pacific attitude merited contempt from Beveridge in light of the Spanish-American War and the beloved "March of the Flag," in the 1850's an uncompromising antislavery stand, followed by war, appeared unwise in view of the needlessness of the American participation in World War I. Thus rare discerning readers could note that in Beveridge's *Lincoln,* to quote J. Franklin Jameson, "Douglas is the hero."[20]

The former senator was in his sixties at the time he started his study, rejected by and rejecting his first love, politics. He interrupted his work to try for a political comeback; when that failed, he vented his disgust with politicians, and perhaps with his own past, in *Lincoln*. Indeed, he appears to have gone through something of a metamorphosis while writing the book. His correspondence, as well as his finished work, bespoke a deep revolt against "the teachings of my youth," which, as he wrote to Edward Channing, were "sheer bunc." From his mountains of freshly unearthed facts Beveridge saw, to paraphrase Beard, a blinding new vision. If at the end of his labors he still expected to find a giant of a President, the volumes he did complete ran through much muck of his own raking. An unfairly negative view permeated his biography, clothed in brilliant scholarship. Perhaps it was this latter quality, together with his penchant for not voicing his views directly, that prevented Lincoln scholars from seeing what a layman like Oliver Wendell Holmes noted immediately: Beveridge did not like his subject. Students thus generally failed to treat his unspoken yet plain judgments with much needed caution.[21]

VI. THE BEVERIDGE SCHOOL

During the decades that followed the appearance of the Beveridge masterwork, historians successfully challenged many of the Herndonian tales the book had overenthusiastically embraced. The same cannot be said of its overall conception of the prepresidential Lincoln — disregarding the romanticisms and the generalizations left unsupported by scholarly particulars. In Beveridge's wake William E. Baringer's 1937 *Lincoln's Rise to Power* showed the Illinois Republican discreetly wheeling and dealing his way to his party's presidential nomination — but not possessing any higher motives. In 1945, in *A House Dividing*, Baringer continued where the earlier work had left off, in spirit, in chronology, and in a seductive style. During this period, President-elect Lincoln made the most fateful decision of his life, perhaps in the nation's life, by refusing compromise over slavery. The historian, however, found it accurate to portray throughout roughly 95 per cent of his text a politician who spent nearly all of his time scheming to keep the majority of the other politicians, whom he eventually appointed, from entering his cabinet!

Baringer, unlike Beveridge, displayed no hostility toward Lincoln. On the contrary he pictured a good politician, doing well what politicians were supposed to do. Having principles, however, did not appear to be among the desirable qualities. As for elements of true greatness, Lincoln had none. The grip with which such views came to hold the Lincoln establishment, although not the folk religionists, was perhaps measured by the official honors bestowed on the able Baringer: Executive Secretary of the prestigious Abraham Lincoln Association from 1943 to 1947, and later the Executive

Director of the Lincoln Sesquicentennial Commission from 1958 to 1960.

Baringer did not ride the crest of this school of historical thought. Donald W. Riddle published *Lincoln Runs for Congress* in 1948, and followed in 1957 with *Congressman Abraham Lincoln.* The man he portrayed had one seemingly all-overriding goal: "to advance his own political standing."[22] In this view Lincoln began his career of self-seeking as an advocate of special privilege in the Illinois legislature, although his allegiance to the Whigs was a mistake, for they ever remained the minority party. He then moved on to Congress to oppose the war against Mexico, without any real convictions, out of political ambition, albeit again misplaced ambition, for he thus committed political suicide.

In the end, however, after a life of political blunders, he helped whip up a rather artificial crisis over slavery, joined the Republicans and rose to the top position in the land. Riddle does not spell out these last details, or note that the price of Lincoln's personal aspirations could be counted in more than half a million dead Americans. But the cynicism of his portrait is perhaps unmatched in scholarly literature. This fact is not eased by his apparent unawareness of it. Indeed, Riddle unwittingly outdid the latter-day Confederate calumniators of Lincoln, who saw "a man of coarse nature, a self-seeking politician, who craved high office . . . to satisfy his own burning desire for distinction."[23]

VII. THE MODERN SCHISM

The logical outgrowth of the labors of the Beveridge school was the welcome, and at its best circumspect, extension of critical attitudes to the idealized picture of Lincoln's war years. In ways that are discussed in Section VIII, the President was made more *real.* The god, however, did not quite disappear. For, in fact, there was something of what we tend to call the divine in Lincoln.

In 1960 Reinhard H. Luthin published a full-scale biography, *The Real Abraham Lincoln,* and summed up the findings of the post-Beveridge era. Up to 1860 he portrayed a generally self-serving, not very admirable politician. Although Luthin significantly moderated the god image of the White House years, in places too much so, he recognized the unparalleled greatness that was in Lincoln. His work thus gave an up-to-date illustration of the schism created by historians.

The first to have fully exemplified as well as diagnosed the above ailment was John T. Morse. The inspiration for his 1893 *Abraham Lincoln* came from the well-nigh simultaneous appearance of the biographies by Herndon and by Nicolay and Hay. Morse, editor of the *American Statesmen* series, who reserved for himself the greatest plum, Lincoln, wrote of "the insoluble problem of two men — two lives — one following the other with no visible link . . . we have physically one creature, morally and mentally two beings."[24]

The chief scholarly value of his study was in this insight, which defined the problem. But Morse supplied no solutions. He merely presented his two Lincolns; spoke, inadequately, of Lincoln's ability to grow, as have many students to this day; and concluded by admitting that the hero was incomprehensible.[25]

Forty-three years later, in 1935, Roy P. Basler, surveying the field, despaired even of the feasibility of bridging the gap between the man and the god.[26] After another generation passed, students could still observe the spectacle of one scholar proclaiming Lincoln, as President, "the spiritual center of American history," and another speaking of Lincoln in Illinois as "not fighting for a cause" but "using the slavery issue . . . to run for office."[27] The double image became so ingrained that when careful research undermined it — as did William Wolf's study of Lincoln's religion, *The Almost Chosen People* (1959) — the researcher could still see fit to pay lipservice to it. In the face of this dilemma Don E. Fehrenbacher displayed renewed optimism in the 1960's. Yet at the end of the decade his Harmsworth Lecture also remarked on the "common solution" of many historians that presented Lincoln "as the frontier hero down to 1860 and as the national saint after that, along with some vague observations about his remarkable 'growth' in the presidency."[28]

Fehrenbacher's optimism was nonetheless warranted. During the years that had elapsed since Beveridge, the Lincoln schism had narrowed considerably. Indeed, in spite of some aforementioned students, the better part of modern scholarship can be seen as at times a conscious attempt to move toward that end, to build bridges between the two Lincolns.

VIII. THE GLISSADING GOD

The application of the hard-nosed techniques of modern scholarship, which in christology was labeled "higher criticism," could not but bring Lincoln the godly president closer to the antebellum man. Thus what Lamon's ghost, Black, had called "the usual stuff," and Beveridge "Tarbellizing," disappeared in the post-Beveridge era from the forefront of Lincoln studies.[29]

Even before this, there existed a school of writers whose purpose was to bring the god down from his heights and consign him to Inferno. These belligerent students were not concerned with the problem of historical continuity. They wanted to produce the picture of an evil man. A certain body of postbellum Confederate literature must be included in this category, distinguished as much by a hatred of the Civil War President as by a lack of scholarship. To illustrate, however, that on rare occasions a high plane of learning was reached here, one is tempted to include Charles W. Ramsdell's accusatory argument, now rejected by historians, that Lincoln deliberately maneuvered the South into starting the war: "Lincoln and Fort Sumter,"

Journal of Southern History, 3 (1937); [cf. Current, *Lincoln and the First Shot* (1963)].

Edgar Lee Masters' 1931 *Lincoln the Man* must also be noted, a work singular in being perhaps the only full-length hostile biography. This fascinating poet had seen Beveridge's *Lincoln* as the "Definitive Biography," and followed his directions to their extreme. Masters' antihero "surveyed" the American road "toward empire and privilege," or as the poet-biographer wrote in private to Theodore Dreiser, "ruined the institutions of the republic."[30]

A good recent example of anti-Lincoln writing is Lerone Bennett, Jr.'s popular magazine article insisting that Lincoln, as a white supremacist, deserves no honor: ("Was Abe Lincoln a White Supremacist?" *Ebony* (February 1968). The message of this entire group of writers, whether disgruntled Southerners, latter-day Copperheads, or left militants, is summed up well in Bennett's words, that the sixteenth President "is not the light . . . he is in fact standing in the light, hiding our way . . . ." [Cf. Benjamin Quarles, *Lincoln and the Negro* (1962); John Hope Franklin, *The Emancipation Proclamation* (1963); Don E. Fehrenbacher, "Only His Stepchildren: Lincoln and the Negro," *Civil War History,* 20 (1974); George M. Frederickson, "A Man but Not a Brother: Abraham Lincoln and Racial Equality," *Journal of Southern History* 41 (1975); and G. S. Boritt, "The Voyage to the Colony of Linconia; The Sixteenth President, Black Colonization, and the Defense Mechanism of Avoidance," *Historian,* 37 (1975)].

The bitterly antagonistic historians contributed nothing to the bridge-building work of their colleagues — on the contrary. By causing sharp reactions, extreme stands tended to strengthen the divine image. Thus it fell to others to create progress.

A more scholarly approach to dethroning Lincoln was taken by those who, aided by the advance of political science, found a wily politician in the White House. The majority of the outstanding students of the past three decades took part in such labors. Their portrayals of the politician-president were not intentionally belittling. Value judgments were largely left to the reader and depended on the meaning one gave to the term "politician." The findings of these authors amounted to denigration for those who took the god image to heart, and for those who shared Lincoln's angry, early definition of politicians (expressed in a debate over banking) as "a set of men who have interests aside from the interests of the people, and who . . . are, taken as a mass, at least one long step removed from honest men."[31]

Thoughtful recognition of the essential role played by the politician in a democracy led, however, to the conclusion of Harry J. Carman and Reinhard H. Luthin, in *Lincoln and the Patronage* (1943), that to appreciate "the shrewd and practical politician that he was . . . is only to enhance the greatness of Lincoln." Accordingly, they showed a Chief Executive strengthening his own hand through the skillful dispensation of the gifts of government. A year earlier George Fort Milton attempted to demonstrate the President's astute handling of the Copperheads in *Abraham Lincoln and the Fifth Column*. By 1948 Richard Hofstadter, in *The American Political Tradition*, could find it "difficult" to think of any other leader who was as thoroughly the politician as was Lincoln.[32]

In the same year William B. Hesseltine published his *Lincoln and the War Governors*. In this and such other studies as *Lincoln's Plan of Reconstruction* (1960) and *Sections and Politics: Selected Essays of William B. Hesseltine* (1968), edited by Current, he pushed the politician-president interpretation to its detailed, scholarly limits. He saw as Lincoln's central goal in the White House the creation of "a national party," and the Civil War as a war not between but "against" the states. However the student feels about these interpretations, Hesseltine still seemed to admire Lincoln, the *Architect of the Nation* (1959).

Several of Hesseltine's students followed, more or less, in his footsteps. Current's 1958 *The Lincoln Nobody Knows* often emphasized the mundane characteristics of the President while also recognizing his greatness. A single chapter in Kenneth M. Stampp's 1965 study, *The Era of Reconstruction, 1865-1877*, summed up Lincoln's hope for peace in his desire to create a postwar neo-Whig party. Earlier still another outstanding Hesseltine student, T. Harry Williams, found in *Lincoln and the Radicals* (1941) a good man who was heavily involved in politicking, but who had limited skills and who lost out to the radicals within the Republican Party. (Eleven years later, in *Lincoln and his Generals*, Williams produced a substantially different picture of the Commander-in-Chief.)

Williams' work in time became the focus of a debate about whether Lincoln was in substantial agreement with the radicals of his party: Donald, "The Radicals and Lincoln" (1956); Williams, "Lincoln and the Radicals: An Essay in Civil War History and Historiography" (1964); Donald, "Devils Facing Zionwards" (1964); Herman Belz, *Reconstructing the Union, Theory and Policy During the Civil War* (1969); Hans L. Trefousse, *The Radical Republicans: Lincoln's Vanguard for Racial Justice* (1969).

Earlier David Potter's *Lincoln and His Party in the Secession Crisis* (1942) showed a leader who fatally misread the political realities of the South, although not one who plotted to bring about war, as Ramsdell and followers thought. In 1954 William Frank Zornow, in *Lincoln and the Party Divided*, delineated the President's political maneuverings in the crucial election year of 1864. Five years later Norman A. Graebner, in a lecture entitled "Abraham Lincoln: Conservative Statesman," explained that "all successful statesman of the modern world have practiced the art of the possible."[33]

In this new era of Lincoln studies it was not surprising for Donald summarily to declare in his essay "A. Lincoln, Politician" that "the secret of Lincoln's success is simple: he was an astute and dexterous operator of the political machine."[34] Donald and other scholars could speak in such a vein in part because they saw Lincoln's superb statesmanship and his "godlike" qualities as requiring no defense. Their goal was to establish the portrait of a fully believable great man. Although some of them went too far, finding too much politics and too little principle in the sixteenth President, their work was both eminently useful and notably effective. On the whole, they produced the picture of a President who, to quote Williams, illustrated both "principle and pragmatism in politics." They thus delivered sturdy blows at the god image of Lincoln.[35]

The culmination of their work came in the four-volume biography published by J. G. Randall between 1945 and 1955, *Lincoln the President,* the last volume of which was so ably completed by Current. This is the finest scholarly study of the White House years. One can argue about many of its interpretations, but all in all Randall created an aura of totally believable greatness around Lincoln. Significantly, however, the "dean of Lincoln scholars" did not attempt to write a full-scale life. He left the Illinois Lincoln in the hands of his predecessors. Where Randall had ventured to touch the man image, mainly in the 1850's, he underlined the earlier judgments and, like Beveridge, "came very close to making Douglas his real hero. . . ."[36]

IX. THE RISING MAN

If humanizing the god tended toward rescuing Lincoln from his schizoid image, elevating the man served the same purpose. Benjamin Thomas, the biographer who came the closest to bridging the gap between the man and the god, used this method most successfully, although he toned down the godly image, too. His 1952 *Abraham Lincoln: A Biography* is often said to be the best short life of the first century of Lincolniana. Its virtues no more need be enumerated in this essay than those of the other works mentioned. We should note, however, that to eliminate the schism Thomas steered clear of the interpretations of modern students, and this was not always good scholarship. Also, like so many before him, he devoted less than one-fourth of his volume to four-fifths of the hero's life, that before the slavery controversy. This may have been good history but it was not good biography. And in spite of all, and however muted, in the end Thomas presented until 1854 the "politician," "of narrow partisanship and unsure purpose," and after that the "statesman" who grew "to world dimensions."[37]

The students of Lincoln the lawyer also labored in the cause of raising up the man. In the nineteenth century, and early in the twentieth, the majority of writers on this subject indulged in so much romantic nonsense as to elicit from plainspoken recent students comments as "buncombe" and "pop-pycock." Here, too, Beveridge signaled the turning point. In private he declared that Lincoln's law cases, "little and big, put together do not, on their merit, deserve a line in history and not more than a paragraph in any biography." In public, in his biography, he wrote in this same spirit, although not in this substance.[38]

The first historian to disagree with him at length was Albert Woldman in *Lawyer Lincoln* (1936). Much more emphatic and able opposition came from John B. Duff's *A. Lincoln: Prairie Lawyer* (1960). They both indicated advancement in scholarship. Nonetheless they exaggerated the importance of the Illinois attorney's work. To see a great lawyer moving into a great presidency was nice bridge building — but not very realistic. Lincoln had been a very good lawyer; he had not been a great one who made notable national contributions. The first part of Beveridge's statement, about the place of Lincoln's legal work in history, was generally accurate.

The second part of his view, however, that Lincoln's career at the bar deserves no attention even in a biography, is untrue. Studying and practicing law substantially influenced the development of Lincoln's thought patterns. Woldman, Duff, and others before them argued that the Illinoisan's legal life prepared him for the presidency. It remained, however, for John P. Frank's *Lincoln as a Lawyer* (1961) to examine thoroughly Lincoln's legal thinking. Frank convincingly demonstrated that however different were the problems facing the attorney and the Chief Magistrate, "the cast of mind used in their solution was much the same."[39] Thus Frank, much more than any of his predecessors, made a real contribution toward revealing the links between the two Lincolns.

This brings us to the last group of students that took substantial steps toward bridging the Lincoln schism. Basler, in his 1946 essay, "Lincoln's Development as a Writer," by examining literary style, argued against the often quoted but snobbish judgment of Charles Francis Adams, Jr. that Lincoln grew so much in the White House that "he became another being." The Basler essay was convincing but, since it concerned itself primarily with style, its message, and impact, was sharply delimited.[40]

In 1959 Harry V. Jaffa, a political scientist, published his *Crisis of the House Divided; an Interpretation of the Issues of the Lincoln-Douglas Debates*. He, like others, before him, totally missed the meaning of Lincoln's economic views, which he called "petty bread-and-butter party questions."[41] Yet searching for the origins of the debator of 1858, he found them in the young Whig. He did this, often brilliantly, through an examination of two early, nonpolitical Lincoln speeches which nonetheless commented on political processes. Even if these speeches were outside of the Illinois Whig's immediate work, more than any scholar before him, Jaffa unified the portrait of Lincoln.

And yet, partly because of faults in the style and techniques of his book (at least according to the historians' canons), and partly because of the limitations of the Lincoln audience, the *Crisis of the House Divided* did not obtain the wide influence it deserved. A measure of this sad fact was given by Richard Allen Heckman's 1967 *Lincoln vs. Douglas: The Great Debates Campaign* and again in 1970 by John S. Wright's neorevisionist *Lincoln and the Politics of Slavery*. Both of these studies concentrated on the same period as did Jaffa's book, yet neither of them were significantly affected by it. Wright did not even list it in his bibliography.

In 1959, the year of Jaffa's study, Donald delivered a lecture at the University of Illinois under the title "Abraham Lincoln: Whig in the White House." He argued that, however fashionable it was for historians to dismiss Whig ideology, it had largely shaped Lincoln's exercise of the presidential powers. His piece dealt with political format rather than substance, but its important and Jaffa-like implication was that Whiggery had been a most serious business for the Illinois politician. Yet again, illustrating in part the endurance of Beveridge's *Lincoln,* despite Donald's towering stature in the historical fraternity, and despite the publication of his paper in two different collections of essays, its weight has been insufficiently felt so far.[42]

The most recent and the most successful of the bridge builders is Fehrenbacher, whose 1962 *Prelude to Greatness: Lincoln in the 1850's* tackled the Beveridge interpretation head on. It found during the last antebellum decade a man whose admitted ambitions were "leavened by moral convictions and a deep faith in the principles upon which the republic had been built." And it concluded that "the Lincoln of the 1860's was much the same man under greater challenge."[43] Fehrenbacher thus made a major dent in the image of the Illinois Lincoln drawn by Beveridge and his followers. He pushed back to 1854, to Lincoln's entrance into the slavery controversy, the demarcation line between the man and the god. But at that point the two Lincolns still remained.

It is worth repeating that great progress had been made since Morse's day in softening the sharp contrast of the double image. Yet the road to a more unified, a more real Lincoln remained elusive. Folklore had solved the problem long before by having the god and man "inextricably scrambled," to quote Donald.[44] For the students in the 1970's, however, the most noted connection between the two Lincolns remained the platitudes about his remarkable growth.

X. HERMES' LINCOLN

At this point we can turn our attention to the investigators of the area which in this writer's view supplies the sturdiest support for the bridge between man and god: Lincoln's economic persuasion. The notable fact about it is the absence of investigators. In 1944 James W. Kerley, in a master's thesis at Columbia University, addressed himself to "A Discussion of the Determinants of Lincoln's Political and Economic Philosophy." The result was wholly dismal, and with him the list of professionally trained students largely ends in this field.[45]

From time to time, questions about the need to research Lincoln's political economy were raised. To cite examples, the able economist George Gunton brought the subject up in 1895, in the *Social Economist,* having discovered the Whig lawmaker's 1839 speech on banking. So did Randall, passingly, forty-one years later, in "Has the Lincoln Theme Been Exhausted?" Harold Hyman spoke in a like manner in his 1965 lecture, "Lincoln and the Presidency." There were more questioners. But no answer was forthcoming.[46]

Randall himself began his massive *Lincoln the President* by devoting some of his first few paragraphs to a pre-war Lincoln who was concerned with machines, labor, "the problem of fifty bushels of wheat to the acre," social mobility — sketching out a very real Lincoln. With that, Randall's interest in the topic largely ended, excepting his brief argument in *Lincoln the Liberal Statesman* (1947) about the Civil War President's having been no Hamiltonian.[47]

So it was with the fellowship of Lincoln scholars as a whole. Few took any note of Lincoln's economic views. Indeed, perhaps the most penetrating brief appraisals came from non-Lincoln specialists, Vernon L. Parrington and Richard Hofstadter, (though they also made some horrendous errors): *Main Currents in American Thought,* volume II (1930) and *The American Political Tradition* (1948). In a chapter labeled "Abraham Lincoln and the Self-Made Myth" Hofstadter came to emphasize, more than any other historian, the fundamental importance of social mobility to Lincoln — something his student Eric Foner developed fully for the entire Republican party. The brilliant Hofstadter, however, also came close to mocking his subject. Indeed, his Lincoln seemed only a step removed from Bounderby of Dickens' *Hard Times:*

> A man who could never sufficiently vaunt himself a self-made man. A man who was always proclaiming, through that brassy speaking-trumpet of a voice of his, his old ignorance and his old poverty. A man who was the Bully of humility.

Among the other works that groped, often unwittingly, along related lines were two important addresses, nearly three-quarters of a century apart: Charles Sumner, "Promises of the Declaration of Independence, and Abraham Lincoln;"[48] and Arthur C. Cole, *Lincoln's "House Divided" Speech: Does It Reflect a Doctrine of Class Struggle* (Chicago, 1923).

Among Lincolnists Williams, Fehrenbacher, and Current paid explicit if fleeting attention to Lincoln's political economy. None of them went into details, however, and although they were academicians none of them seemed to have encouraged their students to do so. Fehrenbacher summed up their common view, that Lincoln did "not adequately embody the economic spirit of nineteenth-century America," and his economic philosophy was "only casually related to his main lines of thought." Therefore it was not a promising endeavor to raise the subject.[49]

Actually, one segment of Lincoln's economic persuasion, the tariff, had received persistent and at times careful attention. In large part this was a historical spillover of the political controversies surrounding protectionism. At first, though, no disagreement appeared: Lincoln's contemporaries agreed about his high-tariff opinions. By the turn of the century, however, the debate commenced. Crusading Ida M. Tarbell, abandoning an earlier, grudging admission of her hero's misguided tariff views, became the first serious student to deny his orthodoxy on what by then was Republican dogma, in *The Tariff in Our Times* (1911). She, and the lesser lights of her faith were met squarely by the defenders of the Grand Old Party's creed. Thus George B. Curtiss produced what appears to be the earliest consideration of Lincoln's economic views that had any merit — even if he claimed that the Great Martyr was also "one of the Great Protectionists of the World": "Abraham Lincoln, Protectionist," *The Defender,* Document 1, 1916; cf. W. F. Wakeman, "Abraham Lincoln on the Tariff," *Ibid.,* Document 11, 1912.

Zealots of the protectionist school, unsatisfied by, or ignorant of, the ample evidence, supplemented Lincoln's views with suitable forgeries. (See, for example, F. W. Taussig's articles in the *Quarterly Journal of Economics* 28, 29, 35 (1914, 1915, 1921); and also his *Free Trade, the Tariff and Reciprocity* (1927). After long years of debate, which coincided with the beginning of a new American definition of virtuous economic policy, a somewhat new Lincoln of the historians emerged. If Charnwood, Sandburg, and Beveridge still presented a high-tariff man, later students produced a figure whose views were either unclear or leaned toward free trade (Baringer, Randall, Nevins, Current, J. A. Rawley). This new interpretation reached a point where Herndon's self-castigations of the 1870's, which bemoaned his partner's having led him into the unrighteous path of high-tariff advocacy, could be seen by Donald as superfluous because it was doubtful whether Lincoln had really been a protectionist in the first place![50]

The subject proved to be sufficiently interesting for two historians to explore it in detail: Luthin, "Abraham Lincoln and the Tariff," *American Historical Review,* 49 (1944); and Boritt, "Old Wine Into New Bottles: Abraham Lincoln and the Tariff Reconsidered," *Historian,* 28 (1966). Yet when all was said and done, no important new light had been shed on Lincoln.[51]

One other scholar must be mentioned here, even though his work did not deal with economics. In 1956 Robert V. Bruce's *Lincoln and the Tools of War* depicted with careful craftsmanship a President who was greatly attracted to technology. This was a Lincoln who *might* have been interested in political economy, too. Never again could an able critic like Edmund Wilson write, as he did in 1953 for the *New Yorker*, that "the value to humanity of language and the art of writing, [was] the only discovery, invention or improvement that appears to have excited his [Lincoln's] enthusiasm."[52]

XI. SOURCES OF MYTH

Thus we arrive at the most important question of this essay. Fine studies on Lincoln, as the previous listing indicates, abound; some are brilliant. Yet one hundred and fifteen years after the appearance of the first Lincoln books, and thousand of volumes later, his economics has remained unexplored. Why have historians persistently ignored the subject of the present study?

As so often when searching for the origins of a Lincoln myth, the first leads point to Lincoln himself. His early ventures in crafting economic policy in the Illinois General Assembly ended unhappily. The banking and improvement calamities of his state did not shake his economic convictions. They did, however, provide him, and also his friends, with an incentive to minimize the significance of economic matters. Then after 1854 Lincoln made a large effort powered by high morality and pragmatic politics, to disengage himself from his Whig past, to make economic questions into nonissues, and so keep alive the Democratic-Whig alliance of Republicanism. The picture he thus painted of himself vis-à-vis the new, post-Kansas-Nebraska Act politics became dominant. Even in the White House he took some studied steps toward remaining uninvolved with strictly legislative matters, among which he counted economics. In the middle of the twentieth century, Sandburg could thus combine both scholarship and folklore in his *War Years* and declare, in a way that would have pleased the Republican Lincoln, that political economy was a subject Lincoln "did not pretend the grasp of. . . ."[53]

Of course,when faced with other issues, both history and folklore frequently penetrated deeply beyond surface appearances. One fact that must be noted here, therefore, is the professional historians' traditional disdain for local history. By contrast, the popularly oriented writer drawn to the local scene has been generally uninterested in economics. Even John Hay saw fit to apologize to his editor for a chapter he entitled "Financial Measures," as "not in itself amusing — though necessary to the history."[54]

The imaginative professional's negative view of local history has changed substantially in recent years. In our case, however, antilocal bias was reinforced by the "Lincoln-the-man" image, and perfected by the Beveridge school, which exuded the teaching that his early work was of little real historical interest or consequence. Thus, although there have been some charming local histories by Lincolnists, to this day not a single trained historian

(Beveridge was a politician) covered in detail the first stage of Lincoln's political life, which ended with his retirement from the Illinois General Assembly. Without a careful delineation of the starting point, the story could not run on true course. Without an understanding of the young man's economic outlook, its later effect could not be seen. This was particularly true because, with the rise of the slavery controversy, direct economic questions in fact became relatively insignificant to both Lincoln and the nation.

One able student — Illinois state legislator, later lieutenant governor and Congressman, Paul Simon — did produce in 1965 a study of Lincoln's legislative years, having found to his astonishment that in the mountains of Lincolniana no such work existed. He made his most telling contribution through a careful disproval of the foul tale that made the Whig representative cast his votes for internal improvement projects in exchange for votes to make his future home town, Springfield, the state's capital. This myth, which originated with Lincoln's Democratic opponents, implied that he helped plunge Illinois into economic disaster in order to advance his own political standing. Thus it presaged the later man who opposed the Mexican War for like purposes, and who rode the slavery issue to power, heedless of consequences.

Simon made other contributions, too, but his lack of professional training took its toll. His fact-packed volume largely ignored the greater historical forces, including the economics, of the Age of Jackson. Although Simon entitled his book *Lincoln's Preparation for Greatness,* and he rescued his hero from many a Beveridge excess, he failed to reach much beyond Stephen Vincent Benét's "crude small-time politician." He thus failed to make the title of his book meaningful.[56]

Sixteen years earlier, Baringer's brief *Lincoln's Vandalia* had narrated the middle segment of the young politico's legislative service. His book was captivating and it included much useful information. It also led Baringer to think of examining in another work Lincoln's economic views. He did not do this.[55] But if Baringer, having searched some of the Illinois House records, recognized at least the need to study Lincoln's economics, most others could not. It is not cynical to state that to many Lincoln students economics appears to have been a wholly strange sphere. It is no coincidence that the only scholar to speak, however briefly, with admiration of Lincoln's grasp of political economy was Bray Hammond, an economic historian.[57]

Even Lincolnists with some mastery of the beautiful science could make the mistake of judging Lincoln's views against sophisticated twentieth-century standards, find them wanting, and dismiss them as something that should not be taken seriously. Randall classified Lincoln's tariff arguments under the curious heading of "tiresome or labored economics,"[58] although in the hands of Henry Carey, similar thinking had been the best America could offer at mid-century. Even those who might have been prepared to avoid such pitfalls could not, until recently, take advantage of the spectacular development of economic history during this past generation.

Another, closely related problem also weakened Lincoln scholarship. The Whig politician had championed banks, railroads, tariffs, and such. Edmund Wilson's 1953 essay spoke also for many, if not most, professional historians in its misjudgment that the young Illinoisan had belonged to the party of aristocracy. Such a view, with its Jacksonian bias, consigned nearly half of the antebellum Americans, who had generally voted Whig, to the class of the politically ignorant, who failed to understand their own interests and thus undermined their own chance to a better life.[59]

This kind of historiography also failed to distinguish between the pioneering sustenance of the struggling Alton and Sangamon Railroad of the 1840's, for example, and the defense of Edward Harriman's giant corporation in the 1900's, into which the Alton and Sangamon had by then been incorporated. Thus, instead of seeing Lincoln as the bringer of a brave new world, one who would

launch out on trackless seas,
Fearless for unknown shores,

to quote Walt Whitman, historians saw a supporter of "vested interests," to quote Beveridge. Since all in all most students conceded the cause of the common man as Lincoln's ultimate passion, his economics had to be dismissed as unrelated to his central story, not really worth investigating unless as an antiquarian escape.

Yet all this is not enough to explain the myth of the noneconomic Lincoln. The myth survived practically unscathed even a period of American historical writing during which economic interpretations played a pivotal role. It must be noted, too, that not all the writers of the modern epoch nurtured Democratic, hence anti-Whig leanings. And while political economy was not the forte of the majority of Lincoln scholars, Ida Tarbell, for example, reached fame with the *History of the Standard Oil Company;* and Robert Bruce for many years taught economic history at Boston University.

In some cases Lincoln's connections with economic matters were so obvious that only a deep psychological block could have prevented students from seeing them. The facts of his promotion of national banking from the White House, for instance, are so accessible that it is no exaggeration to say that no scholar thinking to look into the question should have had any difficulties in revealing them. Yet the great historian Randall's four-volume masterpiece says no more on the subject than do the great poet Sandburg's six volumes or Nicolay and Hay's ten — although the last two men could not have helped but have some firsthand information on the subject, in some hidden recesses of their minds. Thus in the final analysis we must seek the solution to our riddle in the dominant double image of Lincoln which even the professional historians could not entirely escape.

XII. OF GOD, MAN, AND ECONOMICS

Gods in our epoch do not deal in money. They do not concern themselves with mundane matters such as economics. Lincoln himself had quoted the Bible: you cannot serve both "God and mammon."[60] In Western Civilization, however much money is coveted, it has been held ever in bad repute. There-fore Lincoln's image as a god required that he be drastically severed from the science of man. All the factors that had made people regard him as a near deity — from his truly God-like, superbly moral outlook on life, through his martyrdom at the moment of victory in battle and on the an-niversary of Christ's crucifixion, to the *broad* needs of his nation and of his party denied Lincoln his economics. Even his politicking, which was his everyday business, had been largely taken away from him until three gener-ations after his death.

But there is more. Lloyd Lewis, student of his apotheosis into "the Ameri-can God," noted that the Illinoisan became a very particular god, a Yankee incarnation of the myriad primitive deities of the soil, one who "died to save Man's barns from Jefferson Davis' raiders. . . ."[61] The American god had to be an Arcadian god, for the New World Olympus, more than the Greek ever was, was primeval. But if deification denied Lincoln his economic beliefs, deification in the American mind's Arcady did so doubly, for the Lincolnian economics brought "the machine in the Garden," to borrow the felicitous phrase of Leo Marx. Breaking away from such a captivating god image re-quired perhaps a breaking away from the American confines.

If divinty robbed Lincoln of his economic faith, seemingly his man image should have recaptured it. This did not happen, however. Lincoln the man could no more be permitted to have his beliefs than could Lincoln the god for he was not simply a man — his picture was essentially that of a fron-tiersman. Nature "choosing sweet clay from the breast of the unexhausted West" — this was Lincoln — as James Russell Lowell's Harvard Commem-oration Ode chanted. The image of the plain Westerner clashed sharply with the image of economics as a sophisticated discipline. The log cabin and the bank seemingly could not be mixed. Historians did not even try.

Thus, although Bishop Matthew Simpson's symbolic slip at Oak Ridge Cemetery, which turned Lincoln's 1839 probank commentary into an anti-slavery one, was caught by Nicolay and Hay, again by Henry C. Whitney, and no doubt by others since, the substance of the Bishop's error (for such it was despite an ultimate justification) remained uncorrected. Perhaps it could not be otherwise. The error stood firmly upon the American ethos — indeed upon the American Dream[62]

For the elemental strength, perhaps the indestructibility of the god-man Lincoln legend is in this: it provides the mythological, fairy-tale foundations of man's dream of rising. It is a modern and nobler version of the Old World's fable of the poor peasant lad who wins the hand of the princess. It takes a very ordinary but decent mortal, quite like the average man, and abruptly catapults him to the pinnacle of success and fame.

No matter that in a large sense this denies what Lincoln preached ("work, work, work is the main thing") and what he lived.[63] The Lincoln mythos, with all its religious symbolism, is the living evidence for the common man that the American Dream of the right to rise is true. It is a humane myth that gives solace and hope. One should dare write that Herndon who started it all — if it was not Lincoln, indeed modern mankind in general — sketched out the man and the god not only to show, as he explained, by vivid contrast the glorious heights reached by the man from Illinois. In part he made the two Lincolns to hold out hope that he, Herndon, would yet "make it" in this world. And so he hoped to the end of his seventy-two hard years. And so hope Americans to this day — and modern man everywhere.

Appendix B

Abbreviations

Used in the Footnotes and Bibliography

AER	*American Economic Review*
AH	*Agricultural History*
AHR	*American Historical Review*
ALAB	*Abraham Lincoln Association Bulletin*
ALQ	*Abraham Lincoln Quarterly*
C.W.	*The Collected Works of Abraham Lincoln,* Roy P. Basler, *et al.* eds., 9 vols., 1953-55
C.W.S.	*Ibid., Supplement,* 1974.
CWH	*Civil War History*
EEH	*Explorations in Economic History*
Hist.	*The Historian*
ISHL	Illinois State Historical Library
JAH	*Journal of American History*
JEH	*Journal of Economic History*
JISHS	*Journal of the Illinois State Historical Society*
JNH	*Journal of Negro History*
LC	Library of Congress
LH	*Lincoln Herald*
MA	*Mid-America*
MHSP	*Massachusetts Historical Society Proceedings*
MVHR	*Mississippi Valley Historical Review*
RES	*Review of Economics and Statistics*

cAppendix G
Notes

CHAPTER 1

[1]James Quey Howard's interview with George Close [May, 1860], Abraham Lincoln Papers, Library of Congress (hereafter LC); see also William Dean Howells, *Life of Abraham Lincoln* (Springfield, Ill., 1938 ed.) 28; and William H. Herndon's interview with John Hanks [1865], Herndon-Weik Papers, LC.

[2]Why central Illinois became Whig is a question that has long troubled historians. The subject invites investigation via modern techniques.

[3]John G. Bergen to David B. Ayres, Jan. 1, 1830, in J. Van Fenstermaker, "A Description of Sangamon County, Illinois, in 1830," *Agricultural History*, 39 (1965), 136-41 (hereafter *AH*); Josiah Francis in a letter of Simeon Francis to his brother [Charles?], [1831], Simeon Francis Papers, Illinois State Historical Library (hereafter ISHL).

[4]John Reynolds, *My Own Times: Embracing also the History of My Life* (Belleville, Ill., 1855), 152.

[5]The most adequate picture of the political geography of central Illinois for this period is in Donald Riddle, *Lincoln Runs for Congress* (New Brunswick, N.J., 1948), 22-59: Paul M. Angle provides the best description of the economy of the Springfield area in *"Here I Have Lived": A History of Lincoln's Springfield, 1821-1865* (Springfield, Ill., 1935), *passim*.

[6]Roy P. Basler, ed., Marion Dolores Pratt and Lloyd A. Dunlap, asst. eds., *The Collected Works of Abraham Lincoln* (9 vols., New Brunswick, N.J., 1953-5), I, 5-9 (hereafter *C.W.*)

[7]John H. Krenkel, *Illinois Internal Improvements, 1818-1848* (Cedar Rapids, Ia., 1958), 30f. For the choice between railroads and canals see the bibliography for the works of Albert Fishlow, Stanley Lebergott, Peter D. McClelland, Roger L. Ransom, and Julius Rubin(2). A number in parenthesis after an author's name, in this case #2, indicates that the reference is to the 2nd work listed under that author's name in the bibliography.

[8]Herndon to Ward H. Lamon, Feb. 25, 1870; see also Herndon to Jesse K. Weik, June 13, 1888, Herndon-Weik Papers; Paul M. Angle, ed., *Herndon's Life of Lincoln* (Grenwich, Conn., 1961), 119. [Some of the best of the Herndon manuscripts were published in Emanuel Hertz, *The Hidden Lincoln* (New York, 1940) but careless editing precludes the book's use as a final source]

[9]*C.W.*, I, 13; *Sangamo Journal*, Feb. 16, March 29, 1832; Krenkel, *Illinois Improvements*, 11, 15.

[10]*Annals of Congress*, Feb. 4, 1817, 14:2, 851-4; and March 31, 1824, 18:1, 2001.

[11]*C.W.*, I, 34, 36, 39-40, 42, 46-7; *Journal of the House of Representatives of Illinois*, 1835-6, 324-6 *et passim*; see also William Baringer, *Vandalia, A Pioneer Portrait* (New Brunswick, N.J., 1949), 60. The best review of the state's early transportation history is Krenkel, *Illinois Improvements*, 9-25.

[12]*Ill. House Journal*, 1835-6, 41; *C.W.*, I, 40; *Sangamo Journal*, Feb. 20, 1836; [Paul M. Angle], "Lincoln's Land Holdings and Investments," *Abraham Lincoln Association Bulletin* (hereafter *ALAB*), 16 (Sept. 1929), 1-2.

[13]*C.W.*, I, 32; Paul Simon, *Lincoln's Preparation for Greatness: The Illinois Legislative Years* (Norman, Okla., 1965), 39. Clay called only for 10 per cent distribution.

[14]*C.W.*, I, 21; Krenkel, *Illinois Improvements*, 61.

[15]*C.W.*, I, 43; *Laws of Illinois*, 1836, 145-6, 149-50; Krenkel, *Illinois Improvements*, 37-40.

[16]*C.W.*, I, 48-50; Herndon's interview with James Gourley, 1866, Herndon-Weik Papers; Robert L. Wilson to Herndon, Feb. 10, 1866, Herndon-Lamon Papers, Henry E. Huntington Library. It was during this campaign that Lincoln and his mentor, Whig leader John T. Stuart, were falsely accused of opposing the payment of a state loan. Lincoln objected vigorously to his name being thus "done up in large capitals." He labeled the spreader of the tale "a *liar* and a *scoundrel*" and promised his "proboscis a good wringing." *C.W.*, VIII, 429.

[17]Reynolds, *My Own Times*, 38; *C.W.*, I, 54.

[18]Nathaniel Hamerson to Henry Eddy, Feb. 19, 1836, Henry Eddy Papers, ISHL; Seward as quoted in Glyndon G. Van Deusen, *William Henry Seward* (New York, 1967), 47.

[19]Herndon's *Lincoln*, 153; Carter Goodrich, *Government Promotion of American Canals and Railroads* (New York, 1960), 49-165. I also benefited by the state studies, listed in the bibliography, by Oscar and Mary Flug Handlin, Louis Hartz(1), Milton Sidney Heath, Nathan Miller, Robert J. Parks, James Neal Primm, and Harry N. Scheiber(3). A roll of early Illinois county names is in John Moses, *Illinois Historical and Statistical* (2 vols., Chicago, 1889-92), I, 547.

[20]Ford, *A History Of Illinois from the Commencement as a State in 1818 to 1847* (Chicago, 1854), 181; *Sangamo Journal*, March 4, 1837.

[21]*C.W.*, III, 385; cf. 108-15, 271-9; see also Chapter XVI and the bibliography for Arthur A. Ekirch, Jr., Rush Welter, and Major L. Wilson.

[22]Crocker as quoted in Joseph Dorfman, *The Economic Mind in American Civilization* (5 vols., New York, 1946-59), II, 619. The most reliable work on Lincoln's reading is David C. Mearns, "The Great Inventions of the World: Mr. Lincoln and the Books He Read," in *Three Presidents and Their Books* (Urbana, Ill., 1955), 45-88.

[23]*Ill. House Journal*, 1836-7, 292-5, 363-76, 413, 432-3, 441-3, 674-6.

[24]*Ibid.*, 36; McClernand to Eddy, Feb. 2, 1837, Eddy Papers; Robert L. Wilson to Herndon, Feb. 10, 1866, Herndon-Lamon Papers.

[25]*C.W.*, I, 45-6, 52, 53-4, 60, 69-70, 70-1, 72-3, 76, 82-3, 85-7, 121; *Ill. House Journal*, 1836-7, 230-7, 247-55, 674-5.

[26]Samuel D. Lockwood to Mary Nash, Feb. 26, 1837, Nathaniel Pope Papers, ISHL; *Sangamo Journal*, March 4, 1837.

[27]Simon, *Preparation for Greatness*, 76-105, shattered this segment of the Lincoln Apocrypha. Krenkel, an economic historian, was the first scholar to question the connection of internal improvements to capital relocation, in *Illinois Improvements*, 72-5.

[28]*C.W.*, I, 126-7. Lincoln, of course, did trade votes as he readily conceded. He bargained, however, for the allocation of improvement projects and not for the location of the capital. As in the improvement systems of other states, such a course was a requisite. In Illinois to cite a representative with firsthand knowledge of the matter, "every member wanted a [rail]road to his county town." Usher F. Linder, *Reminiscences of the Early Bench and Bar in Illinois* (Chicago, 1879), 59.

CHAPTER 2

[1]As quoted in Gerald T. Dunne, *Justice Story and the Rise of the Supreme Court* (New York, 1970), 143.

[2]The best work on the subject is dated: George William Dowrie, *The Development of Banking in Illinois, 1817-1863* (Urbana, Ill., 1913). See also the bibliography for R. E. Davis, C. H. Garnett, F. M. Huston, F. C. James, and F. R. Marckhoff. This and the following chapters are particularly indebted to Bray Hammond, *Banks and Politics in America: From the Revolution to the Civil War* (Princeton, N.J., 1957).

[3]*Sangamo Journal*, Sept. 22, Nov. 24, 1832; Feb. 9, Sept. 29, 1833; Dec. 13, 1834; *Ill. House Journal*, 1834-5, 504-8, 511-2; *Laws of Ill.*, 1835, 7-14; Ford, *History*, 170-2; Dowrie, *Banking in Illinois*, 6-61.

[4]"Stephen T. Logan talks about Abraham Lincoln," ALAB, 12 (Sept. 1, 1928), 2; *Ill. House Journal*, 1834-5, 212, 215-7, 258-63, 285, 356, 358-9; 1835-6, 60-2; 1836-7, 70-1; 1838-9, 26-30, 98-103, 108, 231-2, 257-63, 299-300; 1840-1, 167, 170-1; *C.W.*, I, 140-2, 143.

[5]*Laws of Ill.*, 1836-7, 23-4; Dowrie, *Banking in Illinois*, 79-81; see also Leonard C. Halderman, and William Gerald Shade in the bibliography.

[6]*C.W.*, I, 61-9; *Ill. House Journal*, 1836-7, 195-9, 235-7, 247, 288-97, 302-6; cf. Albert J. Beveridge, and Paul Simon in the bibliography.

[7]Gouge, *A Short History of Paper Money and Banking in the United States* (2 parts, Philadelphia, 1833), I, 62; *Ill. House Journal*, 1839-40, 21; "Stephen T. Logan talks about Abraham Lincoln," 2. Antebellum understanding of elasticity is evaluated in Henry E. Miller, *Banking Theories in the United States Before 1860* (Cambridge, Mass., 1927), 70-5.

[8]Ford, *History*, 175; see also Linder, *Reminiscences*, 260-1; Alexander Davidson and Bernard Struve, *History of Illinois, 1763-1884* (Springfield, Ill., 1884), 419-20; Dowrie, *Banking in Illinois*, 65-6.

[9]He slighted laws empirically time and again. For examples, see the following paragraph, or his views on usury, or his plan for taxing speculators, *infra*. Once he defended a constitutionally questionable stance by pointing

out that "each and all" rival positions were "equally unconstitutional." *C.W.*, I, 127.

[10]Ford, *History*, 179; Dowrie, *Banking in Illinois*, 70.

[11]Hammond, *Banks and Politics,* 273; see also Davis R. Dewey, *State Banking Before the Civil War*, Senate Doc. 581, 61:2 (1910), 100f.

[12]Yet in good Jacksonian form the Attorney General of the United States, Benjamin F. Butler, viewed the establishment of the state bank as contrary to the Illinois constitution. Dowrie, *Banking in Illinois*, 76. Hammond, *Banks and Politics*, 106-13, succinctly reviews the question of the legality of paper currency under the U.S. Constitution.

[13]For Linder see the information file of the ISHL, and the works in the bibliography by C. H. Coleman, Merton L. Dillon, G. K. Holbert, and Leonard F. Richards.

[14]*C.W.*, I, 69 (the italics are the author's); cf. 65: "the reward of their industry."

[15]Hugh Rockoff, "Money, Prices and Banks in the Jacksonian Era," in Robert W. Fogel and Stanley L. Engerman, eds., *The Reinterpretation of American Economic History* (New York, 1971), 448-58.

[16]Linder, *Reminiscences*, 260-1. Linder was elected attorney general by the legislature, so he thought, because of his assault on the bank. *Ibid.* His tenure was short-lived, however.

[17]Meyers, *The Jacksonian Persuasion: Politics and Belief* (Stanford, 1960), 13 *et passim*. Banking histories of the period that, as I read them, support the Meyers view include those by Fritz Redlich, Hammond, Shade, and James Roger Sharp — all listed in the bibliography; see also Douglas T. Miller, and Karl Polanyi. Of course there were other factors dividing the nation and these should be investigated via quantitative techniques in Illinois. For Lincoln, however, these factors seemed to carry small importance: see chapter 8.

[18]See the economic historians in the above note; those in Chapter 1, note 19; and the bibliography for Rondo Cameron, and Carter Harry Golembe.

[19]Linder as quoted in *Ill. State Register*, Jan. 12, 1837; *C.W.*, I, 43, 68; *Ill. House Journal*, 1835-6, 126.

[20]*Sangamo Journal*, Jan. 28, 1837, reprinting *Vandalia Free Press*, in *C.W.*, I, 61-9; and *Sangamo Journal*, Feb. 4, 1837.

[21]*Ill. House Journal*, 1836-7, 288, 299-300, 496-9, 616-22; Dowrie, *Banking in Illinois*, 82.

[22]*Sangamo Journal*, Feb. 11, 1837; Ford, *History*, 197.

CHAPTER 3

[1]*C.W.*, I, 77, 82-3, 85-7; Krenkel, *Illinois Improvements*, 111-2. The governor was Joseph Duncan.

[2]*Ill. State Register*, Nov. 9, 1838.

[3]*C.W.*, I, 132-4, 135-8; cf. *Ill. House Journal*, 1828-9, 10-39; cf. Ninian Edwards, *History of Illinois from 1778 to 1883, and Life and Times of Ninian Edwards* (Springfield, Ill., 1870), 104-23.

[4]*C.W.* provides confusing figures about Lincoln's plan. I, 133, copies the report of the *Vandalia Free Press*, Jan. 24, 1839, which erroneously ascribed to Lincoln the estimate of ten million acres of unsold public lands in Illinois. He thought in terms of about twenty million acres, the correct figure. This latter statistic is accurately reported and credited to Lincoln in the *Ill. House Journal*, 1838-9, 223-5, and is reprinted in *C.W.*, I, 136. The calculations checking Lincoln's predictions are based on Arthur H. Cole, "Cyclical and Sectional Variations in the Sale of Public Lands, 1816-60," *RES*, 9 (1927), 52, and Krenkel, *Illinois Improvements*, 149.

[5]For a modern argument tying high population growth to high growth in total output, see Richard A. Easterlin in the bibliography.

[6]*C.W.*, I, 181; see also *Ill. House Journal*, 1839-40, 221, 250, 254, 269-70; 1840-1, 32. For Calhoun's plan see the bibliography for the works of Charles M. Wiltse, and Roy M. Robbins.

[7]*C.W.*, I, 135.

[8]*Ibid.*, 147-9; see also *Ill. House Journal*, 1838-9, 52, 197, 436, 510.

[9]*C.W.*, I, 122-3; *Ill. State Register*, March 15, April 5, 8, June 21, July 6, 1839.

[10]Ford, *History*, 192; see also Krenkel, *Illinois Improvements*, 100.

[11]North, *The Economic Growth of the United States, 1790-1860* (New York, 1961), 190, 201; and *Growth and Welfare in the American Past* (Englewood Cliffs, 1967), 32. Peter Temin, *The Jacksonian Economy* (New York, 1969), 155-7, raises important questions about the severity of the depression but not about the great distress of the financial system.

[12]*C.W.*, I, 144; *Ill. House Journal*, 1838-9, 150, 153. About the same time Lincoln wrote to a troublesome friend, William Butler, concerning a private matter: "I am willing to pledge myself in black and white to cut my throat from ear to ear, if when I meet you, you shall *seriously* say, that you believe me capable of betraying my friends for any price." *C.W.*, I, 139-40.

[13]The Representative was John Crain. *C.W.*, I, 146-7; *Sangamo Journal*, Feb. 16, 1839; cf. Krenkel, *Illinois Improvements*, 93-4.

[14]*C.W.*, I, 280; Sumner to George Livermore, [Dec. 25, 1862], in "Paper Read by William R. Livermore," *MHSP*, 44 (1920-11), 596.

[15]*C.W.*, I, 153, 181, 184. Thus Lincoln showed that his political perceptions were not confused by his preferences. About the same time the leading antiimprovement Whig of the House reached identical conclusions. John J. Hardin to Stuart, Jan. 5, 1840, Hardin Papers, Chicago Hist. Soc. — "Benefit of Clergy" referred to an old English law which originally saved clerics from capital punishment.

[16]*C.W.*, I, 200-1, VIII, 437; *Ill. State Register*, Jan. 20, 1840; *Ill. House Journal*, 1839-40, 177-80, 287-9; 1840-1, 195, 196, 447-50, 514-7, 520-1, 560, 569. The political advantage of having the Governor carry the burden of some of these decisions is nicely discussed in Simon, *Preparation for Greatness*, *passim*

[17]*C.W.*, VIII, 437; *Ill. House Journal*, 1840-1, 71-2.

[18]Thomas J. Nance to his wife Catherine, Dec. 19, 1839, in Fern Nance Pond, ed., "Letters of an Illinois Legislator, 1839-40," *ALQ*, 5 (1949),

121-2; *C.W.*, I, 196; James William Putnam, *The Illinois and Michigan Canal, A Study in Economic History* (Chicago, 1918), 102-4 *et passim*; cf. the work of Hartz (1) Heath, Rubin (1), Harvey H. Segal, and Ronald E. Shaw in the bibliography.

19*C.W.*, I, 195-7; *Ill. House Journal*, 1839-40, 201, 204, 232-3, 235, 236, 242-3, 315-6, 323.

20*C.W.*, I, 243-4; *Ill. State Register*, Dec. 25, 1839; *Ill. House Journal*, 1840-1, 479, 518, 521, 547-9, 565; *Ill. Senate Journal*, 1840-1, 439.

21Krenkel, *Illinois Improvements*, 168-9, 175; Putnam, *Illinois and Michigan Canal*, 54-60; *C.W.*, I, 243-4, 181; D. Davis to W. P. Walker, Nov. 16, 1840, Davis Papers, ISHL; Chas. V. Dyer to John J. Hardin, Sept. 3, 1838, Hardin Papers.

22Goodrich, *Government Promotion*, 121-65, and "Revulsion Against Internal Improvements," *JEH*, 10 (1950), 145-69; see also the various state studies mentioned in Chapter 1, note 19.

23Most students blame the Todd affair for Lincoln's mental breakdown. The inference is reasonable. So is, however, the laconically expressed view of Willard L. King, that sees the economic collapse as the source of Lincoln's ailment. *Lincoln's Manager: David Davis* (Cambridge, Mass., 1960), 40. Probably the two crises exacerbated each other. Only a thorough psycho-historical analysis is likely to shed further light on the subject. See also the bibliography for the work of W. F. Petersen.

24*C.W.*, I, 206, 208; Theodore Calvin Pease, *Illinois Election Returns, 1818-1848* (Springfield, Ill., 1923), 309, 321, 328, 333, 344.

25Orville Browning to John J. Hardin, Jan. 14, 1841, and Hardin to Joseph Gillespie, March 25, 1841, Hardin Papers; *Ill. State Register*, Aug. 15, 1846. See also Chapters IV and V.

26Davis to Walker, June 25, 1847, Davis Papers, ISHL

27*C.W.*, I, 135; *Sangamo Journal*, Jan. 6, 1837; *Ill. House Journal*, 1836-7, 674-6; *Ill. Senate Journal*, 1836-7, 487. Douglas, for example, attacked in a public letter a legislator who opposed the System. A. H. Buckner to John J. Hardin, Jan. 28, 1837, Hardin Papers. Robert W. Johannsen, ed., *The Letters of Stephen A. Douglas* (Urbana, Ill., 1961), 67, and *Stephen A. Douglas* (New York, 1973) 50-1, note only that Douglas wisely backed away from his stance as early as 1838.

28Henshaw in *Peoria Register*, March 9, 1839; Harvey H. Segal, "Cycles of Canal Construction," in Carter Goodrich, ed., *Canals and American Economic Development* (New York, 1961), 23n40; Krenkel, *Illinois Improvements*, 146-8; *Ill. House Journal*, 1836-7, 682; Ford, *History*, 185.

29Krenkel, *Illinois Improvements*, 103.

30Ford, *History*, 184; Krenkel, *Illinois Improvements*, 94-9, 127-48, 178-9.

31*C.W.*, I, 212; see also 74, 129, 221-4, 227-8; *Ill. House Journal*, 1840-1, 86; *Ill. State Register*, Dec. 11, 1840.

32Krenkel, *Illinois Improvements*, 73-4; Ford, *History*, 186-7; *Ill. House Journal*, 1835-6, 36, 47, 274; 1839-40, 302-3.

33*C.W.*, III, 511.

³⁴*Ill. House Journal, Special Session*, 1837, 179; 1839-40, 128 (see also 136, 232); *Ill. State Register*, Jan. 8, 1840.

³⁵Herndon to Weik, Nov. 24, 1882, Herndon-Weik Papers; *C.W.*, V, 166; VII, 24.

³⁶D. Peter Brown, "The Economic Views of Illinois Democrats, 1836-1861," Ph.D. Dissertation, Boston University, 1970, 31-6.

³⁷*C.W.*, II, 248.

³⁸*Ibid.*, I, 233, 482-4; IV, 435.

CHAPTER 4

¹No recent study of taxation considers the ante-bellum period in detail but useful information is available in the works of Sumner Benson, Richard T. Ely, Randolph E. Paul, Sidney Ratner(1), and E.R.A. Seligman, listed in the bibliography.

²Ford, *History*,90; Robert Murray Haig, *A History of the General Property Tax in Illinois* (Champaign, Ill., 1914), 25-73; see also Theodore Calvin Pease, *The Frontier State, 1818-1848* (Chicago, 1922), 52-69; Rodney O. Davis, "Illinois Legislators and Jacksonian Democracy, 1834-1841," Ph.D. Dissertation, University of Iowa, 1966, 247-66.

³*C.W.*, I, 74; Linder, *Reminiscences*, 59-60; Haig, *Taxation in Illinois*, 78.

⁴*Ill. House Journal*, 1834-5, 69, 449-50. The vote for repeal was 41 to 6. Cf. *Sangamo Journal*, Sept. 17, 1836; *Ill. State Register*, July 8, 1836.

⁵My research has forced a modification of my earlier conclusions reached as a graduate student and reported in "Lincoln and Taxation during the Illinois Legislative Years," *JISHL*, 61 (1968), 365-73.

⁶*C.W.*, I, 8; *Ill. House Journal*, 1835-6, 131-2; 1838-9, 374f; 1839-40, 47, 164, 325; Simon, *Preparation for Greatness*, 30-1, 65-6, 112-3, 277-8; Davis, "Illinois Legislators," 432-7. In part, however, something more than a distaste for levies seems to have motivated him. Not atypically of either the Age of Jackson or the self-made man, Lincoln had an ambivalent attitude toward formal education. This attitude stayed with him for life. "In this country," his 1852 eulogy on Clay declared, if a man *"will* he *can"* without much formal schooling "get through the world respectably." In Lincoln's 1860 autobiography, written in third person, there stands the proud, bold sentence about his own training as a lawyer: "He studied with nobody." Even in the White House, where his annual message placed before the nation the major (and sometimes minor) legislative achievements of his administration, he failed to take any notice of the 1862 Agricultural College Land Grant Act. This oversight, pregnant with implication, stands in stark contrast to his enthusiastic advocacy of self education and "booklearning" for farmers. *C.W.*, II, 124; III, 65, 480-1. Lincoln's attitude toward education deserves further investigation.

⁷*Ill. House Journal*, 1838-9, 374, 380-2, 390, 400-1, 419, 426-7, 429, 508.

⁸Davis to Walker, Jan. 19, 1840, Davis Papers; *C.W.*, I, 147-9; *Ill. House Journal*, 1839-40, 21; Haig, *Taxation in Illinois*, 81-2; Krenkel, *Illinois Improvements*, 155-6. In a letter Lincoln attempted to convince William S. Wait of

the virtues of the new tax but he failed to do so. *Ill. State Register*, March 29, 1839.

[9]For further detail see Boritt, "Lincoln and Taxation," 368.

[10]*Laws of Ill.*, 1838-9, 3-9; Emil Joseph Verlie, ed., *Illinois Constitutions* (Springfield, Ill., 1919), 42; Pease, *Frontier State*, 64; Haig, *Taxation in Illinois*, 78-82.

[11]*Ibid.*

[12]*Ill. State Register*, March 29, 1839; see also March 22, Apr. 19, June 14, 21, 28, Nov. 30; *Sangamo Journal*, Aug. 16, 1839; *Quincy Whig*, Jan. 4, 1840; see also Pease, *Frontier State*, 219-21; Krenkel, *Illinois Improvements*, 155-9.

[13]*C.W.*, 215-20, 221.

[14]*C.W.*, I, 238, 243; *Ill. House Journal*, 1840-1, 490.

[15]*Peoria Register*, Dec. 11, 1840; *Sangamo Journal*, Dec. 11, 1840.

[16]John J. Hardin to John T. Stuart, Jan. 20, 1841, Hardin Papers; *Laws of Ill.*, 1840-1, 165; Haig, *Taxation in Illinois*, 83-5. How much of the final bill was Lincoln's handiwork is uncertain. The editors of *C.W.* include the act, and Simon believes that "probably a major part" was written by Lincoln. *Preparation for Greatness*, 235. For party performance on fiscal matters see Davis, "Illinois Legislators," 254-64.

[17]*Ill. House Journal*, 1842-3, 23; *Laws of Ill.*, 1842-3, 228. The minimum valuation was abolished in 1849. *Laws of Ill.*, 1849, 124. For depression land prices see David Davis to Walker, Jan. 22, 1841, Davis Papers, and numerous entries in the Tillson Ledger, ISHL.

[18]*C.W.*, I, 222; *Sangamo Journal*, Jan. 21, June 11, Nov. 19, Dec. 24, 1841; *Ill. State Register*, March 29, Oct. 1, 29, Nov. 5, Dec. 24, 1841; William S. Wait to Gustave Koerner, June 5, 1843, J.F. Snyder Papers, ISHL; cf. Krenkel, *Illinois Improvements*, 171-2. For the national scene see the bibliography for the work of Ralph W. Hidy, R. C. McGrane, and B. U. Ratchford.

[19]*Ill. House Journal*, 1840-1, 331, 378, 411, 469, 472-5, 528-9; *Laws of Ill.*, 1840-1, 121-3; Brownson v. Kinzie, 1 Howard 311 (1843) (cf. *infra* p. 57-8); see also Peter J. Coleman, Harry E. Pratt (2), and Charles Warren in the bibliography.

[20]*C.W.*, I, 218, 234, 243; III, 7; *Ill. House Journal*, 1840-1, 40, 89-90, 106-7, 146-7, 490-1; Johannsen, *Douglas*, 115-6.

[21]*C.W.*, I, 81-2, 181-2, 183-4, 252; *Ill. House Journal*, 1839-40, 116, 252; 1840-1, 203-4, 553-4; *Laws of Ill.*, 1839-40, 61-5.

[22]See for ex.: *Ill. House Journal*, 1836-7, 741-3; 1838-9, 478; 1839-40, 292, 307-8; 1840-1, 144, 332-3, 430.

[23]*Ibid.*, 1839-40, 220-1, 269-70, 318-9; 1840-1, 108.

[24]*Ibid.*, 1840-1, 353-4. The West Point vote also indicated a certain anti-military sentiment which I will investigate elsewhere.

[25]*C.W.*, I, 312; cf. 283, 288-9; and Herndon wrote to the Mass. Hist. Soc.: "poverty is staring us all in the face." March 29, 1842, Herndon Papers, Mass. Hist. Soc.

[26]Ford, *History*, 370-95; Krenkel, *Illinois Improvements*, 177-99; 218-27; Pease, *Frontier State*, 316-26; Haig, *Taxation in Illinois*, 74f.

[27]*American Railroad Journal*, 8 (1839), 61, as cited in Goodrich, *Government Promotion*, 276; Jeriah Bonham, *Fifty Years' Recollections* (Peoria, Ill., 1883), 459.

[28]*C.W.*, I, 311-2, 291-7 *passim*.

[29]*C.W.*, I, 136; Nicol v. Ames, 173 U.S. 509 (1899). I am indebted to Paul A. Samuelson for identifying the source of this quotation. Cf. John Marshall in McCullock v. Maryland, 4 Wheaton 316 (1819), and Panhandle Oil C. v. Knox, 277 U.S. 223 (1928).

CHAPTER 5

[1]This change in attitudes is evident from newspapers, manuscripts, and also the record of the General Assembly where 42% of the Democratic majority voted against banks in 1837, but 76% did so between 1838-41. Computed from Davis, "Illinois Legislators," *passim*. The same pattern appeared in other parts of the country: see the bibliography for the works of Erling A. Erickson, George D. Green, Shade, and Sharp.

[2]*Sangamo Journal*, Oct. 13, 1838; Governor's Message, Dec. 11, 1839, *Ill. House Journal*, 1839-40, 14-24; A. Snyder to G. Koerner, Feb. 14, 1841, Snyder Papers.

[3]To Walker, July 1, 1837 [misdated 1835], Davis Papers.

[4]*Ill. House Journal*, Special Session, 1837, 18, 28, 29-32, 52-3, 70-2, 83-6, 90-1, 98-102, 132-6, 152-3; *Laws of Ill.*, Special Session, 1837, 6-7. The bank restrictions included prohibitions on dividends, on increased circulation, and on dealing out specie selectively. The bank was further required to file monthly statements, allow installment payment on debts, and handle state funds without charge.

[5]*C.W.*, I, 134; *Ill. House Journal*, 1838-9, 275-6, 288-93, 305-6, 424-5, 486, 556-8; see also Davis to Walker, Jan. 19, 1840, Davis Papers.

[6]*C.W.*, I, 159; cf. *Peoria Register*, Dec. 28, 1839.

[7]*C.W.*, I, 179, 185-95; *Ill. House Journal*, 1839-40, 7, 9, 14-24, 56-8, 66; *Ill. Reports*, 1839-40, 243-348; *Sangamo Journal*, Oct. 11, 1839; *Ill. State Register*, Oct. 12, 1839, Jan. 22, 1840; cf. Dowrie, *Banking in Illinois*, 90-4.

[8]*Sangamo Journal*, Nov. 8, 1839, carried a cordial history of the State Bank, signed "A Looker-on" that may have been written by Lincoln. *C.W.*, VIII, 436; Simon, *Preparation for Greatness*, 188; see also *Ill. State Register*, Nov. 8, 1839; Earl Schenck Miers, William E. Baringer, C. Percy Powell, eds., *Lincoln Day by Day* (3 vols., Washington, 1960), I, 120. The report in addition to Lincoln's signature carried those of another Whig and two "tenderfeet" Democrats.

[9]*Ill. House Journal*, 1839-40, 65-9, 71-2, 80, 109, 136-7; *Laws of Ill.*, 1839-40, 15-7.

[10]*Vandalia Free Press*, June 26, 1839; Dowrie, *Banking in Illinois*, 96; Joseph Van Fenstermaker, *The Development of American Commercial Banking, 1782-1837* (Kent, Ohio, 1965), 84-95. Working as a state investigator in 1853, Lincoln obtained detailed evidence on the fluctuations of the bank's paper during 1840-42. *C.W.*, II, 173-8.

[11]James Roger Sharp, *The Jacksonians versus the Banks: Politics in the States After the Panic of 1837* (New York, 1970), xv.

[12]*Ill. State Register*, Dec. 12, 1840; Jan. 8, 1841; *C.W.*, I, 292; *Ill. House Journal*, 1840-1, 79-80; for a participant's recollection see Joseph Gillespie to Herndon, Dec. 8, 1866, Herndon-Weik Papers; see also Harry E. Pratt (4) in the bibliography.

[13]To Walker, Jan. 22, 1841, Davis Papers.

[14]George W. Waters to Eddy, Dec. 22, 1840, Eddy Papers; Dowrie, *Banking in Illinois*, 96-102; Hammond, *Banks and Politics*, 512.

[15]*C.W.*, I, 237-8, 240-1, 242-3. The Representative was Peter Green of Clay County.

[16]*New York Evening Post* as cited in the *Sangamo Journal*, Apr. 2, 1841; *Ill. House Journal*, 1840-1, 459-60, 468-9, 480-7, 511; *Laws of Ill.*, 1840-1, 40-2.

[17]Ford, *History*, 179, 227; cf. Wm. Thomas to Eddy, Jan. 4, 1838, Eddy Papers.

[18]In that election weighty noneconomic factors were present, too, but on these matters Lincoln's record was neither very prominent nor very dissimilar to that of other Whigs. Pease, *Frontier State*, 278-82. See also Chapter VI.

[19]Simon, *Preparation for Greatness;* 263-4, offers a different explanation of Lincoln's 1841 vote as resulting from one of the following: 1. Lincoln was ill; 2. he did not at first understand the issues; 3. He changed his mind.

[20]*C.W.*, I, 7-8, 39, 41; *Ill. House Journal*, 1834-5, 335, 364, 378, 401, 33-4, 464, 542; 1835-6, 32, 41; 1839-40, 296; James D. Richardson, ed., *A Compilation of the Messages and Papers of the Presidents, 1789-1897* (10 vols., Washington, 1896-99), II, 536.

[21]*C.W.*, I, 123, 200; II, 109, 162, 201, 224-6; Pratt, *Personal Finances*, 71-82; Simon, *Preparation for Greatness*, 113; Hammond, *Banks and Politics*, ix *et passim*.

[22]*Revised Statutes of Ill.*, 1953, 255.

[23]*Ill. House Journal*, 1844-5, 11; cf. *Ill. State Register*, June 27, 1850.

[24]*Ibid.*, Oct. 18, 1844.

[25]*C.W.*, I, 241; *Ill. House Journal*, Special Session, 1837, 134-5; 1838-9, 254, 486; see also Ford, *History*, 226-7; Dowrie, *Banking in Illinois*, 101-4.

[26]Hammond, *Banks and Politics*, 195; *C.W.*, I, 136.

[27]See the bibliography for the work of W.W. Rostow; cf. M. Abramovitz and Paul A. David, David(1), Robert William Fogel (3), and Robert E. Gallman.

CHAPTER 6

[1]Paul A. Samuelson, *Economics* (New York, 1970), 273, defines the modern central bank as an institution "that the government sets up to help handle its transaction, to coordinate and control the commercial banks, and, most important, to help *control the nation's money supply* and credit conditions." The BUS fits this criterion in a rudimentary manner. On the BUS see the bibliography for R.C.H. Catterall; Davis R. Dewey(2), Hammond(1), Robert V. Remeni, Fritz Redlich, W.B. Smith, E.R. Taus, Peter Temin, and

J. Wilburn. For Lincoln's earlier expressions on national banking see Chapter 2, note 4.

[2] For the independent treasury, in addition to above, see the bibliography for David Kinely, Sister M. Grace Madeleine, and Richard A. Timberlake, Jr.

[3] *C.W.*, 155-6, 157-72; *Sangamo Journal*, Oct. 11, 1839; *Ill. State Register*, Oct. 12, Nov. 23, 30, 1839; Gillespie to Herndon, Jan. 31, 1866; Joshua F. Speed to Herndon, Sept. 7, 1866, Herndon-Weik Papers; cf. Johannsen, *Douglas*, 25, 77-8. Simon, *Preparation for Greatness*, 192-4, provides a fine description of the political milieu of the debates.

[4] See the estimate of one to four made late in the century by the Comptroller of the Currency (a post created during the Lincoln administration) and the like estimate of a modern economist: Temin, *Jacksonian Economy*, 186.

[5] *Niles' Register*, 53 (Dec. 2, 1837), 214-7; Colton, *The Crisis of the Country* (n.p., n.d. [1840]), 9; Dorfman, *Economic Mind*, II, 614, 882; see also David Kinely, *The Independent Treasury of the United States* (New York, 1893), 25-6; Hammond, *Banks and Politics*, 491-9; for the evolution of the quantity theory of money see Schumpeter in the bibliography.

[6] *Sovereignty and an Empty Purse: Banks and Politics in the Civil War* (Princeton, 1970), 24-5; *Banks and Politics*, 404.

[7] *Ibid, 358-68;* Miller, *Banking Theories,* 165-7, 215; and Robert Lincoln Carey, *Daniel Webster as an Economist* (New York, 1929), 79-113 (a work that overstates Webster's erudition). See also the bibliography for the works of Redlich, and Thomas Payne Govan on Biddle; Harold J. Callanan on Adams; Calvin Colton(3), Clement Eaton, and Glyndon G. Van Deusen(1) on Clay; Robert V. Remini on Jackson; Raymond Walters on Gallatin; and Richard N. Current(4), Claude M. Fuess, and Sidney Nathans on Webster.

[8] *C.W.*, I, 157-211 *passim;* VIII, 436-8. The above figures provide a rough illustration of the view that during his thirty-three years of public life Lincoln probably spoke more about broad topics of economics than any other issue. If we multiply the length of this single, fully extant speech by twenty-four (and it would not be unreasonable to multiply it by forty-eight) then Lincoln's speeches on national banking, in a single year alone, had they been recorded, could have taken up a volume in his *C.W.*

[9] For Calhoun's views see *Cong. Debates*, Jan. 13, 1834; 23:1, 206-23; and March 21, 1834, 23:1, 1057-73; see also the works of Hammond(1), and Wiltse in the bibliography.

[10] *C.W.*, II, 402, 519; Lincoln regularly used the Bank analogy against Douglas and the Dred Scott decision. *Ibid.*, II, 496, 516, 517, 519, 526, 552; III, 28, 80, 232.

[11] *Ibid.*, VII, 256. Lincoln's statistics on defalcations were checked against *House Doc.* 122 and 313, 25:3 (1839). His estimates were checked against Kinely, *Independent Treasury*, 83-4.

[12] *Quincy Whig*, Jan. 4, 1840; *Sangamo Journal*, Apr. 10, 1840; Speed to Herndon, Sept. 17, 1866, Herndon-Weik Papers; *C.W.*, I, 184; II, 136; Simon, *Preparation for Greatness*, 212.

[13]*Ill. State Register*, Jan. 1, Feb. 8, 14, 21, 1840; Gillespie to Herndon, Jan. 31, 1866, Herndon-Weik Papers; Joshua F. Speed, *Reminiscences of Abraham Lincoln . . .* (Louisville, 1884), 38; John Palmer, *Bench and Bar in Illinois* (2 vols., Chicago, 1899), II, 752. Douglas was quoted by John W. Forney long after the statement was made. Yet he does sound substantially authentic. *Anecdotes of Public Men* (2 vols., New York, 1873-81), II, 179. I am indebted to Robert W. Johannsen for identifying the source of this quotation.

[14]*C.W.*, IV, 138-9; see also 132, 138, 163-4; Nicolay's Memoranda, Nov. 10, 1860, John G. Nicolay Papers, LC; John G. Nicolay and John Hay, *Abraham Lincoln: A History* (10 vols., New York, 1890), III, 280. The view that the politicians were largely powerless faced with the impersonal economic forces of the 1830's is most ably presented in Temin, *Jacksonian Economy*.

[15]It helps to recall here the story of a fifteen-year-old boy who heard Lincoln's speech. The lad, Thomas Jefferson Henderson, was so impressed that he learned the peroration by heart. Twenty years later he repeated it to an enthusiastic Illinois assembly that ratified Lincoln's presidential nomination. Not long after, he joined the Union Army and was breveted general for his gallantry. J. W. Templeton, "Life and Services of General Thomas J. Henderson," *JISHS*, 4 (1911), 76-7.

[16]The quotations are from the *Sangamo Journal*, May 15, in *C.W.*, I, 210; *Peoria Register*, Feb. 15; Springfield *Old Hickory*, Oct. 5; *Alton Telegraph*, Apr. 11; and *C.W.*, I, 172, 211; see also Albert J. Beveridge, *Abraham Lincoln, 1809-1858* (2 vol., Boston, 1928), I, 263.

[17]Ward, *Andrew Jackson: Symbol for an Age* (New York, 1962), 79; Davis to Rockwell, Feb. 10, 1840 [misdated 1841].

[18]For the 1840 contest see the bibliography for William Nisbet Chambers(2), and Robert Gray Gunderson; for the bank issue see Abbey L. Gilbert; Lincoln's campaign is discussed by Beveridge, Logan Hay, Harry E. Pratt(1), and Simon.

[19]*Belleville Advocate*, Apr. 18, 27, 1840; *Ill. State Register*, May 8, 1840; John A. Ransom to Hardin, July 12, 1840; Hardin Papers; Richard Brown to Eddy, Aug. 25, 1840, Eddy Papers. The conclusion concerning the campaign is based, in addition to manuscript sources, on the extant issues of the Illinois newspapers. For a full list of the latter see the bibliography for William E. Keller.

[20]*Alton Telegraph*, Apr. 11, 1840; *Ill. State Register*, Dec. 25, 1839.

[21]*Register of Debates*, Feb. 2, 1831, 21:2, 54; reproduced in Benton, *Thirty Years' View* (2 vols., New York, 1854-6), I, 193. Walter Buckingham Smith, *Economic Aspects of the Second Bank of the United States* (Cambridge, Mass., 1953), 235-7, attempts to evaluate Benton's charge in specific economic terms.

[22]Colton, *Labor and Capital*, "Junius Tracts, No. VII" (New York, 1844), 15; Weed as cited in Gunderson, *The Log Cabin Campaign* (Lexington, Ky., 1957), 110.

[23]See for example Feb. 15, May 1, June 15, 22, Aug. 24, Sept. 23.

[24]*C.W.*, I, 170; *Ill. State Register*, Sept. 4, 1840.

[25]*Ibid.*

[26]*C.W.*, I, 209-10 (cf. 74-6, 458). I will explore this episode in a separate essay.

[27]Pease, *Illinois Election Returns*, 117-9; *C.W.*, I, 206, 292.

[28]Theodore Calvin Pease and James G. Randall, eds., *The Diary of Orville Hickman Browning* (2 vols., Springfield, Ill., 1925-33), I, 600; *C.W.*, IV, 270; II, 256.

[29]*Ibid.*, I, 316-7; Herndon to Weik, Nov. 24, 1882, Herndon-Weik Papers; see also *C.W.*, II, 136; F. B. Carpenter, *Six Months at the White House with Abraham Lincoln* (New York, 1866), 32.

[30]*Ill. State Register*, April 6, 1840; Herndon to Lamon, Feb. 25, 1870, Herndon-Lamon Papers; *C.W.*, I, 307.

CHAPTER 7

[1]The bucolic ideal has received careful scrutiny in a large number of works, most importantly in those in the bibliography by Leo Marx, Charles L. Sanford, and Henry Nash Smith.

[2]J.P. Thompson in Daniel S. Curtiss, *Western Portraiture and Emigrant's Guide: A Description of Wisconsin, Illinois, & Iowa* (New York, 1852), 313: *C.W.*, III, 463; Greeley as quoted in Allen Nevins, *The Ordeal of the Union* (8 vols., New York, 1947-71), II, 177. During this same period, in Europe, the *Communist Manifesto* of Marx and Engels spoke of *"Idiotismus des Landlebens"* (the idiocy of country life).

[3]*C.W.*, III, 472-3.

[4]*Ill. House Journal*, 1836-7, 322-5, 384-5; 1837-8, 372; 1840-41, 168-9, 260; *C.W.*, I, 8, 27-8, 33; *Sangamo Journal*, Jan. 7, 1840.

[5]*C.W.*, II, 440; III, 472, 480; IV, 440; see also Chapter 13.

[6]*Belleville Advocate*, Apr. 18, 1840; the mishap was also reported in the St. Louis *Missouri Republican*, Apr. 18, 1840, and recalled in the *Memoirs of Gustave Koerner, 1809-1896*, T. J. McCormack, ed. (2 vols., Cedar Rapids, Ia., 1909), I, 443-4.

[7]*Laws of Ill.*, 1835-6, 254-5; *Ill. House Journal*, 1835-6, 344.

[8]Ford, *History*, 107-8.

[9]*C.W.*, III, 474; *Ill. House Journal*, 1836-7, 79-80; for the raising and fencing of cattle see the bibliography for the works of Richard Bardolph, Earl W. Hayter, Charles T. Leavitt, and William Oliver.

[10]Benton, *Thirty Years' View*, I, 102-7 *et passim* provides a fine summary of his efforts; see also the bibliography for the works of T. Donaldson, Paul W. Gates (6,7,8), B. H. Hibbard, Roy M. Robbins, G. M. Stephens, and Reynor G. Wellington. Recent scholarship still debates modified versions of the old issues, although a mild consensus appears to be present that more land aided growth. Whether it impeded industry, however, is less than clear. See the bibliography for Abramovitz and David, F. M. Fisher and Temin, H.J. Habakkuk, P. Passell and M. Schmundt, and Temin (1,3); cf. Thomas LeDuc.(1,2).

[11]*Ill. House Journal*, 1834-5, 269; 1835-6, 236; 1836-7, 149-50; *C.W.*, I, 32,

48; *Sangamo Journal*, Jan. 24, 1835. For a model developing the compatibility of rapid land distribution and a high tariff see Peter Passell and Maria Schmundt, "Pre-Civil War Land Policy and the Growth of Manufacturing," *EEH*, 9 (1971), 35-48.

[12]*Ibid.*, and *C.W.*, I, 50.

[13]*Ill. House Journal*, 1838-9, 88-90; on the last point see Chapter 11 for detail.

[14]*Cong. Globe Appendix*, Jan. 29, 1839, 25:2, 139; *C.W.*, VIII, 435 (cf. I, 108-15).

[15]*C.W.*, II, 487; Osborn H. Oldroyd, ed. *The Lincoln Memorial* (Boston, 1882), 251-3; see also Ford, *History*, 145-6; Davis, "Illinois Legislators," 60-70; for preemption see items in note 10 and the bibliography for Everett Dick. Lincoln's law practice helped him reach full familiarity with the various preemption laws: see for example *C.W.*, II, 333-5, 337-8, 393-4; John P. Frank, *Lincoln as a Lawyer* (Urbana, 1961), 92-3.

[16]*C.W.*, I, 133; for Clay's like arguments see *Cong. Globe Appendix*, Apr. 16, 1832, 22:1, 114; for the lands Lincoln specifically spoke of see Theodore L. Carlson. *The Illinois Military Tract: Land Occupation, Utilization and Tenure* (Urbana, Ill., 1951).

[17]For the role of the land speculator see the bibliography for Bogue and Bogue, Thomas LeDuc, Robert P. Swierenga(1); cf. Gates (3).

[18]*C.W.*, I, 163-4.

[19]*Ibid.*, 132-4.

[20]Davis to Rockwell, July 11, 1841, Davis Papers; *C.W.*, I, 307, 312-4.

[21]As it turned out the most popular Whig document on the subject, Calvin Colton's Junius Tract VIII, *The Public Lands* (New York, 1844), was quite unacceptable to Lincoln. It denied the existence of any conflict of interest between the old and new states while decrying open-handed policies as unfair to the former.

[22]The reconstruction of this episode by Ninian W. Edwards for Herndon is probably substantially accurate. *Herndon's Lincoln*, 178; cf. *C.W.*, I, 320.

[23]Tyler Dennett, ed., *Lincoln and the Civil War, in the Diaries and Letters of John Hay* (New York, 1939), 143.

[24]*C.W.*, I, 411, 414; II, 440; III, 334, 473; V, 46.

[25]*C.W.*, III, 473.

[26]*Principles of Political Economy* (London, 1865), 558.

[27]Legaré and Greeley are quoted in Dorfman, *Economic Mind*, II, 627, 670; the Coolidge aphorism paraphrased above comes from his *Foundations of the Republic* (New York, 1926), 187; Lloyd Lewis, *Myths After Lincoln* (New York, 1929), 405 *et passim*.

CHAPTER 8

[1]*C.W.*, I, 307-8, 309-18. The longer statement also carried two other signatures but Lincoln's authorship is evident from *Ibid.* I, 323. In this chapter some of the views I expressed as a graduate student had to be modified. Boritt, "Old Wine Into New Bottles: Abraham Lincoln and the Tariff Reconsidered," *Hist.*, 28 (1966), 289-312.

[2]The text of the 1832 Pappsville speech is from *Herndon's Lincoln*, 118; for variations see *Ill. Journal*, Nov. 5, 1864; James A. Herndon to Herndon, May 29, 1865; Albert Yates Ellis to Herndon, June 5, 1866, Herndon-Weik Papers.

[3]For an excellent summary of traditional Whig principles see Calvin Colton, ed., *The Works of Henry Clay* (10 vols., New York, 1904), VIII, 208-13. For a similar summary by a leading Illinois Whig see Joseph Duncan to Morgan County Whigs [March, 1843], *Proceed. of Miss. Val. Hist. Ass.,* 5 (1911-2), 177-89.

[4]*C.W.*, I, 287, 307, 309-12, 313.

[5]See also Chapters 4 and 14.

[6]*Ill. State Register*, Sept. 3, 1841.

[7]*C.W.*, I, 323; cf. Clay to T.T.B. Stapp, Nov. 16, 1843, Clay Letters, ISHL.

[8]For additional reasons for his defeat see Riddle, *Lincoln Runs for Congress*, 60-75, and Chapter III. The anti-organizational bias of the Whigs is discussed in various studies but I benefited most by the works of Rodney O. Davis, Lynn L. Marshall, and Richard P. McCormick listed in the bibliography.

[9]*C.W.*, III, 5, 16; *Ill. House Journal*, 1838-9, 527-8. At New Salem Lincoln in fact had sold liquor in larger quantities, but not by the drink as was done in "groceries." For his ancestry see the bibliography for the works of William E. Barton(4), Waldo Lincoln, and Louis Warren; on his religion the literature is large but see, above all, Barton(1), and William J. Wolf; for Lincoln and temperance see Angle(3), J.M. Berquist, Harry V. Jaffa(2), Paul Simon, and William H. Townsend.

[10]Lincoln should be examined in further detail in the light of recent research on the Whigs. I briefly consider his views of immigrants in Chapter 15.

[11]*C.W.*, III, 339; I, 271-9; *Herndon's Lincoln*, 222 (cf. W. Henry Snyder to John F. Snyder, [1842], Snyder Papers).

[12]Current, *The Lincoln Nobody Knows*, 193-7; cf. Current(2) in the bibliography. Lincoln had to exaggerate Clay's antislavery views to identify them with his own views. Mark E. Neely, Jr., "American Nationalism in the Image of Henry Clay: Abraham Lincoln's Eulogy of Henry Clay in Context," *Reg. of Ky. Hist. Soc.*, 73 (1975), 31-60. Lincoln's often quoted statement that Clay was his "beau ideal of a statesman" dates from 1858, *C.W.*, III, 29.

[13]*Ibid.*, II, 121 (cf. III, 511), 126. See the bibliography for the work of scholars who noted the confessional element of the Clay eulogy via *other* ingredients in it: Basler(6), Current(5), Fehrenbacher(3), Neely (2), Potter(2), and Randall(4).

[14]Ward, *Jackson: Symbol for an Age*, 174; Irvin G. Wyllie, *The Self-Made Men in America: The Myth of Rags to Riches* (New York, 1966), 9-10.

[15]Welles, *Diary*, I, 507. The Clay-Lincoln relationship deserves further scrutiny.

[16]The tariff history of the United States is now a neglected field. The most

useful general histories are Sidney Ratner(2), Edward Stanwood, and Frank W. Taussig(6), listed in the bibliography. For sectional and party behavior see the work of Joel H. Silbey. Recent articles indicate a revival of the field, but the effect protection had on development, employment, etc., continues to receive little consideration. For the campaign of 1844 (which requires a new examination) see the bibliography for the work of W. C. Ford, J. C. N. Paul.

[17]For Hardin see the bibliography for Nancy L. Cox. The best study of Baker is by Harry C. Blair and Rebecca Tarshis but he deserves further attention.

[18]One one occasion, for example, Lincoln engaged in formal debates, for three or four nights earning his neighbor's designation of the event, twenty-one years later, as the "great tariff debate." The press barely mentioned the affair. Herndon's interview with Gourley, Herndon-Weik Papers, *C.W.*, I, 334-5. And in private one Lincoln partisan reported that "there was nothing left of the animal save ears & hoofs," another that Lincoln had made his opponent "hang down his under lip," and a third that he had left the Locos "pretty much down in the mouth." Owen M. Long to Hardin, March 19; R.L. Dodge to Hardin, March 27; Simeon Francis to Hardin, Apr. 22, 1844, Hardin Papers; cf. *Ill. State Register,* March 29, 1844. Earlier private letters reported, in like fashion, several of his speeches none of which were so much as mentioned in print. Herndon, Dr. Henry, and William Butler to Hardin, Feb. 12, 15, 21, respectively, Hardin Papers. It is worth recalling that Lincoln's 1839-40 bank speech, except for some segments, was also lost from sight until the 1880's. Templeton, "Life of Henderson," 76-7.

[19]Clipping from the *Chester County Times,* Westchester, Pa., Feb. 11, 1860, enclosed in a letter of Joseph J. Lewis (the writer of the piece) to Jesse W. Fell, Jesse Fell Papers, University of Illinois, Urbana. The article was reprinted in William E. Barton, "The Lincoln of the Biographers," *Trans. of ISHS,* 36 (1929), 81-6. For Lincoln's appeal to oldtimers' memories see *C.W.*, IV, 92, 125.

[20]*Ibid.*, I, 334.

[21]See for ex.: Colton's Junius Tracts, I, *The Test* (New York, 1843), and X, *The Tariff Triumphant* (New York, 1844), Greeley, *The Tariff as it Is* (New York, 1844); Charles Hudson in *The Whig Almanac for 1844; (New York, 1843),* and his *"Report from the Committee on Manufactures, House Doc.,* 420, 28:1 (1844), 37-49.

[22]For others using this argument see the above note and also Junius Tract III, *The Tariff* (New York, 1843); George Evans, *Reply to McDuffie's Second Speech on the Tariff* (Washington, 1844) 5-8; Andrew Stewart, *Speeches on the Tariff and Internal Improvements* (Philadelphia, 1872), 225-6, 239; and in Illinois: *Sangamo Journal,* Feb. 29, March 21, June 27; *Olive Branch,* Apr. 18, July 15, Aug. 11, 1844. For the economic picture in 1844 see the bibliography for Arthur Harrison Cole(2,3), T.S. Berry, and C.W. Wright.

[23]Frank W. Taussig, *The Tariff History of the United States* (New York, 1931),

116-22, discusses the "loose talk" of both protectionists and free traders that connected the business cycle with tariff legislation. Edward Stanwood, *American Tariff Controversies in the Nineteenth Century* (2 vols., Boston, 1903), II, 35-7, indulges in such talk, as Lincoln had in 1844.

[24]See, for example, Clay in *Annals of Congress,* March 21, 1824, 18:1, 1978; Colton, *Tariff Triumphant,* 2; Steward, *Speeches,* 236-7, printed also in *Sangamo Journal,* Apr. 25, and excerpted in *Rockford Forum,* May 29, 1844.

[25]A.G. Henry to Hardin, March 25, 1844, Hardin Papers; cf. *Ill. State Register,* March 29, 1844; *C.W.,* I, 311-2, 313, 334, 408.

[26]Today in contrast to Lincoln's times, economists agree that the tendency of the tariff is to redistribute income from the consumers to the producers of the protected good. One notable exception is the "Metzler paradox" which raises the possibility that a tariff on a certain good could improve the country's terms of trade. This has been applied with less than conclusive results to the antebellum period. See the bibliography for the work of Lloyd Metzler, Clayne Pope, Bennett D. Baack and Edward J. Ray.

[27]*C.W.,* I, 378; III, 463 (cf. I, 386); Herndon's interview with N. Grigsby, [1865], Herndon-Weik Papers.

[28]Bonham, *Fifty Years' Recollections,* 158-60; *Quincy Whig,* June 26; *Sangamo Journal,* June 27, July 4, 1844; for Lincoln's 1844 efforts see also Wm. T. Page to James Brooks, June 11, 1849, Lincoln Papers; Rufus Rockwell Wilson, ed, *Uncollected Papers of Abraham Lincoln* (2 vols., Elmira, N.Y., 1947-8), II, 531-3, 568-9, 572-5.

[29]*C.W.,* I, 327, 334. Herndon's interview with James Gourley, [1865], Herndon-Weik Papers; Herndon to Lamon, March 6, 1870, Herndon-Lamon Papers; Milton Hay to John Hay, Jan. 1887, *ALAB,* 25 (1931).

[30]All the extant Illinois newspapers have been examined for 1844. For a complete listing see Keller in the bibliography. The best source of Whig information for the 1844 campaign, however, is the Hardin Papers, a depository of the crosscurrents of the Illinois party. The speeches in question are identified in notes above.

[31]To Walker, May, 1844, Davis Papers.

[32]Herndon to Hardin, March 10, 1844, Hardin Papers; Herndon to Lamon, March 6, 1870, Herndon-Lamon Papers; "Big Me" in Hertz, *Hidden Lincoln, 395-6.* Herndon's comments on his research work for Lincoln are quoted often, but historians uniformly fail to mention that he spoke of research on the tariff.

[33]*C.W.,* I, 332-3, 338-40; *Sangamo Journal,* July 11, 1844.

[34]Herndon to Hardin, Apr. 3, 1844 (cf. Simeon Francis to Hardin, Apr. 22, 1844), Hardin Papers; *C.W.,* I, 336.

[35]Williams, *The Contours of American History* (Chicago, 1966), 297, however, sees Lincoln as a standard bearer of imperialism. This Lincoln was not. See also Chapter 11.

[36]*C.W.,* I, 337; *Ill. State Register,* June 21, Aug. 11, Oct. 18; *Belleville Advocate,* Oct. 3, 1844.

[37]Henry to Hardin, March 25; H. Lamaster to Hardin, Apr. 16, 1844, Hardin Papers. See also *Sangamo Journal,* March 28, Apr. 25, Aug. 14, 22, Oct. 3, 10, 31; *Olive Branch,* Aug. 15, Sept. 1, 15, Oct. 1, 19; *Quincy Whig,* Sept. 25, 1844; cf. Malcolm Rogers Eiselen, *The Rise of Pennsylvania Protectionism* (Philadelphia, 1932), 88, 169.

[38]*C.W.,* III, 78, 487.

[39]Colton to Hardin, Aug. 3; Josuah Moore to Hardin, May 15, Hardin Papers; *C.W.,* I, 341; Davis to Walker, May 4, 1844, Davis Papers. The view of Charles Manfred Thomson, *The Illinois Whigs before 1846* (Urbana, Ill., 1910), 129, that "the Whigs said little about the tariff," is inexplicable.

[40]See for ex.: March 29, Aug. 23, Sept, 27, 1844.

[41]Clay to A.G. Henry, June 17, 1844, Clay Letters; *C.W.,* III, 78.

[42]*Ibid.,* I, 316-7; Moses Coit Tyler, "One of Mr. Lincoln's Old Friends," *JISHS,* 38 (1936), 249-50; and see the following letters to Hardin: G.M. Davis, Nov. 24, Dec. 16; J. Gillespie, Nov. 25, Dec. 18; N. Edwards, Dec. 11; J.T. Stuart, Dec., 18; F. Arenz, Dec. 22, 1844, Hardin Papers. The movement for Illinois Whig dissolution deserves study.

[43]Ethelbert P. Oliphant to Lincoln, Dec. 186[0], Lincoln Papers.

CHAPTER 9

[1]See also Boritt, "Old Wine Into New Bottles."

[2]*C.W.,* I, 354, 381-4; Lacon, *Ill. Gazette,* May 9, 1846; *Ill. State Register,* Aug. 15, 1846; the most adequate secondary work on Lincoln's campaign is Riddle, *Lincoln Runs for Congress,* see especially, 160-75.

[3]*C.W.,* I, 407-16; Herndon, "Lincoln the Individual," Aug. 20, 1887, and to Weik, Oct. 29, 1885, Herndon-Weik Papers. Why these notes were not used until much later is considered in the following chapter.

[4]Dorfman, *Economic Mind,* II, *passim;* and Carl William Kaiser, *History of Academic Protectionist-Free Trade Controversy in America before 1860* (Philadelphia, 1939).

[5]For fragmentary data on wages see Stuart Bruchey, *The Roots of American Economic Growth, 1607-1861* (New York, 1965), 163; and the bibliography for the works of Victor Clark, H.J. Habakkuk, Alvin H. Hansen, Stanley Lebergett, and Nathan Rosenberg. That the tariff may have raised the real wages of American labor is suggested by Wolfgang F. Stolper and Paul A. Samuelson, but they also concluded that a fall in the real income of the country may be a corollary. The opposite possibility is raised by Lloyd Metzler, whereas Clayne Pope sees little effect on the return of labor. See the bibliography for their works.

[6]*C.W.,* III, 477. During the mid-1820's while Lincoln and his family lived at Pigeon Creek in Indiana, Warren was a member of Robert Owen's nearby New Harmony commune.

[7]Edmund Wilson used these words to characterize Marx's reliance on the same concept. *To the Finland Station: A Study in the Writing and Acting of History* (New York, 1953), 298.

[8]Richard C. Edwards, "Economic Sophistication in Congressional Tariff Debates," *JEH*, 30 (1970), 802-38, found this argument the most prominent as early as 1824, but he excluded by definition quasi and noneconomic rationales which were more important at that early date; see also George Benjamin Mangold, *The Labor Argument in the American Protective Tariff Discussion* (Madison, 1906). Edwards, comparing the sophistication of two Congresses, those of 1824 and of 1896, gave high marks to the former but not the latter.

[9]Paul A. David, "Learning by Doing and Tariff Protection: A Reconsideration of the Case of Ante-Bellum United States Cotton Textile Industry," *JEH*, 30 (1970), 521-601; Marshall, *Industry and Trade* (London, 1919), 761-2.

[10]Hamilton, "Report on Manufactures," in F.W. Taussig, ed., *State Papers and Speeches on the Tariff* (Cambridge, Mass., 1893), 56-7; Alexander H. Everett, *America, or a General Survey* (Philadelphia, 1827), 153-5; Willard Phillips, *A Manual of Political Economy* (Boston, 1828), 201; John Rae, *Statement of some New Principles on the Subject of Political Economy* (Philadelphia, 1834), 364-5; for the same point made at a more popular level see Everett, "British Opinions on the Protecting System," *North Am. Rev.*, 30 (1830), 187, 204; Colton, *Tariff Triumphant*, 2-3; Greeley, *Whig Almanac for 1843*, 9-11, and *for 1846*, 12.

[11]*Essay on the Rate of Wages* (3 vols., Philadelphia, 1858-60), *passim*; his articles in *The Plough, the Loom and the Anvil*, III and IV (1851-2); *The Slave Trade* (Philadelphia, 1853), 59f.; *Principles of Social Science* (3 vols., Philadelphia, 1858-60), I, 228; II, 34, 63, 134-40, 328; III, 432-3; *Financial Crises: Their Causes and Effects* (Philadelphia, 1864), 11 *et passim*; on the central role of the argument in Carey's thought see: Mill, *Principles*, 566-7; Kaiser, *Academic Controversies*, 129.

[12]Herndon to Weik, Jan. 9, 1886, Herndon-Weik Papers.

[13]The terms of trade index between East and West moved from 100 to 176. North, *Economic Growth*, 146; Thomas Senior Berry, *Western Prices before 1861: A Study of the Cincinnati Market* (Cambridge, Mass., 1943), 564.

[14]*C.W.*, II, 15-7 (the second italics are the author's).

[15]Swett is quoted in *Herndon's Lincoln*, 276; Howard K. Beale, ed., *Diary of Gideon Welles* (3 vols., New York, 1960), I, 168; II, 11, 59, 64-5, 179-80.

CHAPTER 10

[1]Cheyney, "Presidential Address Delivered Before the American Historical Association," *AHR*, 29 (1924), 237-8.

[2]Herndon's interview with John T. Stuart, Dec. 20, 1866, Herndon-Weik Papers.

[3]Herndon to Weik, Jan. 1, 1886, Herndon-Weik Papers. Mearns, "Mr. Lincoln and the Books He Read," the best essay on the subject, ignores entirely Lincoln's learning in economics as do the lesser works.

[4]Carey, *Essay on the Rate of Wages; The Harmony of Nature* (Philadelphia,

1836); *Answers to the Questions . . . Currency* (Philadelphia, 1840); *Principles of Political Economy* (3 vols., Philadelphia, 1837-40); *Principles of Social Science;* Dorfman, *Economic Mind,* II, 791-99, provides a fine brief summary of Carey's thought; see also the bibliography for the works of Arnold Green, A.D.H. Kaplan, Rodney J. Morrison, George W. Smith, and Ernest Teilhac.

[5]Herndon to Weik, Dec. 29, 1885; Herndon, "Lincoln the Individual," Aug. 20, 1887, Herndon-Weik Papers; A. S. Miller in Tyler, "One of Mr. Lincoln's Old Friends," 254; *New York Independent,* Sept. 1, 1864; cf. J.D. Caton in 37 Ill. 1 (1865); Speed, *Reminiscences,* 21; Milton Hay to John Hay, Jan. 1887, *ALAB*; *Herndon's Lincoln,* 248, 272; Whitney, *Life on the Circuit,* 121-4, 488.

[6]To Weik, Jan. 1, 1886, Herndon-Weik Papers.

[7]To Weik, Nov. 24, 1882, Herndon-Weik Papers.

[8]Wayland, *The Elements of Political Economy* (New York, 1837), v; Dorfman, *Economic Mind,* II, 758. It is possible that Lincoln's acquaintance with Wayland, through *The Elements of Moral Science* (New York, 1835), goes back to his New Salem years: see James T. Hickey in the bibliography.

[9]*Elements,* 107, 111, 167; and wrote Lincoln in his tariff notes: "In the early days of the world, the Almighty said to the first of our race 'In the sweat of thy face shalt thou eat bread'; and since then, if we except, the *light* and the *air* of heaven, no good thing has been, or can be enjoyed by us, without having first cost labour." *C.W.,* I, 411-2.

[10]*Elements,* vi, 165, 262-9, 273-4, 278-85, 290f., 312-20, 352-7.

[11]Greeley, *The Whig Almanac for 1843,* 16; Herndon to Weik, Jan. 1, 1886, Herndon-Weik Papers.

[12]Eiselen, *Pennsylvania Protectionism,* 132; Tucker, *Progress . . .* (New York, 1843); for M. Carey, Niles, and Tucker see respectively the works of K.W. Rowe, R.G. Stone, and T.R. Snavely in the bibliography.

[13]Herndon to Weik, Jan. 1, 1886, Herndon-Weik Papers. Herndon also felt that, however enthusiastic, Lincoln was a poor student of political economy. It is safe to assume that this view reflected not Lincoln's knowledge but the direction Herndon's economic thinking took in his later years. *Herndon's Lincoln,* 163, 374.

[14]Harold J. Callanan, "The Political Economy of John Quincy Adams," Ph.D. dissertation, Boston University, forthcoming.

[15]*C.W.,* I, 448.

[16]*Ibid.,* 407, 481; *Ill. State Register,* Sept. 25, 1846. For similar Whig thinking see: Colton, *Public Economy for the United States* (New York, 1848); Carey as quoted by Henry Carey Baird, "Carey and Two of his Recent Critics," *Proc. of Am. Phil Soc.,* 29 (1891), 171; G. G. Van Deusen, *Horace Greeley, Nineteenth Century Crusader* (Philadelphia, 1953), 328.

[17]*C.W.,* III, 487.

[18]*Cong. Globe,* Jan. 11, June 19, 1848, 30:1, 142, 852; Dec. 11, 1848, 30:2, 26 (see also Jan. 3, 1849, 30:2, 147), *C.W.,* I, 474.

[19]*Cong. Globe*, April 17, 1848, 30:1, 638-9. The Senate had earlier congratu-lated France on the establishment of a republican form of government and the House concurred with Lincoln voting aye. *Ibid.*, Apr. 3, 10, 1848, 3:1, 572, 598, 603-4. Similarly Lincoln's enthusiasm for Lajos Kossuth, who visited the United States in 1851-2, was not impaired when the Hun-garian at moments appeared not only to be an apostle of freedom but also of free trade, a fact that riled Henry Carey. *C.W.*, II, 115-6, 118; *Ill. Journal* (successor of the *Sangamo Journal*), Jan. 12, 1852; Carey, "Centralization," *The Plough, the Loom, and the Anvil*, IV, (1852), 385.

[20]*C.W.*, I, 394; Verlie, ed., *Illinois Constitutions*, 59-60, 84; see also the bibliog-raphy for S.L. Jones(1).

[21]*C.W.*, I, 395-405. No history of the railroad exists but see the Benjamin Godfrey Papers, and the Alton & Sangamon Railroad Company Stock Subscription Book, ISHL; *The Chicago and Alton Railroad Company: Acts, Deeds, Leases* (Chicago, 1906), Baker Library, Harvard University; *Interstate Commerce Commission Reports*, Vol. 40, "Valuation Reports" (Washington, 1933); see also the bibliography for the works of Paul Gates(2), Richard C. Overton, and D.Y. Yungmeyer.

[22]Davis, "Illinois Legislators," 236-46; Glyndon G. Van Deusen, "Some As-pects of Whig Thought and Theory in the Jacksonian Period," *AHR*, 63(1958), 312-15; Eric Foner, *Free Soil, Free Labor, Free Men: The Ideology of the Republican Party before the Civil War* (New York, 1970), 22-3.

[23]*C.W.*, I, 172; For further discussion see Chapter 13.

[24]*C.W.*, III, 499 (cf. Whitney, *Life on the Circuit*, 237-8); Ozias M. Hatch to Lyman Trumbull, July 14, 1860, Trumbull Papers, LC; Pratt, *Personal Fi-nances*, 104-6.

[25]*C.W.*, I, 480-90; the speech is discussed in detail in Donald W. Riddle, *Con-gressman Abraham Lincoln* (Urbana, Ill., 1951), 86-98. Field's speech ap-peared in the *Democratic Review*, 21(1847), 189-203, and as a pamphlet: *Speech of David Dudley Field at the Chicago Convention* (New York, 1847); it is also in A.P. Sprague in the bibliography. See also *Sangamo Journal*, July 15; *Lacon Ill. Gazette*, July 17; *Rockford Forum*, July 21, 1847; For the conven-tion see the bibliography for Don E. Fehrenbacher(1), Robert Fergus, Bessie Louis Pierce, James Shaw, and Mentor L. Williams.

[26]Richardson, ed. *Messages*, V, 610-26; see also the bibliography for the work of Eugene I. McCormick.

[27]Actually, Riddle, *Congressman Lincoln*, 95-6, points out that Lincoln misread Polk's figure which referred to a ten-year period that ended with the accession of Jackson. Richardson, ed., *Messages*, IV, 612, 621. Even in these circumstances, however, Lincoln's figure was much more realistic.

[28]Samuel F. Vinton, Whig of Ohio, also called for the establishment of a statistical bureau, prior to Lincoln. *Cong. Globe*, Dec. 9, 1847, 30:1, 16-8.

[29]*Ibid.*, Dec. 15, 1847, 30:1, 27:8.

[30]*N.Y. Tribune*, June 22, 1848; for a different evaluation see Riddle, *Con-gressman Lincoln*, 86-9.

[31]*House Journal,* Dec. 22, 1847, Jan. 17, 1848, 30:1, 147, 257-8; *C.W.,* VIII, 419.

[32]*Cong. Globe,* July 18, 20, 22, Aug. 10, 11, 1848, 30:1, 943-8, 954, 1054, 1063, 1070.

[33]June 22, 1848.

[34]Lincoln was a member of the Committee on Post Office and Postal Roads; *C.W.,* I, 423-9, 430; *Cong. Globe,* Dec. 13, 1847, 30:1, 19-20; see also Riddle, *Congressman Lincoln,* 71-2, and Leonard P. White(2) in the bibliography.

[35]*C.W.,* I, 494, 517; *Cong. Globe,* Apr. 11, 1848, 30:1, 616 *et passim.*

[36]*Cong. Globe,* Feb. 3, 7, 1848, 30:1, 298, 304-7; *House Journal,* Feb. 3, 1848, 30:1, 347-8.

[37]*C.W.,* I, 442, 460-1, 464; *Cong. Globe,* Dec. 20, 1847; May 8, 1848, 30:1, 57, 307; Roy M. Robbins, *Our Landed Heritage: The Public Domain, 1776-1936* (Lincoln, Neb., 1962), 156-7.

[38]*Cong. Globe,* Dec. 1, 13, 21, 1848; Feb. 5, 16, 1849, 30:2, 25, 38, 85, 454, 548; Van Deusen, *Greeley,* 111-3; Robbins, *Our Landed Heritage,* 92-116 *et passim*; Paul W. Gates, *History of Public Land Law, Development* (Washington, 1968) 270-6.

[39]*C.W.,* I, 469-71; see also II, 26-7.

[40]*Cong. Globe,* Dec. 28, 1848; Feb. 1, 15, 19, 1849, 30:2, 116, 367, 426, 542, 559; see also Riddle, *Congressman Lincoln,* 143-61 *passim.*

[41]*C.W.,* II, 26-7; *Cong. Globe,* Feb. 13, 1849, 30:2, 532.

[42]Brown, "Illinois Democrats," 161-3; see also Lewis Henry Haney, *A Congressional History of Railroads in the United States to 1850* (Madison, Wisc., 1908), 298-317.

[43]*C.W.,* I, 454.

CHAPTER 11

[1]Herndon to C.O. Poole, Jan. 5, 1886, Herndon-Lamon Papers.

[2]On this subject see the bibliography for Beveridge, Boritt(4), and Riddle(2). For the Whig war opposition in general see Frederick Merk(1,3), John H. Schroeder, and N.E. Tutorow.

[3]*C.W.,* II, 11; Speed, *Reminiscences,* 30.

[4]Wilson, *Space, Time, and Freedom: The Quest for Nationality and the Irrepressible Conflict, 1815-1861* (Westport, Conn., 1974), *passim.*

[5]*C.W.,* I, 311; IV, 25.

[6]*Ibid.,* III, 481.

[7]*Sangamo Journal,* Feb. 16, 1843, June 3, July 11, 1844; June 5, 12, 1845; *Ill. State Register,* July 12, 1844; *Nauvoo Neighbor,* March 27, 1844; *Chicago Democrat,* Feb. 17, July 17, 31, 1846; *Cong. Globe,* Jan. 3, 29, 1846, 19:1, 136, 277-8. On expansion see the bibliography for E. Bradner, R.A. Billington(1), T. D. Clark, N.A. Graebner, F. Merk(2,3), R.W. Van Alstyne, C. Vevier, A.K. Weinberg, W.A. Williams(1,2), and S.S. Zwelling. Frederick Merk judged that Illinois was probably the most expansionist state in the Old Northwest. *Manifest Destiny and Mission in American History: A Reinterpretation* (New York, 1963), 37, 147-8.

[8]*C.W.*, I, 177 (cf. 167), 347, 337; III, 49, 357-8; *Ill. State Register,* May 8, 1846, July 14, 1848; Charles M. Segal, *Conversations with Lincoln* (New York, 1961), 62-3; the interview with Green is described in David Potter, *Lincoln and His Party in the Secession Crisis* (New Haven, 1962), 145 (cf. *C.W.*, IV, 155, 172); for Blair's plans see Randall and Current, *Lincoln,* IV, 326-9.

[9]Smith, *The War With Mexico* (2 vols., New York, 1919), II, 285-6.

[10]*Cong. Globe,* March 23, 1848, 30:1, 534; see also the bibliography for Richard N. Current (3), and Avery Craven(2).

[11]Van Deusen, *Greeley,* 108, and *Jacksonian Age,* 224-5; see also the bibliography for Elgin Williams.

[12]*Alton Telegraph,* March 15, 1845; Richard Bardolph, "Illinois Agriculture in Transition, 1820-1870" *JISHS* (1948), 426-7; William Appleman Williams, *The Roots of the Modern American Empire: A Study of the Growth and Shaping of Social Consciousness in a Marketplace Society* (New York, 1969), *passim.*

[13]*C.W.*, I, 463; Van Deusen, *Greeley,* 121; see also Harlan Horner in the bibliography.

[14]*C.W.*, I, 477; cf. IV, 66.

[15]Taylor to A.G. Henry, referred to in Henry to Lincoln, Dec. 29, 1847, Lincoln Papers (cf. the letter of one of Taylor's officers, *Quincy Whig,* Aug. 4, 1847); *C.W.*, I, 454. Taylor's early stance is examined by Holman Hamilton, *Zachary Taylor* (2 vols., Indianapolis, 1941-51), II, 40-7 *et passim.*

[16]John G. Nicolay erroneously believed that Lincoln's earlier tariff notes also had the purpose of outlining what "Genl. Taylor ought to say." *C.W.*, I, 416n3.

[17]Van Deusen, *Seward,* 121, and *Greeley,* 256; Richard N. Current, *Daniel Webster and the Rise of National Conservatism* (Boston, 1955), 153-7; for Taylor's views see Hamilton, *Taylor,* 76-81; for Lincoln's early activities on his behalf see *C.W.*, I, 423-4, 449, 452, 458, 463-4, 467-8, 474; and J.W. Singleton's recollections in *Tazewell Register,* Sept. 30, 1858.

[18]Robert J. Rayback, *Millard Fillmore* (Buffalo, 1959), 119-21, 130-6, 164.

[19]Henry to Lincoln, Aug. 29, 1847, enclosing editorial from *Tazewell Whig,* Sept. 3, 1847, Lincoln Papers.

[20]*C.W.*, I, 463, 501-16.

[21]For Cass on internal improvements see Mentor L. Williams(3), and Frank B. Woodford in the bibliography.

[22]As quoted in Riddle, *Congressman Lincoln,* 110.

[23]*C. W.*, I, 476; Frederick, Maryland, *Republican Citizen,* Sept. 1, 1848, as quoted in *Day by Day,* I, 318; cf. *C.W.*, I, 501-5; II, 2, 5, 7, 12, 14.

[24]On this subject see the bibliography for the works of Kinley J. Brauer, David Donald(4), Martin B. Duberman(1), and Frank Otto Gatell(1,2).

[25]For the central Whig argument, which was non-economic, see Joseph G. Rayback, *Free Soil: The Election of 1848* (Lexington, Ky., 1970), 254-7, 296, 301-2.

[26]*C.W.*, II, 4, cf. 1-9; Lincoln's Massachusetts campaigning is also considered

in Beveridge, Riddle(2), and the articles of Reinhard H. Luthin(1), A.P. Rugg, and James Schouler, all listed in the bibliography.

[27]*C.W.*, I, 477; II, 14.

[28]*C.W.*, I, 515; II, 12-3.

[29]But in the summer of 1844 Lincoln was listed as one of a nine-member Whig committee whose resolutions passingly mentioned noneconomic principles. It is practically certain, however, that he did not write the resolutions. These, for example, spoke in an un-Lincoln-like euphemistic language of a "sound currency," instead of a national bank. *Supra*, p. 105. There is a great need to attempt to go beyond traditional editing techniques to determine the authenticity of this and other documents — for Lincoln as well as others. Computers and statistics hold out particular promise for such an endeavor.

[30]*C.W.*, II, 60. Those not learned in the Bible should be reminded that Samson's strength was in his locks.

[31]Donald, "Abraham Lincoln: Whig in the White House," in Norman A. Graebner, ed., *The Enduring Lincoln* (Urbana, Ill., 1959), 47-66; also reproduced in Donald, *Lincoln Reconsidered* (New York, n.d. [1961], 2nd ed.), 187-208.

[32]*C.W.*, II, 220-1; for examples of petitions to Lincoln see Philo H. Thompson. Apr. 19 and 23; Isaac Funk, March 1; Henry Eddy, March 22; Samuel D. Marshall, Apr. 6 and 20, 1849, Lincoln Papers; cf. Titan J. Coffey in Allen Thorndike Rice, ed., *Reminiscences of Abraham Lincoln by Distinguished Men of His Time* (New York, 1888), 239-40.

[33]*C.W.*, I, 163.

[34]*C.W.*, I, 500, 510.

[35]*Ibid.*, II, 67; A.J. Murphy to Davis, June 30, 1848, Davis Papers.

[36]*Bristol County Democrat*, Sept. 29, 1848, reprinted in *National Magazine* and reprinted from there in *C.W.*, II, 9.

[37]*Herndon's Lincoln*, 248f. G. S. Boritt, "A Question of Political Suicide? Lincoln's Opposition to the Mexican War," *JISHS*, 67 (1974), 79-100, attempts to demonstrate that the common assumption of Lincoln's temporary political demise has little foundation.

[38]*C.W.*, IV, 203; III, 512 (cf. IV, 67).

[39]*Ibid.*, II, 81.

[40]*Ibid.*, 459.

[41]Hurst, *Law and Economic Growth: The Legal History of the Lumber Industry in Wisconsin, 1836-1915* (Cambridge, Mass., 1964), 171; 17 Ill. 291 (1854); 27 Ill. 64 (1863); 19 Ill. 186 (1857); 13 Ill. 504 (1851); 11 Ill. 254 (1849); *C.W.*, II, 415-6 [67 U.S. 485 (1862)]; of the numerous works on Lincoln as a lawyer the most important are by Frank, and John J. Duff in the bibliography; see also C.L. Brown, E.L. Page, J.T. Richards, and A. Woldman. A new work that uses recent advances in legal history is in order.

[42]6 Fed. Cas. 186 (1853) [or 6 McLean 209], continued as 6 Fed. Cas. 191 [6 McLean 70]; cf. *C.W.*, II, 415-22.

[43]*Ibid.*, 209, 393; III, 381-3, 392, 429; *C.W.S.*, 35-8; G.S. Boritt, "A New Lincoln Text: An Opinion on an Illinois Tax," *LH,* 75 (1973), 152-7; and "Another New Lincoln Text? Some Thoughts Concerning an Outrageous Suggestion about Abraham Lincoln 'Corporation Lawyer,'" *LH,* 77 (1975), 27-33.

CHAPTER 12

[1]Don E. Fehrenbacher, *Prelude to Greatness: Lincoln in the 1850's* (Stanford, 1962), 19-47, dispelled the traditional notions about Lincoln's extreme reluctance to leave the Whigs for the Republicans. For the most scholarly presentation of the older view see the bibliography for the work of Reinhard H. Luthin(3).

[2]The price extracted by Democrats from former Whigs in shaping Republican policy is elucidated in Foner, *Free Soil, Free Labor, Free Men,* 168-76. The same point was made by Boritt, "Old Wine Into New Bottles," 307-8, 313.

[3]*C.W.,* III, 487.

[4]*Ibid.*, II, 151, 152, 158-9.

[5]Harry V. Jaffa, *Crisis of the House Divided: An Interpretation of the Issues of the Lincoln-Douglas Debates* (New York, 1959), 344.

[6]See the bibliography, above all, for the work of William J. Wolf, Basler(2,3,4,6), and Jaffa(1,2,3). Much less satisfactory are the attempts to point to an occasional, early Lincoln utterance about democracy *per se* and tying this to his eloquent presidential statements on the subject.

[7]*C.W.,* IV, 65, I, 74-5.

[8]See for example *C.W.,* I, 74-6, 108-16 (especially 104-10, 112, 113), 271-9 (especially 279), 347-8, 412; II, 20-2, 130-2.

[9]*Ibid.*, II, 247-83.

[10]*Ibid.*, 385; see also IV, 168, 240, 437; cf. A. Whitney Griswold, "The American Gospel of Success," Ph.D. Dissertation, Yale University, 1933, 27, 35; Yehoshua Arieli, *Individualism and Nationalism in American Ideology* (Cambridge, Mass., 1964), 308, 315; Cawelti, *Apostles of the Self-Made Men,* 42f.

[11]*C.W.,* IV, 169; see also for ex.: II, 364, 405; III, 477-86; IV, 25, 203, 240, 438; V, 52; VII, 512; Richard Hofstadter, *The American Political Tradition and the Men Who Made It* (New York, 1948), 105.

[12]*C.W.,* II, 266.

[13]On this point see also V. Jacque Voegeli, *Free But Not Equal: The Midwest and the Negro During the Civil War* (Chicago, 1967), 4, 26.

[14]*C.W.,* II, 222, 406; see also 235, 264, 364, etc.

[15]Ward, *Jackson: Symbol for an Age,* 166-80; Cawelti, *Apostles of the Self-Made Man,* 5, 39-75; Foner, *Free Soil, Free Labor, Free Men,* 11-39 *et passim.*

[16]See further Chapter 19.

[17]*C.W.,* VII, 17 (cf. III, 522-5, IV, 265); Jaffa, *Crisis of the House Divided,* 330-2.

[18]*C.W.,* IV, 169; II, 341; see also III, 522-5; IV, 233, 255; VI, 410; VII, 17 and Chapter 19. See further Stanley Pargellis, "Lincoln's Political Philosophy," *ALQ,* 3 (1945), 284-5; T. Harry Williams, "Abraham Lincoln: Pragmatic

Democrat," in Graebner, ed., *The Enduring Lincoln,* 38; Merrill D. Peterson, *The Jeffersonian Image in the American Mind* (New York, 1962), 221; and Arieli, *Individualism and Nationalism,* 318.

[19]*C.W.,* II, 270, 321-2 (cf. II, 320-1; IV, 393; V, 198). For the same moral judgment in a different context, that of internal improvements, see p. 133.

[20]*C.W.,* II, 270, 276; V, 388; VIII, 332. For the politics of the Greeley letter see Chapter 19.

[21]*Ibid.,* II, 351; see also, for example, II, 271, 365; III, 349, 419; IV, 2-13, 16.

[22]*Ibid.,* IV, 16. For other estimates of the value of slaves see, for example, II, 265, 352, 365, IV, 3, 9, 16.

[23]*Ibid.,* II, 352. For a less bold estimate see 365. For Genovese's work see the bibliography.

[24]*C.W.,* II, 230, 270; III, 462; VIII, 41; see also, for example, II, 492, III, 54-5, 199-200, 370, VIII, 52. For the Republican critique of the Southern economy see Foner, *Free Soil, Free Labor, Free Men,* 40-51. Econometricians have gone a long way to dispell the classical notion that immoral forced labor was inefficient, but the idea held sway for a century after Lincoln.

[25]*C.W.,* II, 352.

[26]*Ibid.,* II, 364, see further Eugene H. Berwanger, *The Frontier Against Slavery* (Urbana, 1967), 123-7 *et passim.*

[27]*C.W.,* II, 268; see also 363-4, 498; III, 312, 437; *C.W.S.,* 45.

[28]*C.W.,* II, 268.

[29]James G. Blaine as quoted in Current, *The Lincoln Nobody Knows,* 97.

[30]Williams, *The Contours of American History* (Chicago, 1966), 296.

[31]*C.W.,* II, 437.

[32]*C.W.,* III, 358; II, 232, 437; *De Bow's Review,* cited in Frederick Jackson Turner, *The Frontier in American History* (New York, 1962), 217 [cf. *De Bow's Review,* 15 (1853), 530].

[33]*Cong. Globe,* March 7, 1850, 31:1, 478-81.

[34]"Expediency and Morality in the Lincoln-Douglas Debates," *The Anchor Review,* 2 (1957), 202.

[35]*Cong. Globe,* March 26, 1850, 31:1, 472.

[36]See for example *C.W.,* II, 514-5; III, 87, 276, 316.

[37]*Cong. Globe Appendix,* Feb. 4, 1845, 28:2, 225; *C.W.,* II, 255.

[38]*Ibid.,* II, 515; III, 78; IV, 7-8, 25.

[39]*Ibid.,* V, 372-3; Benjamin Quarles, *Lincoln and the Negro* (New York, 1962), 26-8; see also *C.W.,* II, 159; III, 518; *Day by Day,* II, 106; *Cong. Globe Appendix,* Feb. 23, 1849, 30:2, 262; and the bibliography for the work of Norman Dwight Harris, Robert S. Starobin, and Richard C. Wade.

[40]Charles Desmond Hart, " 'The Natural Limits of Slavery Expansion': The Mexican Territories as a Test Case," *MA,* 52 (1970), 119-31; yet see also Eugene D. Genovese, *The Political Economy of Slavery* (New York, 1967), 243f.; Robert S. Starobin, *Industrial Slavery in the South* (New York, 1970), 213f. The literature of the economics of slavery extension is extensive. Lincoln may have examined J.E. Cairnes, *The Slave Power . . . .* (New York, 1862): *C.W.S.* 144.

[41]*C.W.*, III, 418, 409; see also II, 246, 264, 493-4; III, 78, 226, 257, 500-1.

[42]Compare in more detail his views on the tariff in the 1847 notes, *C.W.*, I, 410-11, and the above cited words on slave trade from the House Divided Speech, II, 468. Another excellent illustration is in Lincoln's view on labor: compare I, 411-2 and III, 462.

[43]For example *Ibid.*, II, 267-8, 449; III, 88, 404-5 etc.

[44]*C.W.*, III, 231, 435; cf. *C.W.S.*, 42.

[45]*C.W.*, III, 460; II, 274; see also III, 230-2, 313, 545; IV, 5-6, 10-11.

[46]For the Southern view see especially William W. Freehling, *Prelude to Civil War: The Nullification Controversy in South Carolina, 1816-1836* (New York, 1966). Lincoln himself had some awareness of this interconnection and argued, like Freehling does, that "at the bottom" of Nullification, which seemingly stemmed from the tariff controversy, "lay this same slavery question." *C.W.*, III, 310, cf. 86.

[47]*Ibid.*, 16; IV, 24-5; see also, for ex.: II, 222, 266, 405, 498, 520, 526-7; III, 145-6, 204, 222, 226, 315; IV, 3.

[48]*Lincoln and the Negro*, 123; cf. 13-4.

[49]*C.W.*, I, 260; II, 320 (italics are the author's).

[50]Douglass in Rice, ed., *Reminiscences*, 193, and in *The Life and Times of Frederick Douglass. . . .* (New York, 1962), 360 [cf. Philip S. Foner, ed., *Life and Writings of Frederick Douglass* (4 vols., New York, 1950-55), III, 36-7]; Eaton, *Grant, Lincoln and the Freedman* (New York, 1907), 75, 173 [cf. Eaton to Mrs. Frederick Douglass, Feb. 21, 1895, in *In Memoriam Frederick Douglass* (Freeport, New York, 1971), 71].

CHAPTER 13

[1]Dec. 23, 1854, as quoted in Eiselen, *Rise of Pennsylvania Protectionism*, 232.

[2]*C.W.*, III, 379.

[3]For discussions of the definition of labor during this period see, for example, the bibliography for Calvin Colton(4), Joseph Dorfman(1), Eric Foner, Walter Hugins (who adopts the definition of the period), Marvin Meyers, Douglas T. Miller, and Rush Welter.

[4]*C.W.*, III, 477-8; IV, 203; III, 473; see also I, 412; III, 459, 468, and Chapter IX.

[5]*C.W.*, I, 412; Whitney, *Life on the Circuit*, 353; *The United States on the Eve of the Civil War As Described in the 1860 Census* (Washington, D.C., 1963), 66. Yet Lincoln understood the tools used by the master of the small shop as capital, thus blurring his delineation of labor.

[6]*C.W.*, III, 459, 468; I, 412; III, 462, 479; Carpenter, *Six Months*, 308-9.

[7]*C.W.*, I, 412; III, 478-9; see also III, 459, 469; IV, 24-5.

[8]*Ibid.*, VII, 259; IV, 24; see also III, 459, 468. For the Republicans see Foner, *Free Soil, Free Labor, Free Men*, 36-8; and for Carey, Chapter 10, note 4.

[9]Wyllie, *Self-Made Man in America*, provides the most detailed discussion of this subject. See also Foner, *Free Soil, Free Labor, Free Men*, 23f., and the bibliography for the works of Cawelti, Griswold, R.M. Huber, Moses Rischin, R. Weiss, and John William Ward.

[10]*C.W.*, III, 479.

[11]*Ibid.*, V, 374.

[12]*C.W.*, III, 459, 469, 478; V, 52 (cf. Webster's Seventh of March Speech, *Cong. Globe*, March, 7, 1850, 31:1, 482). For social mobility during the antebellum period, see the bibliography, above all, for Stuart Blumin, Merle Curti(3), Clyde Griffen, Peter Knights, Gary B. Nash, Edward Pessen(2), and Stephan Thernstrom.

[13]*Chicago Times*, Oct. 5, 1859.

[14]*C.W.*, III, 468, 541. For a somewhat exaggerated picture of Fitzhugh's role in Lincoln's thought see Harvey Wish, *George Fitzhugh: Propagandist of the Old South* (Baton Rouge, La., 1943), 150f.

[15]Mayor Peter M. Neal quoted in Waldemar Kaempffert, ed., *A Popular History of American Inventions* (2 vols., New York, 1924), II, 415. I am indebted to Harold S. Walker, Director of the Lynn Historical Society for information about Neal who had several interviews with Lincoln.

[16]Dorfman, *Economic Mind*, II, 365, 650, 658, 693, 736-7, 754, 764, 795, 807, 827-9, 840, 869-70, 872, 923, 967.

[17]Richard B. Morris, "Andrew Jackson, Strikebreaker," *AHR*, 55 (1949), 54; Carey, *Webster*, 30; Jeter A. Isley, *Horace Greeley and the Republican Party, 1853-1861* (Princeton, 1947), 199-202; Foner, *Free Soil, Free Labor, Free Men*, 26-7. See also the bibliography for John R. Commons, Philip S. Foner(2), Leonard W. Levy, Pessen(1,2), and Van Deusen(4).

[18]*Chicago Democrat*, Aug. 26, 1859; *Chicago Weekly Democrat*, Sept, 17, 1859; see also *Ill. Journal*, Aug. 29, 1859.

[19]*Chicago Weekly Democrat*, March 17, 1860; and see for example *Chicago Weekly Times*, Jan. 20, 27; *Ill. State Register*, Jan. 21, 24; *Chicago Journal*, Jan. 17; *Chicago Press and Tribune*, Jan. 11, 19, 25; *Chicago Democrat*, April 20, 1859.

[20]*C.W.*, III, 479.

[21]*Ibid.*, IV, 1, 7-8, 12-13, 24-6; VII, 93; 259; Segal, *Conversations*, 65-7.

[22]See for example: Burke McCarty, *Little Sermons in Socialism by Abraham Lincoln* (Los Angeles, n.d. [1910?]); Herman Schlüter, *Lincoln, Labor and Slavery* (New York, 1913), 168-85; Bernard Mandel, *Labor, Free and Slave: Workingmen and the Anti-Slavery Movement in the United States* (New York, 1955), 158-9; Foner, *Free Soil, Free Labor, Free Men*, 21.

[23]Taylor, *Transportation Revolution*, 284-5; Philip S. Foner, *History of the Labor Movement in the United States* (4 vols., New York, 1947-65), I, 241-5; see also the bibliography for Foster Rhea Dulles, and Joseph G. Rayback(1); for the shoe industry see John Philp Hall, and Blanche Evans Hazard.

[24]Fitzhugh, *Sociology for the South: or, The Failure of Free Society* (Richmond, Va., 1854), 65; Herndon to Weik, Oct. 28, 1885, Herndon-Weik Papers; *C.W.*, IV, 8.

[25]Foner, *Free Soil, Free Labor, Free Men*, 25-9. The developing Republican stance toward labor organization deserves further examination.

[26]*C.W.*, II, 221.

[27]*Fincher's Trades Review*, Nov. 28, 1863; March 12, 1864. For Lincoln and

strikes see also the following chapter.

[28]*C.W.*, III, 471-82.

[29]The census of 1860 showed the proportion of farmers to farm laborers in the country to be 3:1. Illinois fared little better. (The accuracy of the data is open to question, however.) Paul Gates, "Frontier Landlords and Pioneer Tenants," *JISHS*, 38 (1945), 205-6, and *Farmer's Age*, 182-3, 196, 272-9; Bogue, *Patterns from the Sod*, 35-40, 85-112, 124, 127; see also the works of Helen Cavanagh, and C.P. McClelland in the bibliography.

[30]*C.W.*, III, 481.

[31]William N. Parker and Judith C.V. Klein, "Productivity Growth in Grain Production in the United States, 1840-60 and 1900-10," in *Output, Employment, and Productivity in the United States After 1800* (New York, 1966), 548, 577.

[32]Gates, "Large Scale Farming in Illinois, 1850 to 1870," *AH*, 6 (1932), 14-5, and *Farmer's Age*, 293-4.

[33]*Chicago Weekly Democrat*, Oct. 23, 1858; cf. Sept. 17, 24, 1859; *Chicago Democrat*, July 9, 14, 1859; *Chicago Journal*, Sept. 8, 1859; *Chicago Times*, Sept. 8, 1859; *Jonesboro Weekly Gazette*, June 18, 1859; *Ill. Journal*, July 19, Aug. 6, Sept. 8, 12, 13, 14, 20, 1859; see also the bibliography for R. Bardolph, Reynold M. Wik, and Charles S. Zane.

[34]*C.W.*, III, 475; Coolidge in *School and Society*, XXVI, Sept. 24, 1927, 397.

[35]See Chapter 11 note 44; *C.W.*, II, 437-42; III, 356-63. Interestingly, one of these lectures relied almost entirely on the Bible as a source — perhaps in part as a failed bid for popularity as a lecturer, and in part to increase the enthusiasm of the religious-minded for technological improvement.

[36]*Ibid.*, IV, 202, 203; Herndon to Trumbull, June 17, 1858, Trumbull Papers, LC; Browning, *Diary*, I, 327; Beveridge, *Lincoln*, II, 570. For the place of free land in Republican thought see Foner, *Free Soil, Free Labor, Free Men*, 27-9 *et passim*. Accepting the presidential nomination in 1860 Lincoln did declare for the whole Republican platform but without going into particulars. *C.W.*, IV, 52.

[37]*Ibid.*, II, 220, 221; cf. Schlesinger, *Age of Jackson*, 516, and Van Deusen, *Greeley*, 26.

[38]Carey as cited in Taussig, *Tariff History*, 118; Isley, *Greeley*, 217-8; Eiselen, *Pennsylvania Protectionism*, 244-55; Foner, *Free Soil, Free Labor, Free Men*, 173-6; see also the bibliography for Madison Kuhn; Arthur M. Lee(1,2), and Thomas M. Pitkin(1, 2).

[39]*Chicago Weekly Democrat*, Oct. 10, 17, 1857; Jan. 22, Feb. 5, March 5, July 16, Sept. 3, 13, Oct. 15, 1859; *Chicago Tribune*, Dec. 10, 1858; Feb. 3, 8, 24, 1859; *Chicago Journal*, June 22, Oct. 11, 18, 1858; Aug. 1, 1859; *Chicago Democrat*, Sept. 20, 1859; *Ill. State Register*, Feb. 8, 9, 18, July 27, Aug. 1, 9, Sept. 9, 1859; Judd to Trumbull, Nov. 21, 1857, Ill. Hist. Survey, Univ. of Ill.

[40]*C.W.*, IV, 14; and see II, 543; III, 314, 326, 379; IV, 49, 91, 119, 125; *Chicago Journal*, Oct. 4, 11, 1858; Alexander K. McClure to Lincoln, June 16, 1860; G. Yoke Tams to Lincoln, Sept. 15, 1860; H. A. Denckla to

Lincoln, Sept. 23, 1860; James E. Harvey to Lincoln, Sept, 25, 1860, Lincoln Papers.

41*C.W.,* III, 487.

42Oldroyd, ed., *Lincoln Memorial,* 189-90; *C.W.,* III, 308, 390; Colfax to Lincoln, July 14, 1859; Lincoln Papers. For Lincoln's work on Republican unity see the bibliography for William E. Baringer(1), and John S. Wright.

43*C.W.,* IV, 49.

44*Ibid.,* 47. Some students, emphasizing Pennsylvania's pivotal status and the importance of protectionism to its electorate, see Lincoln's tariff views as crucial to his nomination and election. See the bibliography, for example, for James G. Blaine, William McKinley, Thomas A. Pitkin(1,2), and Reinhard Luthin(2,4).

45Foner, *Free Soil, Free Labor, Free Men,* 103-225 *et passim.*

46Not surprisingly, Seward, his chief rival for the nomination, came the closest to sharing this quality among the leading candidates.

CHAPTER 14

1*Cong. Globe Appendix,* Jan. 27, 1863, 64; cf. Montgomery Blair to Fremont, Aug. 24, 1861, in Nicolay and Hay, *Lincoln,* IX, 334.

2*C.W.,* I, 454, 510; see also Chapter 11.

3*C.W.,* IV, 214. On the Whig theory of the presidency see especially Leonard D. White, *Jacksonians: A Study in Administrative History, 1829-1861* (New York, 1954), 30-3, 46-8, 563-6.

4*C.W.,* VI, 29; II, 60. See the bibliography for discussions of Lincoln's relations with Congress and his Cabinet: Lewis Henry Croce, Leonard P. Curry, Burton J. Hendrick, Clarence E. Macarthey, John Bruce Robertson, and John Y. Simon.

5*C.W.,* V, 169, 537; cf. II, 327; III, 344; IV, 121.

6*Cong. Globe,* Feb. 10, 1864, 37:3, 845; cf. Sherman, *Recollections of Forty Years* (2 vols., Chicago, 1895), I, 298 *et passim.*

7Curry, *Blueprint for Modern America: Nonmilitary Legislation of the First Civil War Congress* (Nashville, 1968). On the meaning of the Civil War economic legislation see the bibliography for the works of Ralph Andreano, ed., Charles A. and Mary R. Beard, Thomas C. Cochran and William Miller, David T. Gilchrist and W. David Lewis, eds., Louis Hacker, and Harry N. Scheiber(2).

8Dorfman, *Economic Mind,* II, 968. A modern biography of Chase is much needed.

9Segal, *Conversation,* 77; Carey to Lincoln, Jan. 7, 1861, Lincoln Papers; *N.Y. Tribune,* Jan. 5, 1861; see also *C.W.,* IV, 171; Chas. M. Hall to Lincoln, Jan. 7; Lemuel C. Reeves to Lincoln, Jan. 8; Thomas Corwin to Lincoln, Jan. 18; W.C. Bryant to Lincoln, Jan. 22, 1861, Lincoln Papers; Nicolay and Hay, *Lincoln,* III, 361. The best account of the economic aspect of the battle over the Treasury appointment is by Arthur M. Lee, "The Development of an Economic Policy in the Early Republican Party," Ph.D. Dissertation, Syracuse University, 1953, 204-35.

[10]*C.W.*, IV, 421-41; Treasury Department Memorial [July 1, 1861], Lincoln Papers.

[11]Sherman to Lincoln, July 6, 1861, Lincoln Papers.

[12]Holland, *The Life of Abraham Lincoln* (Springfield, Mass., 1866), 429.

[13]Chase, *Diaries*, 192, 224; cf. Chase to Lincoln, Apr. 2, 1861, Lincoln Papers; see also Welles *Diary* II, 11, 59, 63, 65.

[14]See the bibliography for Leonard P. White(1,2,3); and see Donald, "Whig in the White House," 36.

[15]Reports of the Sec. of Treasury, *Senate Ex. Doc.*, 2, 37:2 (1861), 17:20, and 1, 37:3 (1862), 17-22. There is a considerable literature on the establishment of the national banking system. See above all Bray Hammond(2), and Leonard P. Curry in the bibliography; for the role of the West see William Gerald Shade; see also the older works of Don Carlos Barrett, Andrew McFarland Davis, Wesley Clair Mitchell, and E.G. Spaulding.

[16]Hay, *Diaries*, 144-5.

[17]*C.W.*, V, 282-3.

[18]*Ibid.*, 522-3; Chase's draft on national banking, Lincoln Papers #20,662-5. Bray Hammond, who fully appreciates Lincoln's understanding of the subject, errs in contrasting the clarity of the President's writing, in his annual message, with Chase's less able report to Congress. Both were the work of the Secretary though the improvement in the Chase presentation presumably resulted, in part, from consultation with Lincoln who in turn adopted the draft in full. Hammond was misled by the *C.W.*, which includes the annual message without noting the Chase original in the Lincoln Papers. *Sovereignty and an Empty Purse*, 290f.

[19]*C.W.*, VI, 60-2; *Cong. Globe*, Jan. 19, 20, 37:3, 381, 342-3, 401-2; *N.Y. Times*, Jan. 20, 1863.

[20]Stoddard, *Inside the White House in War Times* (New York, 1890), 181-4; see also his *Lincoln: The True Story of a Great Life* (New York, 1884), 372-3; William Stoddard, Jr., ed., *Lincoln's Third Secretary: The Memoirs of William O. Stoddard* (New York, 1955), 104-6. For Howe's views see, for example, *Cong. Globe Appendix*, Feb. 12, 1862, 37:2, 51-6; and his vote: *Cong. Globe*, Feb. 12, 1863, 37:3, 896-7.

[21]*Ibid.*, Feb. 11, 1863, 37:3, 878-9, 882; Welles, *Diary*, I, 237-8; cf. Curry, *Blueprint for Modern America*, 202.

[22]To Thomas S. Pike, March 6, 1864, Roger Taney Papers, LC; cf. Report of the Sec. of Treasury, *Senate Ex. Doc.*, 3, 38:2 (1864), 24.

[23]Chase to Lincoln, Feb. 19, and n.d. [Feb. 20], 1863, Lincoln Papers; the second of these letters is misdated and thus misplaced as June 3, 1864, #33, 510-11; *C.W.*, IV, 321. The House passed the bill 78 to 64. *Cong. Globe*, Feb. 20, 1863, 37:3, 1148. See also Samuel Galloway to John Hay, Apr. 6, 1865, Hay-McLellan Papers, Brown University.

[24]*C.W.*, VII, 41; VIII, 143-44.

[25]*Ibid.;* Carpenter, *Six Months*, 252 (cf. 53-4); Chase to Lincoln, Apr. 14, 25, 1864; Chase to Fessenden, Apr. 11, 1864, Lincoln Papers; Chase to Joseph

Cable, July 11, 1864, cited in Randall and Current, *Lincoln*, IV, 186; Welles, *Diary*, II, 11; see also Jacob Henderson to Lincoln, June 30, 1864, Lincoln Papers.

[26]*C.W.*, VIII, 143-4.

[27]Holmes to John Lothrop Motley, Feb. 3, 1862, in John T. Morse, ed., *Life and Letters of Oliver Wendell Holmes* (2 vols., Boston, 1896), II, 161; *C.W.*, V, 39, 522; VII, 41; cf. Chase ms., n.d. [Dec., 1862]; Lincoln Papers #20,665.

[28]*C.W.*, V, 48; cf. Report of the Sec. of Treasury, *Senate Ex. Doc.*, 2, 37:2, (1861).

[29]*C.W.*, VIII, 143; cf. I, 133, and Report of the Sec. of Treasury, *Senate Ex. Doc.*, 3, 38:2 (1864).

[30]Chase to A.G. Riddle, March 7, 1864, in Robert B. Warden, *An Account of the Private Life and Public Services of Salmon P. Chase* (Cincinnati, 1874), 576; Chase, *Diaries*, 224, 225; Chase to Lincoln, Apr. 14, 15, June 20, 30; Chase's Statement on Public Debt, June 14; Chase to Fessenden, June 20; Chase to Stevens, June 29, 1864, Lincoln Papers. cf. Randall and Current, *Lincoln*, IV, 186.

[31]*C.W.*, VII, 420, 423; Hay, *Diaries*, 198-9; *N.Y. World*, as cited in Carl Sandburg, *Abraham Lincoln: The War Years*, (4 vols., New York, 1939), III, 117. It is worth noting that banker McCulloch, Lincoln's first Comptroller of the Currency, thought that in the war Treasury politicians could succeed when "trained financiers, who are usually conservative and cautious, would have failed." *Men and Measures of Half a Century* (New York, 1889), 185.

[32]*C.W.*, VIII, 142; Harrington to E.G. Spaulding, Aug. 31, 1891, Huntington Library.

[33]*C.W.*, V, 507; VI, 420; VII, 45, 285, 347; VIII., 164, 199; Lincoln to Chase, Aug. 29, 1863, Unpublished Lincoln Papers, ISHL; E. Littell to Lincoln, Jan. 1, 1861; Cassius Clay to Lincoln, Oct. 21, 1862; Clipping in Edgar Conkling to Lincoln, Dec. 31, 1863; Ambrose W. Thompson to Lincoln, Apr. 3, Sept. 24, 1864, enclosing Agent of European Bankers to Thompson, Sept. 22, 1864; Thompson to Cameron, Apr. 3, 1864, Lincoln Papers; W.J. Waldie to Lincoln, Aug. 21, 1864; Waldie Letter, ISHL; Nicolay, Conversation with President, Oct. 2, 1861, memo, Nicolay Papers; "General M.C. Meigs on the Conduct of the Civil War," *AHR*, 26 (1921), 292; Hay, *Diary*, 203; Nicolay and Hay, *Lincoln*, VI, 247; Ellis Paxson Oberholtzer, *Jay Cooke: Financier of the Civil War* (2 vols., Philadelphia, 1907), I, 433f; Irvin McDowell, July 10, 1862, as cited in Sandburg, *War Years*, I, 48; James P. Shenton, *Robert John Walker: A Politician from Jackson to Lincoln* (New York, 1961), 191-2.

[34]*C.W.*, V, 282, 522; Don Piatt, *Memoirs of Men Who Saved the Union* (New York, 1887), 106-10; Lamon, *Recollections*, 215; for Lincoln being claimed on both sides of the latter day monetary disputes see for example Hofstadter(3), and Cora L.V. Richmond in the bibliography.

[35]*C.W.*, V, 522; cf. Chittenden, *Reminiscences*, 307-15; Nicolay and Hay, *Lincoln*, IX, 386-7, 396, 401. Interestingly there is a myth about Lincoln hav-

ing originated the movement for the greenbacks. See for example Lincoln to E.D. Taylor, Dec., 1864, in Hertz, *New Portrait*, II, 957; and Piatt, *Memoris*, 215.

[36]*C.W.*, V, 522; Boutwell, *Reminiscences of Sixty Years* (2 vols., New York, 1902), 29 (cf. Whitlaw Reid in *Cincinnati Gazette*, 1864-5, as cited in Sandburg, *War Years*, III, 599); *Lincoln Catechism*, 1864, in Frank Freidel, ed., *Union Pamphlets of the Civil War, 1861-1865* (2 vols., Cambridge, Mass., 1967), II, 991; for Kellogg see *supra*, 180.

[37]*C.W.*, VI, 61; V, 522, 502; J. Bradley to Lincoln, Sept. 11; O.S. Halsted to Lincoln, Sept. 11, 13, Oct. 1; James W. White to Lincoln, Sept. 15, 1864, Lincoln Papers; Carpenter, *Six Months*, 84 [cf. Benjamin Butler, *Butler's Book* (Boston, 1892), 762-3]; Hay, *Diaries*, 236; Van Deusen, *Seward*, 404.

[38]*C.W.*, VIII, 164; Chase to Lincoln, Apr. 14; Chase to Fessenden, Apr. 12, 1864, Lincoln Papers; *U.S. Statutes at Large*, XIII, 132-3; 344; see also Randall and Current, *Lincoln*, IV, 175-7.

[39]*New York Herald*, Dec. 9, 1860; Chase to Lincoln, Feb. 23, 1863, Lincoln Papers; *C.W.*, V, 444; Stoddard, *Inside the White House*, 69-70 (cf. Thomas C. Durant to Lincoln, Oct. 17, 1863, Lincoln Papers); Lincoln also gave a special cotton trading permit to Durant: *C.W.S.*, 268-9.

[40]Gurowski, *Diary*, (3 vols., Boston, 1862-6), II, 121; James G. Blaine, *Twenty Years in Congress* (2 vols., Norwich, Conn., 1884), I, 429; H. Nicolay, *Personal Traits*, 111 (cf. Carpenter, *Six Months*, 253); *C.W.*, IV, 261.

[41]Chase ms, n.d.[1861], Lincoln Papers, #41,717-8; Chase to Dwight Bannister, May 7, 1864, in Warden, *Life of Chase*, 586; cf. Chase to Leavitt, Jan. 24, 1864, *Ibid.*, 561-2; Chase, *Diaries*, 253; Chase to Lincoln, June 24, 1861, Apr. 14, 25, 1864, Lincoln Papers.

[42]*C.W.*, IV, 210-14. The choice of Pittsburgh disregarded the Republican state chairman's earlier appraisal that the tariff was the "overshadowing question" only in the eastern part of the state. McClure to Lincoln, June 16, 1860 (cf. Carey to Lincoln, Jan. 2, 1861), Lincoln Papers; see also the bibliography for Michael Fitzgibbon Holt.

[43]William H. Mitchell and Pitman Pulsifier, eds., *Tariff Acts Passed by the Congress of the United States from 1789 to 1895*, Senate Doc. 219, 54:1 (1895-6), 157-222; *C.W.*, III, 487.

[44]*Ibid.*, IV, 214; Bruce, *Lincoln and the Tools of War*, 43, 49-50; cf. Chase to Lincoln, July 29, 1861, Lincoln Papers; M. Meigs to Cameron, Aug. 27, 1861, Chase Papers, LC.

[45]*C.W.*, IV, 254; V, 528-9 (cf. Winfield Scott to Lincoln, March 3, 1861; Seward to Lincoln, March 15, 1861, etc., Lincoln Papers). Lincoln did pay routine attention to the tariff, for example Fessenden to Lincoln, June 30, 1864, Lincoln Papers.

[46]Spinner to Lincoln, July 23, Sept. 19, 1860; James A. McDougall and James H. Campbell to Lincoln, July 15, 1862; Henry V. Poor to Lincoln, Oct. 3, 1863; Hugh McCulloch to Lincoln, Sept. 22, 1864, Lincoln Papers; *C.W.*, IV, 120-1; VI, 68, 491, 493, 504-5, 518, 519-20, 525-6, 545; VII, 16,

122, 228, 451-2, 464-5; VIII, 38-9, 89, 192-3; *C.W.S.*, 208. *U.S. Statutes at Large*, XII, 807; Welles, *Diary* I, 228-9; Grenville M. Dodge, *Personal Recollections* (Council Bluffs, Ia., 1914), 8-9, 10-11; and *How We Built the Union Pacific Railway* (Council Bluffs, Is., n.d.), 60. See also the bibliography for the works of Milton M. Shutes(3), John W. Starr, and the best work on the railroad by Robert William Fogel(1).

[47] Hay to John A. Dix, Dec. 1, 1863, Hay-McLellan Collection; Edgar Conkling to Lincoln, Nov. 14, 1864, enclosing his pamphlet *The Pacific Railroad* (n.p., n.d. [1861]), Lincoln Papers.

[48] *C.W.*, V, 526; VII, 122; Nevins, *Ordeal of the Union*, VI, 209-10; Milton H. Shutes, *Lincoln and California* (Stanford, 1943), 155-7; see also James McCague(1) in the bibliography.

[49] Dodge, *Recollections*, 14-7, and *How We Built the Union Pacific*, 61-3 (see also the bibliograpy for Stanley P. Hirshson); Nevins, *Ordeal of the Union*, VI, 210; Haney, *Congressional History of Railways*, II, 62-4; *C.W.*, VIII, 146. The often repeated recollection of Oakes Ames, of Credit Mobilier fame, that Lincoln spoke of doubling the road's subsidies, must be treated with caution. Nor seems to be there evidence to support the Dodge claim of presidential arm twisting on behalf of the 1864 act. On the debate concerning the necessity of federal subsidies see W. D. Farnham, Heywood Fleisig, and Robert William Fogel(1) in the bibliography.

[50] *C.W.*, V, 37; P.J. Staudenraus, ed., *Mr. Lincoln's Washington: Selections from the Writing of Noah Brooks, Civil War Correspondent* (New York, 1967), 307. Curry, *Blueprint for Modern America*, 136-47, traces the legislative history of the proposal but does not mention Lincoln. See also the bibliography for John Y. Simon(1,2), and for the economic picture J.W. Putnam, and Robert B. Sutton(1).

[51] John Ericsson to Lincoln, Apr. 14, 1862; Memorial . . . by Samuel B. Ruggles, June 9, 1862; Arnold to Lincoln, June 9, 1862, Lincoln Papers; *C.W.*, V, 270. Memorials opposing the canals were quietly stashed away among Lincoln's papers. S.C. Morton to Lincoln, July 2, 1862 (Resolutions of the Philadelphia Board of Trade enclosed); Henry C. Carey to Lincoln, July 4, 1862, Nov. 16, 1863, Lincoln Papers.

[52] Ruggles to Edwin D. Morgan, Nov. 28, 1862, Ruggles Letter, ISHL; Bates, *Diary*, 267; *C.W.*, V, 526; *C.W.S.*, 149.

[53] Arnold to Ruggles, Apr. 1, 1863, Lincoln Collection, Univ. of Chicago; *C.W.*, VI, 508, VII, 48, 274. See also the bibliography for the work of Arthur C. Cole(2), and Richard N. Current(1).

[54] *C.W.*, V, 37; VI, 373; VII, 321. Nicolay and Hay, *Lincoln*, V, 67, wrote that Lincoln even went before a Senate committee urging the project. The President indeed felt very strongly about the matter but there appears to be no other evidence for such an extraordinary step by him. See also Hay, *Diary*, 104-5; Henry C. Carey to Lincoln, Nov. 16, 1863, enclosure, Lincoln Papers; and the bibliography for S.R. Kamm.

[55] *C.W.*, V, 314; VI, 66; VII, 224, 237-8; *C.W.S.*, 258-9, 273; Bates, *Diary*, 338,

343; Bates to Lincoln, Sept. 11, 19, 1862; Samuel T. Glover to Lincoln, Jan. 12, 1863; Bates to W.S. Rosecrans, March 19, 1864, enclosing Quartermaster's Dept., St. Louis: Agreement, July 26, 1864, and Frank S. Bond to Lewis B. Parsons, Aug. 18, 1864; Rosecrans to Lincoln, Sept. 15, 1864, Lincoln Papers.

[56]*C.W.*, VI, 68-9, 246; see also Petition for Railroad, Oct. 28, 1862, Lincoln Papers; *Day By Day,* III, 148. Congress provided for other improvements as well which Lincoln approved without comment. He vetoed, however, aid to a railroad in Minnesota for reasons that are not clear. John Bruce Robertson, "Lincoln and Congress," Ph.D. Dissertation, University of Wisconsin, 1966, 340.

CHAPTER 15

[1]*C.W.,* V, 46.

[2]Senators L.S. Foster and Fessenden, *Cong. Globe,* Apr. 22, May 3, 20, 1862, 37:2, 1756, 2014-7, 2216.

[3]*House Reports,* 21, 37:2 (1861); Williams, *Roots of Empire,* 115. I am indebted to Professor Williams for his assistance in unearthing his error.

[4]The best review of the early work of the Department is Paul W. Gates, *Agriculture and the Civil War* (New York, 1965), 301-23; see also the earlier work of John M. Gaus and Leon O. Walcott, T. Swann Harding, Henry Barrett Learned, Earl D. Ross(2), W.W. Stockberger, and W.L. Wanless in the bibliography. For Newton's political intrigues see Bates, *Diary,* 279, 290-1 *et passim*; Browning, *Diary,* I, 591-2.

[5]T. Swann Harding, *Two Blades of Grass: A History of Scientific Development in the U.S. Department of Agriculture* (Norman, 1947); *C.W.,* III, 480; the manuscript of Newton's report is in the Lincoln Papers, #20,762-815; it is printed in *House Ex. Doc.,* 78, 37:3 (1862), 4-25.

[6]*C.W.,* V, 526-7; VI, 343, 367-8; VII, 3-4; cf. Report of the Commissioner of Agriculture, *House Ex. Doc.,* 91, 38:1 (1863); see also J.S. Wright and H.S. Lane to Lincoln, May, 1862 (#15,995); A.D. Bache to Wright, May 14, 1862, Lincoln Papers.

[7]*Senate Ex. Doc.,* 1, 37:2 (1861), 451-2; Gates, *Agriculture,* 323.

[8]*C.W.,* VII, 46-7; IV, 202-3; Report of the Sec. of Interior, J.P. Usher, *House Ex. Doc.,* 1, 38:1 (1863), vol. 3, IV; cf. Report of the Commissioner of Land Office, J.M. Edmunds, *Ibid.,* 6. Lincoln also dealt with routine questions related to agriculture, for ex.: Usher to Lincoln, July 7, 1864, Lincoln Papers.

[9]*C.W.,* VIII, 146; V, 51-3; VII, 259; Bates, *Diary,* 206-7; *Cong. Globe,* Dec. 5, 1861, 37:2, 20; Curry, *Blueprint for Modern America,* 246.

[10]*C.W.,* VII, 44, 271 (cf. VI, 384), 217, 249, 495; see also V, 24; VI, 144, 146, 212, 397, 418, 461; VII, 105, 128, 332-3, 355, 454; VIII, 42, 76, 123, 269, 327-8, 423; *C.W.S.,* 96, 238; George Harrington, "Mr. Lincoln," ms., Huntington Library (HM 19944).

[11]Bancroft's Address before Congress in Nicolay and Hay, *Complete Works of Lincoln,* VIII, xlii-xliii; *C.W.,* VI, 63-5, 88-9; VII, 259-60; Karl Marx and

Frederick Engels, *The Civil War in the United States* (New York, 1961), Richard Enmale (pseudonym), ed., 273, 274, 279-80; Egbert C. Viele in Ward., ed., *Lincoln*, 118; see also the bibliography for Bernard Mandel, Jay Monoghan, J.R. Pole, and Gerald Runkle.

[12]*C.W.*, VII, 259; V, 534-5. On the 1863 riots see the bibliography for Adrian Cook, Albon P. Man, and David Montgomery.

[13]*C.W.*, VII, 466-7; *Day By Day*, III, 309; Randall, *Lincoln*, III, 46. The President's reply to an appeal from Cincinnati seamstresses does not appear to survive. David Montgomery, *Beyond Equality: Labor and the Radical Republicans, 1862-1872* (New York, 1967), 97.

[14]*C.W.*, VII, 100; P. Foner, *History of Labor*, I, 331.

[15]*C.W.*, VII, 81, 84; Address of Working Men's Mass Meeting of Cincinnati to the President, May 10, 1864, enclosing resolutions of May 9, 1864, Lincoln Papers; *Daily Mo. Democrat*, April 15, 19, 26, May 4, 22, 31, April 2, 3, 14, 1864; *Fincher's Trades Review*, May 21, June 4, 11, 1864; Sandburg, *War Years*, II, 621; P. Foner, *History of Labor*, I, 331-3, 354-5. Montgomery, *Beyond Equality*, 100, citing James C. Sylvis, *The Life, Speeches, Labors & Essays of William H. Sylvis* (Philadelphia, 1872), 133-5, errs in claiming that the military broke the strike in St. Louis. For background on labor in Missouri see the bibliography for Walter R. Houf, and Russell Nolen. A detailed history of labor during the Civil War is needed.

[16]*C.W.*, VII, 259; *Fincher's Trades Review*, March 12, 1864.

[17]*Ibid.*, Nov. 28, Dec. 5, March 12, 1864; see also March 5 and April 12, 1864.

[18]*Illinois State Register*, June 21, 1844; *C.W.*, I, 338-40.

[19]*Ibid.*, IV, 203; VIII, 101, 150; Carey to Chase, July 9, 1862, Carey Papers.

[20]*C.W.*, VII, 40.

[21]*Ibid.*, V, 45, 535; *U.S. Statutes at Large*, XIII, 385; Bates, *Diary*, 314; Welles, *Diary*, I, 543; Van Deusen, *Seward*, 512-3; Beard and Beard, *Rise of American Civilization*, II, 100; Charlotte Erickson, *American Industry and the European Immigrant, 1860-1885* (Cambridge, Mass., 1957), vii, 7, 63.

[22]*C.W.*, VIII, 141; *Cong. Globe*, Feb. 7, 23, 24, 27, 1865, 38:2, 653, 1034, 1057, 1070, 1125; P. Foner, *History of Labor*, I, 333-4.

[23]J. Gillespie in Oldroyd, ed., *Lincoln Memorial*, 463; *C.W.*, IV, 138-9; Chittenden, *Recollections*, 74-5, and *Personal Reminiscences, 1840-1890* (New York, 1893), 391-3 (cf. Lawrence Weldon in Ward, ed., *Lincoln*, 254-5); see also the bibliography for Philip S. Foner(1), Richard Lowitt, and Kenneth M. Stampp(2).

[24]Ruggles to Morgan, Nov. 28, 1862, Ruggles Letter, ISHL; for Kennedy see Arthur M. Schlesinger, *A Thousand Days: John F. Kennedy in the White House* (Boston, 1965), 635-6.

[25]*C.W.*, V, 360; and 44, 380, 385, 430; VI, 96, 141, 147, 221, 227-8, 323-4, 403-4, 411-2, 529, 531, 540-1; VII, 202, 242, 363, 368-9; VIII, 97, 268, 417, 422; *C.W.S.*, 220, 261; Enoch T. Casson to S.P. Chase, July 9, 1861; J.W. Forney to Lincoln, Nov. 5, 1864, Lincoln Papers; Browning, *Diary*, I, 654; *Cong. Globe*, Feb. 7, 1865, 38:2, 647-52; *House Ex. Doc.*, 39, 38:2 (1865); see also Sutton(1,2) in the bibliography.

[26]*C.W.*, VI, 138. For the House committee see Fred Nicklason, and Hans L. Trefousse(1,2) in the bibliography. For the Smith brothers see *C.W.*, VII, 522-3; VIII, 240, 364; Welles, *Diary*, II, 7, 53-7, 60, 90, 124-5, 224, 231, 238, 260, 261-6; 334, 359; Carpenter, *Six Months*, 259-60; Edward L. Pierce, *Memoir and Letters of Charles Sumner* (4 vols., Boston, 1893), IV, 232-3; see also the bibliography for Curtis Dahl, H.H. Goodman, John Niven, and Franklin W. Smith. The Widener Library, Harvard University has a fine collection of materials on the Smith case. The question of corruption is considered in the works of Edwin S. Bradley, A.H. Meneely, Fred A. Shannon(1), Richard H. Sewall, Richard S. West, and above all Ludwell Johnson(1,2,3,4,5,6). For the controversial Almaden case in particular see L.A. Ascher(1,2), Milton W. Shutes(1,3), David M. Silver, Benjamin Thomas and Harold Hyman, and Samuel C. Weil.

[27]*C.W.*, V, 37-8, 39, 77, 186, 253, 521; VI, 35-6, 51, 206; VII, 72-3, 87, 147-8, 169, 187-8, 503-4; VIII, 137-8, 145, 203-4, 296; Bates, *Diary*, 284-5, 285-6; George E. Baker, ed., *The Works of William Seward* (5 vols., Cambridge and Boston, 1853-1884), V, 91; Welles, *Diary*, I, 246-7, 259-60, and *Lincoln and Seward* (New York, 1874), 162-4; Pierce, *Memoir and Letters of Sumner*, IV, 129; John Sherman to Lincoln, July 6, 1861, Lincoln Papers; *Day By Day*, III, 71, 96.

[28]*C.W.*, IV, 499-500; V, 24-2; VI, 112-3, 298; VII, 279; VIII, 208; cf. Randall, *Lincoln*, I, 375; III, 247-50.

[29]*C.W.*, VII, 46; VIII, 145; see also IV, 467; V, 189-90, 312, 521, 524-5; *U.S. Statutes at Large*, XII, 170, 711; Report of the Postmaster General, William Dennison, *House Ex. Doc.*, 1, 38:2 (1864), v, 792-3; and J. Duane Squires in the bibliography.

[30]*C.W.*, IV, 558; V, 521; VII, 39; VIII, 138-9, 146; Cyrus Field to Lincoln, Dec. 14, 26, 27, 1861, Lincoln Papers; Homer Bates, *Lincoln in the Telegraph Office* (New York, 1907), 257-9; *U.S. Statutes at Large*, XII, 334; Van Deusen, *Seward*, 513-4; see also the bibliography for Alvin F. Harlow.

[31]Eaton, *Grant, Lincoln, and the Freedmen*, 181.

[32]*C.W.*, V, 521-2; VII, 40, 47; VIII, 146; Report of Sec. of Interior, Caleb B. Smith, *House Ex. Doc.*, 1, 37:3 (1862), vol. II, 4-6; and Report of Commissioner of Land Office, J.M. Edmunds, *Ibid.*, 50-4; and Reports in note 8 *supra; U.S. Statutes at Large*, XIII, 473; A. G. Henry to Lincoln, Jan. 22, 1862, Henry Papers; Edgar Conkling to Lincoln, Dec. 13, 1863 (with enclosures), and July 2, 1864, Lincoln Papers; W.J. Waldie to Lincoln, Aug. 21, 1864, Waldie Letter, ISHL. On mining see also Rodman W. Paul in the bibliography.

[33]The full ms. of the Lincoln message, n.d. [copy of April 15 ms.?], 1865 is in the Schuyler Colfax Papers, Indiana State Library.

[34]*Facts for the People!* . . . , 1862, in Freidel, ed., *Union Pamphlets*, I, 442; Fessenden to James S. Pike, Apr. 5, 1863, Taney Papers.

[35]Chittenden, *Recollections*, 307-8; John N. Kasson in Rice, ed., *Reminiscences*, 379; see also Lewis Henry Croce, "The Lincoln Administration," Ph.D.

Dissertation, University of Maryland, 1968, 114 (cf. Stephen A. Ambrose in the bibliography).

[36]D. Davis to L. Swett, Nov. 26, 1862, Davis Papers; Croce, "Lincoln Administration," 54-5, 83-4; Frank, *Lincoln as a Lawyer,* 151f.

[37]Donald, "Whig in the White House," 60.

[38]Bates, *Diary,* 41, and in Rice, ed., *Reminiscences,* 240.

[39]Chase, *Diaries,* 192. Both confiscation and cotton are discussed in the following chapter.

[40]William Elder to Carey, March 21, June 20, 1861; Carey to Scranton, March 20, 1861, Carey Papers.

[41]Carey to Lincoln, Jan. 2, June 20, Nov. 9, 1861; Carey to Noah H. Swayne, Jan. 29, 1865, Lincoln Papers.

[42]*C.W.,* II, 248; I, 504.

[43]*Ibid.,* V, 43; Noah Brooks, *Washington in Lincoln's Time* (New York, 1895), 50; cf. Brooks, "Personal Recollections of Abraham Lincoln," *Harper's Monthly,* 31 (1865), 227.

[44]Hay, *Diaries,* 6.

[45]Bates, *Lincoln and the Telegraph Office,* 266.

CHAPTER 16

[1]Kenneth A. Bernard, *Lincoln and the Music of the Civil War* (Caldwell, Idaho, 1967), 206-7; *Day by Day,* III, 299.

[2]*C.W.,* II, 275; cf. 255, 274, 406, 546-7.

[3]*Ibid.,* IV, 271, 259, 269; V, 53, 527-9.

[4]*Ibid.,* III, 17-8, 88, 120-1, etc.; cf. Seward's "Higher Law" Speech. *Cong. Globe Appendix,* March 11, 1850, 31:1, 260-9.

[5]*C.W.,* V, 528-9; *Cong. Globe,* July 21, 1846, 29:1, 1124; cf. Henry Carey to Lincoln, Nov. 9, 1861, Lincoln Papers.

[6]One is reminded here of an exchange that took place fourteen years earlier between Herndon and Lincoln after both men had visited Niagara Falls. Back at their law office Herndon rejoiced over the wonder and beauty of the Falls and his partner ("I shall never forget his answer," the startled Herndon wrote) responded with a scientific query about the source of the water. "He had no eye for the magnificence and grandeur of the scene, for the rapids, the mist, the angry waters, and the roar of the whirlpool," the younger man concluded somewhat unfairly. It is true, however, that Lincoln's trip led to the patenting of his "improved method of lifting vessel over Shoals." *Herndon's Lincoln* 249; *C.W.,* II, 32-6 (cf. 10-11). For the growth of the concept of a Nature ordained Union, which reached special intensity in the old Northwest and which, with some, became an economic argument, see the bibliography for Merle Curti(3), Henry Nash Smith, Kenneth M. Stampp(2), and above all Paul C. Nagel(1).

[7]Wendell Phillips, "Lincoln's Election," in *Speeches, Lectures, and Letters* (Boston, 1863), 316.

[8]*C.W.*, V, 530-7. For Lincoln's earlier proposals see *Ibid.*, 29-30, 43, 144-6, 152-3, 160-1, 169, 192, 222-3, 317-9, 324-5, 336, 433-6, 503-4; see also Nicolay and Hay, eds. *Complete Works of Lincoln*, VI, 120-8; Nicolay and Hay, *Lincoln*, V, 201-17; Arnold, *Lincoln*, 251; Browning, *Diary*, I, 512; *Day by Day*, III, *passim;* there is also a considerable body of correspondence addressed to Lincoln on the subject in his Papers.

[9]Randall, *Lincoln the Liberal Statesman* (New York, 1947), 195.

[10]Claudia Dale Goldin, "The Economics of Emancipation," *JEH*, 33 (1973), 84.

[11]His figures were correct but his projections proved to be overly optimistic as the U.S. growth rate tapered off after the Civil War. (cf. Van Deusen, *Clay*, 120, for Clay's much too cautious conjectures (not calculations) about U.S. population growth.) The President obtained the raw data for his calculations from J.C.G. Kennedy, the Superintendent of Census. Kennedy to Lincoln, enclosures, March 14, 1862, Lincoln Papers.

[12]*C.W.*, IV, 432; and *infra* p. 284.

[13]*C.W.*, VIII, 150; V, 534, 537. For the evolution of the materialistic concept of the Union see Curti(4), and Nagel(1) in the bibliography.

[14]Browning, *Diary*, I, 591 (cf. Chase to Lincoln, Nov. 28, 1862, Lincoln Papers); for the democratic charges see for example A.W. Spies to Seward, Sept. 23, 1863, enclosure, Lincoln Papers; "Facts for the People!" and "Lincoln Catechism," in Freidel, ed., *Union Pamphlets*, I, 430; II, 988; "The U.S. Treasury Robbed to Buy Negroes," *The Old Guard*, 1 (1863), 19-20; see also Voegeli, *Free But Not Equal, passim.*

[15]*C.W.*, VIII, 52; see also Charles L. Wagandt in the bibliography.

[16]Browning, *Diary*, I, 611-2; Curry, *Blueprint for Modern America*, 54.

[17]Hay, *Diaries*, 77.

[18]Stampp, *The Era of Reconstruction, 1865-1877* (New York, 1965), 24-49 (see also Ludwell H. Johnson, "Lincoln's Solution to the Problem of Peace Terms, 1864-1865," *JSH*, 34 (1968), 576-86); and compare *C.W.*, I, 318 and IV, 437.

[19]*Ibid.*, VIII, 332; V, 537. Lincoln's words stand in sharp contrast to the easy dismissal of his plan by some recent historians. Cf. Randall, *Lincoln*, II, 141 *et passim*, which speaks of the emancipation proclamation "as of minor importance," "relatively and with a view to the President's main concept" for liberating the slaves.

[20]Thus in the 1970's Richard M. Nixon, following the design of Lyndon B. Johnson, and more remotely Lincoln's 1862 peace plan, offered a multi-billion dollar aid package to North Vietnam hoping to entice her to lay down her arms.

[21]*C.W.*, VI , 408.

[22]Herman Belz, *Reconstructing the Union: Theory and Policy During the Civil War* (Ithaca, N.Y., 1969), 230; *C.W.*, VII, 53-6.

[23]*Ibid.*, 451.

[24]Seward, *Works*, V, 177. The Seward Papers, University of Rochester, and the Nathaniel P. Banks Papers, LC., provide the best information about

the Zacharie mission; see also the numerous Zacharie letters, often enigmatic, in the Lincoln Papers. A selection from the Banks Papers is printed in Fred A. Harrington, "A Peace Mission of 1863," *AHR*, 46 (1940), 76-86. See also the bibliography for works by Fred Harrington(2), Bertram W. Korn, and Van Deusen(5).

[25] Yet see *infra* 381. For these and other peace efforts see Randall, *Lincoln*, III, 242-5; IV, 156-7, 165-7, 322-40; J.G. Randall and David Donald, *The Civil War and Reconstruction* (Lexington, Mass., 1969). 470-4; and the works of Martin Duberman(1), Edward C. Kirkland, and Harriet Chappell Owsley in the bibliography.

[26] The Samuel L. Casey peace mission is lost in myth. Casey corresponded with Lincoln, see especially his curious letters of Dec. 19, 21, 1863, Lincoln Papers (cf. J.W. Maguire to Ward H. Lamon, n.d., Lincoln Collection, Huntington Library (LN 1237). For Casey's cotton business see the bibliography for Harrington(2), and Ludwell Johnson(1). For contraband trade see the bibliography above all for E.M. Coulter(1), R.F. Futrell, Johnson(2,3,4,6), Allan Nevins, T. O'Connor, J.H. Parks, A.F. Roberts, and James Ford Rhodes.

[27] *C.W.*, IV, 487-8; Carey to Lincoln, Nov. 16, 1863 enclosure, Lincoln Papers; see also for ex.: *C.W.*, V, 139, 210, 540; VI, 157, 159-60, 479; VII, 8, 192-3, 229; VIII, 115, 140, 197, 208-9; and see E. Merton Coutler, "Effects of Secession Upon the Commerce of the Mississippi Valley," *MVHR*, 3 (1916), 289-90.

[28] Belmont to Lincoln, May 9, 1862, Lincoln Papers; Whitney, *Life on the Circuit*, 440-1; see also Irving Katz in the bibliography.

[29] *C.W.*, VI, 307; VII, 114-6, 148, 151-2, 156, 166; *C.W.S.*, 220; Ludwell Johnson, "Contraband Trade during the Last Year of the Civil War," *MVHR*, 49 (1963), 635-8; see also Chase, *Diaries*, 143-4; 152-3; Cuthbert Bullitt to Lincoln, May 10, 1864, enclosure; and also the ms. of various trade regulations in the Lincoln Papers (ex.: #36,644-5; #43,591-4).

[30] See Chapter 18.

[31] Welles, *Diary*, II, 167; *C.W.*, VIII, 151. For this particular Lincoln project led by the military governor of Texas, Andrew J. Hamilton, see also Hamilton to Lincoln, Feb. 16, 1863, Dec. 9, 1864, Lincoln Papers; *C.W.*, VI, 465-6; VII, 488-9; VIII, 93-4, 103-4; Welles, *Diary*, II, 159-60, 163, 168; Bates, *Diary*, 414; and the bibliography for the works of Harrington(2), Van Deusen(5), Ludwell Johnson(1,4).

[32] *C.W.*, VIII, 163-5, 175-6, 196-7, 243-4, 267; Hay, *Diaries*, 203; HR 805 and *House Reports*, 24, 38:2 (1865), 1-4; Forbes to E. Atkinson, March 8, 1865, in Harold F. Williamson, *Edward Atkinson: The Biography of an American Liberal, 1827-1905* (Boston, 1934), 20; see also Chase to Lincoln, Feb. 23, 1863, Lincoln Papers; Johnson, "Contraband Trade," 640.

[33] *C.W.*, V, 36; VI, 364, 374; Hay, *Diaries*, 77; Browning, *Diary*, I, 489, 563-4; Chase, *Diaries*, 164-6; Belmont to Lincoln, Feb. 16, 1863, Lincoln Papers; Van Deusen, *Seward*, 321. On the subject of European cotton see above all Frank L. Owsley's revised classic *King Cotton Diplomacy* (Chicago,

1959), and the bibliography for the works of E.D. Adams, D.B. Carroll, L.M. Case and W.F. Spencer, H. Hyman(2), R.H. Jones, R.L. Kerby, and A. Khasigian.

34*C.W.,* VIII, 163-4 (cf. Maguire to Lamon, n.d., Lincoln Collection, Huntington Library [LN 1237]); Atkinson to Lincoln, July 8, 19, 28, August 13, 17, Sept. 3, Oct. 19, Dec. 27, 1864; Feb. 8, 1865; Atkinson to John Hay, Aug. 13, 1864, Lincoln Papers; Welles, *Diary,* II, 66; Hay, *Diaries,* 203; see also Johnson, "Contraband Trade," 636-7, 639-40.

35Atkinson to Lincoln, Sept. 13, 1864 (cf. Crafts J. Wright and Charles Hawkes to Lincoln, Jan. 8, 1864), Lincoln Papers; Lamon's untitled m.s. sequence to his *Life of Lincoln,* p.486, Huntington Library; Browning, *Diary,* II, 5, 11.

36*Ibid.;* see also I, xxii-xxiii, 695, 699; II, 1-15 *passim;* Browning to Lincoln, Jan. 9, 1865, and undated (#39,686), Lincoln Papers; John Hay to Browning, Dec. 27, 1864, Browning Papers, ISHL; see also Maurice Baxter in the bibliography. Randall and Current, *Lincoln,* IV, 330-1, ignores the cotton side of the Singleton mission, whereas Ludwell Johnson(3) largely ignores the peace side.

37*C.W.,* V, 507.

38*Ibid.,* 72, 74, 207; VI, 340; VII, 63-4, 114-5, 146-7, 178, 212, 217, 344; VIII, 7-8, 14-5, 30-1, 35, 288-9, 305-6, 337, 340; *C.W.S.,* 221-2, 268-9. 270, 279; Atkinson to William B. Roger, July 13, 1863, and to L.E. Norton, July 20, 1863, Edward A. Atkinson Papers, Mass. Hist. Soc., Boston; New England Loyal Publ. Society Papers, No. 90.

39"Northern Profits and Profiteers: The Cotton Rings of 1864-5," *CWH,* 12 (1966), 115; see also Frank E. Vandiver, *Rebel Brass: The Confederate Command System* (Baton Route, 1956), 114-24; Johnson, "Trading with the Union: Evolution of Confederate Policy," *Va. Mag. of Hist.,* 308-25, and "Contraband Trade," 643. A.S. Roberts, "The Federal Government and Confederate Cotton," *AHR,* 32 (1926), 272-5, argues that the contraband trade prolonged the war by a full year. Further examination is necessary and might lead to a substantial reevaluation of Lincoln as a war leader. Cf. *House Reports,* 24, 38:2 (1865), 1-4, 19, 21, 61-2, 65, 74, 81, 111, 121.

40*C.W.,* VI, 307; VIII, 163-5.

41*Ibid.,* VII, 419 (the tentative *C.W.,* identification of Atkinson is incorrect); Segal, *Conversations,* 244; for Lincoln's worries over cotton corruption see for ex.: *C.W.,* VI, 294, 307; VII, 78-9, 104, 156, 457; VIII, 201-2; cf. *House Reports,* 24, 38:2 (1865), 116-7, 121. Lincoln probably heard the rumor that he was part of a cotton speculating ring. Welles, *Diary,* II, 60.

42*Ibid.,* 84, 218; *Official Records,* XV, 639; Bates, *Diary,* 404-5; Bruce Catton, *The Centennial History of the Civil War* (3 vols., New York, 1961-5), III, 336-43; Ludwell Johnson, *Red River Campaign: Politics and Cotton in the Civil War* (Baltimore, 1958), 102f.; Randall and Current, *Lincoln,* IV, 145-6.

43*C.W.,* VIII, 163, 267, 268, 343-4; Charles Carleton Coffin and Lawrence Weldon in Rice, ed., *Reminiscences,* 177, 210-13; Bruce Catton, *Grant Takes Command* (Boston, 1969), 411-2.

[44]Welles, *Diary,* II, 280-1; Carpenter, *Six Months,* 285-6. It might be possible to place a weak and hostile construction on Lincoln's activities and see the Unionism of his cotton policy as a mere facade. It might then be argued that his real aim was to provide profits for personal and political friends — however high the price for those profits had to appear if Southern Unionism was not an all important factor.

[45]S.T. Hills to his brother, n.d., Papers of Lincoln's Cabinet Members, Lincoln National Life Foundation; *C.W.,* IV, 532; VII, 259-60, 493, 368.

[46]*Ibid.,* VI, 85, 87, 499; VIII, 78; V, 330; VI, 408; *Day by Day,* III, 93; Browning, *Diary,* 659; Stampp, *Era of Reconstruction,* 42; see also *C.W.,* VI, 501; and George W. Julian in Rice, ed., *Reminiscences,* 58-9 (cf. *C.W.,* V, 330-1).

[47]*C.W.,* VI, 87; VIII, 78; VII, 255; also V, 548; VI, 36-8, 427, 434-5; VII, 131, 149, 254-5, 280, 304, 409; VIII, 27-8, 119, 225, 228, 285, 292-3, 294-6, 297-8, 342-3; James Sidney Rollins *et al.* to Lincoln, Feb. 8, 1864, with Lincoln's pardon, Lincoln Collection, Huntington Library; the Lincoln Papers contain much material on the subject, for ex.: Lazarus W. Powell to Lincoln, Jan. 29, 1862; William A. Hall to Lincoln, Feb. 20, 1863, enclosure; Montgomery Blair to Lincoln, Feb. 16, 1864.

[48]*C.W.,* VII, 255, 54; VIII, 387, 388; *Day by Day,* III, 136. On Lincoln and confiscation see also the bibliography for Harold Hyman(3), J.G. Randall(1,5), Henry D. Shapiro, and J. Syrett. The Lincoln Papers contain much information on the subject, for ex.: M. Blair to Lincoln, Nov. 21, 1861; James R. Doolittle to Lincoln, Dec. 19, 1861.

[49]*C.W.,* VIII, 260-1, 388, 407; Welles, *Diary,* II, 237; Chase, *Diaries,* 268; Alexander K. McClure, *Recollections of Half a Century* (Salem, Mass., 1902), 296-7; J.P. Usher in Rice., ed., *Reminiscences,* 98-9.

[50]*C.W.,* V, 330; James R. Gilmore, *Personal Recollections of Abraham Lincoln and the Civil War* (Boston, 1898), 245; cf. P. Foner, ed., *Life and Writings of Douglass,* IV, 316.

[51]*C.W.,* V, 222; Charles Sumner, *His Complete Works* (20 vols., New York, 1969 reprint), VII, 117; Conservative David Davis used radical Sumner's very expressions to describe the President's devotion to his plan. To Leonard Swett, Nov. 26, 1862, Davis Papers, ISHL.

CHAPTER 17

[1]*C.W.,* I, 114; Carpenter, *Six Months,* 90; cf. 208-9, and *C.W.,* V, 503, etc.

[2]Marx to Engels, Oct. 29, 1862, in Marx and Engels, *The Civil War,* 258.

[3]Tolstoy's interview with S. Stakelberg, N. Y. *World,* Feb. 7, 1909 [see also Albert W. Woldman, *Lincoln and the Russians* (Cleveland, 1952), 272-6]; Marx and Engels, *Civil War,* 352.

[4]*C.W.,* V, 433-6; *Spectator,* Oct. 11, 1862, as quoted in John Hope Franklin, *The Emancipation Proclamation* (New York, 1963), 68-9.

[5]*C.W.,* VI, 28-31. Certain minor areas were excluded from the pattern.

[6]*Cong. Globe,* Feb. 9, 1863, 37:3, 835.

[7]See for example Davis to Henry W. Cleveland, Apr. 13, Nov. 22, Dec. 15,

29, 1887, March 10, 1888, Judd-Stewart Lincolniana, Huntington Library.

[8]Julian in Rice, ed., *Reminiscences*, 61-2; Resolutions of Tammany Hall Young Men's Democratic Club, in James M. McPherson, *The Negro's Civil War: How American Negroes Felt and Acted During the War for the Union* (New York, 1965), 77.

[9]The argument is developed in G. S. Boritt, "The Voyage to the Colony of Linconia: The Sixteenth President, Black Colonization, and the Defense Mechanism of Avoidance," *Hist.*, 37(1975), 619-33. The article is also a guide to the large literature on Lincoln and colonization.

[10]Blair to Lincoln, Nov. 16, 1861, Lincoln Papers.

[11]Martin F. Conway in *Cong. Globe Appendix*, Jan. 27, 1863, 37:3, 64; see also the bibliography for Eric Foner, Harry V. Jaffa(2), and R.H. Zoellner.

[12]Chase, *Diaries*, 112; Charles J. Biddle in *Cong. Globe*, June 2, 1862, 37:2, 2504; for a brief summary of the economic argument against colonization see Lewis Tappan's 1861 essay in Freidel, ed., *Union Pamphlets*, I, 107.

[13]*C.W.*, V, 371, 535.

[14]*Ibid.*, 534-5.

[15]*Ibid.*, VI, 291, 365; VII, 51; V, 29-30, 372; see also VI, 48-9, 52-3, 53-4, 291, 358, 364-6, 407-8; VII, 1-2, 66-7, 141, 144, 154-5, 161, 226-7, 499-502; VIII, 371.

[16]*Ibid.*, VII, 243; see also VI, 358, 409, 410-11; VII, 51, 54, 81, 499-501, 506-8; VIII, 2, 152, 250-1, 403; interview of Alexander Randall and John T. Mills with Lincoln, clipping enclosed in F. S. Corkran to J. G. Nicolay, Sept. 8, 1864, Lincoln Papers.

[17]*C.W.*, V, 373, 374; Nicolay and Hay, *Lincoln*, VI, 358-9; the secretaries view, of course only provides part of the answer about Chiriqui's abandonment.

[18]*Papers Relating to the Foreign Relations of the U.S. 1862* (Washington, 1862), 202-4; James Mitchell, *Report on Colonization and Emigration* (Washington, 1862), 21; see also note #9.

[19]*C.W.*, VI, 457; also 98-9, 453-9; VII, 98-9; VIII, 333; *Day by Day*, III, 106; Willie Lee Rose, *Rehearsal for Reconstruction: The Port Royal Experiment* (New York, 1967), specially 272-96.

[20]*C.W.*, VII, 51.

[21]*Ibid.*, V, 487, 535; VI, 30; VII, 145, 212; (see also VI, 24, 362, 387-8; VII, 146-7, 185, 217; VIII, 306, 317; *C.W.S.*, 141-2; Hay, *Diaries*, 125); Eaton, *Grant, Lincoln and the Freedmen*, 168; Henry Samuels, "My Interview with Lincoln," March 8, 1889, ISHL (see also Randall and Current, *Lincoln*, IV, 320; Voegeli, *Free But Not Equal*, 116).

[22]*C.W.*, VI, 198, 280, 332, 404-6, 432, 440, 482; see also the bibliography for Dudley T. Cornish, James McPherson(2), and Benjamin Quarles.

[23]We should not overemphasize the wage system as an expedient to keep the former slaves in the South. After all Lincoln was willing to declare in his second annual message that the even distribution of the black population over the United States would do no injury. He did not actually expect such a population movement to take place, but in a bitter private letter to Massachusetts Governor John Andrew he lamented the Northern hostility to

blacks and explained that he would be gratified if the Bay State, or any other in the North, would change its attitude. *C.W.*, V, 543-5; VII, 191-2. Lincoln may not have sent his angry letter to Andrew. See also Voegeli, *Free But Not Equal,* 95-117 *passim.*

[24]*C.W.*, VII, 212. On freedmen's labor policy during the war see the bibliography for La Wanda Cox, Louis Gerteis(1,2), and J. Thomas May. Whether the notion of forty acres and a mule could have worked might be investigated via a counterfactual study.

[25]*C.W.*, VI, 387; Carpenter, *Six Months,* 209-11; Lamon, *Recollections,* 126-7.

[26]T. J. Barnet to S.L.M. Barlow, Nov. 30, 1862, Barlow Papers.

[27]*C.W.*, VII, 76-7.

[28]Current, ed., *The Political Thought of Abraham Lincoln* (Indianapolis, 1967), xxvii; on this point see also George W. Julian, *Political Recollections, 1840 to 1872* (Chicago, 1884), 245.

[29]*C.W.*, V, 373; Carpenter, *Six Months,* 21.

[30]Chittenden, *Recollections,* 368; cf. Henry C. Bowen to Lincoln, Dec. 2, 1862, enclosure, Lincoln Papers. The subject of Lincoln and Reconstruction still awaits a careful modern monographer. I have benefited above all by Current, *Lincoln Nobody Knows,* 237-72; Belz, *Reconstructing the Union;* and was most intrigued by Stampp, *Era of Reconstruction,* 24-9; see also the bibliography for the standard biographies and William B. Hesseltine(3), Charles H. McCarthy, and J.G. Randall(3).

CHAPTER 18

[1]Hay, *Diaries,* 91.

[2]*C.W.*, I, 439; VIII, 332.

[3]Williams, *Lincoln and His Generals* (New York, 1952), viii; *C.W.*, V, 208. The analysis of the following pages is indebted to a large body of military literature, but above all to the works listed in the bibliography by Colin R. Ballard, Robert V. Bruce, Bruce Catton(1), Richard N. Current(5), Williams(3,5), and W. Birkbeck Wood and James E. Edmonds.

[4]The noneconomic intellectual roots of Lincoln's military thinking must yet be scrutinized.

[5]Bates memorandum, April, 15, 1861; James Henderson to Lincoln, April 16, 1861, etc., Lincoln Papers; *C.W.*, IV, 457.

[6]*C.W.*, III, 356-63; Bruce, *Lincoln and the Tools of War,* 289-90.

[7]*C.W.*, V, 37; VI, 108; Lincoln to Don Carlos Buell, Jan. 6, 1862, Unpublished Lincoln Papers, ISHL; see also Hay, *Diaries,* 91.

[8]*C.W.*, VI, 409, and Chapter 14.

[9]*C.W.*, V, 426; VI, 257; III, 454; see also, for example, V, 98; VI, 164, 327-8, 466-8; VII, 476.

[10]Stoddard, *Inside the White House,* 178-9; also 199, 220, 242; Cf. *C.W.*, VI, 13. Actually Lincoln's arithmetic, in this case, was based on faulty reporting of casualties.

[11]*C.W.*, IV, 432; VIII, 151; Current, "God and the Strongest Battalions", in David Donald, ed., *Why the North won the Civil War* (London, 1962), 3-22.

For further illustrations of Lincoln's strategic thinking see, IV, 42; V, 39, 111-2; Browning, *Diary*, I, 523; Welles, *Diary*, I, 344. It should be noted that he recognized a second, equally important determinant of war: the preservation of the "public purpose," the national will, to fight. *C.W.*, VIII, 149-51. His labors in this cause are considered in the following chapter.

[12]*C.W.*, V, 49; VI, 374; VIII, 2; Interview with Alexander Randall and John T. Mills, clipping from the Baltimore press, enclosed in F. S. Corkran to J. G. Nicolay, Sept. 8, 1864 (Cf. Frederick Douglass to Lincoln, Aug. 29, 1864), Lincoln Papers; see also, for example, *C.W.*, V, 423; VI, 408-9; VII, 49-50, 282. The best source on the broad subject of black soldiers is Cornish, *The Sable Arm*.

[13]*C.W.*, VII, 395; VIII, 151, 332, 362; see also Welles, *Diary*, II, 222; Brooks, "Personal Recollections of Lincoln," 228. For the action of Congress in Richmond, authorizing in fact the use of black soldiers, see the bibliography for Robert F. Durden, and the earlier work of T. R. Hay, N. W. Stephenson(2), and C. H. Wesley(1).

[14]Ruggles, *Internationality and International Congresses* (New York, 1870), 7; see also the bibliography for Van Deusen(5).

[15]*C.W.*, VIII, 150; Stoddard, *Inside the White House*, 179.

CHAPTER 19

[1]*C.W.*, IV, 438.

[2]*Ibid.*, 426.

[3]Hay, *Diaries*, 205.

[4]*C.W.*, II, 532, 323; VIII, 101.

[5]*Ibid.*, IV, 438; III, 315.

[6]*Ibid.*, VII, 301 (cf. II, 493); VIII, 155 (cf. VII, 368); II, 271, 222 (cf. III, 541-2); I, 412; and *infra* p. 284-6.

[7]*C.W.*, V, 537; VI, 410; VII, 512 (cf. 528-9); Hay, *Diaries*, 19.

[8]*C.W.*, VII, 281; IV, 240, II; 407.

[9]*C.W.*, V, 388.

[10]*Ibid.*, 336-8; Chase, *Diary*, 97-8; Welles, *Diary*, I, 70-1; Carpenter, *Six Months*, 20-1; Bates, *Lincoln at the Telegraph Office*, 138-9; S. H. Gay to Lincoln n.d. [Aug., 1862], Lincoln Papers.

[11]*C.W.*, IV, 264, 233, 432; Wilson, *Patriotic Gore: Studies in the Literature of the American Civil War* (New York, 1962), 99-130; Lamon, *Recollections*, 275. Lincoln made the same point via a less clear metaphor from *Proverbs*, 25:11, in *C.W.*, IV, 169.

[12]Lieber to Charles Sumner, Aug. 31, 1864, Lieber Papers, Huntington Library; Williams, "Lincoln: Pragmatic Democrat" in Graebner, ed., *The Enduring Lincoln*, 37. Cf. Mark E. Neely, Jr.(1), and James A. Rawley(2) in the bibliography.

[13]*C.W.*, IV, 268; V, 51-3; VI, 320.

[14]*Ibid.*, VII, 23.

[15]*Ibid.*, IV, 438; VII, 259; V, 39.

[16]*Ibid.*, VI, 63-5; Abel Haywood to Lincoln, Jan. 1, 1863, *Sen. Ex. Doc.*, 49, 37:3 (1863). Cf. Mary Ellison in the bibliography.

[17]*C.W.*, IV, 439; VII, 259, 529.

[18]Hay, *Diaries*, 7.

[19]*C.W.*, IV, 169; cf. *C.W.S.*, 44. For Lincoln's familiarity with the Book of Isaiah see, for example, Brooks, "Personal Recollections of Lincoln," 229.

[20]*C.W.*, IV, 235-6, 240. The italics in the Trenton speech are the author's. Historians have long accepted the accuracy of Lincoln's recollections without coming to terms with their exact meaning. See for example Benjamin P. Thomas, *Abraham Lincoln: A Biography* (New York, 1952), 15.

[21]*C.W.*, IV, 235; Ida M. Tarbell, *The Life of Abraham Lincoln* (2 vols., New York, 1900) I, 17 (cf. Thomas, *Lincoln*, 3-4, and *C.W.*, IV, 70); Clay in Rice, ed., *Reminiscences*, 297.

[22]*C.W.*, IV, 240.

[23]*C.W.*, V, 52-3; yet see for ex.: VII, 512.

[24]*Ibid.*, VIII, 332-3 (cf. V, 478); VII, 282, 535; *C.W.S.*, 44, 45, etc.

HISTORIOGRAPHICAL ESSAY

[1]Potter, *The Lincoln Theme in American National Historiography;* Fehren-bacher, *The Changing Image of Lincoln in American Historiography* (Oxford, 1968).

[2]Thomas, *Portrait for Posterity: Lincoln and His Biographers* (New Brunswick, N.J., 1947); Donald, "The Folklore Lincoln," in *Lincoln Reconsidered,* 144-66, and *Lincoln's Herndon* (New York, 1948); Basler, *The Lincoln Legend: A Study of Changing Conceptions* (Boston, 1935).

[3]Randall, "Has the Lincoln Theme Been Exhausted?" *AHR,* 41 (1936), 270-94; Angle, "The Changing Lincoln," in O. Fritiof Ander, ed., *The John J. Hauberg Historical Essays* (Rock Island, Ill., 1954), 1-17, and "Where We Stand: Lincoln Scholarship," in Gwendolyn Brooks *et al., A Portion of That Field* (Urbana, Ill., 1967), 23-40; Walton, "An Agonizing Reappraisal: 'Has the Lincoln Theme Been Exhausted?' " in Ander, ed., *Lincoln Images* (Rock Island, Ill., 1960). Johannsen, "In Search of the Real Lincoln: or Lincoln at the Crossroads," *JISHS,* 61 (1968), 229-47.

[4]*C.W.,* I, 112.

[5]Rossiter, *The American Presidency* (New York, 1960), 108. For Lincoln as the central figure of America's political religion see also Glen Edward Thurow, "Abraham Lincoln and American Political Religion," Ph.D. Dissertation, Harvard University, 1968; and Russell E. Richey and Donald G. Jones ed., *American Civil Religion* (New York, 1974), *passim.*

[6]Donald, *Lincoln's Herndon,* 373; Herndon to Lamon, March 15, 1870, Lamon-Weik Papers.

[7]*The Life, Speeches, and Public Services of Abram Lincoln,* "Wigwam Edition" (New York, 1860), 6-7; Herndon to Lamon, March 15, 1870, Lamon-Weik Papers; *Herndon's Lincoln,* viii.

[8]Potter, *Lincoln Theme,* 12; Herndon to Lamon, March 15, 1870, Lamon-Weik Papers; Black to Lamon as cited in Thomas, *Portrait,* 36-7; see also Lavern Marshall Hammand(1.2) and Albert V. House, Jr., in the bibliography.

[9]The unpublished ms. is in the Huntington Library. Lamon's daughter, Dorothy Lamon Teilard, used some of its more interesting portions in her *Recollections of Lincoln* by Ward Hill Lamon.

[10]*C.W.,* III, 511.

[11]To Albert J. Beveridge, Nov. 25, 1924, Beveridge Papers, Library of Congress.

[12]C. T. Hulburd as quoted in Thomas, *Portrait,* 154; Horace White wrote to Herndon, Jan. 18, 1890, that *Herndon's Lincoln* "was the best American biography that has ever been written." Herndon-Weik Papers.

[13]Donald, *Lincoln's Herndon*, 372, and *Lincoln Reconsidered*, 161.

[14]S. Stakelberg's interview with Tolstoy, *N.Y. World*, Feb. 7, 1909; see also Woldman, *Lincoln and the Russians*, 272-6. Interestingly, I was unable to locate this seemingly authentic interview in the definitive edition of Tolstoy's work: *Polnoe sobranie sochinenii*. Pod obshchei red. V. G. Chertkova. Iubilenoe izd. (91 vols., Moscow, 1928-1964).

[15]Quoted in Quarles, *Lincoln and the Negro*, 245.

[16]Beard to Beveridge, Apr. 23, 1925; cf. Apr. 14, 1926, Beveridge Papers.

[17]Beveridge, *Lincoln*, I, 493; Beveridge to C. Worthington Ford, as quoted in Thomas, *Portrait*, 256; Beveridge to Charles A. Beard, March 25, 1925; to J. Franklin Jameson, Jan. 31, 1925; cf. to Beard, June 20, July 26, 1924; to Jameson, April 21, 1924 and March 30, 1925; to William E. Connelly, Feb. 14, March 30, 1925; to Frank Hodder, May 5, 1925; to George R. Poage, March 30, 1925; to N. W. Stephenson, Apr. 14, 1925; to James A. Woodburn, May 4, 1925. All the above and subsequent citations of Beveridge letters refer to carbon copies in his Papers unless otherwise noted.

[18]Beveridge to Beard, July 26, 1924; Beveridge, *Lincoln*, 236.

[19]Beveridge to Connelly, Apr. 25, 1925, etc.; to N. W. Stephenson, May 30, 1925; to S. E. Morison, June 28, 1925. Boritt, "A Question of Political Suicide?" 83-6, discusses the weaknesses of the Beveridge interpretation.

[20]Jameson to Beveridge, Sept. 20, 1926, also July 9, 1926; cf. Beard to Beveridge, March 3, Apr. 14, 1926. See also Fehrenbacher, "Disunion and Reunion," in John Higham, ed., *Reconstruction of American History* (New York, 1962), 113, and *Changing Image*, 10.

[21]Beveridge to Channing, May 26, 1926, as cited in Claude G. Bowers, *Beveridge and the Progressive Era* (Cambridge, Mass., 1932), 577; (cf. to Angle, Oct. 14, 1926); Holmes to Beveridge, Nov. 17, 1926. For more positive evaluations of Beveridge as a historian see the bibliography for the works of Bowers, John Braeman, Tracy E. Strevey, and Thomas(2).

[22]*Congressman Lincoln*, 249.

[23]George Edmonds [Elizabeth Avery Meriwether], *Facts and Falsehoods Concerning the War on the South, 1861-1865* (Memphis, 1904), 90. Mrs. Meriwether's words are quoted here as an illustration because they are the very ones that Donald chose to exemplify hostile Southern thought toward Lincoln. *Lincoln's Herndon*, 370. On the latter subject see also Michael Davis, *The Images of Lincoln in the South* (Knoxville, Tenn., 1971), *passim*.

[24]*Abraham Lincoln* (2 vols., Boston, 1893), I, 31-4.

[25]*Ibid.*, II, 355-6.

[26]Basler, *Lincoln Legend*, 193.

[27]Sidney E. Mead, *The Lively Experiment: The Shaping of Christianity in America* (New York, 1963), 73 [Mead's essay on Lincoln first appeared in 1954]; Riddle, *Congressman Lincoln*, 249.

[28]Fehrenbacher, "Changing Image," 6. Wolf's revised book was published in 1963 under the title *The Religion of Abraham Lincoln*, and reprinted in 1970 under the title *Lincoln's Religion*.

[29]Black to Herndon, Feb. 16, 1875, Herndon-Weik Papers; Beveridge to Beard, Sept. 26; to Jameson, Oct. 1; to Stephenson, Oct. 21, 1924, etc., Beveridge Papers.

[30]Masters's Review of Beveridge's *Lincoln, N.Y. Tribune,* Sept. 9, 1928; *Lincoln the Man* (New York, 1931), 498; Masters to Dreiser, Jan. 2, 1940, as quoted in Lois Hartley, "Edgar Lee Masters — Biographer and Historian," *JISHS,* 54 (1961), 65.

[31]*C.W.,* I, 65-6. By the 1960's, however, Donald could create a caricature of Lincoln, describing his reconstruction policies thus: "A rather simple computer installed in the White House, fed the elementary statistical information about election returns and programed to solve the recurrent problem of winning re-election, would emerge with the same strategies and the same solutions." Donald, *The Politics of Reconstruction, 1863-1867* (Baton Rouge, La., 1965).

[32]The quotations are from Carman and Luthin, *Lincoln and the Patronage,* 336; Hofstadter, *The American Political Tradition,* 95.

[33]Graebner, ed., *The Enduring Lincoln,* 67.

[34]*Lincoln Reconsidered,* 57, 65.

[35]Williams, "Abraham Lincoln — Principle and Pragmatism in Politics: A Review Article," *MVHR,* 40 (1953), 89-106.

[36]Fehrenbacher, "Disunion and Reunion," in Higham, ed., *Reconstruction of American History,* 113; cf. *Changing Image,* 10. Angle had intended to create for the Illinois Lincoln the counterpart of Randall's President and thus supplant Beveridge. But he gave up the idea. Ruth Painter Randall, *I Ruth: Autobiography of a Marriage* (Boston, 1968), 130.

[37]*Lincoln,* 142.

[38]Duff, *Prairie Lawyer,* 58, 92-3; Beveridge to Henry M. Bates, Jan. 9, 1926; cf. to William H. Townsend, Jan. 3, 1925, etc.

[39]P. 153.

[40]The essay is reprinted in Basler, *A Touchstone for Greatness: Essays, Addresses, and Occasional Pieces About Abraham Lincoln* (Westport, Conn., 1973), 53-100. The piece first appeared in Basler, ed., *Abraham Lincoln: His Speeches and Writings* (Cleveland, 1946), as an expanded version of earlier articles: "Abraham Lincoln — Artist," *North American Review,* 245 (1938), 144-58, and "Abraham Lincoln's Rhetoric," *American Literature,* 11 (1939), 167-82. Basler's work did not prevent the most recent study of Lincoln's literary style from attempting to perpetuate the two Lincolns: David D. Anderson, *Abraham Lincoln* (New York, 1969). For Lincoln as a writer see also the bibliography, especially for the works of Jacques Barzun, Theodore L. Blegen, Daniel Kilham Dodge, and Herbert J. Edwards and John E. Hankins.

[41]P. 185.

[42]See for example the bibliography for the related work of Lewis Henry Croce, Leonard P. Curry, and John Bruce Robertson, all of which ignore Donald's lecture that appeared in both Graebner, ed., *The Enduring Lincoln* and the 1961 ed. of Donald's *Lincoln Reconsidered.*

[43]P. 161.

[44]*Lincoln Reconsidered,* 162.

[45]Kerley's work may help explain why Allan Nevins turned down another Columbia graduate student's idea of a dissertation on Lincoln's economic views with the curt comment: "He had none." This anecdote was related to me by a reliable historian but I was unable to substantiate it by finding the student in question.

[46]"Lincoln and the Goverment Bank," *Social Economist,* 9 (July 1895), 1-11; Randall, "Has the Lincoln Theme Been Exhausted?" 286-7; Hyman, *Lincoln and the Presidency* (Lincoln, Ill., 1965), 8.

[47]*Lincoln the President,* I, 2; and *Lincoln the Liberal Statesman,* 179-81.

[48]Sumner, *Works,* IX, 367-428.

[49]Williams, ed., *Selected Writings of Abraham Lincoln* (New York, 1943), xiv-xvii; "Principle and Pragmatism in Politics," 99-101, and "Lincoln: Pragmatic Democrat," in Graebner, ed., *Enduring Lincoln,* 34-7; Fehrenbacher, ed., *Abraham Lincoln: A Documentary Portrait through His Speeches and Writings* (New York, 1964), xxi-xxii; Current, ed., *The Political Thought of Lincoln,* xiv-xv. David R. Wrone, "Abraham Lincoln's Idea of Property," *Science & Society,* 33 (1969), 54-70, says almost nothing about the subject.

[50]Herndon, *Address on Free Trade vs. Protection. . . .* [n.p., n.d. (Springfield, Ill., 1870)]: a copy of this pamphlet is in the Widener Library, Harvard University. (Cf. Herndon to Horace White, Aug. 26, Nov. 8, Nov. 26, 1890, Horace White Papers, ISHL); Donald, *Lincoln's Herndon,* 260-4.

[51]Another aspect of Lincoln's economic outlook, his views on labor and capital, received some popular attention. See, for example, the bibliography for works by L. Abbott, W. E. Barton(2), O. T. Corson, W. J. Ghent, and W. U. Meese; see also Chapter XIII, note 24; and John G. Nicolay to George C. Hackstaff, Feb. 8, 1896, Nicolay Papers.

[52]Reprinted in *Patriotic Gore,* 126.

[53]I, 651.

[54]To Richard Watson Gilder, Nov. 17, [1888], Hay Correspondence, Huntington Library. In the end the chapter included very little information about Lincoln. Similarly, Herndon's suggestion to Weik that Lincoln's early ideas on internal improvements should be "explained truly and more fully" was ignored. Herndon to Weik, June 13, 1888, Herndon-Weik Papers.

[55]Correspondence between Baringer and the author, in author's possession. Rodney O. Davis, the most thorough student of the Illinois General Assembly during Lincoln's tenure, also recognized, independently, the need to study Lincoln's economics. Davis to author, March 2, 1972.

[56]See also Don E. Fehrenbacher, "Review of Paul Simon, *Lincoln's Preparation for Greatness," AHR,* 72 (1966), 309-10.

[57]Hammond, *Banks and Politics,* 404; and *Sovereignty and an Empty Purse,* 24-5.

[58]*Liberal Statesman,* 177.

[59]*Patriotic Gore,* 108; cf. 121-2.

[60]*C.W.*, II, 275.
[61]*Myths After Lincoln*, 405.
[62]Nicolay and Hay, *Lincoln*, I, 77; Whitney, *Life on the Circuit*, 465.
[63]*C.W.*, IV, 121; cf. L. Chittenden to editor of *Lyceum Herald* n.d. [c. 1891], Judd Stewart Lincolniana, Huntington Library.

cAppendix D
Bibliography
of the items cited in the footnotes

   I. Manuscripts
  II. Newspapers and Periodicals
 III. Law Cases
 IV. Government Documents
  V. Articles, Books, Dissertations, Pamphlets

I. MANUSCRIPTS:
ALTON & SANGAMON RAILROAD COMPANY Stock Subscription Book, ISHL
EDWARD A. ATKINSON PAPERS, Massachusetts Historical Society
NATHANIEL P. BANKS PAPERS, LC
T.J. BARLOW PAPERS, Huntington Library
ALBERT J. BEVERIDGE PAPERS, LC
LETTERS to G. S. BORITT in possession of the author
SIDNEY BREESE PAPERS, ISHL
ORVILLE BROWNING PAPERS, ISHL
HENRY CAREY PAPERS, Historical Society of Pennsylvania
SALMON P. CHASE PAPERS, LC
HENRY CLAY LETTERS, ISHL
DAVID DAVIS PAPERS, Chicago Historical Society
DAVID DAVIS PAPERS, ISHL (all references to the Davis Papers are to this collec-
    tion unless otherwise noted)
HENRY EDDY PAPERS, ISHL
JESSE W. FELL PAPERS, University of Illinois, Urbana
AUGUSTUS C. FRENCH PAPERS, ISHL
SIMEON FRANCIS PAPERS, ISHL
JOSEPH GILLESPIE PAPERS, Chicago Historical Society
BENJAMIN GODFREY PAPERS, ISHL
JOHN J. HARDIN PAPERS, Chicago Historical Society
GEORGE HARRINGTON LETTERS, Huntington Library
GEROGE HARRINGTON mss. (various), Huntington Library
JOHN HAY CORRESPONDENCE, Huntington Library
HAY-MCLELLAN PAPERS, Brown University
WILLIAM H. HERNDON PAPERS, Massachusetts Historical Society
HERNDON-LAMON PAPERS, Huntington Library
HERNDON-WEIK PAPERS, LC

ILLINOIS HISTORICAL SURVEY, University of Illinois, Urbana
KENNEDY FAMILY CORRESPONDENCE, Bidwell Papers, University of California, Berkley
WARD H. LAMON'S untitled ms. sequence to his *Life of Lincoln,* Huntington Library
ABRAHAM LINCOLN ASSOCIATION PAPERS [Lincoln reference file], ISHL
ABRAHAM LINCOLN PAPERS, LC
LINCOLN COLLECTION, University of Chicago
LINCOLN COLLECTION, Huntington Library
UNPUBLISHED LINCOLN PAPERS, ISHL
PAPERS OF LINCOLN'S CABINET MEMBERS, Lincoln National Life Foundation
HUGH MCCULLOCH PAPERS, Indiana University, Bloomington
JOHN G. NICOLAY PAPERS, LC
NATHANIEL POPE PAPERS, ISHL
CHARLES H. RAY PAPERS, Huntington Library
SAMUEL RUGGLES LETTER, ISHL
HENRY SAMUELS ms., ISHL
WILLIAM HENRY SEWARD PAPERS, University of Rochester
WILLIAM HENRY SMITH PAPERS, Ohio State Archives and Historical Society
J. F. SNYDER PAPERS, ISHL
JUDD STEWART LINCOLNIANA, Huntington Library
ROGER TANEY PAPERS, LC
TILLSON CORRESPONDENCE LEDGER, ISHL
LYMAN TRUMBULL PAPERS, LC
W. J. WALDIE LETTER, ISHL
HORACE WHITE PAPERS, ISHL
RICHARD YATES PAPERS, ISHL

II. NEWSPAPERS AND PERIODICALS
A. Illinois:
Alton Telegraph
Belleville Advocate
The [Charleston] *Republican*
Chicago Democrat
Chicago Journal
Chicago Press and Tribune
Chicago Times
Illinois State Register [Springfield]
Jonesboro Gazette
Illinois Gazette [Lacon]
Nauvoo Neighbor
Old Hickory [Springfield]

366

Old Soldier [Springfield]
Olive Branch [Springfield]
Peoria Register
Quincy Whig
Rockford Forum
Sangamo Journal; from 1847 *Illinois Journal;* from 1855 *Illinois State Journal*
  [Springfield]
Tazewell Register
Tazewell Whig
Vandalia Free Press

B. Other:
The American Laborer [New York]
Chester County Times [Pennsylvania]
De Bow's Review [New Orleans]
Fincher's Trades Review [Philadelphia]
The Log Cabin [New York]
Missouri Democrat [St. Louis]
Missouri Republican [St. Louis]
National Intelligencer [Washington, D.C.]
National Magazine [Washington, D.C.]
New York Herald
New York Independent
New York Times
New York Tribune
New York World
Niles' Register [Baltimore]
North American Review [Boston]
The Old Guard [New York]
School and Society [New York]
Social Economist [New York]

III. LAW CASES:
  4 Wheaton 316 (1819)
  1 Howard 311 (1843)
  11 Ill. 254 (1849)
  13 Ill. 504 (1851)
  6 Fed. Cas. 186 (1853) [6 McLean 209]
  6 Fed. Cas. 191 (1853) [6 McLean 70]
  17 Ill. 291 (1854)
  19 Ill. 186 (1857)
  67 U.S. 485 (1862)

27 Ill. 64 (1863)
37 Ill. 1 (1865)
173 U.S. 509 (1899)
277 U.S. 223 (1928)

IV. GOVERNMENT DOCUMENTS:

Annals of Congress
Congressional Globe
Illinois House Journal
Illinois Senate Journal
Illinois Reports
Laws of Illinois
Official Records of the Union and Confederate Armies, The War of Rebellion. 4 series, 70 vols. in 128, Washington, 1880-1901.
Papers Relating to the Foreign Relations of the U.S. 1862. Washington, 1862
Register of Debates
U.S. House Journal
U.S. House Executive Documents
U.S. House Reports
U.S. Senate Executive Documents
U.S. Statutes at Large

V. ARTICLES, BOOKS, DISSERTATIONS, PAMPHLETS:

ABBOTT, LYMAN. "Lincoln as a Labor Leader," *Outlook,* Feb. 27, 1909.

ABRAMOVITZ, MOSES, and DAVID, PAUL. "Reinterpreting Economic Growth: Problems and Realities," *AER,* 63 (1973), 428-39.

ADAMS, EPHRAIM DOUGLAS. *Great Britain and the American Civil War.* 2 vols., New York, 1925.

AMBROSE, STEPHEN A. "Lincoln and Halleck: A Study in Personal Relations," *JISHS,* 52 (1959), 208-16.

ANDER, O. FRITIOF, ed. *The John H. Hauberg Historical Essays.* Rock Island, Ill.; 1954.

———. ed. *Lincoln Images.* Rock Island, Ill., 1960.

ANDERSON, DAVID D. *Abraham Lincoln.* New York, 1970.

ANDREANO, RALPH. ed. *The Economic Impact of the American Civil War.* Cambridge, Mass., 1967.

ANGLE, PAUL M. "Lincoln's Land Holdings and Investments," *ALAB,* 16 (Sept., 1929).

———. ed. *New Letters and Papers of Lincoln.* Boston, 1930.

———. "Lincoln and Liquor," *ALAB,* 19 (June-Sept., 1932).

———. *"Here I Have Lived": A History of Lincoln's Springfield, 1821-1865.* Springfield, Ill., 1935.

————. ed. "Recollections of William Pitt Kellogg," *ALQ*, 3 (1945), 319-39.

————. ed. *Prairie State: Impressions of Illinois, 1673-1967, By Travelers and Other Observers*. Chicago, 1968.

ANKLI, ROBERT A. "Agricultural Growth in Ante-Bellum Illinois," *JISHS*, 58 (1970), 387-98.

ARIELI, YEHOSHUA. *Individualism and Nationalism in American Ideology*. Cambridge, Mass. 1964.

ARNOLD, ISSAC. *The History of Abraham Lincoln and the Overthrow of Slavery*. Chicago, 1866.

————. *The Life of Abraham Lincoln*. Chicago, 1885.

————. *Reminiscences of the Illinios Bar Forty Years Ago*. [Chicago], 1881.

ASCHER, LEONARD WILLIAM. "The Economic History of the New Almaden Mine, 1845-1863." Ph.D. Dissertation, University of Southern California, 1934.

————. "Lincoln's Administration and the New Almaden Scandal," *Pacific Hist. Rev.*, 5 (1936), 38-51.

BAIRD, HENRY CAREY. "Carey and Two of his Recent Critics," *Proc. of Am. Phil. Society*, 29 (1891), 166-73.

BALLARD, COLIN R. *The Military Genius of Abraham Lincoln: An Essay*. London, 1926.

BAKER, GEORGE E. ed. *The Works of William Seward*. 5 vols. Cambridge and Boston, 1853-1884.

BARDOLPH, RICHARD. "Illinois Agriculture in Transition, 1820-1870," *JISHS*, 61 (1948), 244-64, 415-37.

BARINGER, WILLIAM E. *Lincoln's Rise to Power*. Boston, 1937.

————. *A House Dividing*. Springfield, Ill., 1945.

————. *Lincoln's Vandalia: A Pioneer Portrait*. New Brunswick, N.J., 1949.

BARRETT, DON CARLOS. *Greenbacks and Resumption of Specie Payments, 1862-1879*. Cambridge, Mass. 1931.

BAACK, BENNETT D. and RAY, EDWARD J. "Tariff Policy and Income Distribution: The Case of the United States, 1830-1860," *EEH*, 11 (1973-4), 103-17.

BARTON, WILLIAM E. *The Soul of Abraham Lincoln*. New York, 1920.

————. "Lincoln and Labor," *Life and Labor*, Feb., 1921, 35-9.

————. *The Life of Abraham Lincoln*. 2 vols. Indianapolis, 1925

————. *The Lineage of Lincoln*. Indianapolis, 1929.

————. "The Lincoln of the Biographers," *Trans. of ISHS*, 36 (1929), 81-6.

BARZUN, JACQUES. "Lincoln as a Writer," in *Jacques Barzun on Writing, Editing, and Publishing*, Chicago, 1971.

BASLER, ROY P. *The Lincoln Legend, A Study of Changing Conceptions*. Boston, 1935.

_____. "Abraham Lincoln — Artist," *North Am. Rev.,* 245 (1938), 144-58.

_____. "Abraham Lincoln's Rhetoric," *Am. Literature,* 11 (1939), 167-82.

_____. ed. *The Abraham Lincoln: His Speeches and Writings.* Cleveland, 1946.

_____. ed., Pratt, Marion Dolores, and Dunlap, Lloyd A. asst. eds. *The Collected Works of Abraham Lincoln.* 9 vols., New Brunswick, N. J., 1953-55.

_____. *A Touchstone for Greatness: Essays, Addresses and Occasional Pieces about Abraham Lincoln.* Westport, Conn., 1973.

_____. ed. *The Collected Works of Abraham Lincoln, Supplement, 1832-1865.* Westport, Conn., 1974.

BATES, DAVID HOMER. *Lincoln in the Telegraph Office. . . .* New York, 1907.

BAXTER, MAURICE. *Orville H. Browning, Lincoln's Critic and Friend.* Bloomington, Ind. 1957.

BEALE, HOWARD K. ed. *Diary of Gideon Welles.* 3 vols., New York, 1960.

BEARD, CHARLES A. and MARY R. *The Rise of American Civilization.* New York, 1934.

BELZ, HERMAN. *Reconstructing the Union: Theory and Policy During the Civil War.* Ithaca, N. Y., 1969.

BENNET, LERONE, JR., "Was Abe Lincoln a White Supremacist?" *Ebony,* Feb., 1968, 35, 40, 43.

BENSON, LEE. *The Concept of Jacksonian Democracy: New York as a Test Case.* Princeton, N.J., 1961.

BENSON, SUMNER, in C. S. Benson, *et al. The American Property Tax: Its History, Administration, and Economic Impact.* Clarement, Cal., 1965.

BENTON, THOMAS HART. *A Refutation of the Calumnies of the British Whig Party.* Washington, 1839.

_____. *Thirty Years' View. . . .* 2 vols. New York, 1854-56.

BERNARD, KENNETH. "Lincoln and Civil Liberties," *ALQ,* 6 (1951), 375-399.

_____. *Lincoln and the Music of the Civil War.* Caldwell, Idaho, 1966.

BERQUIST, JAMES M. "People and Politics in Transition: The Illinois Germans, 1850-60," in Fredrick C. Luebke, ed., *Ethnic Voters and the Election of Lincoln.* Lincoln, Neb., 1971.

BERRY, THOMAS SENIOR. *Western Prices Before 1861: A Study of the Cincinnati Market.* Cambridge, Mass. 1943.

BERWANGER, EUGENE H. *The Frontier Against Slavery: Western Anti-Negro Prejudice and the Slavery Extension Controversy.* Urbana, Ill. 1967.

BEVERIDGE, ALBERT J. *Abraham Lincoln, 1809-1858.* 2 vols., Boston, 1928.

BIDWELL, PERCY WELLS and FALCONER, JOHN I. *History of Agriculture in the Northern United States, 1620-1860.* Washington, 1925.

BILLINGTON, RAY ALLEN. *The Far Western Frontier, 1830-1860.* New York, 1956.

BIRD, RICHARD M. and OLDMAN, OLIVER, eds., *Readings on Taxation in Developing Countries,* Baltimore, 1964.

BLAINE JAMES GILLESPIE. *Twenty Years of Congress: from Lincoln to Garfield.* 2 vols., Norwich, Conn. 1884-86.

BLAIR, HARRY C. AND TARSIS, REBECCA. *Lincoln's Constant Ally: The Life of Colonel Edward D. Baker.* Portland, Ore., 1960.

BLEGEN, THEODORE C. *Lincoln's Imagery: A Study in Word Power.* LaCrosse, Wisc., 1954.

BLAU, JOSEPH LEON, ed. *Social Theories of Jacksonian Democracy.* New York, 1947.

BLUMIN, STUART. "Mobility and Change in Ante-Bellum Philadelphia," in Thernstrom, Stephen and Sennett, Richard, eds. *Nineteenth-Century Cities: Essays in the New Urban History.* New Haven, Conn., 1969.

BOGUE, ALLEN G. *From Prairie to Corn Belt: Farming on the Illinois and Iowa Prairies in the Nineteenth Century.* Chicago, 1963.

_____. and Bogue, Margaret Beattie. " 'Profits' and the Frontier Land Speculator," *JEH,* 17 (1957), 1-24.

BOGUE, MARGARET BEATTIE. *Patterns from the Sod: Land Use and Tenure in the Grand Prairie, 1850-1900.* Springfield, Ill., 1959.

BONHAM, JERIAH. *Fifty Years' Recollections.* Peoria, Ill., 1883.

BOORSTIN, DANIEL J. *The Mysterious Science of the Law.* Cambridge, Mass., 1941.

BORITT, G.S. "Old Wine Into New Bottles: Abraham Lincoln and the Tariff Reconsidered," *Hist.,* 28 (1966), 289-317.

_____. "Lincoln and Taxation during the Illinois Legislative Years," *JISHS,* 61 (1968), 365-73.

_____. "Lincoln and the Economics of the American Dream: The Whig Years, 1832-1854," Ph.D. Dissertation, Boston University, 1968.

_____. "A Question of Political Suicide? Lincoln's Opposition to the Mexican War," *JISHS,* 67 (1974), 79-100.

_____. "A New Lincoln Text: An Opinion on an Illinois Tax," *LH,* 75 (1973), 152-7.

_____. "Another New Lincoln Text? Some Thoughts Concerning an Outrageous Suggestion about Abraham Lincoln 'Corporation Lawyer,' " *LH* 77 (1975), 27-33.

_____. "The Voyage to the Colony of Linconia: The Sixteenth President, Black Colonization, and the Defense Mechanism of Avoidance," *Hist.* 37 (1975), 619-33.

_____. "The Thrust of Abraham Lincoln," in Sidney Fine and Gerald S. Brown, eds. *The American Past: Conflicting Interpretations of the Great Issues.* 2 vols. New York, 1976.

BOUTWELL, GEORGE S. *Reminiscences of Sixty Years in Public Affairs.* New York, 1902.

BOWERS, CLAUDE G. *Beveridge and the Progressive Era.* Boston, 1932.

371

BOYLAN, JOSEPHINE. "Illinois Highways, 1700-1848, Roads, Rivers, Ferries, Canals," *JISHS*, 26 (1917), 5-59.

BRADLEY, ERWIN S. *Simon Cameron, Lincoln's Secretary of War: A Political Biography*. Philadelphia, 1966.

BRADNER, ERIC JOHN. "The Attitude of Illinois Toward Western Expansion in the 1840's." Ph.D. Dissertation, Northwestern University, 1942.

BRAEMAN, JOHN. *Albert J. Beveridge, American Nationalist*. Chicago, 1971.

BRAUER, KINLEY J., *Cotton versus Conscience: Massachusetts Whig Politics and Southwestern Expansion, 1843-1848*. Lexington, Kentucky, 1967.

BRODIE, FAWN M. *Thaddeus Stevens, Scourge of the South*. New York, 1959.

BROOKS, GWENDOLYN, *et al*. *A Portion of that Field*. Urbana, Ill., 1967.

BROOKS, NOAH. *Washington in Lincoln's Time*. New York, 1895.

————. "Personal Recollections of Abraham Lincoln," *Harper's Monthly*, 31 (1865), 220-30.

BROWN, CHARLES LEROY. "Abraham Lincoln and the Illinois Central Railroad, 1857-1860," *JISHS*, 35 (1943), 121-63.

BROWN, D. PETER. "The Economic Views of Illinois Democrats, 1836-1861." Ph.D. Dissertation, Boston University, 1970.

BRUCE, ROBERT V. *Lincoln and the Tools of War*, Indianapolis, 1956.

BRUCHEY, STUART W. *The Roots of American Economic Growth, 1607-1861*. New York, 1965.

BUTLER, BENJAMIN. *Autobiography and Personal Reminiscences . . . Butler's Book*. Boston, 1892.

CAIRNES, JOHN E. *The Slave Power. . . .* New York, 1862.

CALLANAN, HAROLD J. "The Political Economy of John Quincy Adams." Ph.D. Dissertation, Boston University, forthcoming.

CAMERON, RONDO. *Banking in the Early Stages of Industrialization: A Study in Comparative Economic History*. New York, 1967.

CAREY, HENRY C. *Essay on the Rate of Wages. . . .* Philadelphia, 1835.

————. *Answers to the Questions. . . . Currency*. Philadelphia, 1840.

————. "Centralization," in *The Plough, the Loom and the Anvil*, 3 and 4, 1851-52.

————. *Principles of Political Economy. . . .* 3 vols. Philadelphia, 1837-40.

————. *The Slave Trade*. Philadelphia, 1853.

————. *Principles of Social Science*, 3 vols., Phildelphia. 1858-60.

————. *Financial Crises: Their Cause and Effects*. Philadelphia, 1864.

CAREY, ROBERT LINCOLN. *Daniel Webster as an Economist*. New York, 1929.

CARLSON, THEODORE L. *The Illinois Military Tract: A Study of Land Occupation, Utilization and Tenure*. Urbana, Ill., 1951.

CARMAN, HARRY J. and LUTHIN, REINHARD H. *Lincoln and the Patronage*, New York, 1943.

CARPENTER, F.B. *Six Months at the White House with Abraham Lincoln.* New York, 1866.

CARROLL, DANIEL B. *Henri Mercier and the American Civil War.* Princeton, N.J. 1971.

CASE, LYNN M. and SPENCER, WARREN F. *The United States and France: Civil War Diplomacy.* Philadelphia, 1970.

CATTERALL, RALPH C. H. *The Second Bank of the United States.* Chicago, 1903.

CATTON, BRUCE. *The Centennial History of the Civil War.* 3 vols., New York, 1961-65.

————. *Grant Takes Command.* Boston, 1969.

CAVANAGH, HELEN M. *Funk of Funk's Grove.* Bloomington, Ill., 1952.

CAWELTI, JOHN G. *Apostles of the Self-Made Man: Changing Concepts of Success in America.* Chicago, 1965.

CHAMBERS, WILLIAM NISBET. *Old Bullion Benton, Senator from the New West: Thomas Hart Benton.* Boston, 1956.

————. "Election of 1840," in Arthur M. Schlesinger, Fred L. Israel, and William P. Hansen, eds., *History of American Presidential Elections, 1789-1968.* 3 vols., New York, 1973, I, 643-90.

CHARNWOOD, LORD, *Abraham Lincoln.* New York, 1917.

CHITWOOD, O. P. *John Tyler, Champion of the Old South.* New York, 1939.

CLARK, JOHN G. *The Grain Trade of the Old Northwest.* Urbana, Ill. 1966.

CLARK, THOMAS D. *Frontier America.* New York, 1969.

CLARK, VICTOR. *History of Manufactures in the United States.* 2 vols., Washington, D.C. 1916-28.

CLEAVES, FREEMAN. *Old Tippecanoe: William Henry Harrison and His Time.* New York, 1939.

COCHRAN, THOMAS C. and MILLER, WILLIAM. *The Age of Enterprises: A Social History of Industrial America.* New York, 1961.

COLE, ARTHUR C. *Lincoln's "House Divided" Speech: Does It Reflect a Doctrine of Class Struggle?* Chicago, 1923.

————. *The Civil War Era, 1848-1870.* The Centennial History of Illinois, Vol. III. Springfield, 1919.

COLE, ARTHUR H. *The American Wool Manufacture.* 2. vols., Cambridge, Mass. 1926.

————. and SMITH, WALTER BUCKINGHAM. *Fluctuations in American Business, 1790-1860.* Cambridge, Mass. 1935.

————. *Wholesale Commodity Prices in the United States, 1700-1861, Statistical Supplement.* Cambridge, Mass., 1938.

COLEMAN, CHARLES H. *Abraham Lincoln and Coles County, Illinois.* New Brunswick, N.J., 1955.

COLEMAN, PETER J. *Debtors and Creditors in America: Insolvency, Imprisonment, and Bankruptcy, 1607-1900.* Madison, Wisc. 1974.

373

COLTON, CALVIN. *The Crisis of the Country.* By "Junius." Philadelphia, 1840.

————. *The Junius Tracts.* New York, 1844.

————. *The Life and Times of Henry Clay.* 2 vols., New York, 1846.

————. *The Rights of Labor.* New York, 1847.

————. *Public Economy for the United States.* New York, 1848.

————. ed., *The Works of Henry Clay.* 6 vols., New York, 1855.

COMMONS, JOHN R., *et al., History of Labour in the United States.* 4 vols., New York, 1918-35.

CONNOR, SEYMOUR V. and FAULK, ODIE B. *North America Divided: The Mexican War, 1846-1848.* New York, 1971.

COOK, ADRIAN. *The Armies of the Streets: The New York City Draft Riots of 1863.* Lexington, Ky., 1974.

COOKE, JACOB E. ed. *Frederick Bancroft, Historian.* Norman, 1957.

COOLIDGE, CALVIN. *Foundations of the Republic.* New York, 1926.

COOPER, THOMAS. *Lectures on the Elements of Political Economy.* Columbia, S.C., 1826.

CORNISH, DUDLEY. T. *The Sable Arm: Negro Troops in the Union Army, 1861-1865.* New York, 1956.

CORSON, O. T. "Lincoln on the Relation of Labor to Capital." *Ohio Ed. Monthly,* Jan., 1923, 1-4.

COULTER, E. MERTON. "Effects of Secession Upon the Commerce of the Mississippi Valley," *MVHR,* 3 (1916), 275-300.

————. *The Confederate States of America, 1860-1865.* Baton Rouge, 1950.

COX, LaWANDA F. "Tenancy in the United States, 1865-1900: A Consideration of the Validity of the Agricultural Ladder Hypothesis," *AH,* 18 (1944), 97-105.

————. "The Promise of Land to the Freedman," *MVHR,* 45 (1958), 413-40.

COX, NANCY L. "A Life of John Hardin of Illinois, 1810-1847." M. A. Thesis, Miami University, 1964.

CRAVEN, AVERY. *The Repressible Conflict, 1830-1861.* University, La., 1939.

————. *The Coming of the Civil War.* New York, 1942

CROCE, LEWIS HENRY. "The Lincoln Administration." Ph.D. Dissertaion, University of Maryland, 1968.

CUNLIFEE, MARCUS, ed. *The Life of Washington* by Mason L. Weems, Cambridge, Mass., 1962.

CURRENT, RICHARD N. *Old Thad Stevens: A Story of Ambition.* Madison, 1942.

————. "Lincoln and Daniel Webster," *JISHS* 48 (1955), 307-21.

————. *Daniel Webster and the Rise of National Conservatism.* Boston, 1955.

————. *The Lincoln Nobody Knows.* New York, 1958.

————. "God and the Strongest Battalions," in David Donald, ed., *Why the North Won The Civil War,* London, 1962, 3-22.

_____. *Lincoln and the First Shot*. Philadelphia, 1963.

_____. ed. *The Political Thought of Abraham Lincoln.* Indianapolis, 1967.

CURRY, LEONARD P. *Blueprint for Modern America: Nonmilitary Legislation of the First Civil War Congress.* Nashville, 1968.

CURTI, MERLE, E. "Young America," *AHR*, 32 (1926), 34-55.

_____. "The Impact of the Revolution of 1848 on American Thought," in Edward N. Saveth, ed., *Understanding the American Past.* Boston, 1956, 134-50.

_____. *The Making of an American Community: A Case Study of Democracy in a Frontier County.* Stanford, 1959.

_____. *The Roots of Loyalty.* New York, 1968.

CURTIS, JAMES C. *The Fox at Bay: Martin Van Buren and the Presidency, 1837-1841.* Lexington, Ky., 1970.

CURTISS, DANIEL S. *Western Portraiture and Emigrant's Guide: A Description of Wisconsin, Illinois and Iowa.* New York, 1852.

CURTISS, GEORGE B. "Abraham Lincoln Protectionist," *The Defender*, Doc. 1, 1916.

DAHL, CURTIS. "Lincoln Saves a Reformer," *Am. Heritage*, 23 (Oct., 1974).

DAVID, PAUL. A. "The Growth of Real Product in the United States Before 1840: New Evidence, Controlled Conjectures," *JEH*, 27 (1967), 151-97.

_____. "Learning by Doing and Tariff Protection: A Reconsideration of the Case of Ante-Bellum United States Cotton Textile Industry," *JEH*, 30 (1970), 521-601.

DAVIS, ANDREW MCFARLAND. *The Origin of the National Banking System.* Washington, 1910.

DAVIS, JEFFERSON. *The Rise and Fall of the Confederate Government.* 2 vols. New York, 1881.

DAVIS, MICHAEL. *The Images of Lincoln in the South.* Knoxville, Tenn., 1971.

DAVIS, RODNEY OWEN. "Illinois Legislators and Jacksonian Democracy, 1834-1841." Ph.D. Dissertation, University of Iowa, 1966.

DAVIS, R. EDWARD. *Early Illinois Paper Money.* Chicago, [n.d.]

DENNETT, TYLER, ed. *Lincoln and the Civil War, in the Diaries and Letters of John Hay.* New York, 1939.

DEW, THOMAS R. *Essay on the Interest of Money and the Policy of Laws Against Usury.* Shellsbanks, Va., 1834.

DEWEY, DAVIS R. *State Banking Before the Civil War.* Washington, 1910.

_____. *The Second United States Bank.* Washington, 1910.

DEYRUP, FELICIA. "Social Mobility as a Major Factor in Economic Development," *Social Research*, 34 (1967), 333-46.

DICK, EVERETT. *The Lure of the Land: A Social History of the Public Lands From the Articles of Confederation to the New Deal.* Lincoln, Neb., 1970.

DILLON, MERTON L. *Elijah P. Lovejoy, Abolitionist Editor.* Urbana, Ill. 1961.

DODGE, DANIEL KILHAM. *Abraham Lincoln: The Evolution of His Literary Style.* Urbana, 1900.

_____. *Abraham Lincoln: Master of Words.* New York, 1924.

DODGE, GRENVILLE M. *How We Built the Union Pacific Railway.* Washington, 1910.

_____. *Personal Recollections.* Council Bluffs, Iowa, 1914.

DONALD, DAVID HERBERT. *Lincoln's Herndon.* New York, 1948.

_____. *Lincoln Reconsidered: Essays on the Civil War Era.* New York, 1956, 1961.

_____. ed., *Why the North Won the Civil War.* London, 1962.

_____. *Charles Sumner.* 2 vols., New York, 1961-70.

_____. *The Politics of Reconstruction, 1863-1867.* Baton Rouge, 1965.

DONALDSON, THOMAS. *The Public Domain.* . . . Washington, 1884.

DORFMAN, JOSEPH. *The Economic Mind in American Civilization.* 5 vols., New York, 1946-59.

_____. "The Jackson Wage-Earner Thesis," *AHR,* 54 (1949), 296-306.

DOUGLASS, FREDERICK. *The Life and Times of Frederick Douglass.* . . . New York, 1962.

DOWRIE, GEORGE WILLIAM. *The Development of Banking in Illinois, 1817-1863.* Urbana, 1913.

DUBERMAN, MARTIN. *Charles Francis Adams.* Boston, 1961.

_____. ed. *The Antislavery Vanguard.* Princeton, 1964.

DUFF, JOHN J. *Abraham Lincoln, Prairie Lawyer.* New York, 1960.

DULLES, FOSTER RHEA. *Labor in America.* New York, 1949.

DUNNE, GERALD T. *Justice Story and the Rise of the Supreme Court.* New York, 1970.

DURDEN, ROBERT F. *The Gray and the Black: The Confederate Debate on Emancipation.* Baton Rouge, 1972.

EASTERLIN, RICHARD A. in Lance E. Davis, *et al., American Economic Growth.* . . . New York, 1972.

EATON, CLEMENT. *Henry Clay and the Art of American Politics.* Boston, 1957.

EATON, JOHN. *Grant, Lincoln and the Freedmen,* New York, 1907.

EDMONDS, GEORGE [Elizabeth Avery Meriwether] *Facts and Falsehoods Concerning the War on the South, 1861-1865.* Memphis, Tenn., 1904.

EDWARDS, HERBERT J. and HANKINS, JOHN E. *Lincoln as a Writer: The Development of His Literary Style.* Orono, Maine, 1962.

EDWARDS, NINIAN, *History of Illinois From 1778 to 1883, and Life and Times of Ninian Edwards.* Springfield, Ill., 1870.

EDWARDS, RICHARD C. "Economic Sophistication in Congressional Tariff Debates," *JEH,* 30 (1970), 802-38.

EISENDRATH, JOSEPH L. "Lincoln's First Appearance on the National Scene, July, 1847," *LH,* 76 (1974), 59-62.

EISELEN, MALCOLM ROGERS. *The Rise of Pennsylvania Protectionism.* Philadelphia, 1932.

ELAZAR, DAVID J. "Gubernatorial Power and the Illinois and Michigan Canal: A Study of Political Development in the Nineteenth Century," *JISHS,* 58 (1965), 396-423.

EKIRCH, ARTHUR A. *The Idea of Progress in America, 1815-1860.* New York, 1944.

ELLISON, MARY. *Support for Secession: Lancashire and the American Civil War.* Chicago, 1972.

ELY, RICHARD T. *Taxation in American States and Cities.* New York, 1888.

ERICKSON, CHARLOTTE. *American Industry and the European Immigrant, 1860-1885.* Cambridge, Mass., 1957.

ERICKSON, ERLING A. *Banking in Frontier Iowa, 1836-1865.* Ames, Ia. 1971.

EVANS, GEORGE. *Reply to McDuffie's Second Speech on the Tariff.* Washington, 1844.

EVERETT, ALEXANDER H. *America, or a General Survey.* Philadelphia, 1827.

—————. "British Opinions on the Protecting System," *No. Am. Review,* 30 (1830), 160-216.

FARNHAM, W. D. "'The Weakened Spirit of Government': A Study in Nineteenth Century American History," *AHR,* 68 (1963), 662-80.

FEHRENBACHER, DON E. *Chicago Giant: A Biography of "Long John" Wentworth.* Madison, Wisc., 1957.

—————. *Prelude to Greatness: Lincoln in the 1850's.* Stanford, 1962.

—————. ed. *Abraham Lincoln: A Documentary Portrait Through His Speeches and Writings.* New York, 1964.

—————. "Review of Paul Simon, *Lincoln's Preparation for Greatness,*" *AHR,* 72 (1966), 309-10.

—————. *The Changing Image of Lincoln in American Historiography.* Oxford, 1968.

—————. "Only His Stepchildren: Lincoln and the Negro," *CWH,* 20 (1974), 293-310.

FERGUS, ROBERT. compiler, *Chicago River and Harbor Convention.* Chicago, 1892.

FIELD, DAVID DUDLEY. *Speech of David Dudley Field at the Chicago Convention.* New York, 1847. Also in *Democratic Review,* 21 (1847), 189-202.

—————. *Speeches, Arguments, and Miscellaneous Papers of David Dudley Field.* ed. by A. P. Sprague, 3 vols., New York, 1884.

FIELD, HENRY M. *The Life of David Dudley Field.* New York, 1898.

FISHER, F. M. and TEMIN, PETER. "Regional Specialization and the Supply of Wheat in the U.S., 1867-1941," *RES,* 52 (1970), 134.

FISHLOW, ALBERT. *American Railroads and the Transportation of the Ante-Bellum Economy.* Cambridge, Mass., 1965.

377

FITE, EMERSON DAVID. *The Presidential Campaign of 1860*. New York, 1911.

FITZHUGH, GEORGE. *Sociology for the South: or, The Failure of Free Society*. Richmond, Va., 1854.

FLEISIG, HEYWOOD. "The Union Pacific Railroad and the Railroad Land Grant Controversy," *EEH*, 11 (1973-4), 155-72.

FOGEL, ROBERT W. *The Union Pacific Railroad*. Baltimore, 1960.

_____. *Railroads and American Economic Growth*. . . . Baltimore, 1964.

_____. and Engerman, Stanley L. *Time On the Cross*. 2 vols., Boston, 1974.

_____. and Engerman, Stanley L. eds. *The Reinterpretation of American Economic History*. New York, 1971.

FONER, ERIC. *Free Soil, Free Labor, Free Men: The Ideology of the Republican Party before the Civil War*. New York, 1970.

FONER, PHILIP S. *Business and Slavery: The New York Merchants and the Irrepressible Conflict*. Chapel Hill, 1941.

_____. *History of the Labor Movement in the United States*. 4 vols., New York, 1947-65.

_____. *Life and Writings of Frederick Douglass*. 4 vols., New York, 1950-55.

FORD, THOMAS. *A History of Illinois from the Commencement as a State in 1818 to 1847*. Chicago, 1854.

FORD, WORTHINGTON CHAUNCY. *The Campaign of 1844*. Worcester, Mass., 1909.

FORNEY, JOHN W. *Anecdotes of Public Men*. 2 vols., New York, 1873-81.

FRANK, JOHN P. *Lincoln as a Lawyer*. Urbana, 1961.

FRANKLIN, JOHN HOPE. *The Emancipation Proclamation*. New York, 1963.

FREDERICKSON, GEORGE M. *The Black Image in the White Mind: The Debate on Afro-American Character and Destiny*. New York, 1971.

_____. "A Man but Not a Brother: Abraham Lincoln and Racial Equality," *JSH*, 41 (1975), 39-58.

FREEHLING, WILLIAM W. *Prelude to Civil War: The Nullification Controversy in South Carolina, 1816-1836*. New York, 1966.

FREIDEL, FRANK, ed., *Union Pamphlets of the Civil War, 1861-1865*. 2 vols., Cambridge, Mass., 1967.

FRIDEMAN, MILTON. "The Role of War in American Economic Development: Price, Money and Monetary Change in Three War-Time Periods," *AER*, 42 (1951), 612-625.

FUESS, CLAUDE M. *Daniel Webster*. 2 vols., Boston, 1930.

FUTRELL, ROBERT F. "Federal Trade with the Confederate States, 1861-1865: A Study of Governmental Policy." Ph.D. Dissertation, Vanderbilt University, 1950.

GALLMAN, ROBERT E. "Commodity Output, 1839-1899," in William N. Parker, ed., *Trends in the American Economy in the Nineteenth Century*. Princeton, 1960.

GARNETT, CHARLES HUNTER. *State Banks of Issue in Illinois*. Urbana, 1898.

GATELL, FRANK OTTO. "Consciousness and Judgment: The Bolt of the Massachusetts Conscience Whigs," *Hist,* 21 (1958), 18-45.

_____. *John Gorham Palfrey and the New England Conscience.* Cambridge, Mass., 1963.

GATES, PAUL W. "Large-Scale Farming in Illinois, 1850 to 1870," *AH,* 6 (1932), 14-25.

_____. *The Illinois Central and Its Colonization Work.* Cambridge, Mass., 1934.

_____. "The Role of the Land Speculator in Western Development," *Pa. Mag. of Hist. and Biog.,* 66 (1942), 314-33.

_____. "Frontier Landlords and Pioneer Tenants," *JISHS,* 38 (1945), 143-206.

_____. "Frontier Estate Builders and Farm Laborers," in Walker D. Wyman and Clifton B. Krocher, eds., *The Frontier in Perspective.* Madison, Wisc., 1965.

_____. *The Farmer's Age: Agriculture, 1815-1860.* New York, 1960.

_____. *Agriculture and the Civil War.* New York, 1965.

_____. *History of Public Land Law Development.* Washington, 1968.

GAUS, JOHN M. and WOLCOTT, LEON O. *Public Administration and the United States Department of Agriculture.* Chicago, 1940.

GENOVESE, EUGENE. *The Political Economy of Slavery.* New York, 1965.

_____. *Roll, Jordan, Roll: The World the Slaves Made.* New York, 1974.

GERHARD, FRED. *Illinois As It Is.* Chicago, 1857.

GERTEIS, LOUIS S. *From Contraband to Freedman: Federal Policy Towards Southern Blacks, 1861-1865.* Westport, Conn., 1973.

_____. "Salmon P. Chase, Radicalism, and the Politics of Emancipation, 1861-1864," *JAH,* 60 (1973), 42-62.

GHENT, W. J. "Lincoln and Labor," *Independent,* 66 (Feb., 11, 1909), 301-5.

GILBERT, ABBY L. "Of Banks and Politics: The Bank Issue and the Election of 1840," *W. Va. Hist.,* 34 (1972), 18-45.

GILCHRIST, DAVID T. and LEWIS, W. DAVID, eds. *Economic Change in the Civil War Era.* Greenville, Da., 1965.

GILMORE, JAMES R. *Personal Recollections of Abraham Lincoln and the Civil War.* Boston. 1898.

GILMER, FRANCIS WALKER. *Vindication of the Laws. . . .* Richmond, Va. 1820.

GOLDIN, CLAUDIA. DALE. "The Economics of Emancipation," *JEH,* 33 (1973), 66-85.

GOLEMBE, CARTER HARRY. "State Banks and the Economic Development of the West," Ph.D. Dissertation, Columbia University, 1952.

GOODMAN, H. H. *The United States against Franklin W. Smith.* Boston, 1865.

GOODRICH, CARTER. "The Revulsion Against Internal Improvements," *JEH,* 10 (1950), 145-69.

_____. *Government Promotion of American Canals and Railroads.* New York, 1960.

_____. ed. *Canals and American Economic Development.* New York, 1961.

_____. "Internal Improvements Reconsidered," *JEH,* 30 (1970), 289-311.

GOUGE, WILLIAM. *A Short History of Paper and Money and Banking in the United States.* London, 1833.

GOVAN, THOMAS PAYNE. *Nicholas Biddle, Nationalist and Public Banker, 1786-1844.* Chicago, 1959.

GRAEBNER, NORMAN A. *Empire in the Pacific: A Study in American Continental Expansion.* New York, 1955.

_____. ed. *The Enduring Lincoln.* Urbana, 1959.

GRAY, LEWIS CECIL. *History of Agriculture in the Southern United States to 1860.* 2 vols., Washington, 1933.

GREELEY, HORACE. *The Tariff as it Is.* New York, 1844.

GREEN, ARNOLD W. *Henry Charles Carey, Nineteenth Century Sociologist.* Philadelphia, 1951.

GREEN, GEORGE D. *Finance and Economic Development in the Old South.* Stanford, 1972.

GRIFFEN, CLYDE. "Making it in America: Social Mobility in Mid-Nineteenth Century Poughkeepsie," *N. Y. History,* 51 (1970), 479-500.

GRIFFIN, CLIFFORD S. *Their Brothers' Keeper: Moral Stewardship in the United States, 1800-1865.* New Brunswick, N. J., 1960.

GRISWOLD, A. WHITNEY. "The American Gospel of Success." Ph.D. Dissertation, Yale University, 1933.

GUNDERSON, ROBERT GRAY. *The Log Cabin Campaign.* Lexington, Ky., 1957.

GUNTON, GEORGE. "Lincoln and the Government Bank," *Social Economist,* 9 (July, 1895), 1-11.

GUROWSKI, ADAM. *Diary.* 3 vols., Boston, 1862-6.

HABAKKUK, H. J. *American and British Technology in the Nineteenth Century: The Search for Labour Saving Inventions.* Cambridge, Mass., 1962.

HACKER, LOUIS M. *The Triumph of American Capitalism: The Development of Forces in American History to the Beginning of the Twentieth Century.* New York, 1947.

HAIG, ROBERT MURRAY. *A History of the General Property Tax in Illinois.* Champaign, Ill., 1914.

HALDERMAN, LEONARD G. *National and State Banks: A Study of Their Origins.* Boston, 1931.

HALL, JOHN PHILIP. "The Gentle Craft: A Narrative of Yankee Shoemakers." Ph.D. Dissertation, Columbia University, 1953.

HAMAND, LAVERN MARSHALL. "Ward Hill Lamon: Lincoln's Particular Friend." Ph.D. Dissertation, University of Illinois, 1949.

————. "Lincoln's Particular Friend," in Donald F. Tingley ed., *Essays in Illinois History in Honor of Glenn Huron Seymour.* Carbondale, Ill., 1968, 18-36.

HAMILTON, HOLMAN. *Zachary Taylor.* 2 vols., Indianapolis, 1941-51.

HAMMOND, BRAY. *Banks and Politics in America: From the Revolution to the Civil War.* Princeton, 1958.

————. *Sovereignty and an Empty Purse: Banks and Politics in the Civil War.* Princeton, 1970.

HANDLIN, OSCAR and MARY FLUG. *Commonwealth: A Study of the Role of Government in the American Economy, Massachusetts 1774-1861.* New York, 1947.

HANEY, LEWIS HENRY. *A Congressional History of Railroads in the United States to 1850.* Madison, Wisc., 1908.

HANSEN, ALVIN. H. "Factors Affecting the Trend of Real Wages," *AER,* 15 (1925), 27-42.

HARDING, T. SWANN. *Two Blades of Grass: A History of Scientific Development in the U. S. Department of Agriculture.* Norman, 1947.

HARLOW, ALVIN F. *Old Wires and New Waves: A History of the Telegraph, Telephone, and Wireless.* New York, 1936.

HARRINGTON, FRED A. "A Peace Mission of 1863," *AHR,* 46 (1940), 76-86.

————. *Fighting Politician: Major General N. P. Banks.* Philadelphia, 1948.

HARRIS, NORMAN DWIGHT. *The History of Negro Servitude in Illinois.* Chicago, 1906.

HART, ALBERT BUSHNELL. *Salmon Portland Chase.* Boston, 1899.

HART, CHARLES DESMOND. " 'The Natural Limits of Slavery Expansion': The Mexican Territories as a Test Case," *MA,* 52 (1970), 119-31.

HARTLEY, LOIS. "Edgar Lee Masters — Biographer and Historian," *JISHS,* 54 (1961), 56-83.

HARTZ, LOUIS. *Economic Policy and Democratic Thought: Pennsylvania, 1776-1860.* Cambridge, Mass., 1948.

————. *The Liberal Tradition in America: An Interpretation of American Political Thought since the Revolution.* New York, 1955.

HAY, LOGAN. "Lincoln One Hundred Years Ago," *ALQ,* 1 (1940), 82-91.

HAY, THOMAS R. "The South and the Arming of the Slaves," *MVHR,* 4 (1919), 34-73.

HAYTER, EARL W. *The Troubled Farmer, 1850-1900: Rural Adjustment to Industrialization.* De Kalb, Ill., 1968.

HAZARD, BLANCHE EVANS. *The Organization of the Boot and Shoe Industry in Massachusetts Before 1875.* Cambridge, Mass., 1921.

HEATH, MILTON SIDNEY. *Constructive Liberalism: The Role of the State Government in Georgia to 1860.* Cambridge, Mass., 1954.

HECKMAN, ALLEN. *Lincoln vs. Douglas: The Great Debates Campaign.* Washington, 1967.

HELPER, HINTON ROWAN, *The Impending Crisis of the South: How to Meet It.* New York, 1857.

HENDRICK, BURTON J. *Lincoln's War Cabinet.* Boston, 1946.

HERNDON, WILLIAM. *Address on Free Trade vs. Protection.* n.p., n.d. [Springfield, Ill., 1870]

_____. *Herndon's Lincoln: The True Story of a Great Life.* 3 vols., New York, 1889.

_____. *Herndon's Life of Lincoln.* ed. by Paul M. Angle, Greenwich, Conn., 1961.

HERTZ, EMANUEL. *Abraham Lincoln: A New Portrait.* 2 vols., New York, 1931.

_____. *The Hidden Lincoln: From Letters and Papers of William H. Herndon.* New York, 1938.

HESSELTINE, WILLIAM B. *Lincoln and the War Governors.* New York, 1948.

_____. *Abraham Lincoln: Architect of the Nation.* Fort Wayne, Ind., 1959.

_____. *Lincoln's Plan of Reconstruction.* Tuscaloosa, Ala., 1960.

_____. *Sections and Politics: Selected Essays of William B. Hesseltine.* ed. by Richard N. Current. Madison, Wisc., 1968.

HIBBARD, BENJAMIN H. *A History of Public Land Policies.* New York, 1924.

HICKEY, JAMES T. "Three R's in Lincoln's Education: Rodgers, Riggin, and Rankin," *JISHS*, 52 (1959), 195-207.

HICKS, FREDERICK C. "David Dudley Field," in *Dictionary of American Biography.* 22 vols., New York, 1928-46, VI, 360-2.

HIDY, RALPH. *The House of Baring in American Trade and Finance: English Merchant Bankers at Work, 1763-1861.* Cambridge, Mass., 1949.

HIGHAM, JOHN. ed. *Reconstruction of American History.* New York, 1962.

HIRSHSON, STANLEY P. *Grenville M. Dodge: Soldier, Politician, Railroad Promoter.* Bloomington, 1967.

HOFSTADTER, RICHARD. "The Tariff Issue on the Eve of the Civil War," *AHR*, 44 (1938), 50-5.

_____. *The American Political Tradition and the Men Who Made it.* New York, 1948.

_____. *The Age Of Reform.* New York, 1954.

HOLBERT, GEORGE K. "Lincoln and Linder in Kentucky and Illinois," *LH*, 44 (Feb., Oct.-Dec., 1942), 2-3, 10-12, 2-5.

HOLLAND, J.G. *The Life of Abraham Lincoln.* Springfield, Mass., 1866.

HOLT, MICHAEL FITZGIBBON. *Forging a Majority: The Formation of the Republican Party in Pittsburgh, 1848-1860.* New Haven, 1969.

HOMER, SIDNEY. *A History of Interest Rates.* New Brunswick, N. J. 1963.

HORNER, HARLAN. *Lincoln and Greeley.* Urbana, Ill., 1953.

HOUF, WALTER "Organized Labor in Missouri Politics Before the Civil War," *Mo. Hist. Rev.,* 56 (1962), 244-54.

HOUSE, ALBERT V., JR. "The Trials of a Ghost-Writer of Lincoln Biography —

Chauncy F. Black's Authorship of Lamon's Lincoln," *JISHS*, 31 (1938), 262-96.

HOWARD, ROBERT P. *Illinois: A History of the Prairie State.* Grand Rapids, Mich., 1972.

HOWE, WALTER A. comp., *Documentary of the Illinois and Michigan Canal: Legislation, Litigation, and Titles.* Springfield, Ill. 1957.

HOWELLS, JAMES DEAN. *Life of Abraham Lincoln.* Springfield, Ill., 1938.

HUBER, RICHARD M. *The American Idea of Success.* New York, 1971.

HUGINS, WALTER. *Jacksonian Democracy and the Working Class: A Study of the New York Workingmen's Movement.* Stanford, 1960.

HURST, JAMES WILLARD. *Law and Economic Growth: The Legal History of the Lumber Industry in Wisconsin, 1836-1915.* Cambridge, Mass. 1964.

HUSTON, FRANCIS MURRAY. *Financing an Empire: History of Banking in Illinois.* 4 vols., Chicago, 1926.

HYMAN, HAROLD M. *Lincoln and the Presidency.* "Abraham Lincoln Memorial Lecture." Lincoln, Ill., 1965.

————. ed. *Heard Round the World: The Impact Abroad of the Civil War.* New York, 1969.

————. *A More Perfect Union: The Impact of the Civil War and Reconstruction on the Constitution.* New York, 1973.

Interstate Commerce Commission Reports, vol. 40, "valuation reports." Washington, 1933.

ISLEY, JETER A. *Horace Greeley and the Republican Party, 1853-1861.* Princeton, 1947.

JAFFA, HARRY V. "Expediency and Morality in the Lincoln-Douglas Debates," *The Anchor Review,* 2 (1957), 179-204.

————. *Crisis of the House Divided: An Interpretation of the Issues in the Lincoln-Douglas Debates.* New York, 1959.

————. *Equality and Liberty: Theory and Practice in American Politics.* New York, 1965.

JAMES, F. CYRIL. *The Growth of Chicago Banks.* 3 vols., New York, 1938.

JELLISON, CHARLES A. *Fessenden of Maine, Civil War Senator.* Syracuse, New York, 1962.

JOHANNSEN, ROBERT. ed., *The Letters of Stephen A. Douglas.* Urbana, 1961.

————. "In Search of the Real Lincoln, or Lincoln at the Crossroads," *JISHS,* 61 (1968), 229-47.

————. *Stephen A. Douglas.* New York, 1973.

JOHNSON, LUDWELL. *Red River Campaign: Politics and Cotton in the Civil War.* Baltimore, 1958.

————. "Contraband Trade during the Last Year of the Civil War," *MVHR,* 49 (1963), 635-52.

————. "Beverly Tucker's Canadian Mission, 1864-1865," *JSH,* 29 (1963), 88-99.

————. "Northern Profits and Profiteers: The Cotton Rings of 1864-1865," *CWH,* 12 (1966), 101-15.

————. "Lincoln's Solution to the Problem of Peace Terms, 1864-1865," *JSH,* 34 (1968), 576-86.

————. "Trading with the Union: The Evolution of Confederate Policy," *Va. Mag. of Hist. and Biog.,* 78 (1970) 308-325.

JONES, ROBERT H. "Long Live the King?" *AH,* 37 (1963), 166-69.

JONES, STANLEY LEWELLYN. "Anti-Bank and Anti-Monopoly Movements in Illinois, 1845-1862." Ph.D. Dissertation, University of Illinois, 1947.

————. "Agrarian Radicalism in Illinois' Constitutional Convention of 1862," *JISHS,* 58 (1955), 271-82.

JULIAN, GEORGE W. *Political Recollections, 1840-1872.* Chicago, 1884.

KAEMPFFERT, WALDEMAR. ed. *A Popular History of American Invention.* 2 vols., New York, 1924.

KAISER, CARL WILLIAM. *History of the Academic Protectionist-Free Trade Controversy in America Before 1860.* Philadelphia, 1939.

KAMM, SAMUEL RICKEY. *The Civil War Career of Thomas A. Scott.* Philadelphia, 1940.

KAPLAN, A. D. H. *Henry Charles Carey: A Study in American Economic Thought.* Baltimore, 1931.

KATZ, IRVING. *August Belmont: A Political Biography.* New York, 1968.

KELLER, WILLIAM E., comp., *Newspapers in the Illinois State Historical Library.* Springfield, Ill., 1970.

KELLOGG, WILLIAM. *Labor and Other Capital: The Right of Each Secured. . . .* New York, 1849.

KERBY, ROBERT L. *Kirby Smith's Confederacy: The Trans-Mississippi South, 1863-1865.* New York, 1972.

KINDLEBERGER, CHARLES P. *Economic Development.* New York, 1965.

KING, WILLARD L. *Lincoln's Manager: David Davis.* Cambridge, Mass., 1960.

KINLEY, DAVID. *The Independent Treasury of the United States.* New York, 1893.

KIRKLAND, EDWARD. *The Peacemakers of 1864.* New York, 1927.

KNIGHTS, PETER R. *The Plain People of Boston, 1830-1860.* New York, 1971.

KORN, BERTRAM W. *American Jewry and the Civil War.* New York, 1961.

KRAUSE, WALTER, *Economic Development, The Underdeveloped World and the American Interest.* San Francisco, 1961.

KRENKEL, JOHN H. *Illinois Internal Improvements, 1818-1848.* Cedar Rapids, Ia., 1958.

KRUG, MARK M. *Lyman Trumbull: Conservative Radical.* New York, 1965.

KUHN, MADISON. "Economic Issues and the Rise of the Republican Party in the Northwest." Ph.D. Dissertation, University of Chicago, 1940.

LeDuc, Thomas H. "Public Policy, Private Investment, and Land Use in American Agriculture, 1825-1875," *AH,* 37 (1963), 3-9.

————. "History and Appraisal of U.S. Land Policy to 1862," in Howard W. Ottoson, ed., *Land Use Policy and Problems in the United States.* Lincoln, Nebr. 1963.

Lambert, Oscar Duane. *Presidential Politics in the United States, 1841-1844.* Durham, N. C., 1936.

Lamon, Ward H. *Life of Abraham Lincoln from His Birth to His Inauguration as President.* Boston, 1872.

————. *Recollections of Abraham Lincoln, 1847-1865.* ed. by Dorothy Lamon Teilard. Washington, D. C. 1911.

Learned, Henry Barrett. *The President's Cabinet: Studies in the Origin, Formation and Structure of an American Institution.* New York, 1972.

Leavitt, Charles T. "Attempts to Improve Cattle Breeds in the United States, 1790-1860," *AH,* 7 (1933), 51-67.

Lebergott, Stanley. *Manpower in Economic Growth Since 1800.* New York, 1964.

————. "United States Transportation Advance and Externalities," *JEH,* 26 (1966), 473-61.

Lee, Arthur M. "The Development of an Economic Policy in the Early Republican Party." Ph.D. Dissertation, Syracuse University, 1953.

————. "Henry C. Carey and the Republican Tariff," *Pa. Mag. of Hist.,* 81 (1957), 280-302.

Lee, Judson Fiske. "Transportation — A Factor in the Development of Northern Illinois Previous to 1860," *JISHS,* 10 (1917), 17-85.

Levy, Leonard W. *The Law of the Commonwealth and Chief Justice Shaw.* Cambridge, Mass., 1967.

Lewis, Lloyd. *Myths After Lincoln.* New York, 1929.

Lincoln, Levi. *Remarks in the U. S. House of Representatives, April 6, 1840.* Boston, 1840.

Lincoln, Waldo. *History of the Lincoln Family. . . .* Worcester, Mass., 1923.

Linder, Usher F. *Reminiscences of the Early Bench and Bar in Illinois.* Chicago, 1879.

Lipset, Martin S. and Bendix, Reinhard. *Social Mobility in Industrial Society.* Berkley, 1959.

Lively, Robert A. "The American System: A Review Article," *Business History Review,* 29 (1955), 81-96.

Livermore, Thomas L. *Numbers and Losses in the Civil War in America, 1861-1865.* Boston, 1901.

Logan, Stephen T. "Steven T. Logan Talks About Lincoln," *ALAB,* 12 (1928), 1-5.

Lowitt, Richard. *A Merchant Prince of the Nineteenth Century: William E. Dodge.* New York, 1959.

Luthin, Reinhard H. "Abraham Lincoln and the Massachusetts Whigs in 1848," *New England Qtly.*, 14 (1941), 619-32.

————. "Abraham Lincoln and the Tariff," *AHR*, 49 (1944), 609-29.

————. "Abraham Lincoln Becomes a Republican," *Pol. Sci. Qtly.*, 59 (1944), 420-438.

————. *The First Lincoln Campaign.* Cambridge, Mass., 1944.

————. *The Real Abraham Lincoln: A Complete One Volume History of His Life and Times.* Englewood Cliffs, N. J., 1960.

Macartney, Clarence Edward. *Lincoln and His Cabinet.* New York, 1931.

McCague, James. *Moguls and Iron Men: The Story of the Transcontinental Railroad.* New York, 1964.

————. *The Second Rebellion: The Story of the New York Draft Riots of 1863.* New York, 1968.

McCarthy, Charles H. *Lincoln's Plan of Reconstruction.* New York, 1901.

McCarty, Burke. *Little Sermons in Socialism by Abraham Lincoln.* Los Angeles. n.d. [1910].

McClelland, Clarance P. "Jacob Strawn and John T. Alexander," *JISHS*, 34 (1914), 177-208.

McClelland, Peter D. "Railroads, American Growth, and the New Economic History: A Critique," *JEH*, 27 (March, 1968), 102-23.

McClure, Alexander K. *Recollections of Half a Century.* Salem, Mass., 1902.

McCormack, T. J. ed., *Memoirs of Gustave Koerner, 1809-1896.* 2 vols., Cedar Rapids, Ia., 1909.

McCormick, Eugene I. *James K. Polk: A Political Biography.* Berkley, 1922.

McCormick, Richard P. "Political Development and the Second Party System," in William Nisbet Chambers and Walter Dean Burnham, eds., *The American Party Systems, Stages of Political Development.* New York, 1967, 90-119.

McCulloch, Hugh. *Men and Measures of Half a Century: Sketches and Comments.* New York, 1888.

McFaul, John M. *The Politics of Jacksonian Finance.* Ithaca, N.Y., 1972.

McGrane, Charles. *The Panic of 1837.* Chicago, 1965.

McGrane, Renginald C. *Foreign Bondholders and American State Debts.* New York, 1935.

McKinley, William. *The Tariff in the Days of Henry Clay and Since.* New York, 1896.

McPherson, James M., *The Struggle for Equality: Abolitionists and the Negro in the Civil War and Reconstruction.* Princeton, 1964.

————. *The Negro's Civil War: How American Negroes Felt and Acted During the War for the Union.* New York, 1965.

386

McVickar, John. *Outlines of Political Economy.* New York, 1825.

McWhiney, Grady. ed. *Grant, Lee, Lincoln and the Radicals: Essays on the Civil War* (Evanston, Ill., 1964).

Madeleine, Sister M. Grace. *Monetary and Banking Theories of Jacksonian Democracy.* Philadelphia, 1943.

Malone, Thomas J. "Lincoln's Schooling in Finance," *The Burroughs Clearing House,* 14 (Feb., 1930).

Man, Albon P. "Labor Competition and the New York Draft Riots of 1863," *JNH,* 36 (1951), 375-405.

Mandel, Bernard. *Labor, Free and Slave: Workingmen and the Anti-Slavery Movement in the United States.* New York, 1955.

Mangold, George Benjamin. *The Labor Argument in the American Protective Tariff Discussion.* Madison, 1906.

Marckhoff, Fred R. "Currency and Banking in Illinois Before 1865," *JISHL,* 52 (1959), 365-418.

Marshall, Lynn L. "The Strange Stillbirth of the Whig Party," *AHR,* 72 (1967) 445-68.

Marshall, Alfred. *Industry and Trade.* London, 1919.

Marx, Karl and Engels, Frederich. *The Civil War in the United States.* ed., Richard Enmale, (pseudonym), New York, 1937.

Marx, Leo. *The Machine in the Garden: Technology and the Pastoral Ideal in America.* New York, 1964.

Masters, Edgar Lee. "Review of Beveridge's *Lincoln,*" *New York Tribune,* Sept. 9, 1928.

_____. *Lincoln the Man.* New York, 1931.

May, S. Thomas. "Continuity and Change in the Labor Program of the Union Army and the Freedmen's Bureau," *CWH,* 17 (1971), 247-51.

Mead, Sidney E. *The Lively Experiment: The Shaping of Christianity in America.* New York, 1963.

Mearns, David C. " 'The Great Inventions of the World': Mr. Lincoln and the Books He Read," in *Three Presidents and Their Books.* Urbana, 1955.

Meese, William U. "Abraham Lincoln und Wassewege," *Deutsch-Amerikanische Geschictsblatter,* 8 (July, 1908), 81-99.

Meier, Hugo. "Technology and Democracy, 1800-1860," *MVHR,* 43 (1956), 618-40.

Meneely, A. N. *The War Department, 1861.* New York, 1928.

Merk, Frederick. *Manifest Destiny and Mission in American History: A Reinterpretation.* New York, 1963.

_____. *The Monroe Doctrine and American Expansionism, 1843-1849.* New York, 1966.

_____. "Dissent in the Mexican War," *MHSP,* 81 (1969), 120-36.

METZLER, LLOYD. "Tariffs, the Terms of Trade, and the Distribution of National Income," *Jn. of Pol. Economy,* 57 (1949), 1-29.

MEYERS, MARVIN. *The Jacksonian Persuasion: Politics and Belief.* Stanford, 1957.

MIERS, EARL SCHENCK, BARINGER, WILLIAM E., POWELL, C. PERCY, eds., *Lincoln Day By Day.* 3 vols., Washington, 1960.

MILL, JOHN STUART. *Principles of Political Economy.* London, 1865.

MILLER, DOUGLAS T. *Jacksonian Aristocracy: Class and Democracy in New York, 1830-1850.* New York, 1967.

MILLER, E. *Banking Theories in the United States Before 1860.* Cambridge, 1927.

MILLER, NATHAN. *The Enterprise of a Free People: Aspects of Economic Development in New York State during the Canal Period. 1792-1838.* Ithaca, N.Y., 1962.

MILTON, GEORGE FORT. "The Eve of Conflict: Stephen A. Douglas and the Needless War. Boston, 1934.

————. *Abraham Lincoln and the Fifth Column.* New York, 1942.

MITCHELL, JAMES. *Report on Colonization and Emigration.* Washington, 1862.

MITCHELL, WESLEY CLAIR. *A History of the Greenbacks, 1862-65. . . .* Chicago, 1903.

MONOGHAN, JAY. *Diplomat in Carpet Slippers: Abraham Lincoln Deals with Foreign Affairs.* Indianapolis, 1945.

MONTGOMERY, DAVID. *Labor and the Radical Republicans, 1862-1872.* New York, 1967.

MORRIS, RICHARD B. "Andrew Jackson, Strikebreaker," *AHR,* 55 (1944), 54-68.

MORRISON, RODNEY J. "Henry C. Carey and American Economic Development," *Exp. in Ent. Hist.,* Ser. 2, V (Winter, 1968).

MORSE, JOHN T. *Abraham Lincoln.* 2 vols., Boston, 1893.

————. ed., *Life and Letters of Oliver Wendell Holmes.* 2 vols., Boston, 1896.

MOSES, JOHN. *Illinois, Historical and Statistical.* 2 vols., Chicago, 1889-92.

MOYAN, ROBERT J. *A Whig Embattled: The Presidency under John Tyler.* Lincoln, Nebr. 1954.

NAGEL, PAUL C. *One Nation Indivisible: The Union in American Thought, 1776-1861.* New York, 1964.

————. *This Sacred Trust; American Nationality, 1789-1898.* New York, 1971.

NASH, GARY B. "The Philadelphia Bench and Bar, 1800-1861," *Comp. Studies in Society and History,* 7 (1965), 203-20.

NATHANS, SIDNEY. *Daniel Webster and Jacksonian Democracy.* Baltimore, 1973.

NEELY, MARK E. JR. "Abraham Lincoln's Nationalism Reconsidered," *LH,* 76 (1974), 12-28.

————. "American Nationalism in the Image of Henry Clay: Abraham Lincoln's Eulogy of Henry Clay in Context," *The Register of the Ky. Hist. Soc.,* 73 (1975), 31-60.

NEVINS, ALLEN. *The Ordeal of the Union.* 8 vols., New York, 1947-71.

NICKLASON, FRED. "The Civil War Contracts Committee," *CWH*, 17 (1971), 232-44.

NICOLAY, JOHN G. and HAY, JOHN. *Abraham Lincoln: A History.* 10 vols., New York, 1890.

————. eds., *Complete Works of Abraham Lincoln.* 12 vols., New York, 1905.

NIVEN, JOHN. *Gideon Welles: Lincoln's Secretary of the Navy.* New York, 1973.

NOLEN, RUSSELL. "St. Louis Labor Movement Prior to the Civil War," *Mo. Hist. Rev.,* 34(1939), 18-37.

————. "The Labor Movement in St. Louis from 1860-1890," *Mo. Hist. Rev.,* 34(1940), 157-81.

NORTH, DOUGLAS C. *The Economic Growth of the United States, 1790-1860.* Englewood Cliffs, 1961.

————. *Growth and Welfare in the American Past: A New Economic History.* Englewood Cliffs, 1967.

OBERHOLTZER, ELLIS PAXSON. *Jay Cooke: Financier of the Civil War.* 2 vols., Philadelphia, 1907.

O'CONNOR, THOMAS H. "Lincoln and the Cotton Trade," *CWH,* 7 (1961), 20-35.

————. *Lords of the Loom: the Cotton Whigs and the Coming of the Civil War.* New York, 1968.

OLDROYD, OSBORN H. *The Lincoln Memorial. . . .* Boston, 1882.

OLIVER, WILLIAM, *Eight Months in Illinois with Information to Emigrants.* Newcastle upon Tyne, 1843.

Output, Employment, and Productivity in the United Statues After 1800. National Bureau of Economic Research, Studies in Income and Wealth. No. 30, New York, 1966.

OVERTON, RICHARD C. *Burlington Route: A History of the Burlington Lines.* New York, 1965.

OWSLEY, FRANK L. and OWSLEY, HARRIET C. *King Cotton Diplomacy: Foreign Relations of the Confederate States of America.* Chicago. 1959.

OWSLEY, HARRIET CHAPPELL. "Peace and the Presidential Election of 1864," *Tennessee Historical Review,* 18 (1959), 3-19.

PAGE, EDWIN L. "The Effie Afton Case," *LH,* 58 (1956), 3-10.

PALMER, JOHN. *Bench and Bar in Illinois.* 2 vols., Chicago, 1899.

PARKS, JOSEPH H. "A Confederate Trade Center Under Federal Occupancy, Memphis, 1862 to 1865," *JSH,* 7 (1941), 289-314.

PARKS, ROBERT J. *Democracy's Railroads: Public Enterprise in Jacksonian Michigan.* Port Washington, N.Y., 1972.

PARGELLIS, STANLEY. "Lincoln's Political Philosophy," *ALQ,* 3 (1945), 284-5.

PASSELL, PETER AND SCHMUNDT, MARIA. "Pre-Civil War Land Policy and the Growth of Manufacturing," *EEH,* 9 (1971), 35-48.

PAUL, JAMES C. N. *Rift in the Democracy.* Philadelphia, 1951.

PAUL, RANDOLPH E. *Taxation in the United States.* Boston, 1954.

PAUL, RODMAN W. *California Gold: The Beginning of Mining in the Far West.* Cambridge, Mass., 1947.

_____. *Mining Frontier of the Far West, 1848-1880.* New York, 1963.

PEASE, THEODORE CALVIN. *The Frontier State, 1818-1848.* The Centennial History of Illinois, Vol. II. Chicago, 1922.

_____. *Illinois Election Returns 1818-1848.* Springfield, Ill., 1923.

_____. and Randall, J. G. eds., *The Diary of Orville Hickman Browning.* 2 vols., Springfield, Ill., 1925-33.

PESSEN, EDWARD. *Most Uncommon Jacksonians: The Radical Leaders of the Early Labor Movement.* Albany, N. Y. 1967.

_____. *Jacksonian America: Society, Personality, Politics.* Homewood, Ill., 1969.

_____. *Riches, Class and Power Before the Civil War.* Lexington, Mass., 1973.

PETERSEN, WILLIAM F. *Lincoln-Douglas: The Weather as Destiny.* Springfield, Ill., 1943.

PETERSON, HENRY J. "Lincoln at the Wisconsin State Fair as Recalled by John W. Hoyt," *LH,* 51 (Dec. 1949), 6-10.

PETERSON, MERRILL D. *The Jeffersonian Image in the American Mind.* New York, 1960.

PHILLIPS, WENDELL. *Speeches, Lectures, and Letters.* Boston, 1863.

PHILLIPS, WILLARD. *A Manual of Political Economy.* Boston, 1828.

PIATT, DON. *Memories of Men Who Saved the Union.* New York, 1887.

PIERCE, BESSIE LOUISE. *A History of Chicago.* 3 vols., New York, 1940.

PIERCE, EDWARD L. *Memoir and Letters of Charles Sumner.* 4 vols., Boston, 1893.

PITKIN, THOMAS M. "The Tariff and the Early Republican Party," Ph.D. Dissertation, Western Reserve University, 1935.

_____. "Western Republicans and the Tariff of 1860," *MVHR,* 17 (1940), 401-20.

POLANYI, KARL. *The Great Transformation: The Political and Economic Origins of Our Time.* Boston, 1957.

POLE, J. R. *Abraham Lincoln and the Working Classes of Britain.* London, 1959.

POPE, CLAYNE. "The Impact of the Ante-Bellum Tariff on Income Distribution," *EEH,* 9 (1972), 375-421.

POTTER, DAVID. *Lincoln and His Party in the Secession Crisis.* New Haven, 1942.

_____. *The Lincoln Theme in American National Historiography.* Oxford, 1948.

PRATT, HARRY E. "Lincoln — Campaign Manager and Orator in 1840," *ALAB,* 50 (1937), 3-8.

_____. "Lincoln and Bankruptcy Law," *Ill. Bar Journal,* 31 (Jan. 1943), 201-6.

_____. *The Personal Finances of Abraham Lincoln.* Springfield, Ill., 1943.

_____. "Lincoln's 'Jump' from the Window," *JISHS,* 48 (1955), 456-61.

PRESSLY, THOMAS J. *Americans Interpret Their Civil War.* New York, 1962.

PRIMM, JAMES NEAL. *Economic Policy in the Development of a Western State: Missouri 1820-1860.* Cambridge, Mass., 1954.

PUTNAM, JAMES WILLIAM. *The Illinois and Michigan Canal: A Study in Economic History.* Chicago, 1918.

QUARLES, BENJAMIN. *Lincoln and the Negro.* New York, 1962.

RAE, JOHN. *Statement of Some New Principles on the Subject of Political Economy.* Philadelphia, 1834.

RAMSDELL, CHARLES W. "The Natural Limits of Slavery Expansion," *MVHR,* 16 (1929), 151-71.

_____. "Lincoln and Fort Sumpter," *JSH,* 3 (1937), 259-88.

RANDALL, J. G. *Constitutional Problems Under Lincoln.* Urbana, 1964.

_____. "Has the Lincoln Theme Been Exhausted," *AHR,* 41 (1936), 270-94.

_____. *Lincoln and the South.* Baton Rouge, 1946.

_____. *Lincoln the Liberal Statesman.* New York, 1947.

_____. *Lincoln the President.* 4 vols., New York, 1945-1955. Vol. IV completed by Richard Current.

_____. and DONALD, DAVID. *The Civil War and Reconstruction.* Lexington, Mass., 1969.

RANDALL, RUTH PAINTER. *I, Ruth: Autobiography of A Marriage. . . .* Boston, 1968.

RANSOM, ROGER C. "Canals and Development: A Discussion of the Issues," *AER,* 54 (1964), 365-76.

RATCHFORD, B. U. *American State Debts.* Durham, N. C. 1941.

RATNER, SYDNEY. *American Taxation: Its History as a Social Force in a Democracy.* New York, 1942.

_____. *The Tariff in American History.* New York, 1972.

RAWLEY, JAMES A. "Lincoln and Governor Morgan," *ALQ,* 6 (1951), 272-300.

_____. "The Nationalism of Abraham Lincoln," *CWH,* 9 (1963), 283-98.

RAYBACK, JOSEPH G. *A History of Labor.* New York, 1958.

_____. *Free Soil: The Election of 1848.* Lexington, Ky., 1970.

RAYBACK, ROBERT J. *Millard Fillmore.* Buffalo, 1959.

REDLICH, FRITZ. *The Molding of American Banking: Men and Ideas.* New York, 1951.

REMINI, ROBERT V. *Andrew Jackson and the Bank War: A Study in the Growth of Presidential Power.* New York, 1967.

REYNOLDS, JOHN. *My Own Times, Embracing also the History of My Life.* Belleville, Ill., 1855.

RHODES, JAMES FORD. *History of the United States from the Compromise of 1850.* 7 vols., New York, 1892-1922.

391

RICE, ALLEN THORNDIKE, ed. *Reminiscences of Abraham Lincoln by Distinguished Men of His Time.* New York, 1888.

RICHARDS, JOHN T. *Abraham Lincoln, The Lawyer-Statesman.* Boston, 1916.

RICHARDS, LEONARD F. *"Gentlemen of Property and Standing": Anti-Abolition Mobs in Jacksonian America.* New York, 1970.

RICHARDSON, JAMES D. ed. *A Compilation of the Messages and Papers of the Presidents, 1789-1897.* 10 vols., Washington, 1896-1899.

RICHMOND, CORA L. V. *Abraham Lincoln . . . on the Financial Question.* Chicago, 1896.

RICHEY, RUSSELL E. and JONES, DONALD G. eds. *American Civil Religion.* New York, 1974.

RIDDLE, DONALD. *Lincoln Runs for Congress.* New Brunswick, N. J. 1948.

_____. *Congressman Abraham Lincoln.* Urbana, 1957.

RISCHIN, MOSES. ed. *The American Gospel of Success: Individualism and Beyond.* Chicago, 1965.

ROBBINS, ROY M. *Our Landed Heritage: The Public Domain, 1776-1936.* Princeton, N. J., 1942.

ROBERTS, A. S. "The Federal Government and Confederate Cotton," *AHR,* 32 (1926), 262-75.

ROBERTSON, JOHN BRUCE. "Lincoln and Congress." Ph.D. Dissertation, University of Wisconsin, 1966.

ROBINSON, MARSHALL A. "Federal Debt Management: Civil War, World War I, and World War II," *AER,* 45 (1955), 388-401.

ROSE, WILLIE LEE. *Rehearsal for Reconstruction: The Port Royal Experiment.* Indianapolis, 1964.

ROSENBERG, NATHAN. "Anglo-American Wage Differences in the 1820's," *AER,* 27 (1967).

ROSS, EARL D. "Lincoln and Agriculture," *AH,* 2 (1929), 51-66.

_____. "The United States Department of Agriculture During the Commissionship: A Study in Politics, Administration, and Technology, 1862-1889," *AH,* 20 (1946), 129-43.

ROSSITER, CLINTON. *The American Presidency.* New York, 1960.

ROSTOW, W. W. *The Stages of Economic Growth.* Cambridge, 1960.

RUBIN, JULIUS. "An Innovating Public Improvement: The Erie Canal," in Carter Goodrich, ed., *Canals and American Economic Development.* New York, 1961, 15-66.

_____. "Canal or Railroad? Imitation and Innovation in the Response to the Erie Canal in Philadelphia, Baltimore, and Boston," *Trans. of Am. Philo. Soc.,* No. 51 Part 7 (1961).

RUGG, ARTHUR P. "Abraham Lincoln in Worcester," *Worcester Soc. of Antiq. Proceedings.,* 25 (1910), 226-42.

Ruggles, Samuel. *Internationality and International Congresses.* New York, 1870.

Runkle, Gerald. "Karl Marx and the American Civil War," *Comp. Std. in Soc. and Hist.,* 6 (1964), 112-41.

Sabin, Edwin L. *Building the Pacific Railway.* . . . Philadelphia, 1919.

Sandburg, Carl. *Abraham Lincoln: The Prairie Years and the War Years.* 6 vols., New York, 1926-1939.

Sanford, Charles L. *The Quest for Paradise: Europe and the American Moral Imagination.* Urbana, Ill., 1961.

Saveth, Edward N. ed. *Understanding the American Past: American History and Its Interpretations.* Boston, 1954.

Scheiber, Harry N. "Urban Rivalry and Internal Improvements in the Old Northwest," *Ohio Hist. Qtly.,* 71 (1962), 227-39.

————. "Economic Change in the Civil War Era: An Analysis of Recent Studies," *CWH,* 11 (1965), 396-411.

————. *Ohio Canal Era: A Case Study of Government and the Economy, 1820-1861.* Athens, Ohio, 1969.

Schlesinger, Arthur M. *The Age of Jackson.* Boston, 1946.

————. *A Thousand Days: John F. Kennedy in the White House.* Boston, 1965.

Schluter, Herman. *Lincoln, Labor and Slavery.* . . . New York, 1913.

Schouler, James. "Abraham Lincoln at Tremont Temple in 1848," *MHSP,* 42 (1908), 70-83.

Schroeder, John H. *Mr. Polk's War: American Opposition and Dissent, 1846-1848.* Madison, 1973.

Schumpeter, Joseph A. *History of Economic Analysis.* ed. by Elizabeth Boody Schumpeter. New York, 1974.

Segal, Harvey H. "Cycles of Canal Construction," in Carter, Goodrich, ed., *Canals and American Economic Development.* New York, 1961.

Segal, Charles M. *Conversations with Lincoln.* New York, 1961.

Sellers, Cha rles. *James K. Polk, Continentalist, 1843-1846.* Princeton, 1966.

Seligman, E. R. A. *The Income Tax.* New York, 1914.

Sewall, Richard H. *John P. Hall and the Politics of Abolition.* Cambridge, Mass., 1965.

Shade, William Gerald. *Banks or No Banks: The Money Issue in Western Politics, 1832-1865.* Detroit, 1972.

Shannon, Fred A. *The Organization and Administration of the Union Army, 1861-1865.* 2 vols., Cleveland, 1928.

————. *The Farmer's Last Frontier: Agriculture, 1860-1897.* New York, 1945.

Shapiro, Henry D. *Confiscation of Confederate Property in the North.* Ithaca, N. Y., 1962.

Sharp, James Roger. *The Jacksonians versus the Banks: Politics in the States After the Panic of 1837.* New York, 1970.

SHAW, JAMES. "A Neglected Episode in the Life of Abraham Lincoln," *Trans. of the Ill. State Hist. Soc.,* 29 (1922), 51-8.

SHAW, RONALD E. *Erie Water West: A History of the Erie Canal, 1792-1854.* Lexington, Ky., 1966.

SHERMAN, JOHN. *Recollections of Forty Years in the House, Senate and Cabinet: An Autobiography.* 2 vols., Chicago, 1895.

SHUTES, MILTON H. "Abraham Lincoln and the New Almaden Case," *Chicago Hist. Soc. Qtly.,* 15 (1936).

————. "Henry Wager Halleck, Lincoln's Chief of Staff," *Chicago Hist. Soc. Qtly.,* 16 (1937).

————. *Lincoln and California.* Stanford, 1943.

SILBEY, JOEL H. *The Shrine of Party: Congressional Voting Behavior, 1841-1852.* Pittsburgh, 1967.

SILVER, DAVID. M. *Lincoln's Supreme Court.* Urbana, 1957.

SIMON, JOHN Y. "Congress Under Lincoln." Ph.D. Dissertation, Harvard University, 1960.

————. "The Politics of the Morill Act," *AH,* 37 (1963), 103-11.

SIMON, PAUL. *Lincoln's Preparation for Greatness: The Illinois Legislative Years.* Norman, 1965.

SMITH, ADAM. *The Wealth of Nations.* London, 1904.

SMITH, DONALD. *Chase and Civil War Politics.* Columbus, Ohio, 1931.

SMITH, FRANKLIN WEBSTER. *The Conspiracy in the U.S. Navy Department against Franklin W. Smith of Boston, 1861-1865.* n.p., n.d. [New York, 1890].

SMITH, GEORGE WASHINGTON. *When Lincoln Came to Egypt.* Hurrin, Ill., 1940.

SMITH, GEORGE WINSTON. *Henry Carey and American Sectional Conflict.* Albuquerque, 1951.

SMITH, HENRY NASH. *Virgin Land: The American West as Symbol and Myth.* Cambridge, Mass., 1950.

SMITH, JUSTIN H. *The War With Mexico.* 2 vols., New York, 1919.

SMITH, WALTER BUCKINGHAM. *Economic Aspects of the Second Bank of the United States.* Cambridge, Mass., 1953.

SNYDER, JOHN FRANCIS. *Adam W. Snyder and his Period in Illinois History, 1817-1842.* Virginia, Ill., 1906.

SPAULDING, E. G. *History of the Legal Tender Paper Money.* Buffalo, N. Y., 1869.

SPEED, JOSHUA F. *Reminiscences of Abraham Lincoln. . . .* Louisville, 1884.

SQUIRES, J. DUANE. "Some Enduring Achievements of the Lincoln Administration, 1861-1865," ALQ, 5 (1948), 191-211.

STAMPP, KENNETH M. *Indiana Politics During the Civil War.* Indianapolis, 1944.

————. *And the War Came: The North and the Secession Crisis, 1860-61.* Baton Rouge, 1950.

————. *The Era of Reconstruction, 1865-1877.* New York, 1965.

STANWOOD, EDWARD. *American Tariff Controversies in the Nineteenth Century.* 2 vols., Boston, 1903.

STAROBIN, ROBERT S. *Industrial Slavery in the South.* New York, 1970.

STARR, JOHN W. *Lincoln and the Railroads: A Biographical Study,* New York, 1927.

STAUDENRAUS, P. J., ed. *Mr. Lincoln's Washington: Selections from the Writing of Noah Brooks, Civil War Correspondent.* New York, 1967.

STEPHENS, ALEXANDER H. *Recollections of Alexander H. Stephens.* New York, 1910.

STEPHENSON, NATHANIEL WRIGHT. *Lincoln: An Account of His Personal Life, Especially of Its Springs of Action as Revealed and Deepened by the Ordeal of War.* Indianapolis, 1922.

————. "The Question of Arming the Slaves," *AHR,* 18 (1913), 295-308.

STEWART, ANDREW. *Speeches on the Tariff Question and On Internal Improvements.* Philadelphia, 1872.

STOCKBERGER, WARNER W. *Personnel Administration Development in the United States Department of Agriculture: The First Fifty Years.* Washington, 1947.

STODDARD, WILLIAM O. *Lincoln: The True Story of a Great Life.* New York, 1884.

————. *Inside the White House in War Times.* New York, 1890.

STODDARD, WILLIAM O. JR., ed., *Lincoln's Third Secretary: The Memoirs of William O. Stoddard.* New York, 1955.

STOLPER, WOLFGANG F. and SAMUELSON, PAUL A. "Protection and Real Wages," *RES,* 9 (1941) 58-73.

STREVEY, TRACY E. "Albert J. Beveridge," in William T. Hutchinson, ed., *The Marcus W. Jernegan Essays in American Historiography.* Chicago, 1937, 374-93.

STRUNSKY, ROSE. "Lincoln's Social Ideals," *Century,* 87 (1914), 588-92.

STUDENSKI, PAUL and KROOSS, HERMAN E., *Financial History of the United States.* New York, 1963.

SUMNER, CHARLES. *His Complete Works.* 20 vols., New York, 1969, reprint.

SUMNER, WILLIAM GRAHAM. *History of Banking in the United States.* New York, 1896.

SUTTON, ROBERT B. "The Illinois Central Railroad in Peace and War, 1858-1868." Ph.D. Dissertation, University of Illinois. 1948.

————. "The Illinois Central: Throughfare for Freedom," *CWH,* 7 (1961) 278-84.

SWIERENGA, ROBERT P. "Land Speculators 'Profits' Reconsidered: Central Iowa as a Test Case," *JEH,* 17 (1957), 1-24.

————. *Pioneers and Profits on the Iowa Frontier.* Ames, Ia., 1968.

SYLVIS, JAMES C. *The Life Speeches, Labors and Essays of William H. Sylvis,* Philadelphia, 1872.

Syrett, John, "The Confiscation Acts: Efforts at Reconstruction During the Civil War." Ph.D. Dissertation, University of Wisconsin, 1971.

Tarbell, Ida M. *The Life of Abraham Lincoln.* 2 vols., New York, 1900.

_____. *The Tariff in Our Times.* New York, 1911.

Taus, Esther Rogoff. *Central Banking Functions of the United States Treasury, 1789-1941.* New York, 1943.

Taussig, Frank W. ed., *State Papers and Speeches on the Tariff.* Cambridge, Mass., 1893.

_____. "Abraham Lincoln and the Tariff: A Myth," *QJE,* 28 (1914) 814-20.

_____. "Lincoln and the Tariff: A Sequel," *QJE,* 29 (1915) 426-9.

_____. "The Lincoln Tariff Myth Finally Disposed Of," *QJE,* 35 (1921) 500.

_____. *Free Trade, the Tariff and Reciprocity.* New York, 1927.

_____. *The Tariff History of the United States.* New York, 1931.

Taylor, George Rogers. *The Transportation Revolution, 1815-1860.* New York, 1951.

Teilhac, Ernest, *Pioneers in American Economic Thought in the Nineteenth Century.* Trs. E.A. Johnson, New York, 1936.

Temin, Peter. "Labor Scarcity and the Problem of American Industrial Efficiency in the 1850's," *JEH,* 26 (1966), 277-98.

_____. *The Jacksonian Economy.* New York, 1969.

_____. "Labor Scarcity in America," *Journ. of Interdisciplinary Hist.,* 1 (1971), 251-64.

Templeton, J.W. "Life and Services of General Thomas J. Henderson," *JISHS,* 4 (1911), 67-81.

The Life, Speeches, and Public Services of Abraham Lincoln. "Wigwam Edition." New York, 1860.

The Tribune Almanac for the Years 1838 to 1864. . . . New York, 1868.

Thernstrom, Stephan. *Poverty and Progress; Social Mobility in a Nineteenth Century City.* Cambridge, Mass. 1964.

Thomas, Benjamin P. *Lincoln's New Salem.* Springfield, Ill., 1934.

_____. *Portrait for Posterity: Lincoln and His Biographers.* New Brunswick, N.J. 1947.

_____. *Abraham Lincoln: A Biography.* New York, 1952.

_____. and Hyman, Harold, *Stanton: The Life and Times of Lincoln's Secretary of War.* New York, 1962.

Thompson, Brinton. *Ruggles of New York: A Life of Samuel B. Ruggles.* New York, 1946.

Thomson, Charles Manfred. *The Illinois Whigs before 1846.* Urbana, Ill., 1910.

_____. "Attitude of the Western Whigs Toward the Convention System" *Proceed of Miss. Valley Historical Ass.,* 5 (1911-12) 177-89.

396

THUROW, GLEN EDWARD. "Abraham Lincoln and American Political Religion." Ph.D. Dissertation, Harvard University, 1968.

TIMBERLAKE, RICHARD A. JR. "The Independent Treasury and Monetary Policy Before the Civil War," *Southern Econ. Jr.* 27 (1960) 92-103.

TOLSTOY, LEV NIKOLAEVICH. *Polnoe sobranie sochinenii.* Pod obshchei red. V. G. Chertkova, Iubilenoe izd. 91 vols., Moscow, 1928-1964.

TOWNSEND, WILLIAM H. *Lincoln and Liquor.* New York, 1934.

TREFOUSSE, HANS L. *The Radical Republicans: Lincoln's Vanguard for Racial Justice.* New York, 1969.

_____. "The Joint Committee on the Conduct of the War: A Reassessment," *CWH,* 10 (1964), 5-19

TRUEBLOOD, ELTON, *Abraham Lincoln: Theologian of American Anguish.* New York, 1973.

TURNER, FREDERICK JACKSON, *The United States, 1830-50: The Nation and Its Sections.* New York, 1965.

_____. *The Frontier in American History.* New York, 1962.

TURNER, GEORGE EDGAR. *Victory Rode the Rails: The Strategic Place of the Railroads in the Civil War.* Indianapolis, 1953.

TURNER, JOHN R. *The Ricardian Rent Theory.* New York, 1921.

TUTOROW, NORMAN EUGENE. "Whigs of the Old Northwest and the Mexican War." Ph.D. Dissertation, Stanford University, 1967.

TYLER, MOSES COIT. "One of Mr. Lincoln's Old Friends," *JISHS,* 38 (1936), 247-57.

UNGER, IRWIN. *The Greenback Era: A Social and Political History of American Finance, 1865-1879.* Princeton, 1964.

VAN ALSTYNE, R. W. *The Rising American Empire.* New York, 1960.

VAN DEUSEN, G. G. *The Life of Henry Clay.* Boston, 1937.

_____. *Horace Greeley: Nineteenth Century Crusader.* Philadelphia, 1953.

_____. *The Jacksonian Era, 1828-48.* New York, 1959

_____. "Some Aspects of Whig Thought and Theory in the Jacksonian Period," *AHR,* 63 (1958), 312-15.

_____. *William Henry Seward.* New York, 1967.

VANDIVER, FRANK E. *Rebel Brass: The Confederate Command System.* Baton Rouge, 1956.

VAN FENSTERMAKER, J. "A Description of Sangamon County, Illinois, in 1830," *AH,* 39 (1965), 136-41.

_____. *The Development of American Commercial Banking, 1782-1837.* Kent, Ohio, 1965.

VERLIE, EMIL JOSEPH, ed. *Illinois Constitutions.* Springfield, Ill., 1919.

VEVIER, CHARLES. "American Continentalism: An Idea of Expansionism, 1845-1910," *AHR,* 65 (1960), 323-35.

VOEGELI, V. JACQUE. *Free But Not Equal: The Midwest and the Negro During the Civil War.* New York, 1967.

VOGEL, VIRGIL J. *Indian Place Names in Illinois.* Springfield, Ill., 1963.

WADE, RICHARD C. *Slavery in the Cities: the South, 1820-1860.* New York, 1964.

WAGANDT, CHARLES L. *The Mighty Revolution: Negro Emancipation in Maryland, 1862-1864.* Baltimore, 1964.

WAKEMAN, W. F. "Abraham Lincoln and the Tariff," *The Defender,* Doc. 11, 1912.

WALTERS, RAYMOND, *Albert Gallatin: Jeffersonian Financier and Diplomat.* New York, 1957.

WANLOSS, WILLIAM. *The United States Department of Agriculture: A Study in Administration.* Baltimore, 1920.

WARD, JOHN WILLIAM. *Andrew Jackson: Symbol for an Age.* New York, 1962.

WARDEN, ROBERT B. *An Account of the Private Life and Public Services of Salmon Portland Chase.* Cincinnati, 1874.

WARREN, CHARLES. *Bankruptcy in United States History.* Cambridge, Mass., 1935.

WARREN, LOUIS A. *Lincoln's Parentage and Childhood.* New York, 1926.

WAYLAND, FRANCIS. *The Elements of Moral Science.* New York, 1835.

_____. *The Elements of Political Economy.* New York, 1837.

WEBER, THOMAS. *The Northern Railroads in the Civil War, 1861-1865.* New York, 1952.

WEBSTER, DANIEL. *The Writings of Daniel Webster.* 18 vols., Boston, 1903.

WEEMS, MASON. *The Life of Washington.* Ed. by Marcus Cunlife. Cambridge, Mass., 1962.

WEIL, SAMUEL C. *Lincoln's Crisis in the Far West.* San Francisco, 1949.

WEINBERG, ALBERT K. *Manifest Destiny.* Baltimore, 1935.

WEISS, RICHARD. *The American Myth of Success: From Horatio Alger to Norman Vincent Peale.* New York, 1969.

WELLES, GIDEON. *Lincoln and Seward.* New York, 1874.

WELLINGTON, RAYNOR G. *The Political and Sectional Influence of Public Lands, 1828-1842.* Cambridge, Mass. 1914.

WELTER, RUSH. *The Mind of America, 1820-1860.* New York, 1975.

WESLEY, CHARLES H. "The Employment of Negroes as Soldiers in the Confederate Army," *JNH,* 4 (1919) 239-53.

_____. "Lincoln's Plans for Colonizing Emancipated Negroes," *JNH,* 4 (1919), 7-21.

WEST, RICHARD S. JR. *Gideon Welles: Lincoln's Navy Department.* New York, 1943.

WHITE, LEONARD D. *The Federalists: A Study of Administrative History.* New York, 1948.

_____. *The Jacksonians: A Study in Administrative History, 1829-1861.* New York, 1954.

_____. with SCHNEIDER, JEAN. *The Republican Era, 1869-1901: A Study in Administrative History.* New York, 1968.

WHITNEY, HENRY CLAY. *Life on the Circuit with Lincoln.* Ed. by Paul M. Angle. Cladwell, Idaho, 1940.

WIK, REYNOLD M. "Steam Power on the American Farm, 1830-1880," *AH,* 25 (1951), 181-6.

WILBURN, J. *Biddle's Bank.* New York, 1967.

WILLIAMS, ELGIN. *The Animating Pursuits of Speculation: Land Traffic in the Annexation of Texas.* New York, 1949.

WILLIAMS, KENNETH P. *Lincoln Finds a General: A Military Study of the Civil War.* 5 vols., New York, 1949-59.

WILLIAMS, MENTOR L. "The Chicago River and Harbor Convention, 1847," *MVHR,* 35 (1949), 607-26.

_____. "The Background of the Chicago River and Harbor Convention, 1847," *MA,* 30 (1948), 219-32.

_____. "A Shout of Derision: A Sidelight on the Presidential Campaign of 1848," *Mich. Hist.,* 32 (1948), 66-77.

WILLIAMS, T. HARRY. *Lincoln and the Radicals.* Madison, 1941.

_____. ed. *Selected Writings of Abraham Lincoln.* New York, 1943.

_____. *Lincoln and His Generals.* New York, 1952.

_____. "Principle and Pragmatism in Politics: A Review Article," *MVHR,* 40 (1953), 89-106.

_____. "The Military Leadership of the North and South," in David Donald, ed., *Why the North Won the Civil War.* London, 1962 33-54.

WILLIAMS, WILLIAM APPLEMAN. *The Contours of American History.* Cleveland, 1961.

_____. *The Roots of the Modern American Empire: A Study of the Growth and Shaping of Social Consciousness in a Marketplace Society.* New York, 1969.

WILLIAMSON, HAROLD F. *Edward Atkinson: The Biography of an American Liberal, 1827-1905. Boston, 1934.*

WILSON, EDMUND. *To the Finland Station: A Study in the Writing and Acting of History.* New York, 1953.

_____. *Patriotic Gore: Studies in the Literature of the American Civil War.* New York, 1962.

WILSON, MAJOR. *Space, Time, and Freedom: The Quest for Nationality and the Irrepressible Conflict, 1815-1861.* Westport, Conn., 1974.

WILSON, RUFUS ROCKWELL, ed. *Uncollected Works of Abraham Lincoln.* 2 vols., Elmira N. Y. 1947-8.

WILTSE, CHARLES M. *John C. Calhoun.* 3 vols., Indianapolis, 1944-51.

WISH, HARVEY. *George Fitzhugh: Propagandist of the Old South.* Baton Rouge, 1943.

399

WOLDMAN, ALBERT W. *Lawyer Lincoln*. Boston, 1936.

————. *Lincoln and the Russians*. Cleveland, 1952.

WOLF, WILLIAM J. *Lincoln's Religion*. Philadelphia, 1970 (Previous titles: *The Almost Chosen People*, 1959, and *The Religion of Abraham Lincoln*, 1963.)

WOOD, W. BIRKBECK and EDMONDS, JAMES E. *A History of the Civil War in the United States, 1861-5*. New York, 1937.

WOODFORD, FRANK B. *Lewis Cass: The Last Jeffersonian*. New Brunswick, N. J. 1950.

WRIGHT, CHESTER WHITNEY. *Wool-Growing and the Tariff*. . . . Boston, 1910.

WRIGHT, JOHN S. *Lincoln and the Politics of Slavery*. Reno, 1970.

WRONE, DAVID R. "Abraham Lincoln's Idea of Property," *Science & Society*, 33 (1969), 54-70.

WYLLIE, IRWIN G. *The Self-Made Men in America: The Myth of Rags to Riches*. New Brunswick, N. J., 1954.

YUNGMEYER, D. Y. "An Excursion Into the Early History of the Chicago and Alton Railroad," *JISHS*, 38 (1945), 7-37.

ZANE, CHARLES S. "Lincoln as I Knew Him," *JISHS*, 14 (1921), 74-84.

ZOELLNER, ROBERT H. "Negro Colonization: The Climate of Opinion Surrounding Lincoln, 1860-65," *MA*, 42 (1960), 131-50.

ZORNOW, FRANK WILLIAM. *Lincoln and the Party Divided*. Norman, Okla., 1954.

ZWELLING, SHOMER S. *Expansion and Imperialism*. Chicago, 1970.

INDEX

A Separate Index to Historiographical Essay begins on p. 415

Adams, Charles Francis, 219, 242
Adams, Henry, 199
Adams, John Quincy, 4, 5, 67, 125, 139
Agrarian myth, 79
Agricultural College Land Grant Act, 321n6
Agriculture, x, 2, 7, 17, 20-1, 27, 59, 79-91, 117, 141, 176, 185-9, 215-7. *See also* Public Lands.
    education and, 187, 321n6
    expansionism and, 139, 187, 188
    industry and, 88-91, 326n10
    farming, business of, 187, 189
        intensive 185-6
    mechanization of, 115, 187, 188
    productivity of, 186, 187
Agriculture Department, 215-7, 229
Alaska, 140
Alexander II, 276
American Dream, ix, x, xii, xxiv, 1, 11, 20, 22-3, 34, 72, 74-5, 81, 89-90, 112-3, 117, 127, 131, 137, 138-9, 149, 150-1, 155f, 158-62, 180, 187, 198, 269. *See also* Common man, Lincoln: economic outlook.
    as central idea of America, 158-62, 275, 276, 279, 281, 284-7
    Civil War and, 275-87
    colonization of blacks and, 258
    created by Fathers, 160, 162
    democracy and, 276-9
    economic independence and, 180-1, 185, 188
    emancipation and, 256, 262-3, 266
    Gettysburg Address and, 282
    institutionalization of, 161
    international significance of, 281, 283
    labor strikes and, 184

Lincoln's silence and, 175f
military strategy and, 273-4
political power and, 218, 256, 262-3, 266
as political religion, 160, 286-7
roots of, 161, 173, 284-5
Second Inaugural Address and, 286-7
slavery and, 155-74
as spiritual goal, 160, 282, 284-7
as symbol, 277
Union and Constitution and, 161-2, 276, 280-1
American Laborer, The (New York), 114
American Notes (Dickens), 110
American Party. *See* immigrants.
American Revolution, 4, 41, 118, 160, 237, 284-5
American System, 4, 22, 87, 99, 106, 210
Ames, Oakes, 347n49
Andrew, John, 357n23
Army of the Potomac, 271
Arnold, Isaac, 211-2, 229
Articles of Conferederation, 210
Ashmun, George, 249
Astor, John Jacob, 178, 223
Atkinson, Edward, 245, 246, 247, 248
Auden, W. H., 158

Bacon, Nathaniel, 138
Baker, Edward D., 29, 33, 101, 139
Baltimore American, 145-6
Bancroft, George, 219
Bank of England, 60, 63
Bank, Illinois State, 322n1
    created, 15
    evaluated, 60
    fails, 59
    investigated, 16-24, 53-4

401

national banking system and, 199-203
peace missions and, 242
war finance and, 203-6, 208
Cheeves, Langdon, 66
Cheyney, Edward P., 123
Chicago and Alton Railroad, 183
Chicago Democrat, 182, 183
Chicago Journal, 191
Chicago Internal Improvement Convention (1863), 213
Chicago River and Harbor Convention (1847), 129-30
Chiriqui, 261-2
Chittenden, Lucius, 266
City v. country, 33, 48
Civil War, ix, xiii, 38, 42, 44, 93, 96, 98, 118, 119, 158, 161, 172, 185, 195-287
Clay, Cassius, 285
Clay, Henry, 2, 3, 5, 67, 73, 107, 109, 126, 144, 320n6, 352n11
  on Bank of the United States, 68, 96
  Lincoln, influenced by, 98-9
  on public lands, 83, 84, 87
  on slavery, 328n12
  on tariff, 118
  on Whig theory of executive, 93-4
Clayton, John M., 148
Clinton, DeWitt, 7, 36
Colfax, Schuyler, 19, 226
Colonization of blacks, 235
  economics of, 258-61
  and expansionism, 258-9
Colton, Calvin, 66, 104, 106
  on self-made man, 75
Common man, 20, 23, 43, 45, 69, 79, 82, 84, 86, 89, 95, 112, 133, 135, 147, 217, 261, 282-4
Common Sense School, 110
Commonwealth v. Hunt, 182
Confiscation, 208, 249-52, 265
Confederate Debt, 242, 251
Connecticut, 184

Constitution
  Illinois, 45, 127
  Michigan, 7
  U.S., 4, 41, 63, 68, 72, 129-30, 161, 162, 171, 195, 250, 317n12. *See also* American Dream: Union and Constitution.
Conway, Martin F., 195
Coolidge, Calvin, 91, 189
Cooke, Jay, 206
Cooper, James Fenimore, 21
Corporations, 128, 181. *See also* Banks.
Corwin, Thomas, 140
Cotton trade
  Civil War, prolonged by, 354n39
  corruption and, 248
  failure of, 247-9
  international relations and, 245
  Lincoln and, 206, 228, 244-9
  Lincoln's economic outlook and, 243
  Northern economy and, 245
  patronage and, 247, 355n44
  peace, 246-7
  regulation, 243-4
  Union, 244
Cox, LaWanda, 264
Credit. *See* Banking.
Credit Mobilier, 347n49
Crevecoeur, J. Hector St. John, 79
Crocker, Noah, 8
Currency, 14, 16-7, 59, 65, 69, 85, 123, 124, 144, 145, 200, 206-7, 247, 317n12
Current, Richard, 266, 271
Curry, Leonard, 197
Curtin, Andrew, 220

Davis, David, 52, 149
  bank opponents, condemned by, 52, 55
  "hurrah boys" condemned by, 73
  Improvement System condemned by, 34
  Lincoln praised by, 106

403

Expansionism. *See* Agriculture: expansionism, Lincoln: expansionism.

Experiment, 25

Farming. *See* Agriculture.
Fathers of United States, 4, 63, 160, 162, 199, 210, 284
Faust (Gounod), 233
Federal Reserve System, 67
Federalist Party, 41, 72, 106
Fell, Jesse, 101
Fessenden, William Pitt,
    Agriculture Department, opposed, 215
    Civil War economic legislation, supported, 226
    and Lincoln, 205, 206, 228, 229
    national banking system, supported, 202
Field, David Dudley, 129, 130
Fillmore, Millard, 144
First International, 219
Fiscal Bank of U.S., 144
Fiscal Policy. *See* Taxation.
Fitzhugh, George, 138, 180, 184
Florville, William, 169
Foner, Eric, 161
Forbes, John Murray, 245
Ford, Thomas, 7, 17, 29, 36, 47, 82
    on Illinois banks, 59, 166
    on Illinois debt, 49
Founding Fathers. *See* Fathers.
France, 127, 245, 334n19
Franklin, Benjamin, 161
Fredricksburg, Battle of, 271
Freedmen's Bureau, 264, 265
Free Labor. *See* Labor.
Free Soil Party, 146, 147, 149-50.
Frost, Robert, 1

Gallatin, Albert, 4, 67
Gates, Paul, 217
General Welfare Clause. *See* Lincoln: general welfare clause.
Genovese, Eugene, 163

Geographical mobility, 138. *See also* Lincoln: expansionism, Western movement.
George III, 49
Georgia, 33
Gilmore, J.R., 242
Gillespie, Joseph, 74
Gouge, William, 16
Gounod, Charles, 233
Graduation. *See* Public Lands.
Grant, Ulysses, 250, 273
Greeley, Horace, 73, 114, 118, 196, 189
    on farming, 80, 189
    on homestead legislation, 134
    on labor unions and strikes, 182, 183
    on manufacturing, 90
    on Mexican War, 141
    Prayer of Twenty Millions, 162, 279-80
    on Taylor, Zachary, 142, 144
    Whig principal of, cardinal, 124
Green, Duff, 140
Greenbacks. *See* Currency.
Gersham's Law, 59
Guercino (Giovanni Francesco Barbieri), 79
Gurowski, Adam, 208

Hafiz, xiii
Hamilton, Alexander, 48, 94, 203
    and Bank of U.S., 63
    and internal improvements, 4
    and tariff, 114, 116, 117
Hamlin, Hannibal, 208, 213
Hammond, Bray, 18, 63, 201
    on Lincoln, 67
Hampton Road's Conference, 251-2, 264, 265
Hardin, John J., 29, 46, 101, 105, 139
Harmony of Interests, 176, 181
Harriman, Edward H., 129
Harrington, George, 205

405

406

banking, ignorance of, 67
creditors, attacked by, 57
on labor strikes, 182
ridiculed by Lincoln, 140
Jacksonians. *See* Democratic Party.
Jaffa, Harry V., 157, 167
Jaquess, James, 242
Japan, 89-90
Jawboning, 224, 227
Jefferson, Thomas, 7, 41, 155. *See also* Declaration of Independence.
Johnson, Andrew, 134, 264
Johnson, Ludwell, 248
Johnson, Lyndon B., 353n20
Johnson, William Cost, 66
Johnston, Albert Sidney, 274
Johnston, John D., 117, 138
Julian, George, 258
Junius Tracts. See Colton.

Kansas, 128, 195
Kansas-Nebraska Act, viii, ix, 155, 156, 175
Kellogg, Edward, 180, 202, 207
Kennedy, J.C.G., 352n11
Kennedy, John F., 224
Kentucky, 1, 99, 213, 285
Keynes, John Maynard, 94
Know Nothing Party. *See* Immigrants.
Kossuth, Lajos, 334n19

Labor, 176-85, 217-21. *See also* Slavery, Strikes.
capital and, 122, 123, 176-7, 181-2, 184, 218
employment of, 114, 226
slavery contrasted with, 135f
Labor and Other Capital (Kellogg), 180
Labor theory of value, 111-3, 123, 124, 176, 218
Lamon, Ward Hill, 206, 246
Lee, Robert E., 246, 250, 270, 271, 272
Legal tender. *See* Currency.
Legaré, Hugh, 90

Lieber, Francis, 281
Life of Washington (Weems), 285
Lincoln
as agricultural deity, 91
background, social, 97
on banking, 13-24, 51-61, 197-203, 346n35
Bank of the United States, 15, 60-1, 64-78, 85, 135
investigator, 53-4, 322n10
Illinois, defended, 16-24, 51-61
national system, role in creation of, 199-203
report on, 53-4
speeches on, 1837, 16-24
1839, vii, 65-71, 156, 325n14
1840, 67, 72-3
blacks and, 255-65, 356n23. *See also* Blacks.
elite, 261
land for, 264, 265
masses, 262-5
soldiers, 261, 271-2
wage labor, 263-4
Cabinet, 197-8, 227-8
capitalist class, 223-5
defined, 123, 177
as "respectable scoundrels," 71, 223-4
war on, 184

Civil War
goals of, 275, 277, 278
will to fight, 352n11
on Clay, 99
Congress, relations with in White House, 227, 228-30. *See also* Whig theory of executive.
Congressman, economic record summarized, 135
commercial treaties and, 225
corruption and, 225. *See also* Cotton.
debts, personal, 47, 58
on deflation, 66
Discoveries and Inventions, lecture, 189, 342n35

407

408

409

supports, 43-50
tariff, compared to, 94-5
war finance and, 203-8
temperance and, 97-8, 99
on telegraph, 225
on Union, ix, x, 161-2. *See also* Union.
westward movement and, 1, 117, 138. *See also* Lincoln: expansionism.
Whig policy, resolutions on, 1843, 86, 93
Whig policy, address on, 1843, 86-7, 93-7, 111
Whiggery of, 107-8, 178. *See also* Whig Party, Whig theory.
defined, 21-3, 93-7, 147
presidency and, 195f, 201, 209
sources of, 97-9
Wisconsin Fair Address, 1859, 80, 90, 139, 176, 185-9, 216, 218
Lincoln-Douglas Debates, 48, 71, 191, 234, 280
and Bank of U.S., 68
Lincoln, Mary Todd, 33, 233, 319n23
Lincoln, Thomas, 30, 138
Linder, Usher, 19, 20
Little Bull Law, 81-2
Loco Focos, 106
Logan, Stephen T., 15
Log Cabin (New York), 73
Log Cabin Campaign. *See* Elections, 1840.
"Long Nine" of Sangamon, 10, 30
Louisiana, 129, 263
Louisiana Purchase, 26
Lovejoy, Elijah, 19
Lovejoy, Owen, 215
Lowe, T.S.C., 269
Lowell, James Russell, 240

Machinists and Blacksmiths Union, 185
Malthus, Thomas R., 125
Manifest Destiny. *See* Expansionism.

Mark, 97
Marshall, Alfred, 115
Marx, Karl, 20, 160, 219, 255
Maryland, 33, 238
Massachusetts, 149, 184
Masters, Edgar Lee, 28
Matthew, 41
McClellan, George, B., 270
McClernand, John A., 9, 56, 134
McCormick, Cyrus, 166
McCulloch, James R., 121, 125
McCulloch, Hugh, 205, 345n31
McDuffie, George, 104
McKay, Gordon, 181
Mechanization. *See* Agriculture: mechanization.
Meyers, Marvin, 22
Mexico, 140, 141, 183, 245
Mexican War, 109, 126, 133, 135, 142-3, 149
Military strategy, xiii, 267-74
and black soldiers, 271-2
and blockade, 268
and cordon offense, 271
and economic power, 270-2
and Mississippi Valley, 269
and railroads, 269
and technology, 269
and unified command system, 269-70
Mill, James, 121, 125
Mill, John Stuart, 90, 121, 125
Michigan, 23
Mississippi, 54
Missouri, 7, 33, 239
Missouri Compromise. *See* Kansas-Nebraska Act.
Mobility. *See* geographical-, social-, mobility.
Mobs. *See* Social order.
Money. *See* Currency.
Morgan, Edwin D., 205, 224, 229, 246
Morrill bill (tariff), 209
Mussolini, Benito, 281

Napoleon, 191
Nash, Ogden, 57
National bank. *See* Bank of the United States.
National Debt. *See* Debt.
National Intelligencer (Washington), 70
Nativism. *See* Immigrants.
New Hampshire, 184
New Mexico, 140, 141, 166
New Salem, Illinois, 2, 10, 37, 38
New South, 247, 266
Newton, Isaac, 216
New York, 33, 35, 55, 129, 184, 185, 199, 206, 224
New York Canal. *See* Erie and Oswego.
New York Draft Riots, 219
New York Herald, 207
New York Times, 132, 133, 182, 190, 280, 285
New York World, 205
New York Workingmen's Association, 218, 219
Nicolay, John G., and Hay, John, 262
Niles, Hezekiah, 125
Niles' Register, 125
Nixon, Richard M., 352n20
Nord contre Sud (Verne), vii
North Carolina, 33
North, Douglas C., 29
Northern Cross Railroad, 8, 31, 35 132
Northwest Ordinance, 162
Nullification, 100, 340n46

Ohio, 7, 23, 26, 33, 87
Old Hickory. *See* Jackson.
Old Soldier (Springfield, Illinois), 75

Pacific Railroad, 208, 210-11, 212, 213, 229
Panic
  1819, 14
  1837, 15, 25, 29, 30-1, 33, 51, 54, 64, 71, 81, 102, 206

1857, 187, 190-1
1860 (crisis), 71
Pauline theology, 18
"Peculiar Institution." *See* Slavery.
Pennsylvania, 33, 101, 106, 156, 175, 190, 191, 197, 209, 343n44, 346n42
Petöfi, Sándor, 7n
Philadelphia Public Ledger, 175
Phillips, Wendell, 235, 252
Philosophe, 79
Physiocratie, 79
Pilgrim's Progress, The (Bunyan), 108
Polk, James K., 105, 107, 126, 129, 130, 132, 140, 144
Poor
  charity for, 148-9, 184
  Lincoln's attitudes on, 178
Porter, David D., 249
Preemption. *See* Public Lands.
Progress of the United States. . . . (Tucker), 125
Protectionism. *See* Tariff.
Protestant ethic, 138, 161
Public Lands, 26-7, 28, 42, 66, 132, 133-4, 191, 217. *See also* Agriculture.
  distribution, 5, 83, 86-7, 94
  graduation, 83, 84, 85-6
  history of, 83, 217, 327n21
  preemption, 83, 84-5
    laws studied by Lincoln, 327n15
  speculation, 5, 7, 27, 42, 47, 85, 141

Quantity theory of money
  Americans use, 66
  Lincoln uses, 65, 66, 81
Quarles, Benjamin, 169, 173
Quesnay, Francois, 79

Rabelais, Francois, xiv
Randall, J.G., 236, 259
Reconstruction, 196, 227, 258-66. *See also* Blacks.
Renaissance, 71, 161

411

South Carolina, 33, 100
Spectator, The (London), 256
Speculation. *See* Public Lands.
Spinner, Francis E., 210
Springfield, Illinois, 2, 23, 25
  relocation of state capital to, 10
Springfield and Alton Railroad,
  127-9, 141
Squatter Rights. *See* Preemption.
Stampp, Kenneth M., 239, 250
Stanton, Edwin M., 220, 228, 246,
  268
Stay law, 47
Steuart, James, 114
Stevens, Thaddeus, 205, 218
Stewart, Andrew, 104, 127, 148
Stoddard, William O., 201-2, 271,
  273
Story, Joseph, 13
State Register. See Illinois State Register.
Strickland, William, 74
Strikes, 181-5, 220-1, 223. *See also*
  Lincoln: labor.
  American views of, 182
  Civil War, 220
  Illinois views of, 182
Stuart, John T., 15, 31, 54, 70, 121,
  315n16
Subtreasury. *See* Independent
  Treasury.
Sumner, Charles, 253, 257, 301
Supreme Court
  California, 211
  Illinois, 19
  U.S., 13, 47, 50, 68, 96
Swayne, Noah H., 229
Swett, Leonard, 118-9

Tamaulipas, Mexico, 141
Taney, Roger, 68
Tariff, 83, 87, 90, 93-5, 100-19, 122,
  124, 125, 126-7, 135, 138, 140,
  141, 143, 144, 145, 148, 156, 170,
  175, 190, 192, 197, 209-10, 225,
  229, 322n9, 325n19, 329n18,
  340n16

Act of 1833 (Compromise), 94
Act of 1842, 102, 107, 115, 126
Act of 1846 (Walker Act), 109,
  114, 115, 126
effect of, 95, 100, 101-3, 110f,
  332n5
history, 100
Taxation, x, 5, 27, 41-50, 51, 58, 85,
  94, 135, 152, 203-8, 238, 241. *See*
  also Lincoln: taxation.
  graduated, 43, 44, 47, 96
  history, Illinois, 42
  U.S., 41-2
Taylor, George Rogers, 183
Taylor, Zachary, 216
  Linicoln supports for presidency,
    142-8
  principles of, 144
Taylorism, 149
"Tenderfoot." *See* Democratic Party.
Tennessee, 2, 213, 257
Texas
  Annexation, Lincoln on, 105, 106,
    139
  "iniquity," 141
Thoreau, Henry David, 34
Time Magazine, 113
Tod, David, 205
Todd, Mary. *See* Mary Todd Lincoln.
Tolstoy, Lev Nikolaievich, 255
Trade with Confederacy. *See* Cotton.
Transportation. *See* Internal im-
  provements.
Treatise (Say), 123
Treaty of Guadalupe-Hidalgo, 140
True Whig (Washington), 106
Trumbull, Lyman, 47, 190
Turner, Frederick Jackson, 38
Tucker, George, 66, 125
Tyler, John, 93, 96, 144

Union. *See also* American Dream:
  union, Lincoln: union.
  economic argument for, 210,
    234-5
  Nature and, 235, 351n6

413

INDEX

to Historiographical Essay

Hamiltonian, non-. *See* Lincoln images.
Hammond, Bray, 308
Hard Times (Dickens), 305.
Harriman, Edward, 309
"Harvard Commemoration Ode" (Lowell), 310
"Has the Lincoln Theme Been Exhausted?" (Randall), 291, 305
Hay, John, 307-8. *See also* Nicolay and Hay.
Historians of Lincoln, compared to priests, 292, 294
Heckman, Allen, 304
Herndon, William, 292-4, 298, 311
  Beveridge, influenced by, 295, 297
  frontier thesis, harbinger of, 294
  Lamon, sells ms. to, 293
  Lincoln biography, nature of, 292
  Lincoln's economics, 306
  Morison on, 294
  public reaction to, 294
  Weik, coauthor of, 293
Herndon's Lincoln. See Herndon.
Hesseltine, William B., 301
"Higher criticism," 299
Historiography. *See* Lincoln: historiography.
History of Abraham Lincoln and the Overthrow of Slavery, The, (Arnold), 295
History of the Standard Oil Company (Tarbell), 309
Hofstadter, Richard,
  Lincoln as politician, 301
  Lincoln, mocked by, 305
  Lincoln's economics, 305
Holland, J.G., 295
Hostility to Lincoln. *See* Lincoln: hostility.
House Dividing, A. (Baringer), 297
Hyman, Harold, 305

Illinois General Assembly
  Lincoln's economics, 307, 308

record, a morass, 295-6
Internal improvements. *See* Lincoln: internal improvements.

Jaffa, Harry V., 303-4
Jesus, Lincoln compared to, 291, 292, 294, 299
Johannsen, Robert W., 291

Kansas-Nebraska Act, 307
Kerley, James W., 305

Lamon, Ward Hill, 293, 294, 299
Lawyer. *See* Lincoln images.
Lawyer Lincoln (Woldman), 303
Lewis, Lloyd, 294, 310
Life of Abraham Lincoln, The (Arnold), 295
Life of Abraham Lincoln (Holland), 295
Life of Abraham Lincoln (Tarbell), 295
Life of Abraham Lincoln (Lamon), 293
Lincoln (Stephenson), 295
"Lincoln and Fort Sumter" (Ramsdell), 299
Lincoln and His Generals (Williams), 301
Lincoln and His Party in the Secession Crisis (Potter), 301
Lincoln and the Economics of the American Dream (Boritt), 291
Lincoln and the First Shot (Current), 300
Lincoln and the Negro (Quarles), 300
Lincoln and the Party Divided (Zornow), 301
Lincoln and the Patronage (Carman and Luthin), 300
Lincoln and the Politics of Slavery (Wright), 304
Lincoln and the Radicals (Williams), 301
"Lincoln and the Radicals: An Essay in Civil War History and Historiography" (Williams), 301
Lincoln and the Tools of War (Bruce), 306

A NOTE ABOUT THE AUTHOR

G.S. Boritt was born in Budapest, educated in South Dakota, at Yankton College and the State University, and received a Ph.D. from Boston University. He is Assistant Professor of History at Memphis State University. He held visiting appointments in Japan and at the University of Michigan, Ann Arbor. He has been a research fellow of the American Philosophical Society, the Huntington Library and Art Gallery, the Newberry Library, and the Social Science Research Council. Most recently he was Postdoctoral Fellow in Mathematical Statistics at Harvard University.